ACROSS AMERICA BY MOTOR-CYCLE

Fully Annotated Centennial Edition

Featuring the Complete Original Text by

Captain Charles Kenilworth Shepherd

Annotated by

Captain Mark Leslie Hunnibell

Foreword by

Dr. Charles Drury Shaw, Son of Captain C.K. Shepherd

UNION SQUARE
PUBLISHING

ACROSS AMERICA
BY MOTOR-CYCLE

UNION SQUARE

PORTRAITS OF THE AUTHORS

Captain C.K. Shepherd

Captain M.L. Hunnibell

Published by
Union Square Publishing
301 E. 57th Street, 4th floor
New York, NY 10022
www.unionsquarepublishing.com

The Original Edition of *Across America by Motor-Cycle*, by Captain C. K. Shepherd, was published in 1922 by Edward Arnold & Co. in London and by Longmans, Green & Co. in New York.

Manufactured in the United States of America, or in the United Kingdom when distributed elsewhere.

Hunnibell, Mark L.
    Across America by Motor-Cycle – Fully Annotated Centennial Edition
    LCCN: 2019934916
    ISBN: 978-1948181495
    eBook: 978-1948181501

Cover design by: Joe Potter and Mark Hunnibell

Cover photo by: C.K. Shepherd on or about August 15, 1919, on the California coast using a Butcher's Watch-Pocket Carbine No. 4 camera to create a 6cm x 9cm negative, later printed on a glass slide and hand-tinted by C.K. for use in slide presentations.

Photo credits: Except for photos from the 1922 book noted as being included with permission of Dr. F. Rolt-Wheeler, all photos from the 1922 book were taken by C.K. Shepherd. The source and credits for photos included in this Annotated Edition are noted in the caption beneath each photo.

For more information, errata notices, and supplemental resources, visit:
http://acrossamericabymotorcycle.com/resources/

This book is dedicated to the eternal wandering spirit of the mortal man named Charles Kenilworth ("C.K.") Shepherd, who arrived in this world on May 31, 1895 and—using his words—"shuffled off this mortal coil" on January 16, 1971. I hope I have done you proud.

—Captain Mark L. Hunnibell

CONTENTS

ILLUSTRATIONS FROM THE ORIGINAL WORK

NEW ILLUSTRATIONS FOR *THE CENTENNIAL EDITION*

ABOUT THIS BOOK

by Mark L. Hunnibell

When I discovered this original book title as a free download from the Internet Archive, I was immediately captivated by the story told by a British Royal Air Force Captain, Charles Kenilworth ("C.K.") Shepherd, who came to New York City in June 1919 after World War I, bought a brand new Henderson four-cylinder motorcycle (the same make, model, and year as my own antique motorcycle), and drove it nearly 5,000 miles until he reached San Francisco.

I have since longed to retrace Shepherd's trip on my bike, but I found the book lacked some details and had no maps. So I began the painstaking process of "reverse engineering" the book. I cross-referenced the manuscript with period maps and travel books. Happily, I have completed a route plan that is as accurate as humanly possible. Beyond the details, my critical review led me to wonder, "Whatever happened to C.K. Shepherd?"

After researching and investigating for several years, I finally discovered the answer to that question. I'll provide a quick summary here, but more can be found at the end of this book in "About the Author: Charles Kenilworth Shepherd." In 1939, just before his 44th birthday, Shepherd legally changed his name to Charles Kay Shaw and married a second time. He had two more children, including a son, Charles Drury Shaw, who is now a physician. I located Dr. Shaw, whom I hoped would be tolerant of my inquiries into details of his father's life. I became elated that Dr. Shaw was not only helpful in my efforts, but also patient and wonderful. He provided me with vital information and a number of photographs, many of which appear in this annotated edition.

To retain as much of the spirit and integrity of the book's first edition, the original editorial content of the book is presented in a serif font. My notations have been added in this sans-serif font. Every effort has been made to faithfully transcribe and reset the original manuscript. No changes to spelling or grammar have been made. Consecutive notation numbers have been embedded in the original text, with my new comments, notes, diagrams, and photos included at the end of each chapter as "Notes." Also, rather than use two different names in this book, I most often refer to Charles Kenilworth Shepherd and Charles Kay Shaw by the name he was consistently known on a personal level: "C.K."

FOREWORD

REDISCOVERING MY FATHER

by Dr. Charles Drury Shaw, Son of Captain C. K. Shepherd

My father had been dead for 46 years when Mark Hunnibell brought him back to me. Mark first identified my son from my mother's will and contacted me in July 2017. He introduced himself as an airline pilot, genealogist, and motorbike fanatic, and he asked many questions.

As our correspondence developed, I was increasingly embarrassed to realise how many questions I could not answer about my father and his family—especially during the 1920s and 30s. Certainly I knew about the ride across America and I have a copy of his book, inscribed to Nora Tarpey (who later became my mother) "on the occasion of her 18th birthday" in 1928. I confess I had not read the book critically, nor had I asked my father many questions about this or various other exploits before he married my mother in 1939.

As I grew up, my father—nearly 50 years older and averse to sport—steered my sister and me away from orthodoxy and into interesting places. We were living in Drury Lane when I was born in 1944 at number 12, where my father ran a library and painted maps on the shop window to illustrate progress of the war in Europe and North Africa. Later, in bohemian Bloomsbury, he manufactured and sold artist supplies opposite the British Museum before we moved to a large house in Sussex. There, in the 1950s, he set up a photographic darkroom, a machine shop, and a laboratory; designed and built his own garage and a treetop house for us children; painted Egyptian murals in the bedroom; and laid out a circular lawn depicting the sun, moon, and planets to scale.

Guns are not common (or legal) in English households. It was around 1960 when I discovered an army compass, a dagger, and a Smith and Wesson .38 revolver in a locked filing cabinet. These artifacts stirred my curiosity and prompted me to ask about their history. My father merely replied that they were souvenirs of foreign travels, but he was not inclined then or later to recount his exploits in America, Morocco, Algeria, and Tunisia, or talk about his many inventive business ventures in France and England. I was too young at the time to ask the salient questions, and he was more preoccupied by spiritualism and the next world. It was not until I had finished more years in boarding school, grown out of adolescent rejection of parents, and graduated from medical school that I began to recognize the significance of my father's achievements and failures.

Many years later, I was surprised and delighted to hear of Mark's interest in my father's 1919 ride from New York City to San Francisco and in his plans to replicate that journey 100 years later on a Henderson model of the same year. I was amazed and impressed by how much more Mark knew about my family than I did, most of which he gleaned from internet searches and contemporary archives in the public domain.

This led me to explore nearer to my home the many crates of documents, patents, and publications, as well as two boxes of glass magic lantern slides, which had gathered dust in a series of attics. Some of the slides were original pictures or photographs of postcards relating to the trip across America. Publications ranged from industrial publicity to house building in concrete; manuscripts included details of his crossing the Sahara in a small Rosengart car, touring Tunisia on a Harley Davidson, and living in Montmartre in Paris before the war.

Thanks to Mark, my family and I now have a clearer narrative and independent interpretation of my father's life, and I have a better understanding of genealogy and of the power of internet searching.

MAPS AND NAVIGATION

One of the challenges researching the 1919 route was the lack of schedule/ timetable in the original book. The even greater challenge was establishing C.K.'s actual route over the roads. One hundred years ago, the "state of the art" for maps and navigation intended to be used by touring motorists was in its infancy.

Various approaches were taken by different companies and organizations. The American Automobile Association (AAA) and its affiliated local clubs, in particular, produced illustrated "strip maps" showing detail and distances for key landmarks between two locations. Other companies, such as the Blue Book Company, produced books with detailed "turn-by-turn" instructions to navigate between two locations. Each method had pros and cons.

In his book, C.K. referred to several maps he used, but his descriptions make clear the maps were from differing sources. Some years after his trip, C.K. produced a map showing his route as travelled west of Colorado. That map is included in this book and it was also used to validate the methods by which the *most likely* route and details could be discovered and documented by "reverse engineering." Three main publication types were identified and analyzed to reach conclusions as to the route likely taken, even though C.K. may never have seen or used these actual publications during his journey. They main publications used for research are:

1. The National Old Trails Road Series of Strip Maps from the Automobile Club of Southern California ("*Auto Club*").

This club was arguably the most active of all AAA affiliates in the United States and had gone to great lengths to document and even place signposts from coast to coast along the National Old Trails Road (NOTR) and other main routes, such as the Lincoln Highway. Beginning in 1915, the Auto Club produced two booklets containing strip maps of the NOTR and "side trips" divided into over sixty route segments identified by number. Figure 3 is the title page of the 1916 edition of Part I of this two-volume series. Figure 4 is the index map of the series showing the numbered segments

Figure 3: Cover: *National Old Trails Road to California, 1916.*
Source: Automobile Club of Southern California.

from Los Angeles to Kansas City. One of the known issues with these maps is that they were not drawn completely to scale. Rather, they were created in order to reflect desired detail and key intersections. As a result, they do not line up well when overlaying them onto modern maps.

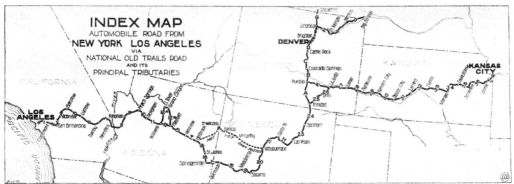

Figure 4: Index Map: *National Old Trails Road to California, 1916.*
Source: Automobile Club of Southern California.

Standards for Identification: The individual Auto Club strip maps referenced in this book are all from 1915 or 1916 and will be identified by their published number. For example, the route segment from Seligman to Peach Springs, AZ, is numbered "10." This map is identified in this book as *Auto Club Map 10*.

2. US Geological Survey (USGS) Topographical Maps.

There is no evidence that C.K. ever used such maps. However, they have been used to research and document key events based upon C.K's descriptions. Every effort has been made to locate the most period correct map, but there are gaps in their availability and the scales vary.

Standards for Identification: The individual USGS maps referenced here identify: a "quadrangle" of the map (including the state and name of the map); its scale series (typically "15 Minute" or "7.5 Minute"); and the year of publication. For example, *Ohio Thurston Quadrangle*, 15 Minute Series, 1909.

3. The Official Automobile Blue Book (*"Blue Book"*).

This resource was published by a private company in a number of volumes annually from 1901-1929. Each volume provided motorists with turn-by-turn instructions for the region using the publisher's unique "Route" numbering system that assigned numbers to each set of instructions. These route numbers were *not* the numbers of any state or national highways.

(Numbering of state or national roads did not begin until the mid-1920s.) Each set of route instructions were prepared by "pathfinders"—some paid and some volunteer—who established and updated the most efficient ways to get from "A" to "B." Each *Blue Book* contained a folded map of the region the volume covered with cities and towns marked by circles with lines drawn between them in the same manner as period railroad maps. The published routes between cities were one way routes. A different number was used to identify the route going the other way. For example, Figure 5 shows a segment of a map in the *Blue Book*.

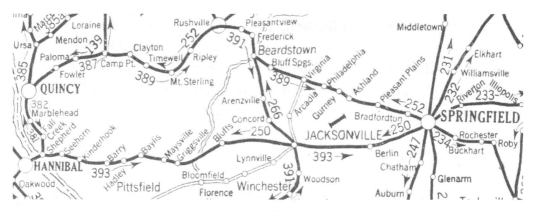

Figure 5: *Blue Book* Routes between Springfield, Illinois and Hannibal, Missouri. This identifies Routes 250 (westbound) and 393 (eastbound) between Springfield and Hannibal, a segment that C.K. wrote about traveling westbound.
Source: *Blue Book*, Vol. 5. 1919. Page 22.

Figure 6 contains the instructions for *Blue Book* Route 250. It includes references to a number of places C.K. described passing, including the ferry across the Illinois River to Valley City.

There is no indication that C.K. used the *Blue Book* for navigation while driving his motorcycle on the road. (It would have been extremely dangerous for him to have done so had he tried.) It is still worth citing, however, since it established the then current "state of the art" of routes. Absent evidence of deviations, the *Blue Book* should be relied upon as a reflection of the route C.K. would have taken.

Route 250—Springfield, Ill., to Hannibal, Mo.—105.3 m.
Reverse Route 393.
Via Berlin, Jacksonville, Valley City and Kinderhook. Dirt roads all the way. This route covers a section of the Pike's Peak Ocean-to-Ocean highway.

MILEAGE   For this and other exits see City Map, page 274.
Total Intermed.

0.0   0.0   **SPRINGFIELD**, 5th & Washington Sts., court house on left. Go south with trolley on 5th St.
1.0   1.0   Grand Ave.; stucco house on right; turn right. Cross RR 1.1.
2.2   1.2   Park Ave.; turn left into Washington Park, leaving trolley.
2.4   0.2   Fork, park building in center; bear left.
2.5   0.1   End of road; turn left. Avoid right fork immediately beyond.
2.9   0.4   Fork; bear right and at diagonal 4-corners, immediately beyond, turn right.
3.0   0.1   Caution, irregular 4-corners; bear sharp left.
3.1   0.1   Fork; bear right, going straight out of park. Cross RR 4.6.
7.9   4.8   Fork, store in center; bear left. Avoid road to left 8.4, keeping right past church on left.
15.2 7.3   **Berlin.** Straight thru. Avoid road to left 17.1. Keep ahead across iron bridge.
19.5 4.3   End of road; turn left.
19.6 0.1   Right-hand road; turn right with poles.
26.5 6.9   End of road; turn left and immediately right with poles. Jacksonville City Map and Points of Interest, page 255.
Turn left under RR 31.7 and immediately curve right onto State St., picking up trolley. Cross RRs at sta. 32.4.
32.9 6.4   **Jacksonville**, State & Main Sts., at public square.
HOTELS—Dunlap Hotel, on W. State St., 1½ blocks west of Public Square.
GARAGES—Modern Garage, 210 W. Court St., ½ blk. W. from N. W. cor. of Public Square.
Keep ahead around green, coming onto West State St.
33.9 1.0   Sandusky St., park on right; turn right. Cross RR 34.4.
34.6 0.7   4-corners; turn left. Avoid road to left 35.3. Curve right with road 35.6.
36.0 1.4   Left-hand road; turn left.
40.5 4.5   3-corners; bear right with poles.
41.9 1.4   Left-hand road, immediately beyond right turn; turn left with poles. Cross RR 43.2.
44.7 2.8   4-corners; turn right and take first left-hand road immediately beyond with poles.
46.9 2.2   End of road; turn left.
47.2 0.3   First right-hand road; turn right.
48.3 1.1   Irregular 4-corners; jog right and left.
51.2 2.9   End of road; meeting poles, turn left.
51.4 0.2   Irregular 4-corners; turn right and immediately left.
52.1 0.7   **Bluffs**, bank on left. Straight thru across RR at sta. Avoid road to right just beyond iron bridge 52.3.
53.5 1.4   Fork; bear left.
54.8 1.3   Left-hand road, just beyond right turn; turn left, avoiding left fork immediately beyond.
55.7 0.9   Right-hand road, immediately beyond iron bridge; turn right. Cross RR 59.1.

59.9 4.2   Ferry across Illinois river.
Charges: Roadster, 75c; touring car, 85c. Runs from 7:00 a. m. until 7:00 p. m.
Leaving ferry, curve left and right going up the main road.
60.3 0.4   End of road; meeting poles, turn right.
60.4 0.1   **Valley City**, irregular 4-corners immediately beyond RR at sta. Bear slightly left, leaving RR.
64.2 3.8   **Griggsville.** Take right-hand drive along small green.
68.1 3.9   **Maysville**, church on right. Straight thru.
70.6 2.5   **New Salem**, 4-corners, store on right. Turn right.
71.4 0.8   4-corners; turn left.
72.2 0.8   Left-hand road; turn left with poles and travel.
74.3 2.1   Right-hand road; turn right.
74.9 0.6   **Baylis**, sta. on left. Straight thru.
75.3 0.4   End of road; turn left across RR.
75.4 0.1   Right-hand road; turn right. Cross RR 77.5.
78.8 3.4   4-corners, school ahead on left; turn left. Cross RR at sta. 79.8.
80.3 1.5   **Hadley**, 4-corners. Turn right.
83.7 3.4   Right-hand road; turn right with travel, leaving poles.
83.8 0.1   4-corners; turn left with travel.
84.0 0.2   **Barry**, 4-corners, park on right. Turn right.
GARAGES—Clough-Reihm Co.
84.1 0.1   4-corners, brick bank on left; turn left one block and at old hotel turn right downgrade. Avoid road to left 84.4.
84.5 0.4   Left-hand road, just before mill; turn left.
84.8 0.3   End of road; bear right.
86.2 1.4   Fork, just beyond long iron bridge; bear left. Jog right and left across RR 87.2.
89.6 3.4   End of road; turn left with poles and travel.
89.9 0.3   Right-hand road; just before RR; turn right with travel.
90.9 1.0   Left-hand road; turn left and take first right-hand street with travel, keeping ahead two blocks.
91.1 0.2   4-corners; turn left three blocks.
91.3 0.2   **Kinderhook**, irregular 4-corners, stores on left and right, mill over to left. Turn right. Avoid road to left 91.6.
91.7 0.4   Fork, just beyond long iron bridge; keep right.
91.9 0.2   Fork; bear left with poles running along bluff.
97.9 6.0   Left-hand road, church on left; turn left with poles and travel. Cross RR at Seehorn 98.1. Avoid road to left 98.4.
Right-hand road at school 102.3 is Route 381 to Quincy.
Cross RR at Shepherd, Ill., 103.2.
103.3 5.4   Right-hand road, sign "Hannibal" on right; turn right.
103.9 0.6   Fork, just before RR viaduct; bear left, crossing Mississippi river on RR bridge (toll 50c), using caution for trains. Wait for signal from flagman.
104.3 0.4   End of road, just before tunnel; turn left. Cross RR 104.5.
Hannibal City Map and Points of Interest, page 425.
105.0 0.7   North St., end of street; turn right and take first left around brick factory onto Main St., keeping ahead three blocks.
105.3 0.3   **HANNIBAL, MO.**, Main St. & Broadway, bank on left.
GARAGES—Clough-Reihm Co.
Jessup's Garage, 105-117 S. 4th St.
SERVICE STA.—United States Tire Sales & Service Depots located here.

Figure 6: *Blue Book* Route 250.
Source: *Blue Book*, Vol. 5. 1919. Pages 295-297.

An effort was undertaken to acquire copies of all nine regional volumes of the 1919 edition of the *Blue Book* series—since that is the year of C.K.'s travels—and eight of the nine volumes were acquired. The 1918 version of the missing Volume 7 was acquired as were two additional volumes from 1920.

Standards for Identification: For brevity, all references to the *Blue Book* herein are to the 1919 editions of the *Blue Book,* unless otherwise noted with year in parentheses—e.g. *Blue Book* (1918). Additionally, the volume number is omitted from in-line references, as this would have been needlessly distracting. A complete list of referenced *Blue Book* volumes has been included in the Bibliography, including identification of all routes cited from that volume.

4. Other Maps and Resources.

There were numerous other "competing" maps and books of the period, including:

A. Strip maps produced by the United States Touring Information Bureau in Waterloo, IA, commonly called "*TIB*" books. Although the quality of the copies of the maps from the *TIB* books obtained during research is poor, they are remarkable because—in many cases—they include the populations of even the smallest communities along the route, an attribute of one of the maps that C.K. mentioned, a piece of data that has not been found on any other maps.

B. In 1913, the Arizona Good Roads Association in Prescott produced a series of strip maps in a 200-page illustrated *Road Maps and Tour Book*. Like the *Auto Club* maps, these strip maps were not drawn to scale, instead focusing on desired detail and key intersections. Unlike the *Auto Club* maps, the Arizona Good Roads Association also included numerous photographs of key intersections or landmarks along the route. Although these photos are almost too small to be useful, the photographs provided users with visual cues they were on the right road. Of critical importance, this *Road Maps and Tour Book* contains the most detailed presentation—compared to all other sources—of the route from Flagstaff to the Grand Canyon—which was really just an old stage coach "road" across the open desert even though it had been sign-posted by the *Auto Club* in 1916.

THE ORIGINAL TEXT
BY CAPTAIN C.K. SHEPHERD

PREFACE

A few months after the Armistice of 1918 was signed,[1] when the talk of everyone concerned was either WHEN they would be demobilized or what they would do when they WERE demobilized, two young men were exchanging views on this same subject in the heavy atmosphere of a very ordinary hotel somewhere in London.

One[2] was wondering how near, or how far, were the days when he would see the old home-folks once again "way back in Dixieland."[3]

The other was wondering what form of dissipation would be best suited to remove that haunting feeling of unrest, which as a result of three or four years of active service was so common amongst the youth of England at that time.

"How about getting married?" suggested the one.[4]

Then followed a long pause, wherein the other was evidently considering the pros and cons of such a unique proposition.

"Nothing doing," he replied eventually—"not exciting enough, old man." Another pause—"And when I come to think, I don't know of any girl who'd want to marry me even if I wanted to marry her." And as if to give a final decision to any proposal of that nature, he added—"Besides, I couldn't afford it!"

"But I tell you what I will do, Steve," said he, "I'll go back with you across yon, herring-pond[5] and have a trot round America."

So that was how it happened.

Two or three months later, when I arrived at New York from Canada,[6] I purchased a motor-cycle and set out to cross the continent to the Pacific, and I have it on the best authority that this was the first time an Englishman had ever accomplished the trip on a motor-cycle. If it is so, I don't wonder at it![7]

The whole trip, which covered just fifty miles short of 5,000, was undertaken quite alone, and although spread over about three months, constituted a day or two short of a month's actual riding. For the benefit of brother motor-cyclists who may be interested in such details I may add that I dispensed entirely with the use of goggles from beginning to end, and except at stops in large towns on the way I wore no hat. I think that when the motor-cyclist gets accustomed to doing without these encumbrances he will find the joys of motor-cycling considerably enhanced.

The total number of replacements to the engine alone comprised the following: Five new cylinders; three pistons; five gudgeon pins; three complete sets of bearings; two connecting rods, and eleven sparking plugs.[8]

The machine was entirely overhauled on four occasions between the Atlantic and the Pacific, and on three of these by the recognized agents of the manufacturers.[9] The engine cut-out switch was the only part of the machine that did not break, come loose, or go wrong sooner or later. I was thrown off 142 times,[10] and after that I stopped counting! Apart from that I had no trouble.

Contrary to what the reader may think, I paid considerable care to the machine, particularly in the early stages. For the first three hundred miles I barely exceeded twenty to twenty-five miles per hour in order to give the machine a good "running-in" before submitting it to harder work. At the end of the trip I had spent more in repairs and replacements than the original cost of the machine,[11] and I sold it at San Francisco[12] for just over a quarter of the amount I paid for it[13] three months before.

And I am still as keen a motor-cyclist as ever!

The machine was of the four-cylinder, air-cooled type, and I have nothing but praise for the smooth running that this type affords.[14] I have ridden scores of machines at one time and another, but never have I driven any motor-cycle that for luxurious travel could I even compare with the one mentioned in this narrative. As regards reliability, however, I must leave the reader to form his own opinion from the facts, which occurred exactly as I have stated them. Nothing in this book is set down in malice, and I can only hope that my case was exceptional so far as the frequent breakdowns were concerned. I must admit that the conditions were exceptional and that anyone crossing the United States on a motor-cycle might expect trouble sooner or later.

The reader may observe that I say little of tyre trouble throughout the story. That is for two reasons: the first is that there is nothing at all interesting in the narrative of repairing a puncture, for instance; the second is that I had very little trouble indeed to complain of. With the smooth, even torque that is so characteristic of four-cylinder engines, tyre trouble is easily halved, and practically all that one has to fear is the terrible condition of most of the roads. I arrived in San Francisco with the same tyres as I had when I started, and they were still good for several hundreds of miles more.

Petrol consumption, too, was excellent. Those who have not known high-powered, four-cylinder motor-cycles would probably think the consumption would be about forty miles to the gallon. On the contrary, I found my machine much more economical than the same-powered V-twin. As far as I know I averaged about 75 m.p.g. "all on."

The journey was comparatively uneventful. I never had to shoot anybody and nobody shot me! In spite of the relative wildness and barrenness of the West, there were always food and petrol available in plenty. I spent most nights at the side of the road and experienced neither rheumatism nor rattlesnakes.

In the following pages I have endeavoured to portray America and Americans exactly as I found them and as they appealed to me. If at times I perchance may give offence to any who are lovers of all and anything American, I do it without intent. Suffice it to say that before I went I had the highest opinion of anything that came from that worthy country, so that it cannot be claimed that I am one of those "Pro-British-every-time" individuals who delight in criticizing other countries and other peoples in order to gratify their own sense of national or other superiority.

Finally, I will ask the reader to be patient, or at any rate, not over-critical when he or she may confess to being bored. For the sake of making this a complete record of my wanderings I have included that which may lack interest, and as I can lay claim to no graceful diction, I may, I am sure, rely on the reader's indulgence towards the narrative of quite an ordinary, unaspiring, British motor-cyclist.

C. K. S.
Birmingham, 1922.[15]

PREFACE NOTES

1. The Armistice signed on November 11, 1918 served as the agreement that ended the fighting on the Western Front in the First World War. It went into effect at 11 a.m. in Paris on November 11, 1918 ("the eleventh hour of the eleventh day of the eleventh month," now known as Veteran's Day in the United States). If "a few months after" was three months later, it would have been about March 11, 1919. This estimation is further supported by his subsequent statement that he arrived in New York from Canada on June 3, 1919, "two or three months" *after* the conversation.

2. The "One" person was "Steve" (Thomas Stevenson, Jr.) and the other was C.K. himself. While on the trip across America, C.K. paid a lengthy visit to Steve and his father, Thomas Senior, in Cincinnati. Both men were born in Scotland. Thomas Senior had emigrated to the United States in 1913. Steve was farming in Alberta, Canada, in 1914 when he visited his parents in Cincinnati on his way back to England to enlist in the Royal Flying Corps (RFC). Steve and C.K. worked together, moving up through the ranks to Captain at the "Engine Repair Shops" in what became the Royal Air Force (RAF), both serving in France during WWI. Thus, this conversation was between two British RAF Officers who had just completed their service together in WWI.

3. As a definite geographic location within the United States, "Dixie" or "Dixieland" is usually defined as the eleven Southern states that seceded in 1860-1861 to form the Confederate States of America. However, Cincinnati, Ohio is north of Kentucky (thus not among the "Confederate States"). It is reasonable that one who is not an American (such as Steve) might think of the entire United States as "Dixieland" and, like many Europeans, refer to all Americans as "Yankees"—in spite of the fact that Americans today (and perhaps in 1919 as well) would associate those terms with different geographic regions across the country.

4. Neither man was married at the time. C.K. married his first wife, Ursula Mary Edwards, on November 21, 1922 within a month or two of when this book was first published. Steve (Thomas Stevenson, Jr.) married Blanch Edna Davis on March 30, 1927.

5. The eastern coast of North America (the Atlantic Ocean) is the habitat of abundant herring fish, hence the basis of the "herring-pond" nickname which, according to the *Oxford English Dictionary, Second Edition*, was first used in 1686.

6. C.K. arrived in Montreal aboard the SS *Megantic* on Tuesday, June 3, 1919 at 4:00 p.m. He entered the United States the same day and was processed by a border post under the auspices of the Border Patrol station at St. Albans, Vermont. He did not necessarily *enter* the US in St. Albans, Vermont, as each border crossing post in the area was administered by the St. Albans office. C.K. completed his US arrival card stating that his destination was Persons Manufacturing Co., 54-68 Bloomingdale Road, Worcester, Massachusetts—a maker of motorcycle saddles. Because his father, Timothy Shepherd, owned the XL-ALL, Ltd.—a manufacturer of saddles, motorcycles, and motorcycle accessories in Hall Green, Birmingham, England—it seems that C.K.'s visit to Persons Manufacturing was business-related. C.K. may have been visiting the company for one of three potential purposes: (a) collect/demand royalties for patent infringement; (b) convince them to distribute the XL-ALL saddles in the US; or (c) determine if Persons would like XL-ALL to distribute their saddles in the U.K. While there are no known records to confirm these theories, numerous period news accounts reported that the purpose of C.K.'s trip was a mix of both business and pleasure.

The June 1918 New York Central Railroad ("NYCRR") timetable indicates that, in order to get from Montreal to Worcester (having arrived in Montreal at 4 p.m. and the US the same day), he would almost certainly have taken the #62 Rutland Line train that departed Montreal at 8:00 p.m. and arrived in Albany at 4:05 a.m. From Albany, he would have taken the Boston and Albany Railroad (B&ARR) #46, departing at 04:55 a.m. and arriving at Worcester at 09:45 a.m. on Wednesday, June 4, 1919. That would allow him to meet the rest of the day with representatives of Persons Manufacturing.

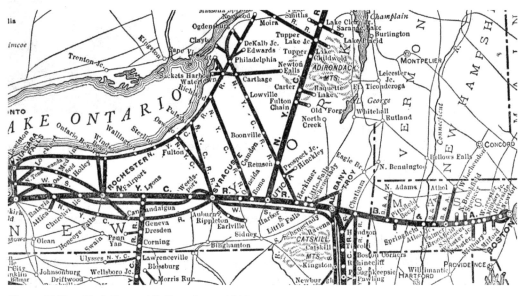

Figure 7: New York Central Railroads, *ca.* 1918.
Source: *The New York Central Railroad Company Timetable.* June 30, 1918.

At the beginning of Chapter 1, C.K. states that he took a Pullman train from Niagara Falls to New York City. There are three trains that he may have taken from Worcester back over to Niagara Falls via B&ARR and NYCRR. There were trains—all of which were overnight rides with sleeper cars—as shown below with scheduled Worcester departure time and scheduled arrival time in Niagara Falls:

(#29) 18:00-08:50
(#59) 21:00-12:20
(#73) 23:00-15:20

C.K. had a photo of the American Falls in his personal slide collection (Figure 8) but it could only have been taken from the Canadian side.

Figure 8: Photo of American Falls from Canada, *ca.* 1919.
C.K. took this photo, but the vantage is from the Canadian side of the falls, so it seems most likely it was taken as he journeyed back to New York from California.
Source: C.K.'s personal slide collection.

Years later, on September 19, 1940, C.K. wrote a letter to Steve in which he compared the noise of British anti-aircraft guns to that of Niagara Falls from the *Maid of the Mist*, the name of the boat tour that still exists as of this writing. It would have been a long day for C.K., but if he arrived at Niagara Falls at 08:50 a.m. on Thursday, June 5, 1919, he would have been able to see the sights—including the boat tour—and still make it aboard a train to New York City the next morning. At the time there were only morning departures from Niagara Falls arriving at Grand Central Station in New York. The train rides were about twelve hours long. It is highly probable he travelled from Niagara Falls on the morning of Friday, June 6, 1919 on one of these trains:

(#58, The Metropolitan) 06:05-18:15
(#40, The Michigan Central Limited) 08:30-19:30
(#20, The New Yorker) 10:00-20:45

This means that C.K. would have arrived in New York City as early as the evening of Friday, June 6, 1919, still only a week before he drove away from the Henderson dealer.

7. C.K.'s use of the words "first…Englishman" is an important qualification because there were accounts of numerous American riders who journeyed back and forth across America by motorcycle before him and set long-distance speed records. Among these notable American motorcyclists were Wells Bennett, Alan Bedell, Hap Scherer, and Erwin George "Cannon Ball" Baker (whom C.K. mentions he spoke to in Chapter 19).

Also, C.K.'s "first…Englishman" claim was implicitly repeated in a series of at least five installments in *Pacific Motorcyclist and Western Wheelman ("Pacific Motorcyclist")* about his ride beginning August 21, 1919. The publication reported that he was the "first *foreign* motorcyclist *of note* to make the transcontinental trip across America" (italics emphasis added), leaving some room for the possibility that others came before C.K. but their achievement was not recorded or they may have been a different nationality (e.g., French, German, etc.).

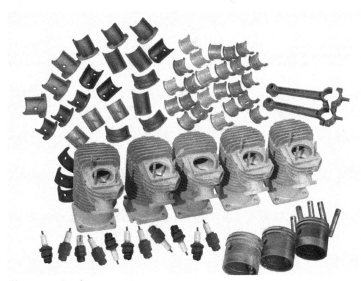

8. The parts depicted in Figure 9 illustrate the replacement parts that C.K. endured. These are unusable parts I set aside during the course of restoring my own 1919 Henderson.

Figure 9: *Replacement Parts*

9. The three Henderson agents he would have used in the cities he cited were:

- *Cincinnati:* Motorcycle Sales Co., 1525 Race St., Cincinnati, Ohio.

- *Kansas City:* Excelsior-Henderson Motorcycle Co., 211 East 15th St., Kansas City, Missouri.

- *Los Angeles:* Henderson Motorcycle Sales Co., 977 S Main St., Los Angeles, California.

10. The number of times he says he was thrown off varies depending on publication. In this book, C.K. reports that he stopped counting at one hundred and forty two. However, in his 1968 work *Introduction to Spiritualism* he states that he stopped counting after having been thrown off one hundred and thirty seven times.

Figure 10: 1919 Henderson Four Advertisement.
Source: *Popular Science Monthly,* Vol. 93, No. 96. December 1918. Page 103.

11. The 1919 Henderson Four was dubbed "the Aristocrat of Motorcycles" and was advertised at a price of $435 for the 1919 Model Z-2-E full electric (generator, battery, horn, lights, etc.) as shown in Figure 10.

C.K. added a luggage rack and speedometer to his machine. Assuming these extras cost another $45, he would have paid $480. A newspaper article in New Mexico reported that C.K. stated he paid $550, but he may have been including costs for repairs. Accounting for inflation over one hundred years, the $480 amount would be equal to about $7,225, which is a rather low price for one of the highest-end motorcycles on the market.

12. In the Epilogue, C.K. states that he sold the bike for $125.

13. If $125 was "just over ¼ of what he paid for it," and "just over" is $5, then 4 x $120 would equal a sale price of $480—a value supposedly confirmed by the Henderson agency in San Francisco as described in the Epilogue.

14. Figure 11 is from the Henderson Operating Manual for the 1919 Z-2. The model depicted is not an electric model like the one C.K. rode, nor does it have a speedometer or luggage rack. It also does not have the double-brake on the rear wheel, which was made of both Excelsior and Henderson parts on the 1919 model.

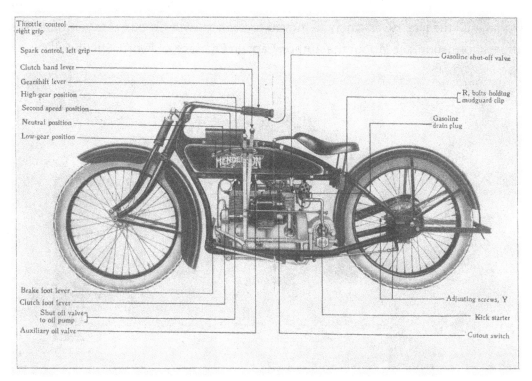

Figure 11: 1919 Henderson Z-2.
Source: *Instructions for Operation and Care of Henderson Four-Cylinder Motorcycles - 1919 Model Z-2.* Excelsior Motor Mfg. & Supply Co. Pages 16-17.

15. When he separated from the RAF in early 1919, and even upon his entrance to the US on June 3, 1919, C.K. provided "Newbie, Wythall [near] Birmingham, England" as his address. At the time, Newbie House (see Figure 12) was the home of his brother, George Frederick Shepherd. It is not known if C.K. ever actually lived there, but the house still stands today at 68 Westfield Rd., Birmingham, England, B15 3QQ. C.K. called Birmingham home until the late 1930s when he moved to London with his business ventures. (For more information, see "About the Author: Captain Charles Kenilworth Shepherd.")

NEWBIE HOUSE, WYTHALL, NEAR BIR-
MINGHAM. J. B. SCOTT, ARCHITECT

Figure 12: Newbie House, Wythall, Near Birmingham, J.B. Scott, Architect.
Source: *The International Studio*, Vol. 43, No. 171, May 1911. Pages 212-216.

PROLOGUE

One bright morning in June—to be exact, the thirteenth (the significance of that number will be apparent later), in the year of Our Lord 1919 and in the year of American Prohibition 1, a small assembly of mechanics, passers-by, and urchins witnessed my departure[16] from a well-known Motor Cycle Agency in New York.[17]

The machine, a perfectly new and very powerful motor-cycle, was dazzling in her pristine beauty. No spot or blemish could be seen on her enamel of khaki hue. No ungainly scratch or speck of rust marred her virgin form. Her four little cylinders, gaily murmuring as the engine joyfully sprang into life, seemed to hide a world of romance as if they were whispering to each other of the days that were to come, the adventures and experiences they were to encounter, and the strange lands they were to see. The purr of her exhaust, healthy though muffled, smooth and even in its rhythm, was music in my ears. A thing of beauty is a joy for ever, and to those who know the call of the open road and who love to feel the rush of the wind and the glamour of speed, such was this machine. Although she was in reality but an organized combination of various pieces of unfeeling, soulless metal, without even a name, and known only by a sordid number embossed on a tinplate provided by the Law, she was soon to develop a character and personality of her own. She was to play the rôle[18] of sole companion in the weeks and months to follow. There would be times when I should curse her profanely and at the same time love her passionately. I pictured vast prairies and deserts where we should be alone together, far from the haunts of man or animal or perhaps of any living thing— times when it would depend upon HER to bear me on to civilization. So I trust, reader, that you will not think I was waxing too sentimental on that memorable day in June.

* * * * *

The mileage indicator just flicked to 4,422.[19]

I was hungry, hungry as a dog. I was thirsty too, and tired oh, so tired! The skin on my face was tanned dark with the desert sun and bore the dirt of many days' accumulation. The growth of the previous week was upon my chin. My hair was

1

bleached and dishevelled, my clothes and boots laden with the sand and dust of Arizona and California. With a bandaged, broken finger, and the rest skin-cracked and bloodstained with the alkali sand, I held the handles with the palms of my hands. The sole was missing altogether from my right boot, and the left contained many a piece of stone or gravel from far away. A couple of empty water-bags flapped up and down on the handlebar, and as the old bus dragged her weary way on three cylinders through the crowded streets of Los Angeles her hideous clatter told many a tale of woe. I decided at that moment that the best thing in all the world was to get something to eat and drink.

"What's the day of the month?" I asked, when with a final "clank" of the engine we drove into the Agency Garage.[20]

"The seventh."

"The month?"

"August."

"And what's the year?"

"Nineteen nineteen."

"The seventh of August nineteen nineteen,"[21] I mused, and relapsed into contemplative silence. . . .

Some one spotted the registration plate "N.Y. 8844"[22] and "rumbled" that I had come from New York.

"When did you start?" they asked in curious tones. The question pulled me up with a jerk and brought me back to normal existence, so inadequately measured by time.

"Oh, seems like ten years ago!" I replied, and relapsed once more into reverie.

PROLOGUE NOTES

16. Although he says the significance of *13* will become apparent later, nothing else in the book seems to address the relevance of "13" or "June 13th." Additionally, in an August 21, 1919 article in *Pacific Motorcyclist,* C.K. stated that, "on the afternoon of June 14th last I could be seen sailing along New York's Broadway." If both dates are accurate, it suggests he picked up the motorcycle at the dealer on June 13, 1919, or—more likely—purchased the motorcycle before then and stopped at the dealer shortly before leaving town.

17. It may never be possible to positively identify the dealer where C.K. purchased his machine, but most of the Excelsior and Henderson motorcycles shipped to New York were delivered to exporters like Melchior, Armstrong & Dessau, Inc. and Martin C. Van der Wal. Although Edwards & Crist Co. did some exporting, they were a national "chain" with showrooms around the United States. Therefore, it seems more likely that C.K. bought his bike at Edwards & Crist Co., 938 Eighth Avenue, New York, which was about a mile north on Broadway from his room at the Hotel McAlpin.

18. *"rôle":* This word is of French origin and is synonymous with the modern "role."

19. A comparison of this 4,422 odometer reading to those cited later in the book indicate that he drove an extra 113 miles between Kansas City, Missouri, and Los Angeles, California. This extra mileage is certainly understandable given the various detours and excursions he took between the two cities which, using published roads of the period amounted to almost 2,387 miles, with the extra 113 miles being just 5% over the accumulated published distance.

20. This "Agency Garage" was Henderson Motorcycle Sales Co., 907 S Main St., Los Angeles.

21. August 7, 1919.

22. I have been unable to determine if 8844 was his actual plate number. In 1919, New York plates were white letters on black. Auto numbers were hyphenated (e.g. 123-456 or 12-345, etc.). Motorcycle plates in New York were four or five white numbers on black (see Figure 13).

Figure 13: Example of a 1919 New York Motorcycle License Plate.
Source: Ebay.

CHAPTER I

TRAFFIC IN NEW YORK

I spent the better part of two days in the survey of New York City from all points of view.[23] In the Pullman from Niagara[24] I had decided that America would probably be just as bad as any European country for robbing the alien. I would therefore simulate the gentle habits and customs of these (hitherto) worthy people. Having some slight knowledge of their language I would endeavour to acquire perfection in the art of American self-expression.

I would cultivate the correct pose of the hat and wear boots with knobbly toes. Only a little practice would be required before I should be able to gyrate a cigar at the accepted velocity from one corner of my mouth to the other. In a little while, methought, I should feel much more at ease in tight-fitting clothes with ridiculously small sleeves and three inches of projecting shirt-cuffs.[25] Maybe I should improve my outlook on the world if I viewed it through a pair of large, round, ebony-rimmed spectacles. There was just a possibility that I should some day appreciate the soothing charm of a much-overworked morsel of chewing-gum. With all these splendid accomplishments I could no doubt dispense with the less attractive habits of Modern America.

Let me say at the outset that I proved a dismal failure. I would sooner master the Chinese than the American lingo. The infinite variations of nasal accomplishment outnumber by far the tribal dialects of India[26] and leave the poor student to wonder and despair. Why! the number of orthodox ways of translating the plain English word "Yes" is probably beyond the scope of mathematical deduction! The shades and blends between "Yep" and "Ye-oh" alone are sufficient to put a spectrograph of the sun to shame.[27]

For four months[28] I travelled through the wilds of New York, Ohio, and Illinois, and even into the civilized states of Colorado, New Mexico, and Arizona, in a vain search for the man who pronounced "Yes" with a final "s." In the end I found him, lurking in a little restaurant in Los Angeles. I gazed in wonderment intense and rapturous when I heard it. I have his pedigree. He said he came from Boston.

Boston, according to all well-informed Bostonians, represents the acme of perfection in all things relating to education, etiquette, and propriety. As such it is unassailable by any other city in America.

There was a time early on when I thought I was succeeding well. I found that I did better by dispensing with speech altogether. If I dressed in a "Palm Beach" suit,[29] walked on people's feet, elbowed my way through passers-by, and continually repeated to myself "The earth is mine and all that therein is," there was never any doubt but that I was a "Native Son."

It is superfluous for me to say, however, that after many trials and more rebuffs, I ultimately abandoned the idea of becoming Americanized. "After all," thought I, "what sane Englishman wants to be an American?" The project had been but a brain-wave to combat the "H.C. of L." To the uninitiated, that is the recognized "Hearst"[30] abbreviation for the "High Cost of Living,"[31] a topic which so frequently appears in American newspapers that editors were forced to face the question of either referring to it in symbols or of cutting out the "Want-Ads." Finally, therefore, I consoled myself that it was better for hotel bills, cinemas, ice-cream sodas, petrol, and other necessities to rise 200 per cent, on my approach than for me to lose my own soul.[32] Incidentally, virtue does not always have its own reward. On my return to England I heard many accusations against me.

"What an awful American accent you have!" was the greeting of many one-time friends.

. . . Some have recovered. Others are still in hospital!

* * * * *

It took me some time to get accustomed to the traffic of New York—rather should I say, to its habits and practices. New York itself consists of a network of streets and avenues ingeniously arranged on an island which is about five or six times longer than it is broad. The avenues run the length of the island and the streets run at right angles across them. In addition, "Broadway" wobbles across from one end of the island to the other, cutting the avenues at a weird angle of anything between nothing and twenty degrees.

At all the important street crossings was stationed a "traffic cop" whose duty was apparently to hold up at the most inconvenient intervals all the traffic going one way until all the traffic going the other way had passed. Then he blew his whistle and Hey, presto! the traffic in the other street began to move. It was fatal to move before the whistle was blown. I didn't know that!

I had been sailing down Sixth Avenue, just trying the machine for the first time, as a matter of fact. Everything went smoothly. I felt at peace with all the world. Here was I on my iron steed of ten little horses, about to begin a long holiday wherein I should forget the Kaiser and his deeds[33] and the four or more years of my existence that had gone in helping to bring about his everlasting undoing. But all of a sudden:

"Why the jooce don't yer stop, yer Goldarn young son of a gun?" bellowed an irate "cop" who gesticulated but a few feet from my front wheel.

"Well, why the blankety blank SHOULD I blankety well stop, anyway?" I returned, not to be outdone, as I pulled up in the exact centre of 34th Street, Sixth Avenue, and Broadway.[34]

I could see a crowd beginning to collect. I don't like crowds at any time. I have a keen antipathy for publicity. My friend the "cop" drew nigh. "See here, young fellar: whar yer from?" he inquired, evidently anxious to investigate further the mental condition of this unique defier of the Law. . . . To cut a long story short, I was finally constrained by good judgment to avoid further constabulary hostilities and, in accordance with the somewhat over-ardent desire of the "cop," retired like a whipped schoolboy to the corner where there was already a long queue of waiting automobiles and taxis. In a few seconds the whistle was blown and the procession sailed across 34th Street, headed by a much-humbled motor-cyclist.[35]

I should explain at this juncture that a motor-cyclist is an altogether despised individual in America. Motor-cycles are not popular over there. With few exceptions they are owned by delivery men, newspaper boys, "traffic-cops" and sundry other undesirables. Personally I do not wonder at it. The roads and streets in the cities are bad enough to ruin the constitution of any but the most confirmed young "blood" who does not mind risking a few broken bones. I have seen places in Broadway where the tram-lines wander six or seven inches above the surface of the road and where the pot-holes would accommodate comfortably quite a family of dead dogs within their depths.

So much for the cities. The roads that traverse the country are with few exceptions nothing better than our fifth-rate country roads on which no self-respecting Englishman would ride.

Here and there, in the far East and the far West, are found stretches of concrete or macadam. Somehow, the Americans think they are great road-builders. A couple of inches of concrete laid over a garden-path or a sheep-track, with the cracks filled in with tar, represents the zenith of road construction in this country of ninety odd million inhabitants. I should like to see some of those concrete roads when they have had a few years' solid wear with heavy lorries and occasional traction engines.

Ninety-five per cent or more, however, of America's highways are dirt roads, or what they are pleased to call "Natural Gravel."[36] In many cases they comprise merely a much worn trail, and as often as not a pair of ruts worn in the prairie. Very often, instead of being a single pair of ruts, there are five or six or perhaps ten, where individual cars have manifested their own personality. When this multiplicity of ruts crosses and re-crosses in a desperate attempt to achieve the survival of the fittest, the resultant effect on the poor motor-cyclist is somewhat disconcerting. But of this more anon.[37] Suffice it to say that on the whole journey of 4,500 miles from one coast to the other, I only saw FOUR other motor-cyclists on the road anywhere.[38]

So the reader will perhaps understand why the poor human who travels in this fashion is to be pitied, and why his associates in the towns and cities are despised by the rest of the community.

When I had acclimatized myself to the traffic of New York and could worm my way successfully in and out of the "hold-ups" or dart between trams, taxis, cars, and other impedimenta without danger either to the community or to myself, I felt that it was time for me to commence my peregrinations in earnest.

I decided first, however, to visit Coney Island, which is within easy reach of New York (it is only a few miles away), and, with a plentiful supply of trains, trams, and 'buses, is fed with a never-ending stream of pleasure-seeking humanity.[39] It has one avenue of perhaps a couple of miles' length running parallel with the beach, and every nook and corner on both sides accommodates a "fun palace" of some kind. There are dancing-halls by the dozen; mountain railways, switchbacks, and roundabouts by the score; soda fountains by the hundred. Fronting the beach are hotels, boarding-houses, and restaurants of all types save the best. Coney Island is decidedly not a place for the élite. Hither flock young couples, married or single, representatives of the American democracy, for a week-end of frivolity. The beach is at all times sprinkled, as by a human pepper-box, with specimens of the "genus anthropomorpha"[40] of all sizes, of all ages, of all shapes, and in all stages of dress and undress. I opined that indeed 'twas no place for me, and with one push of the starting pedal the motor was a living thing. "Enough is as good as a feast," and an hour at the Playground of New York was an hour well spent; but I left it for ever behind me without the slightest desire or intention of ever returning to its whirl of plebeian gaiety.

Arrived once more at New York City, I prepared to make my adieux.[41] I had two handbags only, one a beautiful new dressing-case, resplendent with pig-skin writing pads, ebony brushes, and glass bottles, and the other, a slightly larger one, which accommodated my spare clothing, boots, etc., and the miscellaneous collection of junk that every globe-trotter inevitably carries around with him.

Now I have an inherent contempt for side-cars, although had one been available at New York when I bought the machine I should have taken it and carried all my luggage with me. That would have been the acme of luxury. As it was, however, I contented myself with a good strong carrier[42] and with many straps; the dressing-case, surrounded by a good thick blanket, was securely attached to the back of the machine. The other bag I "shipped" on by train to my predetermined stops across the country.

That dressing-case must have weighed fifty or sixty pounds, and with the blanket around it looked an alarming size when *in situ*.[43] There was no hope for it. I'm that kind of individual who always likes plenty of silk shirts and pyjamas[44] and things, so it didn't occasion me the slightest worry if the people did stare wildly at me as I passed through their towns and villages.

And they "sure" did!

CHAPTER 1 NOTES

23. It is not clear that he did this "survey" on his motorcycle, but given the availability of public transit, it is plausible that he conducted it while he was waiting for his motorcycle to be prepared by the dealer. In any case, he left New York City on his journey across America less than two weeks after arriving in America.

24. In a September 19, 1940 letter sent to Steve, C.K. referenced the "Captain of the *Maid of the Mist* at Niagara Falls" in such a manner as to indicate he did, in fact, tour Niagara Falls at some point. However, C.K.'s precise pre-ride and post-ride itinerary is not known, including this "Pullman from Niagara."

25. It is not known where C.K.'s impression of American fashion originated or why he believed that extended sleeves were not an intentional fashion design. In all likelihood he probably witnessed people wearing clothing designs he disliked or perhaps did not fit well. However, protruding sleeves were a fashion at the time, as evident in Figure 14.

26. This is evidently an extreme exaggeration. Although 1919 data is unavailable, the Indian census of 1961 recognized 1,652 different languages; however, many of these are "foreign" languages (such as English), not "dialects."

Figure 14: The Beltsac (Protruding Sleeves). **Source:** *Saturday Evening Post.* Vol. 189, No. 40. March 31, 1917. Page 2.

27. Another extreme exaggeration, likely intended as humor. The statement is an allusion to the scientific method of determining the composition of the sun by examining the "almost countless number" of lines within its spectrum using methods developed in the 1800s. His reference to the spectrum of sunlight is conspicuous, however. Later in his life, C.K. conducted a great deal of research and investigation into refraction of light and developed specialized luminescent paints.

28. He departed from Liverpool, England on May 23, 1919 and returned there on September 19, 1919 (a few days short of four months). He arrived in the US on June 3, 1919 and departed on September 10, which means he actually spent just over three months "traveling through the wilds" of the country. (The breakdown, therefore, consists of two months on the ride and one month in total using train and public transportation on each end of the journey.)

29. A "Palm Beach suit" (see Figure 15) was a French-faced jacket with or without a butterfly shoulder lining (or no lining at all). Usually made of white linen—or a mohair and cotton blend—it was popular in tropical climates during the 1920s. A company later formed and used the name, but they were just marketing an existing term.

Figure 15: Palm Beach Suit.
Source: *Kansas City Star*, July 11, 1917. Page 24.

30. C.K. is referring to William Randolph Hearst (born April 29, 1863 in San Francisco, CA; died August 14, 1951 in Beverly Hills, CA), the American newspaper publisher who built up the nation's largest newspaper chain—thirty-eight newspapers at its peak—and whose methods profoundly influenced American journalism. Hearst is commonly believed to have been the inspiration for the main character of the 1941 Orson Welles film, *Citizen Kane*.

31. The term "H.C. of L" has not been found in searches of newspapers of the day. The acronym "H.C.L." *does* frequently appear in news articles and advertising spanning 1919-1920, but it is not clear whether a Hearst newspaper first coined the term. Often, it appears to be prefixed with "old" as in "How to beat Old H.C.L."

32. It seems most likely that this 200% inflation reference was C.K.'s way of describing how people "saw him coming" as a gullible foreigner, and therefore charged him twice as much as an American for the same goods or services. While the high cost of living was a major economic issue in 1919, 200% was a significant exaggeration. The US Labor Department had created the Consumer Price Index in 1913 as a means to measure the cost of living and quantify its increases as inflation rates. The chart in Figure 16 reflects the inflation rate for the decade following 1913.

Year	Inflation Rate
1914	1.3%
1915	0.9%
1916	7.7%
1917	17.8%
1918	17.3%
1919	15.2%
1920	15.6%
1921	-10.9%
1922	-6.2%
1923	1.8%

Figure 16: Chart Indicating Inflation Rates Spanning 1914-1923.
Source: Federal Reserve Bank of Minneapolis.

33. Kaiser Wilhelm II (1859-1941), the German Kaiser (emperor) and king of Prussia from 1888 to 1918, was one of the most recognizable public figures of World War I (1914-1918). Beginning in 1919, numerous attempts were made to prosecute him for war crimes, but he had been granted asylum in the Netherlands after his abdication in 1918 and all efforts to extradite him failed.

34. Broadway crosses 6th Avenue between 33rd and 34th Streets. The area is named Herald Square, after the now-defunct *New York Herald* newspaper (see the center of the postcard in Figure 18), which was located on the northern edge of the square until it was demolished in 1921. The Hotel McAlpin, where C.K. stayed while he was in New York, is out of view on the right. Today, the roads have been routed so as to avoid the need for the major six-way intersection that existed in 1919. In addition to the road traffic that filled the streets at the time, there was a new elevated train running above Sixth Avenue. Figures 17 and 18 present a map of the area circa 1920 alongside a postcard of Herald Square from 1919.

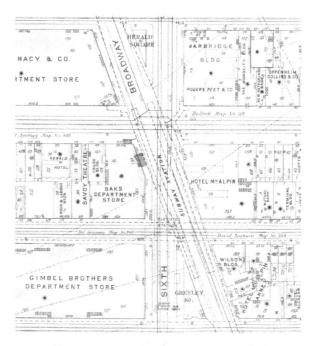

Figure 17: Map of 6th Avenue between 33rd and 34th Streets, Today Known as Herald Square.
Source: *Atlas of the City of New York, Borough of Manhattan.* New York: G.W. Bromley & Co. 1920. Plate 21, Part of Section 3.

Figure 18: North View of the New Elevated Train Tracks Above Sixth Avenue.
Source: Postcard. New York: American Studio. 1919.

35. If C.K. was travelling south on 6th Avenue and stopped by the cop at 34th Street, he would have been riding under the new elevated tracks (which he does not mention). It is likely that he embellished this story, since C.K. tells of other encounters with law enforcement throughout the book. It seems he had a penchant for ignoring or challenging authority later in life as well; in September 1924 he was fined £5 for failing to stop as directed by a constable at Five Ways—a busy intersection in Birmingham, England.

36. A description of "natural gravel" roads is found Figure 19.

11. Natural Gravel Roads

The most common type of gravel road is the one built from natural gravel banks; that is, roads built with unscreened bank material with the possible removal of the larger particles of stone. These roads are ordinarily constructed by dumping the material shovelled from the gravel bank onto the surface of old roads in such a manner as to widen them out and to adjust the cross grades so as to properly drain the surface of the road. A typical cross-section of a natural gravel road is shown in Fig. 1. After the gravel is deposited upon the surface of the road, it should be well handled

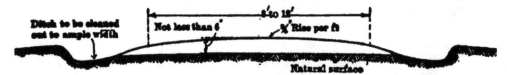

Fig. 1. Natural Gravel Road

over, leaving no piles undisturbed. Otherwise, since a portion of the road is compacted harder when the material is dumped and left in place, there will be a decided bump in the travelled portion of the road which can only be removed by harrowing or continued dragging. For roads under light country travel, this is a satisfactory method of procedure, but the following rules should be followed: If the road to be improved is exceedingly narrow, the grass on the sides should be removed and carted away from the road; the ditches should be deepened and proper drainage outlets provided.

Natural gravel roads are advisable in many instances where the material is easily available and where the road is not liable to be subjected to a large amount of motor travel, nor to a continuous travel thruout the year. Some of the easiest riding and most comfortable roads are those which are built by this method without the use of either roller or other device.

Figure 19: Natural Gravel Roads.
Source: *American Highway Engineers' Handbook, First Edition.* Blanchard, Arthur H., ed. New York: John Wiley & Sons. 1919. Page 535.

37. "More anon" means "more on this subject soon." The book includes many of C.K.'s observations that American roads were poorly paved and not well maintained, so the use of "more anon" provides the reader with a "preview" of coming attractions.

38. C.K. only cites three specific encounters with motorcyclists after New York:

- A young British motorcyclist riding from Atlantic City to Philadelphia (Chapter 2).

- The tinsmith with a customized Indian motorcycle in Pecos, New Mexico (Chapter 14).

- The adventurous youth on an Excelsior motorcycle in the Mojave Desert (Chapter 20).

In Chapter 20, he describes the following as he enters Los Angeles: "hundreds upon hundreds of cars, buses, and motor-cycles passed." It seems likely that he was only referring to experiences with other motorcyclists he had on the open road, not in the cities (or not just "anywhere" as he claimed), which is why the encounter on Riverside Drive in Manhattan he describes at the beginning of Chapter 2 is not included above. However, since he had just left his hotel, he may have considered himself to be "anywhere" and "on the open road" on his trip, so he may have been referring to the encounter described in Chapter 2 as the first of the four motorcyclists.

39. C.K. took a photo (Figure 20, next page) of the scene at Coney Island, but he did not include the photo in the original book.

Figure 20: Coney Island.
Source: C.K.'s personal slide collection.

40. "*Genus anthropomorpha*" is a term coined by 18th Century Swedish naturalist Carl Linnaeus in the first edition of his 1735 book *Systema Naturae*. In an article titled "Rewriting the Savage: The Extraordinary Fictions of the 'Wild Girl of Champagne,'" author Julia Douthwaite characterized Linnaeus' description of the "*genus Anthropomorpha* as a catch-all category for human and human-seeming creatures, including *Homo* (man, described as European, American, Asiatic, African), *Simia* (apes, including the 'Satyrus'), and *Bradypus* (sloths)."

41. The way this is written, it indicates that he went out to Coney Island one day and prepared to leave for California the next. This is particularly likely given the amount of time and effort required for a "same day" departure: It would have taken him at least three hours to get out to Coney Island, linger for an hour, and then return to Manhattan at which point he would prepare for his drive all the way to northern New Jersey. It seems more likely the trip to Coney Island was part of his two days of "surveying the city."

42. This is a reference to an aftermarket optional carrier/rack he had bought with the motorcycle. It was almost certainly installed with the other options by the dealer who had sold the motorcycle to him.

43. *"in situ"*: A Latin phrase meaning "in position." In this case, it refers to the fifty to sixty pound dressing case being in position—-strapped onto the rear rack of the motorcycle.

44. "Pyjamas" is a primarily British spelling of pajamas.

CHAPTER II

NEW YORK TO PHILADELPHIA

"Gotter match?" he inquired as I pulled up near him.

I had left my palatial sky-scraper hotel[45] only fifteen minutes before.[46] Soon, I contemplated, my experiences in and around New York would be past history. Happy and light-hearted, I was humming along that boulevard with the truly wonderful surface which runs along the edge of Manhattan Island. It is known as "Riverside Drive," and here dwell many of America's millionaires.[47] A young fellow and his companion with a Harley-Davidson and side-car[48] at the side of the road attracted my attention. Neither of them looked as though he were a resident of that district. A khaki-coloured shirt, thick corduroy breeches, leggings, and boots were their only attire. One of them held up his hand when he saw me.

"Maybe these fellows know something about the roads," thought I; so I stopped.

To stop a motor-cyclist and ask him for a match seemed quite a unique departure from the well-established English customs with which I was familiar. Feeling benevolent, I silently proffered a box of "England's Glory" wax vestas.[49] Without a word he took one, scrutinized it closely as though it were something wonderful in the art of match-manufacture, and slowly lit his pipe. A dozen puffs ensued. He broke the silence.

"Where you from?"

"When I left it they called it England," I replied.

Another dozen puffs.

"Where you goin'?"

"I may get to San Francisco some day."

"You sure got some bit of pavement in front of you. I said it."

"Well, I guess it's never so bad but what it might be worse," I hinted.

He spat twice, puffed a few clouds, spat again; took another look at me, then glanced at my machine.

"You got SOME bird there," he ventured, and then added, as if to place the assertion beyond all doubt,—

"I said it."

I agreed that it ought to be able to get along.

"Yew said it.—See that bird thar?" he asked, pointing to his machine." Waal, I guess she can move some too; she done eight thousand miles on them roads, an' I guess they warn't mos'ly booleyvards neither."

In the conversation which followed, mainly in reference to many inquiries on my part as to the various "National Highways" which I had learnt were occasionally to be found throughout the country, I gleaned from this worthy native son that it would be better for me to "go back 'ome and pick strawberries" than to continue farther with such an obviously insane desire as to cross the American Continent. I persisted, however, that having come thus far, I would at any rate continue while sanity remained, although I should certainly bear his good advice in mind for future reference.

With a final injunction from him that I should know him when next I saw him if I were fortunate enough to subsist in the land of the living, we parted, and after a trip on the Ferry across the Jersey River,[50] I was soon winding my way out of the drab and dreary suburbs of Newark.

It would be incorrect to say that the best people do not go to Atlantic City. Americans, I believe, reckon this well-known seaside resort to be one of the nine wonders of the world. No free-born American citizen, I do not doubt, would give the credit of the other eight, whatever they may be, to any foreign country. On this assumption I felt I should have no difficulty in identifying the other eight when I had seen more of "God's Own Country."

Now Atlantic City is just one hundred per cent. American. It would be impossible to associate it with any other country but America. To begin with, it has the inevitable "million-dollar" pier. Let me explain that nothing in America is worthy of popular patronage unless it costs at least a million dollars. When I was at Niagara I was told how many million gallons of water flowed over the falls in a year.[51] No one (on the American side) seemed to worry very much about the magnificence of the falls or the grandeur of the river. Such sordid interests do not appeal to them. But ask someone how many million horse-power will be developed in a year,[52] and see with what eagerness he relieves you of your ignorance! The American public WILL have millions in their calculations and their lust for the superlative MUST be appeased.

In Atlantic City there are naturally many objects of interest to the budding student of modern life like myself, but, on the whole, the amusements of this nation do not differ considerably from the modest efforts of our own. There one can see the usual bashful maidens whose main delight is to recline on the sand or parade the beach in the latest thing in bathing costumes, but never under any circumstances to get them wet.[53] Also we find the usual stores where every conceivable variety of picture post card or "present from . . . ." can be bought.

In two hours I was aweary of Atlantic City.[54] In a very superior frame of mind I trod on my feelings and the kick-starter of "Khaki Lizz"[55] (my soubriquet[56] for the machine, which was finished entirely in that delightfully-reminiscent hue) and turned her nose towards the west. Philadelphia, I decided, was to be my resting-place that night.

To be hot on the scent of Philadelphia was one thing; but to get there was quite another. A glorious three-mile stretch of macadamized road out of Atlantic City[57] was indeed a tempting bait, and I admit for a few luscious but brief moments I set at defiance all limits of speed imposed for the general welfare of the public by worthy law-makers upon the motoring population of New York State.[58] I have always contended (privately, not in public!) that laws are only made to be broken. I might perhaps add that I was destined afterwards to supplement this somewhat outrageous dictum with a further "He only is entitled to break laws who thoroughly knows and understands them!"

As every wanderer in this vale of tears discovers, all good things come to an end some time. That three-mile stretch of macadamized road very soon came to an end. It ended, as far as I remember, in an abrupt right-angle corner where in an endeavour to get round at about forty-five miles an hour I nearly met myself coming back, and from that point the road gradually bore resemblance to an elongated dust-heap. They call it "natural gravel,"[59] which means that in the opinion of the road engineers of that time the natural surface of the road did not need any reinforcement in the way of metal. I should imagine that about 99 per cent. of all the roads in America are of this construction, the remaining 1 per cent. being either covered with a layer of concrete, or macadam, as in any civilized European country. At times, very few and far between, this natural gravel forms quite a tolerable surface where there is not much traffic, but it must be remembered that motor-cars are used in the States on a far greater scale than is ever dreamt of in England.

I was, in fact, simply amazed at the tremendous number of cars in the various towns and villages through which I passed. I have sometimes been in a town, and quite a large one too, where it was almost impossible to find a place at the side of the pavement where I could leave my machine. Every available space was taken up with a car, and in some towns, Salt Lake City[60] for instance, I have seen cars "parked" along the side of the road two-deep, so that to cross from one side of the road to the other one has to traverse four separate ranges of automobiles. In the summer, thousands of cars are travelling all day long between Atlantic City and the adjacent large cities, so that the reader can perhaps imagine the state of all the main highways in that direction.

I was here introduced to a diversion which at first seemed quite an interesting one, but which continued familiarity certainly turned to contempt. I refer to the "detour." The unfortunate motorist is perhaps ploughing his way steadily along through the gravel, dust, and sand. He encounters a barrier across the road bearing a notice that repairs are going on and that he must follow the detour indicated. The road selected, I believe, is generally the one with the most pot-holes, ruts, mountains, canyons, etc., in its formation in the surrounding district. Sometimes in these detours one finds further auxiliary detours until finally one has to use the utmost intelligence and a compass in order to get back to the main highway.

I did not, therefore, arrive in Philadelphia strictly to schedule. I was many times tempted to take up my abode at a convenient spot on the side of the road. Several times I dismounted and examined a promising spot, but always there was some very serious objection. This objection either took the form of frogs or of mosquitoes or of both. As we used to read in the days of the War, "the enemy was present in large numbers." I did not relish either the prospect of being kept awake indefinitely with the objectionable gurgling of a battalion of bullfrogs or of being eaten to death in my slumbers by a nation of bloodthirsty mosquitoes.

So I spun onwards, ever onwards towards Philadelphia. Meanwhile the sun was sinking lower and lower in the west. The nearer I got to Philadelphia the more numerous became the cars on the road. It seemed as though the whole of Philadelphia frivolled at Atlantic City on a Sunday afternoon. I was working my way along, dodging tremendous pot-holes and ruts, imagining myself in an hour or two's time reposing comfortably between clean white sheets. All of a sudden a most distressing noise came across my ear. It appeared to be a motor-cycle in pain. At times there was only one cylinder firing. Sometimes there were two. At other times there was none at all. I drew in to the side of the road and waited for the unfortunate author of this disturbance to arrive.

He soon emerged from the darkness. He had no lights, and was only too pleased to stop at the sight of another motor-cyclist.

"Why, I thought I was the only madman about here," I greeted him, surprised but gratified to know that there really were other seemingly sane people who rode motor-cycles in America.

How delighted he was to meet another Englishman! He had, he explained, been in America only a year or two, having come from my old home town of Birmingham during the War.[61] He had got so "fed up" with Americans that it was a treat to set eyes on anyone from the Old Country.

He was a youth of eighteen or nineteen years,[62] and after I had fixed him up with a couple of sparking plugs and attended to a few other urgent requirements, he asked me abruptly, but quite politely, the inevitable question, just as I might have expected." Where you from, an' where you goin'?"

I explained that I was making for Philadelphia, where I hoped to find somewhere to lay my weary head.

"Well, if you don't want anything very luxurious," said he, "I think I can fix you up all right, if you don't mind going on ahead to light the way."

I gladly assented, and by this means, with my brilliant headlight illuminating the road, it did not take us long to reach the Delaware River, on the opposite bank of which stood the fine old city of Philadelphia. It took a quarter of an hour to cross the river by the ferry, but once in Philadelphia my friend was happy. "Now you follow me," he said.

He had no lights whatever, but his engine was running well, so I agreed and followed. This was not in itself very easy. I am perfectly certain that I have never seen ANY motor-cycle ANYWHERE dash along at such a rate through a city. Although it was dark and I could not see my speedometer, I am sure that he must have travelled about forty-five miles per hour through the streets of Philadelphia. They were certainly good and straight and wide. There was a little traffic here and there, but this did not seem to worry our friend in the slightest. Occasionally we saw a "cop" or two standing on a street corner make a half-hearted attempt to step into the road to hold us up. Our friend, however, was desperate and would stop for no one. After about a quarter of an hour's riding, dodging round corners and shooting past obstructions at a tremendous pace, he pulled up at a small corner house in a secluded portion of the town and we dismounted. He lived with his mother, he explained, but she was away in New York. Also he had lost his latchkey. Also it was really a florist's shop, but he was sure I wouldn't mind. "There is nothing for it,"[63] he said, "but to climb the fire escape and get in through the front window."[64]

I shouldered him up to an iron frame projecting from the house. Thence he clambered on to a rickety fire escape leading up the wall into blackness, and he was soon lost to sight. A few moments later the front door opened and we pushed our muddy, dirty machines on to the clean linoleum of the front room, where they remained overnight surrounded by pots of roses, carnations, palms, and ferns.

This, he explained, was quite the usual procedure and his mother would not mind a bit!

It was then about 11.30, and when we had washed some of the dirt from our faces we sallied forth in quest of a meal. We had no difficulty in picking up the scent of a flourishing cafeteria. Neither did we have any difficulty in disposing of disgusting quantities of hot coffee and "waffles," a commodity peculiar to America,[65] resembling pancakes and eaten with jugfuls of maple syrup.

Well after midnight we returned to our domicile, and I laid me down to sleep the sleep of the righteous. At seven o'clock in the morning I bade farewell to mine host. Not a cent would he accept in payment for my night's lodgings. So, with the parting assurance that he would drop in and see me when he was next in England, we each took our several roads—he in the direction of a neighbouring works where he was employed as a mechanic, and I towards Washington, drifting meekly along the streets at certainly nothing like the speed of the night before.

The road for some distance was good, the sun came out, and the day promised to turn out fine and hot. I soon began to feel an inward content. Everything was going smoothly. I was expecting some money to be waiting for me at Washington, and then I should have nothing to worry about for a long time to come.

As it usually happens when one begins to pat oneself on the back, I immediately had a puncture. It was of course in the back wheel. Meanwhile the sun was rising higher and higher, and when, after about half an hour, I had repaired the wheel, I was feeling very thirsty. Another five miles further on I had another puncture. This time it happened to be exactly outside a garage.

I have known places in England where a certain amount of trade is always guaranteed by the ingenuity of some of the garage proprietors who regularly and systematically throw tacks and nails along the road in their vicinity.[66] It occurred to me that this was a practice not confined to England, as examination revealed the cause of the puncture to be a nice long nail driven through from one side of the tube to the other. Not feeling of a very arduous disposition at the time, I wheeled it into the garage to be repaired.

I am afraid I was rather annoyed at the result. In the first place, I had to supply the mechanic with solution. In the second place, I had to take off the tyre for him. In the third place, I supplied a patch; and in the fourth place, I actually had to do the job for him. After settling his account, I finally explained in language as polite as I could muster that in my opinion the practice of strewing discarded nails and other implements on the highway, while not being exactly meritorious in itself, was just as commendable a method of obtaining a business connection as many that were frequently resorted to in other trades or professions of a higher standing. I explained, however, that after having been so successfully victimized by such an artifice, one would consider oneself justified in expecting a much higher standard of workmanship than was apparently forthcoming in his establishment.

Then we parted, the mechanic expressing the hope that he would never (crimson)[67] well see me again, and that if I ever did happen to be coming back that way and got a nail in my (unspeakable) tyre that he would see me in (Arizona) before he would (smoking) well repair it for me!

CHAPTER 2 NOTES

45. In the August 21, 1919 article in *Pacific Motorcyclist*, C.K. stated that he stayed at Hotel McAlpin, at Broadway and 34th Street, commonly known as Herald Square—the same intersection where he had reported being stopped by a traffic policeman. Hotel McAlpin claimed to be the world's largest hotel and contained some 1,500 rooms. Since then, the building has been converted to condominium apartments; it is currently known as Herald Towers.

46. In the same August 21, 1919, article in *Pacific Motorcyclist*, C.K. said his trip "started fairly late in the afternoon" and implies he left Manhattan on June 14, 1919: "On the afternoon of June 14th last I could be seen sailing along New York's Broadway..."

47. "Riverside Drive is New York City's most scenic street. As one of the Upper West Side's main roads, it parallels the West Side Highway and offers panoramic views of the Hudson River. [... It] starts at 72nd Street as it emerges from Riverside Boulevard which stretches all the day down from 62nd St. It then continues north until it eventually merges with the Henry Hudson Parkway." —Edgar Catasus, March 20, 2017.

48. The 1916 Harley-Davidson with sidecar in Figure 21 was sold in 2017 for $44,000 at the Mecum motorcycle auction in Las Vegas.

Figure 21: 1916 Harley-Davidson with Sidecar.
Source: Courtesy of Mecum Auctions.

49. England's Glory has been a brand of matches in the UK since 1871, the year of the launching of the battleship HMS *Devastation*, which is portrayed on the box. It remains one of the most popular "strike anywhere" match brands in the country. Swan Vestas matches—named after Vesta, the Roman goddess of hearth and home—were first introduced in the UK in 1883. Made from cotton wick dipped in wax, they were much more solid than other wax matches available at the time. By the 1930s, Swan Vestas were Britain's best-selling match and, to this day, are the only British match brand consistently asked for by name.

50. C.K. would have crossed the *Hudson* River to New Jersey, not the Jersey River (which does not exist by that name anywhere).

51. Approximately 2.38 trillion (i.e., 2.38 million millions) gallons of water flow over Niagara Falls each year: Horseshoe Falls (2.15 trillion gallons) and American and Bridal Veil Falls (238.9 billion gallons).

52. In 1895, Professor W. Cawthorne Unwin wrote an article for *Mechanical Energy and Industrial Progress* in which he estimated that Niagara Falls theoretically represented seven million horsepower. In 1914, five power companies were developing about 450,000 electrical horsepower, equally divided between the American and Canadian sides of the river.

53. American laws at this time were strict when it came to regulating women's bathing suits. The same year C.K. visited Coney Island, a woman was arrested there for wearing a bathing garment (what basically resembled a long dress with stockings) in public—*under* her normal clothes.

54. Figure 22 is a photo C.K. took of an Atlantic City residential street.

Figure 22: A residential street in Atlantic City.
Source: C.K.'s personal slide collection.

55. C.K.'s mother's name was Elizabeth (as was his grandmother's). "Lizz" or "Lizzie" was possibly used as a nickname in homage to his mother or it may be a nod to "Tin Lizzie," the nickname by which the Ford Model T came to be known.

56. *"sobriquet"*: a descriptive name or epithet: nickname.

57. The *Blue Book* defines two routes from Atlantic City to Philadelphia, both of which begin with what are characterized as newly paved roads followed by gravel:

- Route 116 (64.2 mi): "Via the White Horse Pike, thru Pleasantville, Egg Harbor City, Hammonton, and the Camden Ferry. From Atlantic City the route leads over the new boulevard, which crosses the meadows and is 120 feet wide. From Pleasantville to Philadelphia is tarbound macadam and Jersey state gravel. This is the shortest route… an equally good option is Route 119."

- Route 119 (66.2 mi): "Via Pleasantville, Mays Landing, Malaga, Glassboro, and Gloucester. First 5 miles over new Atlantic City Blvd., Jersey state gravel to Glassboro, balance macadam."

Because Route 119 appears to reflect the appearance of "Jersey state gravel" sooner than on Route 116, it seems fair to conclude C.K. took Route 116.

58. He was in New Jersey, not New York, so the laws of the latter would not apply on the roads between Atlantic City and Philadelphia.

59. The *Blue Book* referred to the road surface here in New Jersey as being "Jersey state gravel." Note 36 in Chapter 1 describes the "natural gravel" method of road construction. By referring to the gravel as "Jersey state gravel," the *Blue Book* may have been stating the geological *source* of the gravel rather than a road construction method unique to New Jersey.

60. On his way back to New York by train, C.K. stopped in Salt Lake City.

61. This elaborate story about meeting up with the young man from Birmingham is conspicuous by its complete absence in his serialized story published immediately after his journey in *Pacific Motorcyclist*. In the second installment of his story in *Pacific Motorcyclist*, published on September 4, 1919, C.K. wrote simply, "I managed to make Philadelphia that night. I forget where I slept, but that doesn't matter, being a stranger in a strange land. Suffice it to say that the early morning found me on the way to Washington."

It seems highly unlikely he forgot about his son-of-Birmingham host in Philadelphia, whom he had met only ten weeks earlier. This—combined with the lack of independently verifiable facts supporting the details in the book (such as the presence of an English-born florist with a son in the area at the time)— strongly suggests this part of the story was fabricated. Perhaps it was added at the urging of C.K.'s publisher, who requested he add a more entertaining story with a "Birmingham connection." It is unlikely we will ever discover if this was the case.

62. Systematic examination of the 1920 US census data for Philadelphia revealed 54 men who were born in England and were age 16-20 in 1919. However, 53 of those (98%) were either not living with their mothers or no occupation was listed for them. The one mother who did have an occupation was a winder at a textile mill, not a florist. Additionally only seven of the 54 (13%) had arrived in the United States in 1917 or 1918. Thus, no Englishmen were living with their mothers in Philadelphia who possessed anything close to the unique demographic and occupation profile described in C.K.'s story.

63. "nothing for it": A British term meaning that "there is no alternative solution."

64. There *was* one England-born florist in Philadelphia: Mrs. Jessie Drew-Bear, who owned and operated the successful London Flower Shop at 1800 Chestnut Street. But this was the bottom floor of a multi-story downtown office building owned by Mrs. Drew-Bear (not a "small corner house in a secluded portion of town"). Mrs. Drew-Bear was either divorced, widowed, or just living apart from her husband, but she did have three children with her in 1919, including two sons, Dudley and Robert, aged 20 and 18, respectively. The 1920 census indicates that Robert was a mechanical engineer living with his mother one block away from the flower shop. However, the census also indicates that Robert had been in the U.S. for as long as thirteen years. While some facts resemble details about the individual in C.K.'s story, too many are inconsistent to conclude that C.K. slept on the floor of the London Flower Shop at 1800 Chestnut Street in Philadelphia.

65. Another anomaly appears in the fourth installment of his story in the October 2, 1919 edition of *Pacific Motorcyclist*. In that article, he states that he first had waffles in Cincinnati, further suggesting that he embellished reporting about his activities in Philadelphia.

66. In 1919 Philadelphia, there were city ordinances against throwing rubbish—including nails—in the streets, but this was largely a "littering" and "clean streets"

policy. Still, the illicit practice of throwing nails into the streets to generate tire repair business was common enough in the U.S. that state laws were enacted to prohibit it. Although C.K. was apparently still in Pennsylvania when this puncture occurred, the law in effect at that time in Maryland (Maryland Code, Article LVI, Chapter 85, Section 155, Throwing Tacks, Nails, Glass, Etc., on Highways) explicitly prohibited the placement of sharp objects in the street that injured people, animals, or vehicle tires and allowed fines of up to one hundred dollars for anyone doing so. A search for comparable provisions of the Motor Code of Pennsylvania in effect in 1919 has been unsuccessful, but it seems doubtful C.K. would have sought to research the law and prosecute anyone for violating it.

67. Among other word substitutions made to convey—as politely as possible— the mechanic's generally harsh diction, C.K. used "crimson" in lieu of "bloody," which was generally regarded as an unprintable swear word in the UK; it was believed to imply a blasphemous reference to the blood of Christ. Because the crude use of the word "bloody" in this context was probably outside the normal vocabulary of a mechanic in the Philadelphia area in 1919, the mechanic probably did not actually say "bloody," but rather that is the sentiment that C.K. "heard" and sought to convey to his British readers.

CHAPTER III

PHILADELPHIA TO WASHINGTON

The scenery now began to look charming. Rolling ranges of hills extending into the distance clustered around as we drew nearer to the Chesapeake River,[68] which flows into the well-known bay to which it gives its name.

"All aboard for Chesapeake Bay."

... I hummed the air to myself as the road abruptly ended and a suspension bridge continued the course across the broad, peaceful mouth of the river.[69] The whole country around seemed to be permeated with a comfortable, wholesome vigour. Nothing seemed shabby, discontented, or poverty-stricken. I passed through many small towns and embryo cities. All were prosperous and all extended a hearty welcome to the traveller or visitor. Stretched across the road between two poles, just before I entered one little town, was a huge white banner bearing the words:

"CONWAY CITY WELCOMES YOU.
WE LIKE TRAVELLERS TO VISIT US.
HAVE A GOOD LOOK AT OUR CITY."

Conway "City" did not prove to be exactly a metropolis.[70] It was probably nothing more than a well-to-do farm town. But the houses were clean and neat, indeed some of them were very beautiful, perfectly up-to-date but never objectionably modern. The roads were a bit bumpy in places but not at all bad as American roads go. As I passed out of the town I saw another notice similar to the first:

"THANK YOU FOR COMING.
WE HOPE YOU LIKE US.
COME AGAIN."

I got so used to being welcomed to every town I came to that I forgot I was a "stranger" in a "foreign land."[71]

There was not a town or village that did not publish its welcome in some form or other. In the main it was by advertisements. But if I stopped at a wayside store to quench my thirst (oh, the sun was hot!) I was met neither with scowls nor incivility. I am reminded of the old joke of *Punch* many years ago:

"Oo's that bloke over theer, Bill?"

"Dunno; stranger, I think."

"'Eave 'arf a brick at 'im."[72]

That is typical of what we *English* think of strangers. The man of better education or more refinement perhaps expresses himself differently, but he feels just the same as a rule.

At this juncture in my reveries the macadam road stopped and gave way to "natural gravel." That was quite sufficient to postpone any soliloquies I may have been indulging in until a later date. The entire sixty seconds in every minute were employed in keeping myself substantially upright. Small pot-holes gave place to larger ones, and they in turn to larger still. The loose sand, which was an inch or two deep at the start, soon assumed more considerable depths. As the detective books of our youth used to say, "The plot grew thicker and thicker."[73] I was floundering about from right to left, prodding energetically on the ground each side with my feet to maintain some kind of balance. At times the back wheel churned up the sand aimlessly in an endeavour to get a grip on something solid. Here and there the sand and gravel were heaped into great ridges as if a mighty plough had been along that way. Getting through this stuff, thought I, was no joke. Furthermore, it was warm work; very warm work. Now and then I would find myself directed absolutely without control from one side of the road to the other, and only with the greatest strain could I keep the machine on its wheels. And with all this the "highway" still maintained its regulation width of 90 feet![74] The casual observer from an aeroplane above would in all probability be attracted by its straightness, its whiteness, and its apparent uniformity." What a splendid road!" he would think.[75]

Not so I. I was on the point of physical exhaustion with the seemingly-endless paddling and pushing and heaving (and don't forget the half-hundred-weight bag on my back!)[76] when I was thrown on to a steeply-cambered part of the road at the side. The back wheel just slid limply sideways down the slope and left everything reposing peacefully in the natural gravel of Maryland.

When I had extricated myself from under the machine, I surveyed the position with a critical eye. What a road for a civilized country! These Yanks must be jolly-well mad to tolerate such roads as this!

* * * * *

Just then an old Ford came by. It was shorn entirely of mudguards, running boards, and other impedimenta. As he wallowed past me, swaying to this side and that, sometimes pointing at right angles to the way he was going and with his old engine buzzing away in bottom gear and clouds of steam issuing from his radiator (it had no cap; it must have blown off!) the driver seemed perfectly at ease. He rolled a cigar stump from one corner of his mouth to the other and gazed nonchalantly ahead. I don't think he even noticed me and my recumbent motor-cycle. I could not repress a grin as his old box of tricks disappeared slowly up the road, wagging its tail this way and that and narrowly averting a catastrophe at every few yards. "You ragtime bunch of tin merchants!"[77] I mused (not so much in reference to the driver as to the nation in general!) as his diminishing form finally side-slipped into the ditch at a bend in the road.

And then a distressing thought struck me: "They'll never believe me when I get back home and tell them!" So I took my little camera out of the tool-box on the top tube and snapped the worst bit of road there and then.[78] A five minutes' struggle followed, in which "Khaki Lizz" was withdrawn from her ditch.

By way of nourishment to sustain me in any further fights with the road, I slowly and meditatively consumed one only orange before proceeding once more.

But things did not improve. Here and there, where the ridges of soil and gravel had not been disturbed, grew tufts of grass and weeds. Huge ruts, crossing and re-crossing in the remaining sand, showed where cars were wont to pass as fancy dictated, and with only two wheels it was barely possible to maintain any progress at all.

By permission of Dr. F. Rolt-Wheeler.

A COMMON OCCURRENCE.

"Hang it all! This is TOO much!" I exclaimed, after a few more precipitate dismounts,—and took another photo[79] and ate another orange.

A mile or two farther on I came to a weird-looking machine at the side of the road. It was a sort of combination of steam tractor and automatic plough,[80] but very much bigger and more complicated. Its main function was to chop down *en masse*[81] the sides and banks of the road and shovel the debris into the middle. Grass, shrubs, bushes, and young trees alike fell victims to its activities. Now this really was the limit! Not satisfied with the condition of the road as it was, they sent forth this "Heath Robinson"[82] mechanism to improve it. I stopped and left the bike standing in the road where it was—there was no need to prop it up against anything—and went back to question the driver of this implement as to its function in life.

He was not perturbed in the slightest either at my question or at the heated state of mind and body in which I approached him. Punctuated by intervals in which he slowly masticated a worn-out chunk of chewing-gum, he explained that all good motorists liked wide roads; that the State Council had decided that motorists should have wide roads; that they had provided machines for widening roads that at present were not up to standard width; and finally that he was there to see that this machine did its work properly!

So I took another photograph,[83] ate another orange, kicked the self-starter once more, and pushed on again. The road got worse and worse. Sometimes there were ruts and sometimes there were strips of unploughed field in the middle of it. But I spent no more films on it. The people at home, I decided, would have to take my word for it after all. About ten miles farther on I came to a cross-road. It was perfectly straight and beautifully paved with concrete and stretched from one horizon to the other. With what joy I gazed upon its countenance! There was a wooden shack on one corner, evidently a saloon. A negro sat on the doorstep, gazing indolently at me.

"Is this the road to Baltimore?" I inquired, indicating the concrete highway.

No reply. But he continued to gaze at me, and spat twice.

"Must be deaf," thought I. "How's this for Washington?" I shouted.

Still no reply.

"Say, brother, which is the road to Baltimore?" I inquired as politely as convenient.

The appellation "brother" had its effect. The negro jerked his thumb over his shoulder, indicating that I was to go straight on (and incidentally follow that excruciating stretch of natural gravel).

Fortunately, Baltimore was not many miles away,[84] and when I got there I breathed many sighs of relief. There were paved roads, good and true; macadam and concrete for miles and miles, all the way to Washington. I picked my way by instinct through

Baltimore,[85] the capital of the State of Maryland, not stopping for food or rest. I would reach my destination before I gave way to such physical necessities. I certainly had an appetite, but I always feel that more than two meals a day when on tour are not only unnecessary, but mean a dead loss of time, money, and distance.

The reports on the state of the road ahead turned out to be true in every detail, and throwing to the winds all respect for such trivialities as speed limits, I made up for at least a good fraction of the time wasted on the road.

When, about 5 p.m., I pulled Lizzie on to her stand outside one of Washington's "cafeterias," I began to feel an incipient timidity.[86] I doubted whether I should be able to get into any respectable hotel. I was covered in dust, and dirt. Headgear of any kind I had dispensed with altogether. My hair was dusty and knotted with the wind. Owing to the heat, I had also found it advisable to remove my collar and tie, so that the wind could circulate as much as possible. How could I in such a condition maintain my self-respect in Washington, the magnificent capital of the United States?

Fortunately, it did not take long for me to overcome such scruples. Another day or two on the road, and I was perfectly at ease during the intervals in which I had intercourse with civilization. Occasionally I experienced a difficulty in entering a drug-store for an iced drink, and sometimes I felt a trifle shy at my bare, sunburnt neck, but no one seemed to mind. I soon found that in America, and particularly when travelling in the West, one could wear absolutely anything that one's fancy might dictate without rousing the slightest disturbance.

After satisfying my requirements at the "cafeteria," the second item on my programme was a visit to the Post Office.[87] This revealed the sordid fact that there was no money awaiting me. It can easily be understood that such a discovery might have proved most distressing. I had been advised not to take much with me, but to cable for a draft from home at intervals.[88] My adviser,[89] as I was afterwards to find out to my cost, had overlooked the utterly chaotic state of the post-war transatlantic mail service.

I still had a little left, however, quite enough to get me comfortably to Cincinnati, my next financial depot, so why worry? I could always work for a living, or at any rate, if I did not feel inclined to that, I might pawn something.

I found a hotel that, from the outside, just suited my fancy.[90] Plain, large and unpretentious, it described itself in an illuminated sign as the "National."[91] I booked a room at three dollars (12s. 6d.)[92] and sallied forth to see the sights.

I was impressed with Washington. It is truly a city of beautiful streets and magnificent buildings. Undoubtedly it is the city de luxe of America. Being the capital, wealth is lavished upon it. No factories or barren wastes disfigure its graceful countenance. Every street or avenue glistens at night with a bewildering multitude of illuminated signs. This method of advertising is typically American. The first impression of a stranger visiting a large American city at night is that he is in a children's luminous palace. There are illuminations and decorations of every conceivable nature. Sometimes a single sign advertising perhaps some particular brand of chewing-gum or cigarette or motor-car has thousands and tens of thousands of lights wonderfully displayed in different colours and arranged in different series, one series flashing into view as another disappears, then a few seconds later giving place to another still more wonderful, and finally there comes a grand climax in which all the colours and all the series and all the figures blaze forth in an indescribable orgy of light.

When I found myself finally back in my hotel I was to be the victim of still another disillusionment. No country anywhere could rival America for hotels, I had thought. But I had not then experienced the "National" at Washington. The room allotted to me was literally an outrage. It was of the very poorest that one would expect to find in an East End boarding-house in the Old Kent Road.[93] It had one window, which faced on to an unimaginably dreary "area." The carpet was threadbare and colourless. The furniture, consisting of one bed, one dressing-table, one wardrobe and one chair was obviously suffering from advanced senile decay. There was a washbasin in one corner that boasted of two taps and a piece of wood to stop the hole up with. The door showed signs of having been minus a lock for many a long day. I was too tired, however, to bother about trivialities of detail, so putting my revolver[94] under the blanket near me in case of possible eventualities, I laid me down in peace to sleep.

Nothing occurred, however, to disturb my peace of mind or body throughout the night. The following morning found me hot on the warpath after a bathroom. After sundry peregrinations I unearthed a clue. It was in the form of a very corpulent negress—evidently a chambermaid. "Bathroom?" "No, dere am no bathroom h'yar," she informed me. But I persisted in my inquiries, suspecting her reply to be a mere excuse for sheer laziness. Finally, as a last resort, I absent-mindedly took my "life preserver" from my hip pocket[95] and looked at it vacuously.[96] Its effect was magical. "Yes, saar, yes, saar, come right h'yar!—I find you bathroom!"[97]

When I came to square up that morning I paid my respects and three dollars to the management.

"See here, Mister Manager," I said in such a tone that everyone within hearing distance had the benefit of it as well, "I've done a bit of travelling here and there, but never in ANY city at ANY time have I struck ANY hotel that for sheer rottenness compares with THIS one!"

I have an idea at the back of my mind that that manager-man doesn't love Englishmen!

Now that I had seen America's capital,[98] I turned my face to the west, and began to make rash estimates and frivolous promises to myself concerning my destination for the day. Could I get to Cincinnati next day? How long would it take to do the odd 550 miles[99] or so? And what would be my reception when I got there? I had some friends in Cincinnati, friends that I had never even seen.[100] What would they think when they saw THIS specimen roll up to their front door in Clifton Avenue? Was Lizzie going to stand up to it all right? When should I get to the coast? What kind of roads should I meet "out West"? And so I wondered on.

CHAPTER 3 NOTES

68. There is no "Chesapeake River." C.K. was crossing the Susquehanna River, one of five main rivers—including the Potomac, Rappahannock, York, and James Rivers—that comprise the bulk of the Chesapeake Bay watershed.

69. In 1919, the bridge at the mouth of the Susquehanna was an iron bridge, *not* a suspension bridge. Figure 23 is a photograph of the automobile toll bridge across the Susquehanna from the Perryville side of the river—facing southwest—with the railroad bridge paralleling it on the right.

Figure 23: The Toll and the P.B.&W. R.R. Bridges, Perryville, Md.
Source: Historical Society of Harford County.

70. There is no such place ("Conway" or "Conway City") found on any maps of the period, or since.

71. This is an apparent biblical reference to a passage in the Bible, Exodus 2:22.

72. This is a reference to a cartoon (see Figure 24) that appeared in *Punch* or, *The London Charivari* in 1854. *Punch* was a satirical British weekly magazine of established in 1841 by Henry Mayhew and engraver Ebenezer Landells. It was most influential in the 1840s and 1850s, when it helped to coin the term "cartoon" in its modern sense as a humorous illustration.

FURTHER ILLUSTRATION OF THE MINING DISTRICTS.

First Polite Native. "Who's 'im, Bill?"
Second ditto. "A stranger!"
First ditto. "'Eave 'arf a brick at 'im."

Figure 24: Cartoon from *Punch*.
Source: *Punch, or the London Charivari,* Vol. 26, No. 660, March 4, 1854. Page 82.

73. "The plot thickens" is at the core of this term. It is intended to convey an increasingly complex story or mystery. It was apparently first used in the 1671 play *The Rehearsal*, by George Villiers, which included the following line: "Ay, now the Plot thickens very much upon us." It continued to be used, as claimed by C.K. in "detective books of his youth," including *The Expressman and the Detective*, by Allan Pinkerton, in 1874 ("The plot thickens!") and "The Fowl in the Pot," by Stanley J. Weyman, a short story published in *Temple Bar* in 1889 ("'The plot thickens,' muttered the king.").

74. Since there were no national road standards in the US in 1919, this is an exaggeration. In the March 1914 edition of *Better Roads and Streets*, George D. Steele described variations: "In most of the middle Atlantic States, the regulation width is 49½ feet for important roads, and 33 feet for secondary roads. In recent years, however, especially in New York, Pennsylvania, and other coast States, there is a tendency to increase this width in securing right-of-way for all new main roads, a minimum of 60 feet being preferred... In nearly all the States through the Mississippi Valley, the roads are either 60 or 66 feet in width... The legal width as laid out by the United States Public Land Surveys in the west and south is 66 feet, which is quite generally acknowledged to be the proper and standard width."

75. As part of a 2016 historical retrospective, this entire paragraph was quoted to illustrate American roads at the time—conditions that fueled the quest for better roads.

76. The use of "hundred-weight" here likely refers to a standard of measurement adopted in the UK in 1835, establishing 112 pounds as a "hundredweight," so C.K. is describing a bag weighing about 65 pounds—which almost certainly was strapped to his luggage rack (not literally worn on his back).

77. Ragtime is the name of a popular musical style that enjoyed its peak popularity between 1895 and 1918 and is characterized by its syncopated, or "ragged," rhythm. In this period, the word also became a slang description of irregular or haphazard things. In the early 20th century, tin merchants had monopolies that allowed designated companies to squeeze the suppliers at the expense of quality and fair trade. It seems C.K. was complaining that the US was being operated in an irregular and unethical manner, which resulted in extremely poor road conditions.

78. The photo C.K. mentions of his motorcycle in the ditch has not survived.

79. C.K. took the photo (see Figure 25) and saved it in his personal collection, titling it "Road to Baltimore." The road does not seem to be particularly bad—nor is his bike stuck in a ditch—but it may be the photo he mentions having taken before his previously described roadside disengagement.

Figure 25: The Road to Baltimore.
Source: C.K.'s personal slide collection.

Figure 26: The Jones Automatic Road Machine.
Source: *The Road-Maker,* Vol. 13, No. 3, March 1919. Page 57.

80. Horse-team-drawn road-building equipment was common in this era. However, since he implied the equipment he encountered was self-propelled by steam engine, he may have seen a Jones Automatic Road Machine, as shown in Figure 26.

81. *"en masse":* French term for "all together."

82. This is not a reference to machinery maker, but rather to British cartoonist William Heath Robinson (1872-1944), best known for drawings of ridiculously complicated machines to achieve simple objectives. The name "Heath Robinson" became part of common British parlance after it was used as a slang term by the British military during the First World War. Shortly thereafter, San Francisco-born Rube Goldberg (1883-1970) became a popular cartoonist in the same vein as Robinson.

83. These photos have not survived.

84. The distance from the Susquehanna River to Baltimore on the roads at that time was just under forty-four miles. C.K. describes several events and distances following his crossing of the Susquehanna River indicating that, at that point, he may have traveled twenty-five miles after crossing of the Susquehanna River, meaning that Baltimore would have been about nineteen miles away (certainly within the range of "not many miles away").

85. This implies that C.K. did not use a map or written directions to navigate through Baltimore.

86. *Boyd's Directory of the District of Columbia* for 1919 lists about 115 restaurants. Fourteen of them had "café" in the name, but only one had "cafeteria" in the name: United Cafeteria: 1008-1010 F Ave NW, Washington, DC. This is 0.6 miles from the National Hotel, so it seems plausible that he ate at United Cafeteria, pictured in Figure 27. If he ate here and the clientele appear was similar to the people in the photograph, it is little wonder that he would feel "incipient timidity" about his appearance, having ridden a motorcycle all the way from Philadelphia on mostly dirt roads.

View of Main Dining Room. United Cafeteria, Inc. 1008-10 F St., N. W. Washington, D. C. Branch at Richmond, Va.

Figure 27: Postcard of the United Cafeteria Dining Room, *ca.* 1920.

87. In 1919, the Washington, DC Post Office building was only five years old. The building remains standing and is located on Massachusetts Avenue next to Union Station, about one mile due east of the United Cafeteria on F Street. Figure 28 is an illustration of the new post office.

Figure 28: Postcard of Washington, DC Post Office, *ca.* 1914.

88. It seems C.K. was regularly sending telegrams to England with instructions for the recipient to send money for pickup at pre-determined points further ahead on the route. No records have survived indicating the identity of this person or the content of the messages.

89. Although it is unknown who provided C.K. with travel advice and financial support, it is likely to have been his father or George, his older brother, since there is evidence C.K. had a business purpose to his trip—working for his father's company.

90. This passage about his stay at the National Hotel was used as the context for a set of eight sample questions in *Cracking the GED® Test* (2016) from Princeton Review. The GED test is taken in order to obtain a high school equivalency certificate.

91. The National Hotel, built in 1827 by John Gadsby from Alexandria, was once a grand hotel. Actor John Wilkes Booth—the assassin who killed Abraham Lincoln— usually stayed at the National while staying in Washington, DC. By 1919, the hotel had

become run down; it officially closed in 1931. The building was subsequently used as a government building until 1942 when it was demolished. Today, the Newseum—an interactive museum that promotes free expression and the First Amendment to the United States Constitution, while tracing the evolution of communication—is now located on the site. The first photograph (Figure 29) is an advertisement for the hotel in the 1917 *Official Hotel Red Book and Directory*. The next two images (Figures 30 and 31) are postcards circa 1907 of the hotel's interior and exterior.

The National Hotel
Washington, D.C.

Appeals especially to the traveling public who appreciates large airy rooms and home-like comforts and service

Handsomest Cafe in Washington

Located midway between Capitol and White House, on Pennsylvania Avenue

American Plan, $2.50 to $4   European Plan, $1 to $2.50

G. F. SCHUTT, Proprietor

Figure 29: Advertisement of The National Hotel.
Source: The Official Hotel Red Book and Directory, 1917. Page 111.

MAIN DINING ROOM, NATIONAL HOTEL, WASHINGTON, D.C.   106611

Figure 30: Postcard of The National Hotel The Main Hotel Dining Room, ca. 1907.

Figure 31: Postcard of The National Hotel Exterior, ca. 1907.

92. In the 1917 *Official Hotel Red Book and Directory*, the National Hotel advertised rates of $1.00 to $4.00 a night, so $3.00 would be reasonable in 1919. C.K. also takes the opportunity to describe the effective exchange rates between US and UK currencies. He explains that $3.00 equaled 12 shillings and 6 pence (using the then-common "£sd" format to describe the "pre-decimal" valuation of pounds that ended in 1971). In 1919, there were 20 shillings per pound, and 12 pence per shilling, with a standard abbreviation of 12*s*. 6*d* for 12 shillings and 6 pence. Thus, $3.00 would have been valued (using a decimal fraction of a pound) at £0.625. This means that $1.00 would be equivalent to £0.208 (and £1.00 equal to $4.80). There was no official exchange rate in 1919, but the common exchange rate was about £1.00 = $4.70. Shortly thereafter, the value dropped as low as £1.00 = $3.40, but by 1922 it had recovered to about £1.00 = $4.43.

93. Old Kent Road was commonly known as one of the least desirable parts of London's East End. The perception was so common that, in the UK version of the *Monopoly* board game, "Old Kent Road" was the first of the two cheapest "purple" properties. The equivalent in the US version of *Monopoly* is Mediterranean Ave.

94. C.K. never mentions what type of revolver he carried. However, he indicates elsewhere that he carried it on his body—most often concealed on a holster. In the 1960s, C.K.'s son found a .38 Smith and Wesson revolver in a locked cabinet in their home and tendered it to UK authorities under the provisions of an "amnesty" program. It is not known if this was the revolver he carried

with him in America in 1919. It is possible, since the .38 Smith and Wesson was available prior to 1919. It could have been the revolver issued to him upon commission as a 2nd Lieutenant in the Royal Flying Corps; however, a review of the record with regard to standard issue of side arms for British officers has proven inconclusive.

95. The understated humor in this story—which would be rather alarming in a modern context—is obscured by the use of "life preserver" in a manner uncommon to Americans today. At the time, this was slang for a "revolver." It can be found in period literature, such as the 1905 story, "A Variation from the Programme," by Leslie Thomas. Here is an excerpt:

> *"... the man found himself looking into the barrel of an ugly revolver, as, with arm uplifted to strike, he slowly stiffened into motionless rigidity.*
> *"'Drop it!' said the 'Duke' quietly; and the life-preserver fell clattering to the floor. 'Now - stand back!'"*

96. "vacuously": a. Lacking intelligence, stupid, or empty-headed. b. Devoid of substance or meaning; vapid or inane: a vacuous comment. c. Devoid of expression; vacant: a vacuous stare. In the context used, it paints a rather vivid picture of what may not have ended well.

97. Special note should be taken with regard to the downplayed nature of this story: C.K. asked hotel staff where the bathroom was located. He was told there was no bathroom, so he pulled out a gun and was "magically" directed to the bathroom. One's imagination runs wild with what might happen if such a stunt were to be attempted today.

98. C.K. does not mention that he visited a patent agent in Washington, DC. However, he wrote about such a visit in the second installment of his serialized story in *Pacific Motorcyclist*, dated September 4, 1919: "That evening I was in Washington and had occasion to visit a patent agent who was getting a patent through for me."

99. The total mileage in the assemblage of eight numbered routes from Washington, DC, to Cincinnati OH, along his *planned* route was 524 miles. But he ended up getting lost in West Virginia. Route analysis indicates that he actually traveled about 554

miles from Washington, DC, to Cincinnati, OH. Regardless, if he thought it was 550 miles to Cincinnati, he was apparently hoping to ride 275 miles a day for two days. It actually took him three days to get to Cincinnati.

100. The home at 3450 Clifton Avenue was owned by Thomas Stevenson, Sr., Steve's father. C.K.'s reference to "friends he had never seen" would be to Steve's parents and others who lived with them whom he befriended during his visit in Cincinnati.

CHAPTER IV

EXCEEDING THE SPEED LIMIT

I did not waste much time on the road. Fortunately there was a good proportion of concrete road, although the inevitable natural gravel was not by any means conspicuous by its absence. I also passed many stretches of brick road.

This variety is confined in England mainly to city streets, and is associated nearly always with trams. Not so in America. On the main roads of the East I have passed many a ten-mile stretch of splendidly paved highway made solely out of good red brick, and of the correct size and shape and camber of surface that literally made one's tyres hum and sing[101] as each brick was momentarily touched in endless procession. I need hardly say that for every good stretch of brick road there are UMPTEEN bad ones though, just to add a spice of life à la grande route.[102] Here and there one would encounter by no means solitary patches where apparently some enterprising farmer had torn up a few bricks from in front of some one's house to repair his cowshed or to build a new pigsty, or maybe to help put another storey on his house. There would seem to the lay mind such as my own to be a most decided disadvantage in this method of road construction! To put it mildly, it is disheartening when one is enjoying a fifty-mile-an-hour sprint on a straight stretch of road visible almost from horizon to horizon, to be rudely awakened from swift but peaceful contemplation of the beauties of nature, the loveliness of the atmosphere and the joys of motoring by being mercilessly thrown on top of the handlebars with one tremendous thump. At one spot of which I have very vivid recollections, the road took a short dip down and up again. In the bottom of the "valley" thus formed was a young but aspiring cañon where a wayward stream had left its prosaic path to strike out in life on its own across the road. Its presence was unfortunately undiscernible until close acquaintanceship was made.

When I came round I was vaguely conscious of something having happened, but as the engine was still running and the front wheel was still fairly circular, I got up and rode on, but not until I had arrived definitely at the conclusion that had I been doing sixty instead of forty-five I should have jumped across the bit of road that wasn't there and been hardly the wiser of it!

Here it was that I began to scratch crosses on the top tube to keep count of the number of times I was thrown off on the whole trip.

When the top tube got too short I put them on the front down tube.

When that was full I scratched them on the bottom tubes.

After that I trusted to memory.[103] But that was when I got to the "Far West."

I made good time, however, in spite of an occasional set-back, and looked forward to completing three hundred and fifty miles that day. With luck I should reach Cincinnati the next, and then, oh for the joys of a good hot bath, clean clothes, well-cooked food, and last, but not by any means least, good company. And I wasn't forgetting either that I had only about twenty-five dollars in my pocket. With no mishaps I should have enough and to spare for even three or four days' travelling.[104]

It was not yet midday, and the sun was getting very hot indeed. Moreover, I was getting hungry. Although I believe the two-meal-a-day system to be an excellent one, one sure gets a roaring appetite for breakfast at the end of a hundred-mile ride. So if I had not a moral excuse for a little real speed work I at least had a physical one. The road surface now changed from red brick to dazzling white concrete as in the far distance the Alleghany Mountains, that inexpressibly beautiful range that stretches parallel with the Atlantic coastline from Maine to Georgia, loomed gradually higher on the horizon, its varying tints growing deeper and deeper as mile after mile flew by.

There was hardly a soul on the road. Occasionally I would pass a touring car loaded up with human freight and with luggage bags, bandboxes and portmanteaux[105] piled up and strapped (and sometimes I think glued!) to every available mudguard, wing or projection that was large enough to accommodate them and quite a lot that weren't. Then a hay wagon flew by, and then, after a few miles, a solitary farmer on horseback—not at all a common sight in this land of Fords and motorcars. And after a few more miles a tiny black speck came into view on the horizon. It took a long time to catch up. When I got closer I made it out to be a Buick roadster,[106] its two occupants, a young man and his (apparent) fiancée, evidently enjoying a little spin in the country. And he wasn't crawling either. A touch of my electric horn (oh, a beautiful horn it was!)[107] aroused his soul from its soliloquy and he drew in to the right, waving me on vigorously as he did so. And as I passed him he seemed to quicken a little. I glanced sideways for an instant and spotted a gleam in his eye. So I accepted his unspoken challenge and glanced now and then over my shoulder. He was hanging on well, his six cylinders to my four. A mile was passed and he was still just a little way behind. The road was clear and straight, so I opened out a little more.

Another glance. He was still there. My speedometer hovered around fifty.

Not to be outdone I twisted Lizzie's right handlebar grip as far as it would go, and like a bolt from the blue we darted ahead. Fifty-five, sixty, sixty-one, sixty-two, sixty-five. The wind was simply screeching in my ears.

Another glance back, our friend was slowly losing distance. A minute or two more and he was fast dwindling behind. In ten miles he was almost back on the horizon.

I had visions of breakfast in "Hagerstown," the next town of importance not so very far ahead.[108] And so I forgot our friend of the Buick. In ten minutes' time I came to a village.[109] As usual the good surface of the highway stopped and the roads through the town turned from the perfect concrete to an infernal hotch-potch[110] of holes, gullies, ruts and mounds. Ironical notice boards warned the traveller that he must reduce his speed to fifteen miles per hour. It was purgatory even to go at four! To plunge into a seething mass of soil-waves at speed is disconcerting. It annoys you. But it is a custom that grows on you in Eastern America. You flounder about from side to side; you take a hop, skip and a jump here, there and everywhere; your very bones are shaken in their sockets; your temper approaches a frenzy of despair; and your language!

Time was when I would blush with shame at the sound of a word that was bad. Then a war came along and I learnt to experience the soothing charm of an occasional flow of language. Occasionally I met a sergeant-major who could swear freely for five minutes without even repeating himself!

And then I motor-cycled across the States. And my heart rejoiced within me that I had received such an excellent education. I found that with very little provocation or practice I could, had I the desire, have graduated to a very much higher stage of perfection in the United States than with the British Army in France. Indeed I will go so far as to aver that when ultimately I reached San Francisco not only could I have put to shame the most cultured sergeant-major that ever drilled recruits on a square, but in his moments of greatest enlightenment his powers of speech would have appeared as the futile prattle of childhood compared to what *I* could have taught him.

So that is why I slowed down when I got to "Victorville."[111]

In a few minutes, who should come alongside but our friend with the Buick racer. He slowed down and put up his hand. "Mind stopping here a minute?" he asked.

"Not at all," I replied, thinking he wanted to ask the way or borrow a sparking plug—or maybe beg a match.

He got out of his car and came along.

"Say, d'ye know what speed you were doing way back there?" he asked casually with a kind of ten-percent.-solution smile.[112]

"Well, I don't know exactly, but I guess I got YOU beat, anyway!" I chuckled.

Whereat he pulled a pocket-book from his coat and opened it. (Going to give me his card, thought I.)

"I'll trouble you for your number," quoth he, as he came to a page that was all nicely printed in columns ready for use.

From that moment I saw things in a different light. Verily the workings of the Law would seem to be getting interesting.

"And your licence, please?" after he had obligingly removed a layer of dust from my number-plate.

"What licence?"

"Your driving licence, of course. What y' think?"

"See here. Mebbe I do look a bit of a mug, but I do know you don't have to have a separate licence in New York State, s'long as your machine is registered. The number-plate is the same thing as a licence."[113]

"Oh, is it? I didn't know that." (Pause) "Well, do you mind following me a short way down the road—next block but one. It isn't far."

Whereat he got in his car again and moved slowly forward, while his lady friend protruded her arm from one side as if to stop me if I was inclined to dash past.

I did think of it in fact, because I knew I could give him a run for his money, but America, I recollected, was noted for its telephone service and I couldn't quite fancy having to resort to a hiding-place near the banks of the Ohio or perchance a field of corn somewhere in Indiana.

So I followed them down to the corner.

We stopped at a small wooden shanty on the door of which was a board bearing the sign "DANIEL S. TOMKIN, ATTORNEY-AT-LAW." My friend the "speed cop" pushed open the door and ushered me into a passage. On the right was another marked "JUSTICE TOMKIN."[114] Come in: come in," shouted a shrill seedy voice as the "cop" knocked at the door.

"I've got a case for you, Judge," said he, when we got inside.

"Oh yes, oh yes!"—and then to me—"Take a seat, sir, please, and er—make yourself at home."

I'm afraid at that juncture I began to laugh. The "Judge" was just the kind of man that we love to see "on the pictures" in England, but who we never believe really exists. I had seen his prototype dozens of times before. Tall and wiry, thin legs and tight trousers, "Uncle Sam" physiognomy with the usual goat's beard and with stars and stripes printed in indelible ink all over him. He sat at a desk bare of papers, books, letters or other impedimenta. How long the desk had been cleared for action

I know not, but his duties as a Justice of the Peace evidently did not involve any overtime from the look of things. The room was small and dingy and its walls were covered with shelves piled with books of all colours, shapes and sizes.

JUDGE.—"And what has this gentleman been doing?"

SPEED COP (producing notebook and reading therefrom).—"Driving a motor-cycle in excess of the legal speed limit, namely at forty-five miles an hour."

JUDGE (after reaching from a bookcase a large red book marked "Laws, Bye-Laws and Regulations existent in the State of Maryland," or words to that effect).—"I will proceed to read Statoot number 51, article 13, section 321b, subsection 2a of the 'Regulation of Traffic in the State of Maryland Act, 1898.'"[115]—(Submerged chuckle from self)—"And it is hereby enacted that anyone found guilty of exceeding 25 miles per hour but not exceeding 30 miles per hour will be liable to a fine of not less than 5 dollars for the first offence and of 50 dollars for a second and any subsequent offence; and anyone found guilty of exceeding 30 miles an hour but not exceeding 35 miles per hour will be liable to a fine of not less than 10 dollars for the first offence, etc., etc.; and anyone found guilty of exceeding 35 miles per hour but not exceeding 45 miles per hour will be liable to a fine of not less than 25 dollars for the first offence, etc., etc."—(Considerable amusement visible on the face of self)—"and anyone found guilty of exceeding 60 miles per hour[116] will be liable to a fine of 100 dollars, etc., etc."—(Feeling of merriment subsides)—"but anyone found guilty of exceeding 60 miles per hour will be liable to a fine of 250 dollars for the first offence and of 1,000 dollars and imprisonment for any subsequent offence. I am afraid, sir, in view of the evidence and of the dictates of Statoot number 51, article 13, section—etc., etc., I shall have to administer the minimum fine of 25 dollars."[117] (I breathe again).

SELF.—"Say, Judge, we seem to have got a bit ahead, don't we? Aren't I going to have a chance to say anything?"

JUDGE (a little "peeved." Evidently that aspect of the case hadn't occurred to him).—"By all means, sir, by all means. Say jest what you like."

Now I have neither the eloquence of a Disraeli[118] nor the declamation[119] of a Demosthenes,[120] but I do claim to have no small power of persuasion when it comes to an argument or a question of opinion. So I mustered up every effort and summoned every resource to convince this malevolent Judge that he had been reading his "Statoots" upside down and that, far from being incriminated, I should, on the contrary, be granted a handsome award.

I invoked the aid of every artifice known to humanity. Every inflexion of the voice; every modulation of speech; every appeal for sympathy, innocence, ignorance and youth known to me was conjured up.

And to what purpose? Did the Judge budge?—I might as well have read him Gibbon's *Decline and Fall of the Roman Empire*[121] in five minutes for all the good it did.

"I am very sorry, sir," he said, "but the Statoot says that the minimum fine is 25 dollars, so it must be 25 dollars."

"But, my dear good Judge," said I, "I've only got about 25 dollars in the world at the present moment."

"Well, I'm very sorry, but the fine is 25 dollars"—(and then an afterthought)—"Oh! and costs as well."

"Costs!" I gasped in amazement.

"Yes, my costs will be 75 cents, and that makes 25 dollars 75 cents altogether."[122]

Then ensued more argument, more persuasion, more eloquence, more appeals, but it was all in vain. I took out my wallet and counted out my belongings.

I had just 25 dollars and a few odd "bits."[123]

And then the humour of the situation appealed to me once more, and stronger than ever before. I laughed at the Cop and I laughed at the Judge and I laughed at myself for laughing and paid over the 25 dollars 75 cents.

"Thank you very much. Good-day, sir," said the Judge as he put the "bucks" loosely in the drawer in his desk.

Here the Cop spoke up: "I have another charge against the defendant, of riding without his registration certificate, but it's getting late, and I think we might as well overlook it in view of the circumstances." (He was evidently thinking of his girl waiting outside.)

I suggested it *would* be as well and left the Judge to gloat over his ill-gotten gains.

The idea of that goat-faced Judge and his sleek-eyed friend the "speed cop" having a good dinner together at my expense did not appeal to my better self. How was I going to travel 450 miles,[124] buy petrol, oil and food with about tenpence[125] in my pocket? On the opposite side of the road stood Lizzie with her carrier piled high and dusty, waiting, patiently waiting, for her lord and master. Ah, pathetic sight!—An idea—I return to the sanctum of the "Attorney-at-Law."

He was counting over the notes again.

"Say, Judge. S'posing you give me those notes back again. What'll it mean in imprisonment?" I had always since childhood cherished a wild desire to spend a night in prison." The Statoot stipulates that there will be an equivalent of one day's imprisonment for every dollar fine."[126] (Depths of despair once more, then enlightenment.) "Can you show me the statute that says that?"

"Sure," and he reached for the volume.

"All right, don't bother," said I, and left him once more to count his 25 dollars 75 cents.

Somehow I couldn't help laughing at everything. Such interesting sidelights into the workings of the ragtime laws of America[127] are not met with every day of the year, I mused. But what fun to be all alone in America with nothing but a motor-bike and tenpence!

I guess the Judge was wondering what I was laughing at as he watched me through the fly-net at his window while I kicked the engine to a roar and rode away.

Truth to tell, I didn't quite know myself.

I was wondering when the petrol would give out.

CHAPTER 4 NOTES

101. C.K. is describing vitrified paving brick. As noted in 1910 in *Vitrified Paving Brick*, "the year 1885 witnessed the first substantial increase in the use of vitrified brick, as during that year it was laid at Columbus, Zanesville and Steubenville, Ohio, and Peoria, Ill."

102. *"à la grande route"*: French term that means "to the main road."

103. He may have "trusted to memory," but never states the total number including those added by memory. He only says in the Preface that he was thrown off 142 times before he stopped counting. Other than saying he was in the "Far West" before he stopped making notches on the frame after each time he was thrown off, he does not precisely state where he was in the "Far West" when he stopped making the notches. Also, in his 1968 book *Introduction to Spiritualism*, C.K. wrote that he was thrown off 137 times before he stopped counting. If either of these figures are accurate, he could easily have been thrown off over 200 times before reaching San Francisco!

104. A budget of $25 for three days would be $8.33 a day, and $6.25 a day for four days.

105. *"portmanteaux"*: This is a plural use of *portmanteau* that—in this context—refers to a type of large suitcase or trunk that opened in half. The word derives from the French *portemanteau* (from *porter*, "to carry," and *manteau*, "coat").

106. The Buick Roadster was one of a number of Buick models available in 1919 (see Figure 32).

Buick Roadster, $1595.
Also Touring, $1595; Limousine, $2195; Coupe,
$2085. Buick Motor Co., Flint, Mich.

Figure 32: Buick Roadster Models.
Source: *Automobile Trade Journal*, Vol. XXIII, No. 7, January 1, 1919. Page 189.

107. The Klaxon #8C horn was standard equipment on the electric version of the 1919 Henderson Model Z-2-E.

108. In the second installment of his story, published on September 4, 1919 in *Pacific Motorcyclist*, C.K. wrote that he was about twenty to thirty miles from Hagerstown when he began accelerating to pass the Buick Roadster that was already traveling relatively fast.

109. The preceding reference from *Pacific Motorcyclist* notwithstanding, ten minutes at an assumed cruise speed of forty-five mph would mean he would have traveled an additional seven-to-eight miles after the encounter with the Buick Roadster, indicating the village he stopped at was twelve to twenty-three miles east of Hagerstown, Maryland. Additionally, in that same September 4, 1919 article, he described his arrival in this village: "A few miles farther, and I came to a tiny little one-horse village where there was a notice—'City limits. Slow down to 12 m.p.h.' So I slowed down to thirty-five to oblige."

110. "hotch-potch": more currently phrased as "hodge-podge," meaning a confused or disorderly mass or collection of things.

111. There is no known place as "Victorville" in that area on any maps or lists of towns and villages from the day (or since). It appears the name "Victorville" was used for convenience, not dishonesty. C.K. may not have been able to recall the name or misread his notes three years after his trip. However, it is a conspicuous fact that a photo taken near Victorville, California was inexplicably placed within C.K.'s story about speeding in Maryland in *Pacific Motorcyclist*, dated September 4, 1919. See the table in Figure 33, which represents the names and distances for all towns and villages he may have traveled through on Route 814 from Washington DC, to Hagerstown, MD.

Miles Remain	City/Town/Village
76.7	Washington DC (White House)
69.6	Bethesda
61.9	Rockville
57.1	Gaithersburg
49.3	Cedargrove
45.2	Damascus
39.3	Ridgeville
33.4	New Market
25.5	Frederick
20.5	Braddock Heights
17.7	Middletown
10.3	Boonsboro
7.3	Benvola
2.3	Funkstown
0	Hagerstown (Potomac & Washington)

Figure 33: Towns and Cities between Washington, DC and Hagerstown, Maryland.
Source: *Automobile Trade Journal*, Vol. XXIII, No. 7, January 1, 1919. Page 189.

There is only one "ville" along that route (Ridgeville), but it is further from Hagerstown than he implicitly states. His distances could be off (they are occasionally inaccurate elsewhere), he may have been recalling from handwritten notes, or he confused it with someplace further along. If it was not Ridgeville, and it *was* a village twelve to twenty-three miles from Hagerstown, it could only have been Braddock Heights or Middletown. Both *were* small communities (perhaps "one horse villages"), so either is a possibility. If it was not Ridgeville, it seems more probable it was Frederick, the county seat, which had a greater likelihood of being able to support a quick hearing. Although the exact date of the excerpt of *Auto Club Map 55* in Figure 34 is not known—it is believed to be from 1913 to 1927—it depicts location detail for all communities between Ridgeville and Hagerstown (including two not identified in the *Blue Book*) but, unfortunately, still does not provide any proof as to the location of these events.

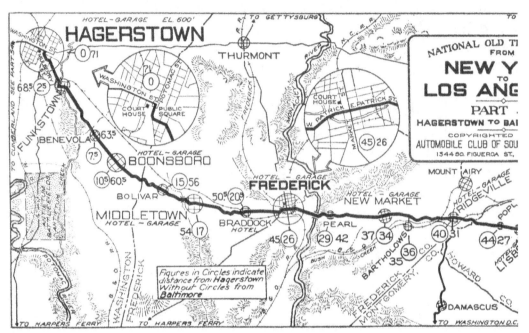

Figure 34: *Auto Club Map 55*, 1915.
Source: Automobile Club of Southern California.

112. "ten-per-cent.-solution": this term was used in period publications to describe a diluted cleaning agent. As used by C.K. here, it is reasonable to infer that C.K. was saying he felt the smile was weak or insincere.

113. In a sense, C.K. was correct stating that "the number-plate is the same thing as a licence." Although "Operator's Licenses" were *available* as early as 1918, they were not *required* by New York State Law until 1924. In 1910, after passage of the "Callan Law" (Chapter 374 of the Laws of 1910), chauffeurs were required to be licensed with photos. Although ordinary drivers could obtain licenses, they did not include a photo and such licenses were not required. Additionally, Maryland's code recognized the validity of licensure in other states so, except for egregious acts, operation of a motor vehicle fully licensed under the laws of New York was legal in Maryland (and vice versa). See the photographs in Figures 35 and 36 for a front-and-back sample of a 1918 Operator's License.

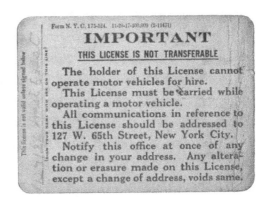

Figure 35 and Figure 36: 1918 New York Operator's License.
Source: Courtesy of Ross Day.

114. Research with local officials failed to reveal any attorney, judge, or justice of the peace named Tomkin (or any variations) in Maryland during this period. It should also be noted that this tale was also included in the second installment of C.K.'s series in *Pacific Motorcyclist & Western Wheelman* on September 4, 1919, but the name of the justice of the peace was not cited (nor the name of the village where he was stopped). It seems that the name of this individual was a fabrication, like the name of the village. There does not appear to be any purpose of deception (the core of this story seems to be true, even if embellished) or concealment (for example, a nervous publisher), but rather, to add "color."

115. These references are literary creations, but they have some statutory basis, even if C.K.'s recollection of their numeric citation or provisions is not entirely accurate. For one thing, the statewide speed limit in Maryland was thirty-five, not twenty-five. It should also be noted that, although C.K. claimed to pass the speed cop at over sixty mph, the "speed cop" alleged he was only doing forty-five mph (although in *Pacific Motorcyclist*, C.K. reported that the speed cop said he had been doing "fifty miles an hour along there"). From the *Maryland Code* in effect in 1919, Article LVI, Chapter 85. LICENSES, MOTOR VEHICLES, PART I. Speed of Motor Vehicles:

> *"(1) General Provisions. 149. No person shall operate a motor vehicle of any kind, as defined in this sub-title, over any public highway of the State recklessly or at a rate of speed greater than is reasonable and proper, having regard to the width, traffic and use of the highway, or so as to endanger the property and life or limb of any person, or without due regard to wear upon said highway, so as not unnecessarily or unreasonably to damage the same.*

"(4) Maximum of Speed. No motor vehicle shall be operated upon any highway of this State at a rate of speed greater than thirty-five miles per hour under any circumstances or conditions.

"(5) Penalties. "Any person violating any of the provisions of sub-sections (1), (2) or (3) of this section shall be deemed guilty of a misdemeanor and subject to a fine of not more than fifty dollars ($50.00) for the first offense. Any person operating a motor vehicle upon any highway of this State at a rate of speed greater than thirty-five miles per hour, shall be deemed guilty of a misdemeanor and subject, upon conviction, to a fine of not less than twenty-five dollars ($25.00) nor more than one hundred dollars ($100.00). Any person operating a motor vehicle upon any highway of this State at a rate of speed greater than sixty miles per hour shall be subject, upon conviction, to a fine of not less than one hundred dollars ($100.00) nor more than one thousand dollars ($1,000.00), or to be imprisoned for not less than thirty days nor more than one year, or to both fine and imprisonment, for the first offense; and any person who shall be convicted of a second or additional such offense, shall be subject to imprisonment for not less than sixty days nor more than two years. Any person convicted shall also be subject, in the discretion of the Commissioner of Motor Vehicles, to a suspension or revocation of his operator's license. The provisions of this section shall apply to the operator and to the owner who causes or permits his motor vehicle to be operated in violation of this section."

116. This is probably a typographical error (the speed limit cited was supposed to be fifty), since the higher fine for exceeding sixty is subsequently stated.

117. Again, although C.K. does not quote the statutes perfectly, he is generally consistent with the actual law that established the minimum fine for exceeding thirty-five mph as "not less than twenty-five dollars ($25.00) nor more than one hundred dollars ($100.00)," just as the judge claimed. Therefore, although C.K. was obviously displeased and might have been successful in appealing the ruling by alleging entrapment (if he wanted to stay for another ten days while the appeal unfolded), it appears that the smallest amount of punishment was imposed once the complaint reached the justice of the peace. If the officer had alleged he was driving over sixty mph, C.K. would have potentially faced a fine of more than $250, since the actual statutes provide, in such cases, for "a fine of

not less than one hundred dollars ($100.00) nor more than one thousand dollars ($1,000.00)."

118. Benjamin Disraeli (1804-1881), the 1st Earl of Beaconsfield, was a British politician and writer well known for his eloquent speech and who twice served as Prime Minister of the UK (in 1868 and later in 1874-1880).

119. "declamation": A recitation delivered as an exercise in rhetoric or elocution.

120. Demosthenes (384-322 BC) was a Greek orator, speechwriter, and lawyer. His speeches provide insight into Greek life and well-developed judicial processes during the 4th century BC.

121. *The History of the Decline and Fall of the Roman Empire* is a large treatise by Edward Gibbon, first published in 1776 and then augmented to such a degree that its complete works are contained in 13 volumes.

122. This is an accurate reflection of the provisions of *Maryland Code* in effect in 1919, Article LVI, Chapter 85. LICENSES, MOTOR VEHICLES, PART V. Enforcement of Motor Vehicle Laws, from with the excerpt from Section 162 below appears:

> *"The fees of Justices of the Peace in cases involving alleged violations of the Motor Vehicle Laws of this State shall be as follows:*
> *"For each State warrant issued upon complaint or at the time the offender is brought before him for an immediate hearing as herein before provided, a fee of fifty cents ;*
> ...
> *"For entry of judgment in contested cases, but not in cases where the accused pleads guilty, twenty-five cents, said entry in all cases to specify the amount of fine and costs respectively."*

Thus, by not pleading guilty, C.K. cost himself an extra twenty-five cents.

123. "bits": C.K.'s use of this word was likely a reference to a colloquial term for small-denomination coins in England. However, a "bit" was also a common term in early America; it was used in reference to some Spanish and Mexican coins that circulated and were worth one-eighth of a peso, or about twelve and one-half

cents. Thus, two bits would have equaled about twenty-five cents and "a few" might be worth fifty cents.

124. This is another distance specification that, if accurate, might have helped locate where this occurred. However, he previously stated that the distance from Washington, DC, to Cincinnati was 550 miles (even though planned route appeared to be 524 miles), so this implies that he was 100 miles from Washington, DC. But Hagerstown was only 76.7 miles from Washington, DC, and these events allegedly transpired about fifteen miles *prior* to reaching Hagerstown, meaning they occurred about fifty miles after leaving Washington, DC. So he actually had 500 more miles to go at that point—not 450.

125. "tenpence": At twelve pence per shilling, twenty shillings per pound, and an approximate exchange rate of £1.00 to $4.70, tenpence was worth about $0.196 (US 20¢), certainly within the range of the value of "a few odd 'bits,'" no matter if it was the American or English use of the word. In 2019, adjusted for inflation in the US, that 20¢ would be worth about $3.00.

126. This is an accurate reflection of the provisions of Maryland Code in effect in 1919, Article LVI, Chapter 85. LICENSES, MOTOR VEHICLES, PART V. Enforcement of Motor Vehicle Laws, from with the excerpt from Section 161, Penalties, below appears:

> *"In default of the payment of any fines imposed for violations of any of the provisions of this sub-title, there shall be imposed an imprisonment in the county or city jail, as the case may be, for a period not exceeding one day for each one dollar of the fine so imposed..."*

127. "Neck and Neck," a short story by an unknown author that was widely circulated in newspapers in the early 1900s, sheds light on the inference that "ragtime laws" are plentiful and ignorant (and, by extension, so is ragtime music):

> *"Let me write the songs of a nation and I care not who makes its laws,"* said the musical young man.
> *"Oh, I don't know,"* replied the practical young woman. *"I guess there are about as many ragtime laws as there are ragtime songs."* - Comfort.

CHAPTER V

ACROSS THE ALLEGHANIES

Strange to say, I felt not the slightest bit "peeved" about this occurrence, but facts have to be faced, and anyone who has ever found himself in a strange land 4,000 miles from home,[128] with a motor-bike and tenpence, will agree that something has got to be done about it sooner or later. All sorts of ways and means of making money quickly—the eternal problem!—occurred to me, but I dismissed them all for one reason or another. I could hold up the next car I passed and shoot the occupants after relieving them of their surplus cash. But that I thought was a distasteful way of getting money. I had seen it done in the "movies," but decided to leave that *modus operandi*[129] for a last extremity. What was it to be—a week's work or "trading away" the watch? I pondered. I got very little inspiration from my surroundings on a problem of such moment. Instead I was exhorted at almost every hundred yards to "Say it with flowers"[130] or to "Chew our famous Smello'mint Gum."[131] A huge yellow sign would then loom in sight bearing the legend "Playtime Biscuit." Every mile or so would appear another and more ominous inscription, "Sell it and buy a Ford."[132] "For all internal ailments 'Kewrit' is the Sovereign remedy,"[133] blurted forth another placard. "The Sovereign remedy," I mused.—But say! What was that? The SOVEREIGN remedy?—Inspiration at last. Lizzie's throttle seemed to close its eyes with a snap. The brakes went on of a sudden and in a few moments I was taking off my tunic at the roadside. The memory had dawned upon me of a kind sister[134] sewing some golden sovereigns[135] in the lining of the belt of that very same tunic months ago way back in good old Brum.[136] She had no doubt imagined me falling into the hands of Mexican bandits at some period in my peregrinations.[137] At first I remembered I had protested against such a seemingly unnecessary precaution. Thank Heaven that argument against a woman is never of any avail!

I searched and I found; a few stitches carefully removed with a pocket-knife revealed two glittering "yellow boys"[138] to my anxious gaze. On we sped once again, bounding, spinning ever faster onward. Truly we toiled not, but we sure did spin. If the sky was blue, it was bluer than ever before. If the road had been good, 'twas never so good as now. Refreshing breezes rolled down from the hills; sweet vistas sprang into sight; charming dells and streamlets flitted by, and never did the call of nature sound so strong.

And all because of two forgotten coins.

Hagerstown hardly welcomed me with open arms. A fair-sized, prosperous little town, it boasted a tramway service[139] and two banks.[140] My heart went not forth in joy at the contemplation of the tramway service. It did at the sight of the banks.

Dusty, dishevelled, and of dilapidated attire, I leant Lizzie up against the kerb and mounted the marble steps of the "First National Bank."[141] The massive swing-doors frowned back as they squeaked and groaned to my command. I stood in the midst of a gilded palace replete with austere-looking deities in white shirt-sleeves behind marble counters and fancy-work grids. Nothing daunted, I flicked my precious sovereigns on the counter before the very quintessence of immaculate manhood with a "Change those, please" as if it were the kind of thing I did every day of my life.

Once upon a time I had often with swelling pride expanded my chest at the thought of a British sovereign being honoured in every country of the world and any corner of the globe. I had reckoned without Hagerstown. It seemed that the austere-looking deity before referred to was not at all impressed by my view of the situation. It must have been the personal *tout ensemble*[142] that put him on his guard. He might oblige me by sending it along to New York to the Head Office, he said. "Couldn't wait a couple of days?" he supposed.

It was no use. He didn't like my face and didn't want my gold.

I scraped the dirt from my boots on his marble steps and crossed the road to the "Incorporated Bank of Holland."[143]

After conducting a lengthy battle of argument and exhortation with all the clerks in succession and all to no avail, I began to realize that British currency was of no more worth than the little sea-shells that in the earliest days of trade were supposed to be used by the enterprising natives of prehistoric communities. With a gallant show of indignation I demanded that the manager be produced forthwith. Strange to say, he appeared. I took him on one side and into my confidence. "Look here, old man," quoth I, "I'm in a bit of a hole. All your worthy satellites[144] here think I'm a sort of cross between a rubberneck[145] and a highway robber. Fact is, I've been rushed for speeding at the last village and I've only got two sovereigns to take me to Cincinnati. Now don't tell me you won't change them." Whereupon he looked warily at me and then at the gold, examining it minutely. "Guess I might fix it for you, but just hang on a minute till I can get some one to identify them. We never see such things as these, y'know."

In a few minutes he returned with an accomplice, who glared with amazement at the coins as they lay on the counter. "Gor' blimey!" said he, "don't that do yer blinkin' eyes good! Strike me pink, an' you've brought these ole yallerboys[146] orl the way from England?" and he picked them up reverently and gloated over their merry chinkle as he dropped them again on the counter. "Lor', I've spent many a one on em! How much d'ye want for them, gev'nor?"

"Four dollars eighty each," I replied.[147]

"Done! Pass him the 'oof, boss. Nuthin' wrong wi' them."[148]

Verily is it said that music hath charms for the savage breast. Once again Lizzie burst into a roar, and once again I turned her nose to the west.

Music? That Cockney's dialect seemed like a wonderful fragrant melody pealing forth through the strains of a ponderous fugue. It was like a sudden rift in the thunderclouds through which burst a cheering shaft of sunlight. It was sacrilege even to think of those nine paper dollars that I had thrust so anxiously into my hip-pocket. "Thank Heaven there is at least one spot in the U.S.A. where the King's English is spoken undefiled," I murmured to myself.

The road to Cumberland was good going. We had now to commence crossing the Alleghany Mountains.[149]

This wonderful range, which also goes by the name of the Appalachians,[150] has, in my opinion, no rival in the American Rockies as regards the loveliness of its scenery and the infinite variations of colour of its slopes. "The best scenery in the world, sir," an American would say, and he would not be so very far wrong either. Perhaps its heights are not so majestic as those of the Rockies; there may be no glaciers on its slopes nor crests of eternal glistening white on its peaks, but there is an unparalleled wealth of natural beauty in the blue and purple pine forests of its less aspiring heights and the myriad glistening streams and rivers that find their source in the thickly-wooded foothills clustering around its borders.

"Cumberland" is a comparatively large town in the middle of the hills and is well named. Undoubtedly the surrounding district reminded the early settlers so forcibly of our own lake district that they were inspired to perpetuate its memory,[151] as they have done in so many other districts, towns and rivers in the far-eastern or "New England" States.[152] Although the descent from the mountains was in places almost precipitous, the road was excellent, and excepting the concrete boulevards of California, afforded undoubtedly the best running that I met in the whole country. Although I stopped several times for considerable periods to allow the brakes to cool, there was nothing left of the brake-linings when ultimately I arrived in Cumberland,[153] where I ministered adequate and well-earned refreshment to the inner man of both Lizzie and myself.

The road now lay clear of obstructions ahead and led over undulating country for several hundred miles. Once more thoughts of Cincinnati in the distance with a vague anticipation of something approaching "England, Home and Beauty"[154]—and money as well—occupied the hours as we sped along, leaving the mileposts quickly behind us. In places travelling was good. In places it was distinctly bad. Here and there were stretches of several miles of brick road, and now and then would reappear our old friend the "Natural Gravel," that so much conspired to make life on two wheels not worth living. At times even that provided quite a respectable surface. My firm intentions not to be baulked in my aim to reach Cincinnati next day, however, kept up the pace even if to our mutual discomfort, and made the going good.

At Uniontown, about seventy-five miles past Cumberland,[155] various trivial little knocks and rattles in the engine disturbed my peace of mind. The speedometer registered only about 800 miles,[156] and I had hardly expected to commence tightening things internally at that stage. A little farther on and one cylinder, after a few peremptory misfires, gave up the ghost altogether, and I proceeded a few miles on three only. I changed the sparking plug, hoping for better results, but in vain. After a few more miles I tried another plug and then another, but always with the same result. After travelling a few dozen miles in this unsatisfactory manner, I put Lizzie once again on her stand. This time I examined closely and found the valves, tappets and clearances all in good condition.[157] There was apparently nothing wrong with the ignition either, or the carburettor, and there seemed no reason at all why such a trouble should arise—particularly, I reflected, as I was anxious to lose no valuable time. On trying still another plug out of one of the other cylinders and finding that No. 1 was still obstinate, I got on again, determined to do the journey on three cylinders only. I found I could touch well over forty-five even at that, so after all there wasn't much to complain about. Every motorist, however, who has a regard for his engine and can sense the "moral fitness" of even running and good rhythm will understand that travelling under such circumstances is decidedly unpleasant and monotonous.

At Waynesburg I passed Pittsburg some miles to the right, the "Birmingham" of America, the centre of a huge coal and iron industry and, next to Philadelphia, the largest town in Pennsylvania. A few miles farther on, and I crossed the borderline and entered West Virginia once again. It was now quite dark and I had to pick out the road as best I could by my headlight. I was getting tired and was very hungry, not having had anything to eat for ten hours. After half an hour the headlight flickered and went out, leaving me with only a "dimmer," as the Americans call the small auxiliary light,[158] with which to keep on the road and find the way. The engine, which before sounded pretty loose, now emitted noises signifying extreme agony of mind.

Then a thick ground mist settled over everything, making it next to impossible to keep on the road at all, much less to keep on the right one. Occasionally I dismounted in an endeavour to bring the headlight back to life. Frequently I narrowly avoided being run down by large cars with powerful searchlights that couldn't see me at all. It generally meant pulling into the side of the road, getting off and waving my arms frantically to signify my presence. Between time I got more hungry and more tired, and kept asking myself the same question, "Why, oh why did I leave England?" The answer always came: "Search me!"

Shortly before midnight I reached the small town of "Moundsville," on the Ohio River and on the borders of West Virginia and Ohio.[159] Every shop in the place was closed except that of a corpulent Italian dealer in bananas, oranges and ice-cream sodas. I entered his door with thanksgiving. The worthy proprietor scrutinized me open-mouthed. Finally he gave it up. I could see he had been wondering to himself, "What is this thing, and whence came it?" I sat on the counter in his presence and consumed three ice-cream sodas, four bananas and two oranges. After witnessing their consumption, he let drop his bottom jaw and ventured, "Whare yer from?"

"Doanchew worry your old think-box about where I'm from, brother, but just tell me where I'm goin'. I wonna get to Cincinnati. Now for the love of Mike don't tell me I'm not on the right road."

His jaw dropped through a further angle of ten degrees. Finally he volunteered the information that I was miles and miles from the road to Cincinnati, and that he hadn't the "goldarnest notion" how I should ever get back on it again. In disgust I filled my pockets with bananas and oranges and presented one more ice-cream soda to the minister for the interior and quitted his establishment.

My next duty was to find somewhere to lay my weary head. I decided to choose a spot where water was convenient, so that I could wash in the morning. The river was quite inaccessible from the road and the only places where there chanced to be a stream were infested with frogs and mosquitoes. After a half-hour of weary searching and climbing of long winding hills in the thick damp fog, I eventually gave it up in disgust. I found an open space at the roadside sheltered by a few trees,[160] and here laid down my rainproof coat with the thick blanket doubled on top of it, and with my suit-case as a pillow, soon convinced myself that I was comfortably settled down for sleep. In a few minutes I was well in the land of dreams. I dreamed that I was journeying to the North Pole on a twelve-cylinder Ford which went so fast that it melted the ice as it passed and ultimately crashed into the Pole at such a terrific velocity that the equilibrium of the earth was entirely upset, as also my own. At this point a lusty mosquito inflicted a tremendous bite on the very tip of my nose, and I woke up with a start. Then I dreamed that I had undertaken a banana-eating tournament with an army of Italians, and was just finishing off the ninety-ninth when another bite in the middle of my left eyelid brought me again to normal consciousness, and thus the night passed.

CHAPTER 5 NOTES

128. 4,000 miles is a reasonable round number to represent as C.K.'s distance from home. According to Google Earth, Birmingham, England is about 3,567 miles away from the approximate location of where C.K. was stopped for speeding.

129. *"modus operandi"*: A Latin term describing someone's habits of working. Often it appears in the context of business or criminal activities, but it can also be applied more generally.

130. The "Say it with Flowers" slogan first appeared in 1917. By early 1918, it was actively promoted by the Society of American Florists, who advocated using posters in shop windows and larger signs on the highway to promote the floral industry and identify member florists. Ironically, by 1921, a dispute arose about the billboards, with objections coming from gardening advocates who opposed all billboards as obstructing the natural (or landscaped) environment. Figure 37 is one of the "Say it with Flowers" advertisements of the period.

Figure 37: "Say It with Flowers" Advertisement. **Source:** *The Literary Digest*, Vol. 60, No. 12, March 22, 1919. Page 13.

131. I have been unable to locate any references to "Smello'mint" gum or anything similar to it. This supposed brand name was reflective of bad recollection, use of "literary license," sarcasm, or to avoid advertising Wrigley's Spearmint Pepsin gum, which had been introduced as early as 1892. Wrigley's Doublemint gum hit the market in 1914.

132. The "Sell it and buy a Ford" slogan was not an *approved* Ford advertising slogan, though some Ford dealers did use it. Figure 38 shows a classified ad in 1918 from a Ford dealer.

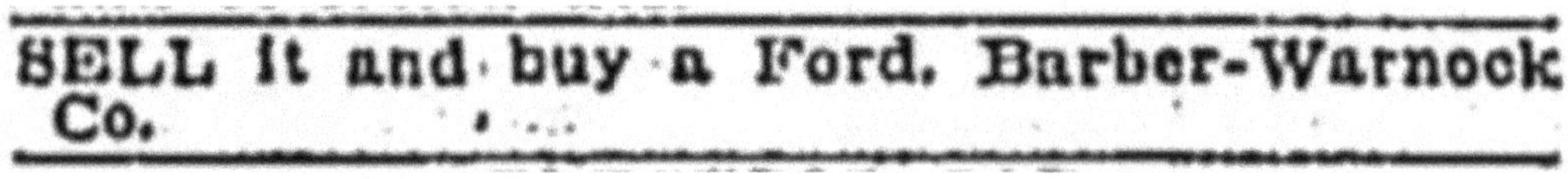

SELL It and buy a Ford. Barber-Warnock Co.

Figure 38: "Sell it and buy a Ford" Barber-Warnock Co. Advertisement.
Source: *Indianapolis Star*, December 10, 1918. Page 14.

However, Henry Ford did not believe in advertising once a product was known. Additionally, his advertising manager, Charles A. Brownell, condemned the slogan in a letter to dealers on March 7, 1919, saying that: "this is an unwholesome type of advertising which has long since been taboo, and we certainly feel that Ford dealers have enough good things to say about our cars without knocking the other fellow."

SELL IT
and buy a Ford
We will trade for anything.
THE MIAMI MOTOR CAR COMPANY
14 Main Street.

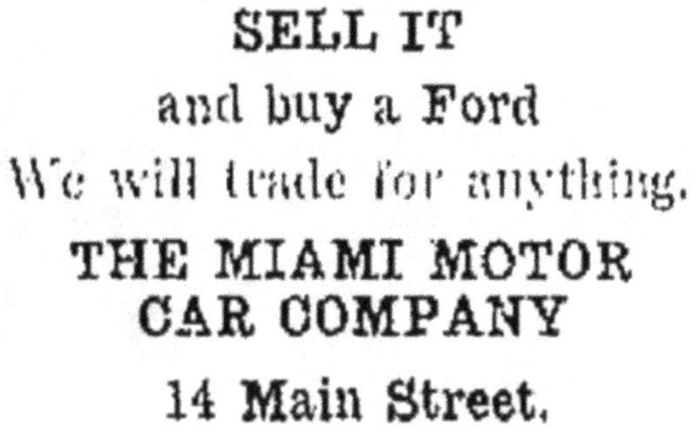

Figure 39: "Sell it and buy a Ford" Miami Motor Car Co. Advertisement.
Source: *Hamilton Evening Journal* (Hamilton, Ohio), April 16, 1919. Page 5.

At least one Ford dealer did not immediately comply. Figure 39 depicts an advertisement six weeks later. However, by 1920, the slogan had all but disappeared from dealer advertising.

133. The name Kewrit in any context was not found during an exhaustive search, but the word "sovereign" before "remedy" was frequently used as term synonymous with "trusted" or "guaranteed" and appeared in numerous advertisements promoting treatments for a variety of conditions, as shown in Figures 40, 41, and 42.

GREEN'S AUGUST FLOWER

In the good old summer time when fruits of all kinds are getting ripe and tempting, when cucumbers, radishes and vegetables fresh from the garden are too good to resist, when the festive picnic prevails and everybody overeats and your stomach goes back on you, then is the time for "August Flower," the sovereign remedy for tired, overworked and disordered stomachs, a panacea for indigestion, fermentation of food, sour stomach, sick headache and constipation. It gently stimulates the liver, cleanses the intestines and alimentary canal, making life worth living. Sold everywhere. Adv.

Figure 40: Green's August Flower Advertisement.
Source: *Hunnewell Graphic* (Hunnewell, Missouri), August 1, 1919. Page 3.

GARNET IS BIRTHDAY STONE FOR JANUARY

Chicago, Dec. 26. — The garnet is the birthstone for January. Consequently it is the luck stone for all born in that month. According to old authorities, "the garnet exercises a calming influence and takes away anger and discord. It is likewise a sovereign remedy for hemorrhages and protects the traveler from all dangers when traveling. When the figure of a lion is engraved upon a garnet, it will protect and preserve the health of the wearer and cure him of all diseases." Moreover—

"No gems save garnets should be worn
By her who in this month was born.
They will insure her constancy,
True friendship and fidelity."

The garnet is a comparatively abundant American stone. It is a beautiful gem and in addition to its January associations, is the symbol of eighteen years of married life.

Figure 41: Garnet Is the Birthday Stone for January.
Source: *Press and Sun-Bulletin* (Binghamton, New York), December 26, 1919.

EXCELLENCE PROVED BY ALL THESE YEARS

Duffee's Cough Syrup is a scientific remedy for the relief of coughs and colds, proved by thirty-five years experience to be unexcelled.

It is used in thousands of homes at the symptoms of a cold, and rarely fails to give quick relief. In combination with Duffee's Fifty-Fifty Tonic Laxative, it will break up the most severe cold and relieve the most aggravated coughs.

No family can afford to be without this sovereign remedy in weather like this. It's protection against the weakness that invites more serious illnesses.

Your druggist or your grocer can supply you with a 25c or 50c bottle. Take one home with you today.

Figure 42: "Excellence Proved by All These Years" Advertisement.
Source: *The Times Recorder* (Zanesville, Ohio), December 12, 1919. Page 2.

134. C.K. only had two sisters who could have sewed the coins into his belt. The youngest of Timothy Shepherd and Elizabeth Dale's seven children, C.K. had two older sisters, Alice Maud Shepherd and Norah Frederica Shepherd. In 1919, they were thirty-five and twenty-eight years old, respectively, and had remained in contact with C.K. as adults.

135. The sovereign is a UK gold coin about twenty-two millimeters in diameter (about 7/8ths of an inch), with a £1 sterling face value weighing about 0.257 ounces or 7.98 grams, although it was only 91.7% pure gold. In 1919, the most recent London minting of the sovereign was two years earlier. The 1917 sovereign was minted in London, Ottawa (Canada), and Melbourne, Perth, and Sydney (Australia). Beginning in 1911, the sovereign depicted King George V on the front (obverse) and Saint George killing a dragon on the back (reverse). The 1917 sovereign minted in London and shown in Figures 43 and 44 is a very rare coin today.

Figure 43: Front of a British Sovereign Coin. **Figure 44:** Back of a British Sovereign Coin.

In 1915, during the early years of World War I, the British Government encouraged citizens to exchange any sovereigns they held for new "treasury notes" or war loans, so that the government could possess sufficient gold to pay for war goods on the international market. Figure 45 was a poster issued by the Parliamentary War Savings Committee in July 1915 proclaiming that "The British Sovereign Will Win."

The public answered the call and soon the new notes replaced the gold coins. By the summer of that year, gold sovereigns had, for most intents and purposes, disappeared from circulation. Two years later, The Royal Mint in

Figure 45: "The British Sovereign Will Win" Poster, *ca.* 1915.
Source: Government of the United Kingdom

London ceased production of sovereigns. Following the war, the sovereign never regained its place in domestic circulation. With the exception of a few rare occasions, it wasn't until 1957 that The Royal Mint began producing gold sovereigns again in the UK, this time as a bullion coin.

Although sovereigns were more commonplace in 1919, it seems conspicuous that the Shepherd household had two sovereigns that could be sewn into C.K.'s belt because, even in 1919, it would have been unusual to find someone with a gold sovereign, which might account for the reaction by the British-born employee at the bank in Hagerstown upon seeing one.

136. "Brum": A colloquial local name for Birmingham used in England.

137. "peregrination": A journey, especially a long or meandering one.

138. This term "yellow boys" suggests that coins C.K. had were the sovereigns depicting King George V, which was minted beginning in 1911. Prior to that, Queen Victoria was on the front (obverse).

139. Hagerstown had local trolley cars running on its streets. Figure 46 is a postcard depicting Hagerstown with automobiles, streetcars, and even a horse-drawn carriage.

Hagerstown was also on an intra-city streetcar line that, by 1919, was operated under the name Hagerstown & Frederick Railway. Part of the H&F Railway, the Hagerstown-Williamsport line ran for over fifty years until 1947.

140. A review of available Hagerstown city directories suggests that this count is inaccurate. There were seven banks in the 1910 Hagerstown directory and eight banks in the 1922 Hagerstown directory.

PUBLIC SQUARE AND POTOMAC STREET, HAGERSTOWN, MD.

Figure 46: Postcard of a Street in Hagerstown, *ca.* 1910.

141. "First National Bank" *is* listed in the 1910-1911 and 1922-1923 directories for Hagerstown. The following banks in Hagerstown were found in both directories, except for the last one which only appears in the later directory:

- City Savings Bank, 58 W. Washington (corner of Jonathan).

- First National Bank, 76/80-84 W. Washington.

- Hagerstown Bank and Hagerstown Trust, 21/33-35 W. Washington.

- Maryland Surety and Trust Co., 63 W. Washington.

- Mechanics Loan and Savings Institute/Bank, 35/55 W. Washington.

- Second National Bank, 12 W. Washington.

- The People's National Bank, Hotel Hamilton/SW Corner of Jonathan & W. Washington.

- Commercial Trust Co., SW Corner of Public Square.

142. *"tout ensemble"*: A French term that, translated literally, means "all together" or "general effect." In this context, C.K. is referring to his "complete outfit and appearance."

143. There wasn't an "Incorporated Bank of Holland" (or anything close to it) across the street from the First National Bank in Hagerstown. (See the list of banks in Note 141). Assuming that he first went into the First National Bank, the closest bank across the street was Maryland Surety and Trust Co. Today, there is a Columbia Bank branch at 83 W. Washington, across the street from where First National Bank stood in 1922. The closest "odd numbered" address listed in the 1922 directory is for Maryland Surety and Trust Co., 63 W. Washington, the present day location of a BB&T bank branch (Branch Banking and Trust Company). It is not known if Maryland Surety and Trust was a bank that one could walk into like C.K. did, but if it was—and if he first entered the First National Bank—then Maryland Surety and Trust is most likely the financial institution where he was ultimately successful in exchanging his British sovereigns for US dollars.

144. "satellite": The word "satellite" is not commonly used in this way, but it can be found in dictionaries as a more archaic context meaning "an attendant or follower of another person, often subservient or obsequious in manner."

145. "rubberneck": This is an antiquated usage of the word that means a "sightseer" or "tourist."

146. "yallerboys": This term suggests it is based on the images on then-recent minting of sovereigns depicting King George V, which was minted beginning in 1911. Prior to that, Queen Victoria was on the front (obverse).

147. The 92% pure gold British sovereign had a one pound face value and was on the UK Gold Standard. C.K.'s valuation of each sovereign at US $4.80 is consistent with the cost he cited for his stay at the National Hotel in Washington, DC (where his valuation indicated that £1.00 was equivalent to $4.72).

148. Although C.K.'s rendition of this story in the September 4, 1919 issue of *Pacific Motorcyclist* cites his transition to a second bank across the street to change his sovereigns, in that article C.K. only says that he made multiple inquiries there: "but I was not so easily put off. I tried the next man; I tried them all. All agreed

that it couldn't be done. I asked to see the manager * * * * * * * A few minutes later I was walking down the marble steps with four dollars and eighty cents burning a hole in my pocket." While it is possible the asterisks were inserted by the *Pacific Motorcyclist* editor to abbreviate the colorful exchange C.K. had with a fellow countryman, it is also possible that these details were added to the story in the book to make it more interesting to British readers.

149. The modern spelling of this range is *Allegheny*, but Alleghany has also been historically used. The range presented a natural barrier to routine travel, with peaks rising to over 4,800 feet in the area where C.K. travelled. The Allegheny range has a northeast–southwest orientation and runs for about 400 miles from north-central Pennsylvania, through western Maryland and eastern West Virginia, to southwestern Virginia.

150. Although it is true that the Allegheny range is a portion of the longer Appalachian mountain range, it is not just "another name." Although definitions of the location of the Appalachian mountain range vary, it is understood to be about 100-300 miles wide, most of which is located in the US. It begins in Newfoundland, Canada and stretches all the way to Alabama.

151. "Cumbria": Often colloquially called "the Lake District" in 1919, Cumbria is a county in northwest England (bordering Scotland) that is famous for its lakes, forests, and mountains, as well as its association with early nineteenth century writings of William Wordsworth and other writers.

152. "New England": This term was first used in 1686 by King James II (King of England, Ireland, and Scotland) when he identified the northern colonies as the "Dominion of New England in America." In 1688, the former Dutch colonies of New York and New Jersey were added to the Dominion. Today, the New England states refer only to Maine, Vermont, New Hampshire, Massachusetts, Connecticut, and Rhode Island.

153. The brakes on a 1919 Henderson were not very good and only existed on the rear wheel. The "dual brakes" on the 1919 Henderson incorporated an Excelsior brake band that squeezed the outside of the drum using one control. Another control applied brake shoes and pads inside the same drum. This motorcycle was made for speed and smooth running, not stopping.

154. This may be a reference to a book, *For England, home and beauty: a story of battle and the breeze*, by Gordon Stables, *ca*. 1895.

155. The current distance over the "Old National Road" (principally US Route 40) between Cumberland, Maryland and Uniontown, Pennsylvania is 61.1 miles. An alternative route of seventy-five miles follows current Pennsylvania State Route 653 to US Route 119. However, C.K. writes nothing about intermediate locations between Cumberland and Uniontown, and it seems unlikely he would have taken a secondary route fourteen miles longer. It is possible that he saw the distance of seventy-five miles on a publication, so that is what he wrote in the book.

156. The total mileage from Manhattan out to Coney Island (and back into Manhattan) and then onward to Uniontown, Pennsylvania using the routes of the day was 591.6 miles. But C.K.'s odometer would have included pre-departure driving around New York acquainting himself with the bike's operation as well as any excursions. So although he says his speedometer registered "about 800" miles, these numbers don't quite add up. He cited his next odometer reading as being 1,000 miles in Springfield, Ohio, which is 267.2 miles before Uniontown, Pennsylvania. If 1,000 miles in Springfield is accurate, his odometer in Uniontown would have been 732.8.

157. A technical drawing of the motorcycle engine appeared in the *1918-1919 Henderson Parts Price List*, an excerpt of which is shown in Figure 47, depicting the components and part numbers for the valves and tappets.

158. According to *Dyke's Automobile and Gasoline Engine Encyclopedia* (1918), "auxiliary headlights are smaller than the head lights. They are placed in front, to be used in place of headlights…They are sometimes called dimmer lights." In 1917, the Society of Automotive Engineers summarized the provisions of the "anti-glare" laws in numerous states and municipalities including those in Chicago requiring "the brilliance of headlights on motor vehicles to be reducible so as not to blind, dazzle or confuse other users of the highway" and in Baltimore, "no motor vehicle, including motorcycle, shall be operated within the limits of Baltimore City equipped with any device by which the headlights can be switched or cut off or on, covered, shaded, deflected, dimmed or lowered from the seat, unless the headlight itself is equipped with some means of preventing glare, which has been approved by this Board. In short, the ordinary 'dimmer' or

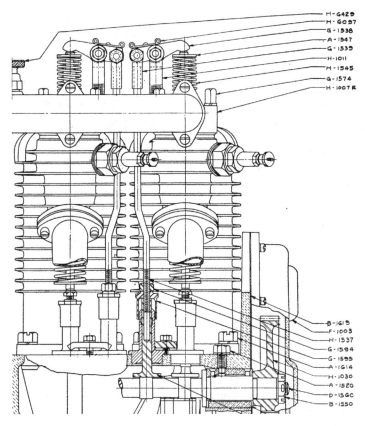

Figure 47: Henderson Engine Sectional Drawing.
Source: *1918-1919 Henderson Parts Price List*. Excelsior Motor Mfg. & Supply Co. Pages 12-13.

auxiliary light operated by a switch from the seat will not be permitted unless the headlight so operated is itself so shaded or constructed that even when cut in from the seat, it will not produce glare."

159. Moundsville is named after the "Grave Creek Mound" at Tomlinson and 9th Streets in Moundsville. It is believed this mound was built by the "Adena culture," a pre-Columbian indigenous population existing from 1000 to 200 BC and ranging from what is now Indiana, across Ohio and into West Virginia and Pennsylvania. They disappeared a thousand years before the "Monongahela culture" began inhabiting the area around 1000 AD, but it seems the "Monongahela culture" were not mound-builders. Europeans arrived as the "Monongahela culture" died out—perhaps due to arrival of unknown diseases carried by the Europeans.

160. The exact location of the campsite cannot be determined, except that it was south of Moundsville. The next day, he describes going back through

Moundsville on his way to the main "pike" through Wheeling. His writings and the map suggest he *meant* to take the westbound *Blue Book* Route 710, northwest from Uniontown and then on to Wheeling, but instead headed due west through the hills until he arrived in Moundsville. Although not depicted in Figure 48, Moundsville is just south of Glendale. Thus, C.K.'s camp site that night was most likely in the area identified as Woodland on the map in Figure 48.

Figure 48: *Blue Book* General Index Map showing Main Automobile Routes.
This excerpt is from the *Blue Book* depicting the primary and secondary roads in the area between Uniontown, PA and Wheeling, WV.
Source: *Blue Book,* Vol. 3, Page 7.

CHAPTER VI

THE DIXIE HIGHWAY

In the morning everything was wet with dew. The mist was disappearing quickly, and I arose refreshed in body and mind. Specialists would have prognosticated acute rheumatism. Doctors would have foretold death within forty-eight hours. But I was never so free from rheumatism as I am now; moreover, I live to tell the tale, with the probability of continued existence for several years to come. Lizzie looked disconsolate and rusty in every nut and bolt, but with a few kicks she rattled into life once more. The driver of a passing Ford informed me that I was twenty miles from the right road, which meant returning into Moundsville and crossing over the broad, muddy Ohio River, spanned by a lofty suspension bridge[161] made almost entirely of wood. The Ohio River, once seen, is never to be forgotten. It is verily a flowing mass of dirty, yellow-brown mud. The natives of Ohio refer to it as the "Golden" River,[162] I believe, but when I first made its acquaintance, I was in no mood to appreciate such poetic nomenclature. Instead I was bent on reaching Wheeling and breakfast.

Wheeling was reached in a couple of hours' riding along the banks of the river.[163] It need hardly be said that I did justice to a substantial breakfast, which put an entirely new aspect on affairs in general. I struck the main "pike" through to Cincinnati,[164] and continued hopefully on three cylinders with the best of intentions of reaching it that evening, although it meant a ride of over 300 miles.[165]

I did 150 in fairly good time and reckoned on having my lunch-tea-dinner-supper meal at Columbus, the State capital, about five in the afternoon. But about twenty miles from that city[166] a most distressing sound arose from the engine. I had previously slackened down to a steady thirty miles an hour so as to give Lizzie the best chance of holding out over the journey. But now a series of violent thumps and bangs disturbed once and for all my hopeful frame of mind. Undoubtedly there was a big breakage somewhere and it was evidently quite impossible to continue another mile. With a final thud the engine stopped and the machine came to a standstill near a little bridge where a tiny streamlet trickled under the roadway.[167] Near the bridge was, as might be expected, the inevitable hoarding: "SELL IT AND BUY A FORD." Strange that Fate should at times be so ironical!

I made myself comfortable on a grassy slope and proceeded to take the engine down. This I soon discovered was no mean task. It took nearly three hours to remove the cylinders. Woe be unto the man hereafter who puts nuts where they cannot be loosened or places cylinders where they cannot be removed save by an Indian sword-swallower! The result of my investigations was that I found the front piston in fragments, mainly in the bottom of the crank-case. The gudgeon pin[168] was broken in half and the connecting rod was waggling about merrily in the cylinder. All the bearings were loose, and although there was plenty of oil in the sump, one was devoid of metal altogether. This was discovered at the bottom in the form of powder. An encouraging outlook indeed!

Although my motto where a refractory[169] motor is concerned—"to get it home somehow"—could have been ignored, I was not even in walking distance of anywhere. There was no town or village for miles around, and only a solitary farmhouse here and there. Further, an empty stomach does not improve one's outlook on life under such circumstances, and mine was very empty. I took stock of the whole situation. What should it be? Walk to Columbus and take the train, or stick by Lizzie and get along somehow? I counted out my money. It amounted to three dollars and thirty-five cents,[170] not even enough for the railway fare. "No, I've set out to cross these infernal States on a motor-cycle, and I'll do it," I resolved, and sat down again to patch Lizzie's engine together.

The rumble of cart wheels on the brick road attracted my attention. The cart was drawn by a weary horse in the charge of a more weary driver.

"Hi, brother, got anything edible on board?" I shouted.

"I gotta lot o' old boots here," he replied, evidently in ignorance of the meaning of the word "edible."[171]

"No, thanks, I gotta good pair of my own to start on before I come to that. Aincher got any oranges?"

"Yep, I got one box left, four fer a quarter."

Bang went seventy-five cents for a dozen, leaving me with two dollars sixty. Now, thought I, I have enough provisions to last a couple of days. Let Old Harry do his worst.[172]

The vendor of boots, furniture, and oranges went on his weary way.

From a bough of a willow tree I shaped a neat gudgeon pin that fitted dead into[173] the loose end of the connecting rod to guide it up and down in the cylinder. I fished out all the big lumps of the broken piston that remained in the crank-case and tightened up the bearings as well as I could. By the time it was dark I had everything replaced ready to start on the road once more.

Before daybreak, I was up and on the road; my plan was to keep on all day at a steady twenty miles an hour and reach Cincinnati about five in the afternoon.[174] The machine ran well considering its wooden gudgeon pin, although it was not easy to avoid being reminded continually of Lizzie's indisposition, and as time went on the rattles became worse, the clanks became gradually louder, and I began to wonder where my next stop would be.

I passed through Columbus about breakfast-time,[175] but did not stop for breakfast. There was no money for breakfasts. Now, although I did not stop at Columbus, I cannot with but a few words dismiss it entirely from consideration. Although not by any means the largest town in Ohio, it is the State capital. That feature, as I have pointed out before, is not at all unique in the States. In fact, I do not think I could name a single State capital that is the largest town of the State, without referring to the authority of one Baedeker.[176] Not only are there over 125,000 people in Columbus,[177] but it appeared to me to be a very fine city. The streets are wider and are better paved than those of most American cities, and in places are illuminated by large electric arches. Although there are seven towns throughout America boasting this title[178] (each one in a different State), I think Columbus, Ohio, must be the *élite* of all the Columbuses.

Outside Columbus I stopped, had lunch—three oranges—and continued. There was really no necessity to stop, but I liked to feel that lunch was just as important an occasion as when it wasn't oranges.

The engine was by now getting rather noisy. People who passed in cars, many of whom I had passed two days before, slowed down as they approached and looked at me wonderingly, as if to ask if I knew anything about it. They probably came to the conclusion that I was a deaf-mute.

Then we got to Springfield, and a noticeable feature at the side of the road, on a special track of its own, was an electric train service connecting up all the large towns in the district,[179] even though the distances amounted to thirty and forty miles, in some cases even fifty, as is the case between Columbus and Springfield. Perhaps I am complimenting them by referring to them as trains, as they are more in the nature of single or double-coach trams, but I was surprised not only by the speed at which they travelled, but also by the number of passengers who availed themselves of the service. In a way, the presence of that track was comforting, particularly when some new noise or rattle emanated from my thrice-weary steed. On the other hand it is distinctly humiliating to be astride a 10 h.p. motor-cycle de luxe,[180] jogging along side-saddle (to ease the growing soreness!) at fifteen or twenty miles per hour on three crotchety cylinders, when a tram-load of disinterested Americans flies past with a shriek at forty or fifty. Generally the driver realized the position and sounded a piercing whistle with a supercilious air, as if to say: "Make way for the fast traffic, please!"

At Springfield the speedometer flicked off the 1,000th mile,[181] and I branched away from the "Pike's Peak" Ocean-to-Ocean Highway[182] (for such it appeared to be), and turned south-westward towards Dayton, a flourishing manufacturing and business centre. "Detours" and sub-detours were the order of the day and were conspicuous by their presence, as also by the general looseness and rottenness of their surface. In theory I was travelling upon the "Dixie Highway,"[183] reputed (by advertisements thereon appearing) to be "the finest and most luxurious highway in the States."[184] As far as my experience was concerned, I found it paved with good intentions and bad cobblestones. Sometimes, when the paving blocks had been pulled up preparatory to new ones being laid down, the surface was tolerably good, but then would appear a "detour" heralded by an insolently-improvised notice-board which led the unfortunate traveller miles and miles from his appointed path and over the most disgusting road-surface imaginable.

I was pleased with Dayton. As I left it behind me, I wished it prosperity. It seemed to have the right kind of air about it. A friendly policeman held up a bunch of traffic for two minutes for me while he put me "wise" to the road to take. He noticed my New York number-plate and finished his chat with "Well, good day, brother, and the best of luck to you." I wouldn't even have killed a mosquito in Dayton!

It was now well after midday. Cincinnati was still about sixty miles away. Would it be safe to have a meal in the next town? I had filled up with "gas" and oil in Dayton and had about fifty cents (2s.) left.[185] With a three days' diet of oranges, I had cultivated an appetite of great latent possibilities. I determined to be rash. Next stop, I told myself, I would look around for a "bakeshop."

An hour later I arrived at a little town called "Lebanon." It was very small, very picturesque, and very unpretentious. But it boasted an excellent "bakeshop." I leant Lizzie against the kerb outside and pressed my nose against the window-pane. The sight of all those nice cakes was almost as good as a feed—but not quite! I espied one, plain and large but tasty-looking. I valued it at twenty-five cents. "Well, it'll last a long time," I thought, and entered meekly to inquire the price. "Five cents," replied the lady of the counter. "Done! It's mine, *all of it!*"

Long live Lebanon!

A few miles out, I halted near a bridge under which ran a little stream of crystal water. It was a treat to be out of the glare of the baking sun, so I sat down on the bank underneath the bridge and settled down in earnest to a sumptuous dinner. The bill of fare was as follows:—[186]

Hors d'œuvres	Gâteau de Lebanon (varié).
Consommé .	Eau Naturelle.
Entrée . .	Gâteau de Lebanon.
Plat du jour	Ditto.
Légumes .	Ditto.
Dessert .	Ditto.
Wines .	Vin blanc d'Adam (direct from the distillery).

And oh, what a meal was there, my countrymen!

There was enough and to spare. The cooking was excellent, the service irreproachable, and there were no gratuities.

After a leisurely half-hour I stuffed what little cake I couldn't contain into the tool-box, took one last, lingering draught from the cool crystal stream, and again kicked Lizzie into a rattle.

Once more towards Cincinnati! Two hours only, now, I reminded myself, and all the trees and birds in hearing. Gradually those two hours became shorter as mile after weary mile rattled past. Sure enough, in about the time I had reckoned the pot-holes in the road grew larger and the ruts deeper, a sure sign of approaching civilization. Then a huge signboard appeared, "CINCINNATI, THE QUEEN CITY OF THE WEST.[187] Make your home in Cincinnati."

The Cincinnati Speedway[188] was passed on the right, and after a couple of miles or more I struck tram-lines. The reader can well imagine how glad and relieved I felt when I spotted trams and tram-lines, those things which in normal life I rightly detest and abhor. Whereas once upon a time I considered them to be the motorist's greatest enemy, I now smiled upon them with friendly gaze.

By the time I was actually on the outskirts of the town, I was "baked to a frizzle." And such a thirst! For three days I had been amassing a good thirst. Ohio mud[189] is not really a good beverage. It might perhaps "put one over" the "near" beer that I have tasted in various American towns, but that's not to be wondered at. The man who first called it "near" beer wasn't much of a judge of distance! Never could I remember having been so hot, so thirsty, and so fed up, all in one. I pulled up at the first drug store and literally squandered twenty-five cents in an orgy of ice-cream sodas. I took the precaution to retain ten cents, however, "in case anything turned up."

At about half-past four[190] WE ARRIVED. A wealth of meaning rests in those two words. My friend Steve heard the noise as he sat reading on the verandah of 3,450 Clifton Avenue.[191] "That can't be Shep. That's somebody wheeling a lawn-mower," he said to himself without looking-up, and went on with his book. But when the lawn-mower had overrun itself and turned round and came back and continued indefinitely to lawn-mow outside the same 3,450, he looked up and saw that it was indeed a motor-cycle or, at any rate, the unmistakable remnants of one. When he saw the rider, he thought: "No, that can't be Shep after all; that's the dustman."[192]

But fact will always triumph over fiction. In the same way soap, thank Heaven, will always triumph over dirt. But what a relief to be once again in a comfortable house, that could almost be considered "home," and once more to know the joys of a good hot bath and feel the luxurious embrace of clean clothes again!

CHAPTER 6 NOTES

161. This sentence contains a juxtaposition of events that seems to suggest that C.K. took a suspension bridge back into Moundsville and then on his way north to Wheeling. However, there was no bridge of any kind across the Ohio River at Moundsville in 1919—only a ferry. There *was* a long suspension bridge spanning the main channel of the Ohio River *north* of Moundsville at Wheeling, WV, a bridge that C.K. would have crossed after heading north from Moundsville. Construction on the Wheeling Suspension Bridge began in 1847 and was completed in 1849. It was the largest suspension bridge in the world from 1849 until 1851, stretching 1,000 feet long. It remains in use to this day as depicted in Figure 49, a photo taken in 2019.

Figure 49: Wheeling Suspension Bridge, 2019.
Source: Photograph by Mark Hunnibell.

162. No evidence has been found indicating Ohio natives or others referred to the Ohio River as the "Golden" river. Although there are numerous publications prior and subsequent to 1919 that document historic names used for the river, none included "Gold" or "Golden." It is possible C.K. heard this characterization from one local and assumed it was true. It is also possible that C.K. conflated this name due to the Ohio River's origin in Pittsburgh, where the Allegheny and Monongahela Rivers merge. This intersection of rivers is where the Ohio River forms, and it is commonly referred to as the "Golden Triangle of Pittsburgh."

163. This describes the road from Moundsville to Wheeling along the east side of the Ohio River, shown on the General Index Map in the *Blue Book* as well as USGS maps of the period.

164. The term "pike" is slang for "turnpike," commonly used in both the US and England to identify a toll road that requires payment to drive upon it. The "main pike" going west into Ohio from Wheeling was the National Old Trails Road. In Ohio in the 1800s, this *had* been a toll road, with tollhouses every twenty miles but, by 1910, tolls were no longer being collected. Still, that section of the National Old Trails Road may have continued to be colloquially called the Ohio Turnpike.

165. It was not over 300 miles from Wheeling WV, to Cincinnati, OH. Using the roads of the day along the route C.K. travelled, it should have been 259.7 miles.

166. The *Blue Book* Route 615 provides distances from downtown Columbus to Zanesville, OH. In Figure 51 (next page), the Route 615 distances from Columbus are added in boxes to the 1909 USGS map of the area. Additional whole mile distances from Columbus distances are identified in circles, based on Etna being 17.3 miles from Columbus. Thus, if twenty miles from Columbus is an accurate approximation, C.K. would have been halfway between Kirkersville and Etna when his engine began acting up.

Town	Distance from Columbus
Etna	17.3
Parkinson Station	19.2
Kirkersville	21.9*
Luray Station	25.5

Figure 50: Distances from Columbus.
* Note: The *Blue Book* erroneously says Kirkersville is 24.9 miles from Columbus.
Source: *Blue Book* Route 615.

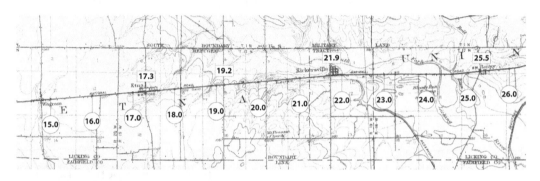

Figure 51: Luray to Etna Miles to Columbus.
Source: USGS: *Ohio Thurston Quadrangle,* 15 Minute Series, 1909.

167. There were two larger streams after the twenty-mile point that fit this general description. The first and larger of the two—an unnamed stream that flows northeast into the South Fork Licking River—is about 18.8 miles from Columbus. This seems to be the most likely stopping point, particularly because there are no waterways for some miles after Etna, and C.K. wrote that he could not drive a mile further after his malfunction.

168. "gudgeon pin": This is a British term for what Americans refer to as a "wrist pin," the dowel that runs through the top of the connecting rod into the piston.

169. "refractory": stubborn or unmanageable.

170. C.K.'s claim of having only $3.35 in his pocket while he was twenty miles short of Columbus seems about right. He wrote that he left the bank in Hagerstown, MD, with $9.60 from exchanging his sovereigns. Before trading them in, he had perhaps thirty-five cents in spare change, so he would have had almost $10.00 in his pocket by the time he reached Hagerstown. From Hagerstown, C.K. drove to Cumberland and may have spent the night there, perhaps at a hotel. During his

stay, he had good food and replaced his brake linings. He pressed on to a campsite near Moundsville, WV, after having consumed oranges and ice cream sodas at a café late at night. If each of C.K.'s "meals" totaled $1.00, and a hotel in Cumberland cost him $2.00, then he would have spent a total of $4.00 for meals and lodging. Add to that another $1.00 for brake parts and shop time, and he would have $5.00, but that does not include fuel and oil, so $3.35 is a reasonable amount.

171. The "weary driver" may not have been ignorant of the meaning of "edible." It could be that he was making reference to the desperate practice of cooking shoe leather and eating it. In a famous scene from the silent film classic *The Gold Rush*, Charlie Chaplin's Tramp character boils and then eats his shoe. Although this film was released six years after C.K.'s travels, it may reflect common beliefs about the eating habits of tramps during the time period.

172. "Old Harry": a British euphemism for "the devil." It first appeared in literature in the mid-nineteenth century.

173. "fitted dead into": A piece that is snugly fit and does not rotate or spin. In this case, it means that C.K.'s replacement wooden pin was snug in the small end of the connecting rod, so that it would not come loose as it moved up and down in the empty cylinder.

174. On June 22, 1919, sunrise near Columbus, OH was at 6:03 a.m. C.K. says he started out before daybreak, so he may be reporting that he left at 5:45 a.m. If C.K. started out that day 18.8 miles from Columbus, he had 142.2 miles to go before he would reach Steve's house in Cincinnati. Riding at twenty mph, it would have taken C.K. seven hours and seven minutes to reach Steve's house in Cincinnati. Thus, without accounting for actual road conditions, traffic, fuel, food, or rest stops, he theoretically could have arrived by 1:00 p.m. So, predicting his arrival at 5:00 p.m. is more than reasonable. Given the major temporary repairs he made to his motorcycle the night before, it seems he might not have actually left before dawn, but rather at around 7:30 a.m.—a departure time that would still have made prediction of 5:00 p.m. arrival quite reasonable.

175. C.K. says he passed through Columbus around breakfast-time. Based on other places in the book where he describes a substantial amount of riding before breakfast, it seems that his "breakfast-time" could have been as late as

8:30 a.m.—a time that fits with the calculation of twenty miles of riding at twenty mph, assuming he had left at 7:30 a.m.

176. German publisher Karl Baedeker (1801-1859) was a pioneer in the business of worldwide travel guides, much like Fodor's and Frommer's travel guides today.

177. In 1919, the population of Columbus was well over 125,000. *The Abstract of the Fourteenth Census of the United States* (1920) reports a population for Columbus of 237,031 in 1920 and 181,511 in 1910.

178. According to the 1920 U.S. Census, there were *fifteen* cities or towns named Columbus with enumerated populations. Five additional small communities also had the name, but without specific populations.

- Ohio: 237,031.
- Georgia: 31,125.
- Mississippi: 10,501.
- Indiana: 8,990.
- Nebraska: 5,410.
- Kansas: 3,155.
- Wisconsin: 2,460.
- New Mexico: 2,110.
- Montana: 987.
- Kentucky: 654.
- Iowa: (Columbus City) 346.
- North Dakota: 332.
- Pennsylvania: 312.
- North Carolina: 168.
- Illinois: 141.
- Minnesota: (small township).
- Missouri: (small village).
- New Jersey: (small village).
- New York: (small village).
- Texas: (small town).

179. This was colloquially known as the Ohio Electric Railway, an amalgamation of companies that, as shown in Figure 52, provided interurban service in western Ohio further west into Indiana.

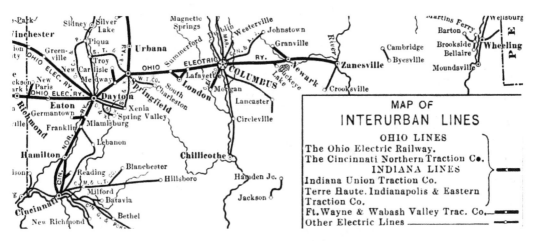

Figure 52: Map of Interurban Lines—Ohio and Indiana.
Source: *Electric Railway Journal,* Vol. 34, No. 15, October 16, 1909. Page 874.

180. The advertised power rating for the 1919 Henderson was 14.2 horsepower, not ten.

181. As previously cited, C.K.'s estimate of 800 miles on the odometer in Uniontown, PA, was about sixty-seven miles more than what could have been if the odometer read 1,000 miles in Springfield, OH. A route analysis of the roads of the day indicates that the actual road miles for his route were 858.8 to reach Springfield, OH. Thus, if it read 1,000 in Springfield, it means that from the time he started driving his motorcycle until he reached Springfield, OH, he had driven an additional 141.2 miles—including orientation in New York City, any excursions on the way, and being lost in West Virginia—a figure that seems reasonable under the circumstances.

182. In Ohio, the Pikes Peak Ocean-to-Ocean Highway ran through Springfield and then southwest to Dayton, after which it resumed a westerly course. The Dixie Highway came through Dayton from the north (through Lima, Wapakoneta, Sidney, and Troy before reaching Dayton) and continued south to Cincinnati.

183. Although C.K. may have traveled on the Dixie Highway south of Dayton for a few miles, he did not take it all the way to Cincinnati. This is known because the Dixie Highway went south through Middletown, OH. However, C.K. went

through Lebanon, OH, which is not on the Dixie Highway (see Figure 53). There is no indication C.K. went through Middletown.

Figure 53: Excerpt of Dixie Highway Map, 1915.
Source: National Highways Association, Washington, DC.

184. C.K. is apparently referring to a sign he saw on the side of the road. However, I have been unable to find any examples of such a sign. The Dixie Highway route was only *proposed* in 1914, at which time the city of Cincinnati aggressively lobbied for it. A newspaper account in November 1919 indicates that it was not yet completed, so any description in the summer of 1919 may have included such promotional rhetoric—even if not the exact words C.K. quoted.

185. C.K.'s financial equation of fifty cents US being the value of two shillings U.K. is accurate and consistent with previous valuations. At an approximate exchange rate of $4.70 per £1.00, one dollar would be about £0.213, so half a dollar would have been £0.106, which is just over two shillings.

186. The menu from which C.K. dined is translated and summarized in the table represented in Figure 54.

Terms	Literal Translation	Meaning
Hors d'œuvres: Gâteau de Lebanon (varié)	Appetizer: Rich cake of Lebanon (diverse)	The cake C.K. bought in Lebanon
Consommé: Eau Naturelle	Soup: Plain water	Water
Entrée: Gâteau de Lebanon	Main course	The cake...
Plat du jour: Ditto	Plate of the day: Same	The cake...
Légumes: Ditto	Vegetables: Same	The cake...
Dessert: Ditto	Dessert: Same	The cake...
Wines: *Vin blanc d'Adam (direct from the distillery)*	White wine from Adam	Water from the stream

Figure 54: Translation of C.K.'s Menu.

In short, this "meal" was the cake he bought in Lebanon and some fresh water from the stream.

187. This description of Cincinnati and its moniker as "Queen of the West" was inspired by the poem "Catawba Wine," by Henry Wadsworth Longfellow.

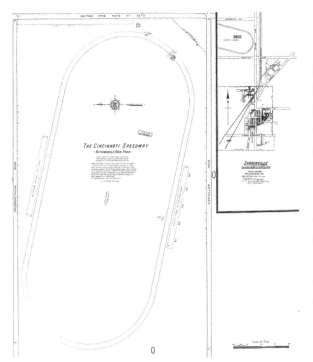

188. The Cincinnati Speedway, built on a 640-acre site just north of Sharonville, OH, (see Figure 55) was a two-mile high-banked oval made of wood. The so-called "board track" had thirty-two-degree banked turns and six-degree banked straightaways to assure extreme speeds. The opening of the speedway in Indianapolis spelled the end for the Cincinnati Speedway, which closed in 1919.

Figure 55: The Cincinnati Speedway.
Source: *Sanborn Fire Insurance Map from Cincinnati, Hamilton County, Ohio.* Sanborn Map Company, Vol. 8, 1917.

189. No slang use of "mud" as a nickname for a beverage during the period has been discovered. It seems more likely that C.K. was simply saying that he did not like the taste of the beer sold in Ohio (or the so-called "near-beer").

190. If C.K. departed his overnight stop east of Columbus at 5:45 a.m. before day-break and arrived at Steve's house at 4:30 p.m., he would have averaged an easy 13.2 mph for nearly eleven hours. If, instead, C.K. departed at 7:30 a.m. and arrived at 4:30 p.m., he would have averaged 15.8 mph for nine hours. This was certainly achievable if he had been cruising at twenty mph at regular intervals as much as possible.

191. The 1920 Census indicates that Thomas Stevenson and his wife, Laura, lived in a 3,600 sq. ft., three-story home at 3450 Clifton Avenue (see Figure 56) along with a thirty-year-old teacher, Annie L. Smith. Additionally, the 1920 Cincinnati City Directory reflected that Cora Bercaw lived there and was also a teacher, at Woodward High School. (This was one of the first public schools in the US. The 27th U.S. President, William Howard Taft, was an alumnus.) Between the 1920 Census and other documents, it is known that Thomas Stevenson, Sr., owned this house and had a mortgage on it. He was age forty-nine at the time and had been born in Scotland from Scottish parents. He immigrated to the US in 1913, but was not yet a citizen. He worked as a photographer in the lithography industry. His house, which still stands, was last sold for $183,000 in 1998, and has since been partitioned into seven apartments available for rent.

192. "dustman": a British term for garbage or trash collector.

Figure 56: 3450 Clifton Avenue, Cincinnati, Ohio, *ca.*1919.
Source: Personal collection of descendants of Thomas Stevenson, Jr.

CHAPTER VII

CINCINNATI AND ONWARDS

I spent in all twelve days in Cincinnati.[193] They were twelve happy days; days of leisure, days of interesting experiences, followed by days of longing to be on the road again.

The first of July, 1919, will live in the mind of every free-born American citizen as the day when Prohibition became law throughout the entire States.[194] Not by design, but by coincidence, was it also the date of my departure[195] from my friends in Cincinnati to explore the "perils" of the West. My sojourn there was brought to a sudden close by the astounding discovery that Lizzie's overhaul was completed. I had a few warm things to observe when I was presented with the repair bill. It amounted to a mere seventy-five dollars, half of which represented the alleged value of the somewhat indifferent labours of a more indifferent mechanic and a small boy. On the various occasions when I had visited the shop, the mechanic was generally conspicuous by his absence, and were it not for the occasional activities of the small boy, who seemed to delight in "salivating" at frequent intervals on every available inch of the floor surrounding Lizzie's remains, I feel inclined to think that I should even now be enjoying myself in Cincinnati. The other half of the bill represented sundry replacements which, to my way of thinking, should have been made free under the firm's guarantee, which had still three-fourths of its term to expire.[196] After much argument, the proprietor and myself agreed to differ on this point.

The early afternoon witnessed my departure.[197] The kindly attentions of mine hostess[198] had provided me with good things for the journey. Meat sandwiches in boxes; fresh butter in tins; fruit and nuts galore. Little packages were squeezed in here and big ones strapped on there. Odd corners and crevices revealed an unsuspected orange or banana and hard-boiled eggs or biscuits in twos and threes lurked amongst the shirts and socks.

With a light heart I spun down the beautiful, well-paved avenues that set at defiance the rigid, straight-edge avenues of more modern American cities. I hummed over the cobble-stones of the lesser streets and swung past trams and over bridges and was soon speeding along the road to Indianapolis, thinking like a true pessimist that Lizzie didn't feel as well as I had hoped, and that I should be hung up again at a not far-distant date.

In America, in the east, it is the easiest thing in the world to take the wrong road. Moreover it is generally the most difficult thing to find out whether one is on the right road or not. I have no objection to make when roads in towns and villages will run either north and south or east and west, because for town life this arrangement spells efficiency. In the country, however, the *raison d'être*[199] of these chess-board roads is somewhat obscure. When combined with old-time roads that originally followed goat-paths or sheep-tracks, its effect is confusing. But when taken to the extreme, and one finds the main highways connecting large cities abound with sharp right-angle turns at every few miles, sometimes going north to make up a little latitude, then continuing west, then returning south to lose the latitude gained, and afterwards continuing west again, the result is ridiculous and sometimes exasperating; very often two, three, four, or more roads run parallel and only a few yards distant, all leading to the same place. Sometimes they lead to different places. Sometimes they lead nowhere at all. Sign-posts are not popular anywhere in the United States. Instead the roads are identified by painting every third or fourth or tenth or *n*th telegraph pole with different colours.[200] When properly carried out, this principle is a very commendable one, and without it travel would be absolutely impossible. But when followed only imperfectly, or when the colours become faded and obliterated, so that one trail can be easily mistaken for another, the traveller has many troubles and trials ahead.

I had ample moral consolation, therefore, for completely losing my way only ten miles out of Cincinnati, and wasted a full hour in trying to get on the right "pike" without going back.[201]

Incidentally the system of decorating telegraph poles in accordance with the trail they follow has its humorous side. There are, all told, over a hundred different trails or "National Highways" in different parts of the States,[202] and each one is supposed to have its distinctive sign. Thus the "Pike's Peak Ocean-to-Ocean Highway" is identified by a circle of scarlet above a circle of white,[203] and the "Lincoln Highway" by circles of red, white, and blue.[204] Sometimes, as in the cases of the "Blackhawk Trail" and "Mackinaw Indian Trail," the sign is of a more or less complex nature,[205] including the profile of an Indian's head, for instance. The humour of the situation will be apparent when a single stretch of road coincides with say four or five separate trails. Each telegraph pole is truly a thing of beauty and a joy for ever, with its inscriptions, circles, squares, profiles, bales of cotton, etc., etc., painted on in various colours from top to bottom![206]

In large towns and cities where several trails meet, it requires the quintessence of alertness and deduction to find one's way by the telegraph poles, which, save for a few exceptions, represent the only means of identification. Strange, in a country using twenty times the number of cars per head found in any other country in the world, that facilities for using them should be so meagre as at times to be almost prehistoric!

It is strange also that some of the roads that were constructed even in modern times were the achievement of personal enterprise and are even now "boosted" and advertised by their "promotors." An outstanding case is that of the "Pike's Peak Highway" just mentioned, which is one of the three trails that cross the Continent from east to west. This road boasts a President, three Vice-Presidents, and a Secretary-Treasurer![207] Between them these worthy gentlemen are responsible for the proper maintenance of the road (experience compels a sarcastic smile), and for the furnishing of information to travellers thereon, etc. Where the money comes from I wot not,[208] unless it be from the various motoring clubs in the country. In a booklet, published apparently by them, it is described as "The Appian Way of America."[209] Permit me to quote passages from this remarkable publication:—

"Increased attention is this year being focussed on the 'See America' idea, and motorists planning a trans-continental trip will naturally select the route of greatest scenic and historic interest. That is why the discriminating tourist will travel over the Pike's Peak Ocean-to-Ocean Highway, the improved central route from the Atlantic to the Pacific coast. From New York it follows the National Old Trails Road to Indianapolis; from that city to Salt Lake City, it has its own DISTINCTIVE ORGANISATION; and west of Salt Lake City it follows the line of the Lincoln Highway. History places the stamp of approval on this as the LOGICAL trans-continental Highway. Etc., etc. (pages of it). . . . The trip has no dreariness and no monotony. . . . (More pages)."

Never was such a grossly misleading impression of ease, comfort, and luxury perpetrated upon an unsuspecting Englishman! It was well said that the pen is mightier than the sword. If ever again I find myself so utterly demented as to motor-cycle across the United States before proper roads have been constructed, may Heaven preserve me from "The Appian Way of America"!

The reader may think that I am dwelling unduly on the subject of roads, but I do so at this juncture because it was a subject which now became of increasing magnitude. Practically the last sign of paved road of any kind between this point and the Pacific Coast (some 2,500 miles away) would be encountered at Indianapolis, and from there onwards were universally the execrable "dirt" roads that so seriously threaten not only the comfort but the safety of motor-cycling. I was not even disappointed at the outlook, because I came to America without even expecting any form of trail or route across its entirety to be at my disposal. But I feel the natural resentment of the Englishman when I am led to believe that there is a luxurious "highway" ahead, only to find an aggravated series of dust-heaps, mud-pools, and cow-paths!

The road, however, to Indianapolis was not of the "Appian Way" variety. It was comparatively good in places, and ran for many miles along the valley of the Miami River,[210] amidst beautiful scenery of ever-changing variety. After a few miles, the Ohio-Indiana boundary was crossed,[211] and here, as many times afterwards, I was struck by the apparently sudden change of landscape, the same as the home tourist can almost always discern by the "feel" of the country whether he is in England or Wales, no matter if he be without his map for reference. I do not mean that either Ohio or Indiana is particularly mountainous. On the other hand, the latter is on the whole somewhat flat, as if in preparation for the weary stretches of monotonous prairie that are to be encountered the more one travels westward until the Rockies are reached.

I made little headway that afternoon, and at 10.30 in the evening[212] I was still some distance from Indianapolis, the capital of the State. I therefore looked around as best I could in the pitch-darkness, with only my lights as a guide, for a likely spot for my night's abode. Water is a *sine qua non*[213] for the camping vagrant, and when I came to a large steel bridge I decided that that was the place for me.[214] It evidently spanned a pretty big river, but it was so far below, or seemed so far, I could not see the water. A lengthy reconnoitre from the road led me to the edge of a field of corn whence I could hear the river but could not see it for dense masses of vegetation.

I propped Lizzie up on her stand and found to my dismay that when the engine stopped the lights went out. Not feeling in the mood for investigating the cause of the trouble, I was satisfied to keep the engine running slowly as long as illumination was necessary in unstrapping my baggage and "making" my bed. Then I set out to find the river and enjoy the luxury of a wash.

Easier said than done! I could find openings in the thick undergrowth where I deemed the river should be, but could find no way of making closer acquaintance with its waters. As I continued my search, the bank suddenly gave way beneath me, and I was plunged up to the waist in the river I had been so diligently seeking!

My exit was more difficult to negotiate than my entrance. The bushes and weeds on the banks were not strong enough to enable me to pull myself out, but came away, roots and all, and left me sinking in the muddy river-bed. I eventually extricated myself, however, and decided to retire unwashed! Pulling off my soaking top-boots was a herculean task, and this done, I hung my wet breeches on a tree to dry in the warm summer night.

I passed a splendid night and awoke with the dawn, only to find my clothes wetter than they were the night before, thanks to a heavy dew. Such conditions, I reflected, were of mere trifling importance in the life of a bona fide tramp, and I was soon humming along once more through the fresh, crisp morning air.

We arrived in Indianapolis at breakfast time and with a hearty appetite.[215] I remember Indianapolis chiefly as a city with long wide streets full of cobble-stones, tram-lines, and traffic policemen. My first duty was to take Lizzie to see the vet. I didn't like the sound of her at all, and she seemed but a rickety shadow of her former self. I was taking no chances now. As if by instinct we went "right there." The Henderson[216] agent took Lizzie under his protecting wing, and while I settled down to consume a hefty breakfast[217] of cantaloupe, puffed rice, and coffee, he took her for a spin along the few miles of concrete road that I had left behind with such regret.

"Waal, I guess there ain't very much wrong with her, boy," was the verdict, although he did not seem over-exuberant about it.

"How far you goin'?" he added.

"Just to the end of the road," I replied.

"Hm, and a tidy ride too, I'll say so. I've done it, but not on one o' them."

Then, after meditation, he added, "But I think she'll take you there. Give my love to 'Frisco, won't you, boy?"

I promised, paid him a dollar, and left to track down the offices of the local branch of the "3 A." Club, or Automobile Association of America, whom, I was informed, I must see before going any further, to inquire about the roads ahead. Dirt roads, it will be understood, vary with the weather. Hardly ever does the English motorist hear of a road being washed away with the rain, but the idea of its being borne away on the wings of the wind would indeed appear strange to him!

I found the "3 A." Club located at one of the large hotels, all alive with "bell-boys" and commissionaires and elevators.[218] I was greeted by the hotel staff with haughty aloofness. "Put that gink outside,"[219] I could imagine the desk clerk saying to the hall-porter. But I was being whisked up the elevator to the umpteenth floor[220] before he had the chance.

At the "3 A." Club office I was greeted most cordially.

The gentleman at the desk was a human encyclopædia of roads and places. Beneath the dirt and dust he believed he perceived some person of high rank, a brigadier or something, and my brown tunic and field-boots must have borne out this assumption. However, that may be, he certainly did his best to give me every assistance. But when I told him I was motor-cycling to the Pacific and wanted to know which was the best road to take, his jaw dropped suddenly. There were two alternative routes to Kansas

City, the "Pike's Peak" through Springfield[221] and the "National Old Trails Highway" through St. Louis. Which should I take?

"Well, sir, the National Old Trail is impossible just now. The rains have been very heavy and there are several places where you couldn't possibly get through. And as for the other—well, I shall have to think."

Which he did. He hummed and ha'd and stroked his chin and hummed and ha'd again, as if struggling with some momentous problem. He spread out maps in rows before him and followed the route with his finger. Then silence.

After a minute or two of this, in which the merits of "washouts" and hold-ups and detours by the score were being weighed together in his troubled brain, he spoke:

"Yes, sir, I think you can get through" and, more deliberately—"I *think* you can get through. Yes, it's a good road," he added.

I learnt then for the first time one outstanding principle in the road-study of America. I confirmed it on innumerable occasions later. There are two classes of roads and two only. They are good roads and bad roads. Any road, ANYWHERE, in the whole of the United States of America (and, I presume, her Colonies as well) is a "good" road if you can "get through." The remainder are bad.

I thanked my benefactor and accepted sheaves of maps and guide-books[222] for which he would take no payment. He was indeed the quintessence of obligation. I on my part was the quintessence of gratitude.

"Now for the fun," I chuckled as I kicked Lizzie to a roar and set out for the highway with red- and white-circled telegraph poles.[223]

CHAPTER 7 NOTES

193. In the fourth installment of his series in *Pacific Motorcyclist & Western Wheelman* dated October 2, 1919, C.K. wrote that he only spent *ten* days in Cincinnati. Figure 57—a photo of C.K. sporting a moustache he had shaved off by the time he arrived in Kansas City—was taken at a park in the Cincinnati area during his visit with Steve and his family, but the exact location remains a mystery. A second photo (Figure 58) was taken in Walton, Kentucky—about twenty-two miles south of Cincinnati—suggesting that C.K. toured greater Cincinnati with Steve, so the park photo could have been taken on such an outing.

Figure 57: C.K. at a Park in Cincinnati.
Source: Personal collection of descendants of Thomas Stevenson, Jr.

Figure 58: Street in Walton, Kentucky.
Source: C.K.'s personal slide collection.

194. The 18th Amendment to the US Constitution, also known as "Prohibition," was passed by the U.S. House of Representatives and U.S. Senate on/by December 18, 1917. The 18th Amendment and its enabling legislation (the Volstead Act) did not ban the *consumption* of alcohol, but prohibited the sale, manufacturing, and distribution of it in the US. The 18th Amendment needed to be ratified by the states before it could take effect. By January 16, 1919, 46 states had ratified Prohibition with only Connecticut and Rhode Island rejecting it. The enabling Volstead Act set the starting date for nationwide Prohibition to begin a year and day after

ratification, on January 17, 1920. Thus, while Prohibition *was* a topic of the times on July 1, 1919, it was not yet legally in effect nationwide. On the other hand, an article in the *Cincinnati Inquirer* on July 1, 1919 described the events of the preceding evening when citizens flocked to drinking establishments to celebrate the "eve of war prohibition"—their last chance to legally purchase alcoholic beverages. Thus, it seems that at least Ohio government officials believed that Prohibition took effect on July 1, 1919 and intended to enforce it accordingly. It is therefore reasonable that C.K. understood this to be its date of effect. On December 5, 1933, the 21st Amendment was ratified, repealing the 18th Amendment.

195. Some of the dates and events in the book can be independently verified or calculated. However, C.K.'s differing explanations as to how long he was in Cincinnati and his itinerary after leaving Cincinnati makes it difficult to confirm he left Cincinnati on July 1, 1919.

196. As shown in Figure 59, the 1919 Henderson came with a "90-day guarantee." If C.K. purchased the motorcycle on June 10, 1919 in New York, he would be twenty-two days into the term of the guarantee on July 1, 1919—exactly one quarter of its duration.

GUARANTEE

Henderson motorcycles are guaranteed under the warranty of the Motorcycle Manufacturers' Association as follows:

1—All Henderson Motorcycles are warranted against imperfections in workmanship and material, and any part proving defective within ninety days from date of the original sale by dealer, when sent to us, transportation charges prepaid, will be replaced free of charge, subject to our inspection and decision, and provided, also, that the owner has filed with this office the registration card furnished with each motorcycle.

2—This guarantee extends to replacement of defective parts only.

3—When machines, or assembled parts, are sent to us, in which defective parts are to be replaced, a reasonable charge for labor will be made.

4—Wear, misuse, abuse or negligence are not guaranteed against.

5—When sending in parts for replacement, customer must tag same with his name and address.

6—A letter giving full and detailed particulars must be sent to us in each case, giving the engine number to avoid delay in identifying the consignment.

7—This guarantee is not operative when parts manufactured by other than this Company are inserted or used for repair.

8—Alteration of our construction in any way whatsoever, or use of devices not approved by us, terminates this guarantee.

9—We do not guarantee any parts of equipment or specialties not of our own manufacture, such as tires, carburetors, magnetos, etc., as these parts are guaranteed by their respective manufacturers, and should be sent direct to them if defects develop.

10—Purchaser accepts the provisions hereof upon purchase of motorcycle, and agrees to rely solely thereon.

Every Henderson motorcycle sold by other than our recognized dealers is sold without our guarantee, unless otherwise provided.

32

Figure 59: 1919 Henderson Guarantee.
Source: *Instructions for Operation and Care of Henderson Four-Cylinder Motorcycles - 1919 Model Z-2.* Excelsior Motor Mfg. & Supply Co. Page 32.

197. Early afternoon is rather subjective, but it seems C.K. could have departed Steve's house on July 1, 1919 as late as 3:00 p.m. because he later reports that, at 10:30 p.m., he stopped and camped by a river that was still some distance from Indianapolis.

198. His "hostess" would have been Steve's mother, Laura, as photographed in Figure 60 with Thomas Stevenson, Sr., Laura, and C.K. on the front porch of 3450 Clifton Avenue.

Figure 60: C.K. with Thomas Stevenson, Sr. and His Wife, Laura.
Source: Personal photo collection of descendants of Thomas Stevenson, Jr.

199. *"raison d'être"*: A French term meaning "purpose."

200. There was no nationally named highway between Cincinnati and Indianapolis. When C.K. reached Indianapolis, he rejoined the Pikes Peak Ocean-to-Ocean Highway, which was marked with a sign consisting of a red rectangle over a white rectangle as shown in Figure 61. Sometimes the sign had the letters "PP OO" printed in the white area at the bottom.

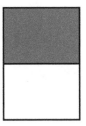

Figure 61: Pikes Peak Pole Marker: Red Band over White Band.

201. It is impossible to know where C.K. got lost, but the correct road from Cincinnati to Indianapolis would have been northwest from Cincinnati toward—and through—Hamilton, Indiana. If he had gone off course, he likely corrected it before crossing the Ohio River—which (if he had crossed it) would have put him well off course in Kentucky—or upon realizing that he had not crossed the Great Miami River about fifteen miles out of Cincinnati.

202. This is a bit of an exaggeration because, even though there were certainly over one hundred named highways in the US at the time, many were shorter roadways that did not cross any state lines. In 1920, AAA began publishing the *Highways Green Book*. In the Second Annual Edition, published in 1921, AAA recognized fifty-six major organized highways. AAA considered twenty-one of those to be of national importance while thirty-five were deemed to be of interstate importance. Additionally, AAA identified fifteen national and interstate roads and affiliated organizations, twenty-four state roads associations, two foreign roads organizations, and countless clubs affiliated with the AAA.

203. The Pikes Peak Ocean to Ocean Highway was marked with signs on poles with the symbol shown in Figure 61, consisting of red over white *horizontal bands* (not circles)—each ten inches wide—at crossroads and forks. They appeared at frequent intervals and were painted on telephone poles, fence posts, trees, or rocks. An additional 1,500 enameled steel signs, 14x20 inches in size, also in red and white, were ordered and placed on individual posts at least every five miles across the country. So although the *colors* cited by C.K. are correct, no evidence was found marking the Pikes Peak Ocean to Ocean Highway using a red circle above a white circle.

Figure 62: Lincoln Highway Pole Marker: Red, White, and Blue Bands with Blue "L."

204. The Lincoln Highway was marked with signs like the one in Figure 62, with a red bar across the top and a blue bar across the bottom. Sections of this highway remain today and are similarly identified for historic purposes. The marker for the Lincoln Highway was highly standardized from its inception in 1913. No evidence has been found of markers on the Lincoln Highway using the red, white, and blue circles C.K. described.

205. C.K. did not travel on either the Blackhawk Trail or the Mackinaw Indian Trail:

- Blackhawk Trail: A sixty-mile route from Dixon, IL, to Beloit, WI.

- Mackinaw Indian Trail: A forty-two mile route between Peoria and Bloomington, IL.

It is not known what signs or symbols were used to identify these trails or if C.K. ever saw them on any maps or pamphlets.

206. The potential for confusion with multiple markers was widely recognized. In a 1916 article titled "The Trail of the Painted Posts—A tale of the organized Middle West Tourist Routes," Raymond S. Spears wrote:

"One finds the public utilities poles, the fences, the trees, and other conspicuous objects decorated with the signs of these many through routes. A telephone pole will have several different markers on some corner or crossroads. There will be a white and yellow band, a red ball, a black and white mark, for example. Sometimes for a few miles one sees two or three different routes indicated. The road is lonesome which does not have a route or two along it.

"I know that many tourists have never heard of these various trails which have local, state, or national significance. But the promoters of the routes have been working on the finds of the people along the painted ways. Out in a little town in Illinois when I turned the wrong way a whole tribe of small boys, seeing my touring outfit, yelled in unison:

"'That ain't the Cannon Ball Trail, mister!' The first I had heard of it."

The telephone pole in Figure 63 (next page) was photographed in Iowa City in 1916 and would not have been on any part of C.K.'s route. However, it provides a good illustration of the highway markers that C.K. describes. Additionally, Figure 64 (next page) is an excerpt from a Gallup's *Official Auto Route and Highway Map of Missouri*, 1922, which identifies over sixty different pole markings used in Missouri and adjacent states.

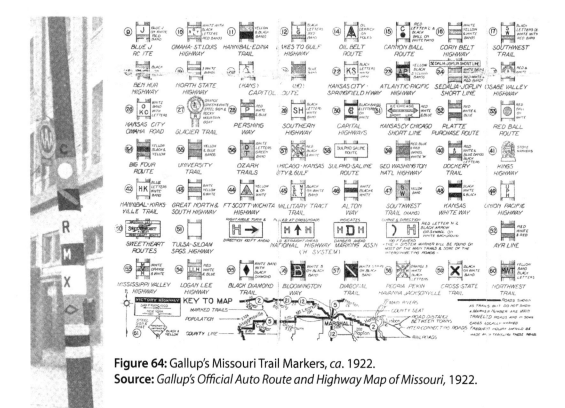

Figure 64: Gallup's Missouri Trail Markers, *ca.* 1922.
Source: *Gallup's Official Auto Route and Highway Map of Missouri, 1922.*

Figure 63: Telephone Pole Photographed in Iowa City, *ca.* 1916.
The original caption from the bulletin reads: "This telephone pole at the corner of Washington and Dubuque Streets bears the unique distinction of bearing the most important tourist road marks of any similar pole in the world-The markings from top to bottom are, American Automobile Association emblem, the Kansas City & Gulf, the Red Ball, the Black Diamond, the River to-River Road, the M. & M., the Red Cross, and The Burlington Way or Orange & White."
Source: *Iowa Service Bulletin* (Iowa State Highway Commission), Vol. IV, No. 11, November 1916. Page 9.

207. In April 1919, the Pikes Peak Ocean-to-Ocean Highway Association split the office of Secretary-Treasurer and elected the following officers:

- C.F. Adams, President (Chillicothe, Missouri).

- W.H. Goodin, Vice President (Lovelock, Nevada).

- George W. Hughes, Vice President (Hume, Illinois),

- Warren R. Jackson, Vice President (Harrisburg, Pennsylvania).

- T.W. Ross, Secretary (Colorado Springs, Colorado).

- A.Q. Miller, Treasurer (Belleville, Kansas).

208. "wot not": An archaic English phrase meaning "know not." In this context it indicates that C.K. did not know the source of funds for road maintenance. However, it is implicit criticism that, whatever the source, it was not *enough* money to properly maintain the roads.

209. The Appian Way of the ancient Roman Empire was built primarily as a route for military supplies. It was one of their earliest and most strategically important roads. At over 300 miles in length, construction began in about 312 B.C. The July 1919 edition of the *Automobile Journal* included an article, "Pikes Peak Highway," that assigned the nickname of the "Appian Way of America" to the Pikes Peak Ocean-to-Ocean Highway, but did not allude to any publication about the highway containing the characterizations quoted by C.K. The article in *Automobile Journal* included this description:

> "The Pikes Peak Ocean-to-Ocean Highway has been termed 'The Appian Way of America.'" The name is fitting. The Appian Way of the Roman empire, designed primarily for military purposes, became during the succeeding centuries, a great line of communication for social and commercial purposes.
>
> "The highway links 12 states. It passes through six state capitals. It traverses 97 counties and passes through more than 500 hamlets, villages, towns and cities, and it serves in these and adjoining countries a total population of nearly 25,000,000.
>
> "The distance from Philadelphia to San Francisco is 3490 miles; from New York City to San Francisco 3564 miles. Road conditions are up to the average."

210. The text implies that the road from Cincinnati to Indianapolis ran parallel to the Miami River. However, although C.K. would have crossed what is now called the Great Miami River on his way out of greater Cincinnati, the first section of "highway" to Indianapolis paralleled the Whitewater River—not the Miami—which runs northeast back into Ohio starting at the Indiana border.

211. Without getting lost, the distance from Steve's house to the Indiana border at West Harrison was about twenty-one miles.

212. The total distance from Steve's house to downtown Indianapolis was about 110 miles. If he averaged twenty miles per hour, it would have taken him five

and a half hours. However, he reported getting lost and losing several hours before leaving greater Cincinnati. This means that, if he left at 3:00 p.m. and spent seven and a half hours on the road, he should have *reached* Indianapolis by 10:30 p.m.—not still been "some distance" from it. Thus, it is most likely that he stopped around 9:00 p.m. when the onset of nightfall was complete. That would leave him about thirty miles from Indianapolis, or about an hour and a half riding in the morning, which seems about right because he later says he arrived in Indianapolis at breakfast time.

213. *"sine qua non"*: A Latin term meaning "absolute necessity."

214. If C.K. stopped near a bridge for the night about thirty miles from Indianapolis, the most likely bridge was over the Big Blue River about twenty-five miles from Indianapolis, just past Morristown. Alternatively, he might have stopped at the bridge over the Little Blue River about thirty-three miles from Indianapolis, just before reaching Arlington. The excerpts from the USGS maps (Figures 65 and 66) are from 1956 and 1960 because no earlier maps of the area have been located.

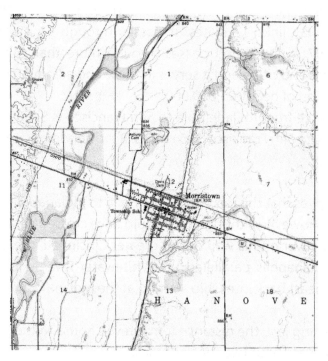

Figure 65: Big Blue River.
Source: USGS: *Indiana Morristown Quadrangle,* 7.5 Minute Series, 1956.

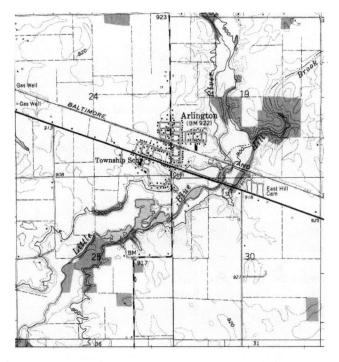

Figure 66: Little Blue River.
Source: USGS: *Indiana Morristown Quadrangle,* 7.5 Minute Series, 1960.

Of the two, it seems more likely C.K. stopped just after Morristown because (a) it is further from the local town and (b) it is likely the bridge over the Big Blue River would be longer and more substantial than over the Little Blue River, which was a narrower crossing. Still, the drop to the water at the Little Blue River seems greater, so either is viable.

215. It would have taken C.K. about an hour and a half at an average of twenty mph to drive from outside Morristown to downtown Indianapolis, so the location fits if he set out at dawn and made Indianapolis at breakfast time.

216. The Henderson agent was Merz Motor Co., 134 E New York St., Indianapolis.

217. If he ate near Merz Motor Co. while waiting for his motorcycle to be evaluated, likely locations were: Thornton's Coffee Shop (see Figure 67, next page) or Cunningham's Coffee Shop (see Figure 68, next page).

Thornton's

Where Thornton's coffee is served with pure cream.

Meats, vegetables and all foods are purchased and censored daily by expert buyers, who demand Thornton quality.

A clean restaurant, where your good health is respected.

Small profit, coupled with volume of business, is one of the factors which contributes to our success.

Courtesy is paramount among all employes, and they will appreciate any suggestions for the betterment of the business.

Thornton's Coffee Shop
138 E. New York St.
Also operating Mars Hill Hotel at Mars Hill.
Established 1916.

Figure 67: Advertisement for Thornton's Coffee Shop.
138 E New York St., Just a Few Doors Down from Merz.
Source: *Indianapolis Star*, December 31, 1920. Page 20.

Special 35c Dinner
Roast Veal.   Roast Beef.
Baked Hash.
Turnip Greens.
Mashed Potatoes. Lettuce Salad.
Corn Bread.   Rice Pudding.
Coffee, Tea or Milk.

SPECIAL SUNDAY.
Boiled Dinner..............35c
Roast Beef or Pork..........50c
Chicken Dinner 75c

Cunningham's Coffee Shop
250 Mass. Ave.
127 E. New York St.

Figure 68: Advertisement for Cunningham's Coffee Shop.
127-129 E New York St., Across New York St. from Merz.
Source: *Indianapolis Star*, May 11, 1918. Page 18.

218. This would have been the Claypool Hotel, located on the northwest corner of Washington and Illinois Streets. The Claypool Hotel was built in 1901 and was demolished in 1969 after a devastating fire in 1967.

219. "gink": A foolish or contemptible person.

220. The 1919 Indianapolis City Directory lists the Hoosier Motor Club (the AAA affiliate) as being on the ninth floor of the Claypool Hotel.

221. The Pikes Peak Ocean to Ocean Highway was a more northerly route than C.K. ended up taking. This is evident in the 1920 advertisement for the Pikes Peak and Jefferson Highways shown in Figure 69.

Figure 69: Crossroads of the Nation Advertisement, *ca.* 1920.
Source: US Department of Transportation.

222. One of the guidebooks C.K. received in Indianapolis would almost certainly have been a 1915 book including dozens of strip maps produced by the Automobile Club of Southern California (probably the largest club affiliated with the AAA), the cover and index of which are included as Figures 3 and 4 in the Maps and Navigation section at the front of this book.

223. As previously discussed in Notes 200 and 203 and depicted in Figure 61 and, the Pikes Peak Ocean-to-Ocean Highway was marked with red and white bands, not circles.

CHAPTER VIII

INDIANA AND ILLINOIS

The first bit of fun was not far ahead. In places the road was passable if one ignored the six-inch layer of loose sand and soil that covered it. The country was flat and uninteresting. Diversion was occasionally encountered in the form of side-slips and here and there an unexpected spill. The quicker I went the easier I got through, as the soil did not cling to the wheels so much and hinder steering. At thirty it was almost impossible to maintain balance. At thirty-five it was tolerable, and at forty it was comparatively simple.

Now and then I would pass a kind of harrow the width of over half the road and drawn along by a team of horses. The function of this was to break up the big lumps of solid mud formed by the recent rains. After this would follow a similar team of horses dragging a "grader"—a kind of snow-plough arrangement which scraped the surface flat and shovelled the surplus sand and mud-lumps into the side.[224] In these districts the farmers are held by law individually responsible for the condition of the roads their farms adjoin,[225] and the process of grading is expected to be carried out within three or four days after the rain. When the farmers are busy with their crops this doesn't get done, and when they aren't, it sometimes does, according, I think, to whether the farmer is a sheriff or a justice of the peace and has to set an example to others. Fortunately all farmers are motorists as well; they have to be able to get about, so when they wish to travel, they grade the roads for their own use if for no more altruistic object.

Once I was passing one of these road-ploughs drawn by a team of three horses abreast, which took up most of the road and showed not the slightest intention of drawing in to the side. In endeavouring to pass it, I struck at too small an angle the huge ridge of solid mud-lumps that it had formed. I was going fast, of course. The handlebar was wrenched out of my hands and I was thrown with great force over it and on to the bank at the side. Lizzie herself lay roaring on her side in the dirt. The horses took fright and galloped off. The only damage done showed itself in some nasty cuts and scratches, some small areas of skin missing from different places, and a few bent levers and controls. From past experience I had learnt that in all such cases the clips and brackets and sharp corners of Lizzie's profile ALWAYS seemed to be in the path of my flight over her handlebars.

A handkerchief bound tightly round the cuts, a few adjustments made, and on we go with smiling faces, only to overtake the wretched thing again!

After twenty or thirty miles of this, we came to mud in earnest—mud measured not by the inch in depth, but by the yard. Never was it soft and squishy and respectable, but always baked rock-hard into ugly contorted shapes that simply defied progress on two wheels alone. The diabolical effect had been heightened by the passing of numerous cars through the roads when the surface was still plastic, and great ruts and cracks and ridges were thrown up at every point between the road-boundaries, each one representing an eternal struggle to "get through." When the fierce sun came out and poured down for days unceasing upon such ugliness as this, the hideous surface was as if petrified by its glare, and the efforts of a "grader" would be futile to alter in the slightest degree its abominable condition.

Riding was out of the question. It was haulage work that had to be done, and many times when I got into a huge solidified "crevasse," I had to leave the machine standing in it on the tubes of its cradle-frame and proceed ahead to chip the edges down until the wheels would reach to the bottom again.

Anyone who has stood on the "Glacier des Bossons," looked upwards towards the summit of Mont Blanc,[226] and seen the contorted, fantastic shapes that the ice assumes as it swells over the ridges in its path, can perhaps imagine the same effect on a smaller scale applied to the dirt roads of Indiana.

Fortunately there were stretches of road, generally when there was a slight gradient, where the surface was well-drained, hard, and flat, and going was good. But invariably at the foot of every slope, or at the dip between two hills, there was a stretch of excruciating "agony" that would reduce the most defiant motor-cyclist to submission.

Thus it was for eighty or ninety miles.[227] The truth began to dawn on me that a fellow has to be a "tough guy" to motor in these parts. Sometimes I would stop and rest awhile to let an occasional car get by. It was funny to see how they all went! The big heavy touring car would roll along as if to devour all that came its way. It would meet a nasty patch and with broken dignity would heave and sigh from side to side as it slowly crawled on bottom gear over the ridges and furrows; and then it would rear proudly into the air as it surmounted some huge lump of solid mud and suddenly flop down with a dull thud on the bottom of the springs as it plunged into the hollow beyond. One could hear every joint groan under the strain and could sometimes see the bottom of the engine scrape ridges in the chunks of earth and watch the little bits knocked off an unfriendly obstruction as the back axle dragged its weary way along.

And then perchance would come some cheeky Ford, the essence of impudence as opposed to the dignity of its wealthier brethren. With a hop, skip, and a jump, it would scramble over the furrows, swinging gaily from side to side, wagging its tail in the air and rattling in every sinew as only a Ford knows how! But the "Flivvers"[228] got through easier than any.

The worst patch I struck was near the small town of Hume.[229] I have never seen in the space of 200 yards a more apt imitation of a volcanic lava-bed. The thick mud of two days before had been churned up into the most fantastic shapes that ever a main highway has taken. Every square inch of the ninety-foot-wide road bore signs of the passage of some vehicle or other. Some of the ruts were so deep that the machine rested on the engine and the frame and not on the wheels at all. Pushing it anywhere but in one of the best ruts was impossible. When the rut got too deep, I had to lift up the back of the machine bodily and wheel it foot by foot, while the rut took the front wheel whither it listed. Here and there were signs where car-drivers, in similar predicaments, but a day or two before, when the mud was not yet baked quite hard, had shovelled away large quantities of the road to allow the engine and chassis to clear. Half-way through was a large hole, deep and broad enough to allow a small car to be hidden therein from view. In this hole the mud was still soft and plastic. A good Samaritan of the road had procured a piece of old corrugated iron from somewhere and propped it against two poles to warn any others who might follow of its presence.

An Awkward Stretch of Road in Indiana.

Lifting four-cwt.[230] Lizzie across this whole stretch took three-quarters of an hour all told, and at the end I was faint with exhaustion. The sun was never hotter and I never perspired more, not even in the middle of the Mohave Desert[231] in California, where the thermometer rises up to 140 degrees or more! I begged a glass of milk from a farmhouse a mile farther on, and thanked God that He made cows and that I was still alive to appreciate them!

And thus we toiled and thus we spun for many miles until late in the afternoon, when I came to parts where the sun had not yet had time to do its work. Every inch of the road was thick, black, slimy mud; mud that stinks with a smell peculiar to itself alone; mud that clings to the tyres and wedges in the forks and fouls the chains and blocks the wheels; mud indeed that sticketh closer than a brother. I stopped at a ramshackle little village of a few dozen shops and houses, all made of wood, and boasting the name of "Murdock," to partake of afternoon tea.[232] Outside an old rickety "store" (this term includes any conceivable kind of retail shop in America), I saw a notice: "HENRY T. HODGES, JUSTICE OF THE PEACE; DRY GOODS STORE; GENERAL MERCHANDISE; POST OFFICE; REAL ESTATE; REFRESHMENTS."[233]

Henry T. Hodges beamed on me benignly from behind a pile of preserved fruit tins as I entered his gloomy establishment.

"See here, dad, I want a good meal," I said; "money's no object. Get me?"

"Sure; an' have ye come far, brother?"

"I should reckon about a thousand miles to-day. Dandy roads you've got in these parts, dad."

"Aye, but you'd 'a seen 'em when we 'ad the rains, brother; they wuz so mighty slick the hottymobiles sunk right down in 'em and 'ad to be dug out wi' a shovel and dragged along wi' a team of four 'osses."

"Why, I shouldn't have thought there were four horses in Murdock," I replied.

"Aye, an' I know there is, brother, cause they're my 'osses."

"Um! Guess you make a pretty good living out of them, don't you, dad?"

"You've said it, brother. Ten dollars a time is my charge, and if a chap don't pay I jest leave 'im there till 'e does!"

"Well, what about this meal, dad? I'm mighty hungry and, say, who's the road commissioner about here?"

He essayed no answer, but disappeared hurriedly to boil the tea. I had no doubt now who the road commissioner was!

After leaving the "Store" of Henry T. Hodges, J.P., I did another twenty miles or so until dark, and sought out a comfortable secluded spot near the road, but far enough from it to avoid the smell of it, and settled down for the night.[234] Mosquitoes were the only source of worry now. Otherwise this roadside sleeping was getting quite a commonplace event.

Up at dawn in the morning! On the road once again; labouring, pushing, hauling, heaving, lifting, cleaning off the mud, speeding a mile or two and then more labouring and more pushing.

THE MIDNIGHT COUCH.

At breakfast-time I reached Decatur, a flourishing town of 20,000 or so inhabitants, and had breakfast at a "get-fed-quick" eat-house[235] where you sit on a stool in front of the counter and the man at the range behind fries you a mutton steak, bakes the "waffles," or poaches the eggs as per your desire.

Then on again towards Springfield, the capital of Illinois State. The mud changes to sand and the sand to dust. More spills, more cuts, more bruises. The country as flat and uninteresting as they make it. More right-angle bends, more losing of the way and more frizzling in the sun. Two villages are passed in forty miles. One has a population of 417 and the other 59.[236]

At 11 a.m. we draw into Springfield,[237] hot, tired, dusty, and sore. Springfield is a mass of roads, trams, telegraph poles, and people. I leave Lizzie leaning against the kerb and go for an ice-cream soda; when I return, Lizzie is no longer visible. Instead there is a large crowd. They are all examining something. Those on the outside elbow their way to the middle. Those in the middle try to keep them out. The passers-by wonder what it's all about and stop to see. They in turn try to make their way to the middle. Many are disappointed and pass on. The traffic cop, seeing the crowd, strolls over to see what's wrong.

When he had moved the crowd away, I got astride Lizzie's saddle and rode away, amid murmurs of astonishment.

"Come quite a ways, I reckon."

"That's the kind of bird to go travelling on."

"Looks as though he's seen some mud somewhere."

"Look, Bill, he's got igh boots on like they have in the movies!"

"Ah, that's what e is, e's a dolgarn movie actor," etc., etc.

All the trails in America seem to go through Springfield, Ill. Consequently the telegraph poles and tram poles were a mass of hieroglyphics. It took a few minutes to get into Springfield. But it took the best part of two hours to get out of it satisfactorily. Once I thought I was well away, but found that for ten miles I had followed a trail that had white stripes on a red background instead of red stripes on a white background, or something of the kind.[238]

Jacksonville was the next town, some forty miles away. There are six smaller towns on the way. I don't remember passing six, but my map vouches for this number. Their respective populations, taken from the said map, are as follows:—Riddle Hill, 25; Berlin, 251; New Berlin, 690; Alexander, 200; Orleans, 38; and Arnold, 15.[239] So America is not full up yet. But fancy showing a village of fifteen inhabitants on the map! If it were in Arizona instead of Illinois they would have called it Arnold "City." Here are some more names, taken at random from the map, to show the endless variety that the American cartographer has drawn upon:—"Daisy," "Whitehall," "Quiver," "Cuba," "Golden," "Siloam," "Time," "Pearl," "Summum," "Birmingham" (population 76), "Illinois City" (population 80), "Bible Grove" (population 10), "Enterprise" (population 7).[240]

After Jacksonville the road seemed to change its mind.

It refused to be a road any longer. It turned instead into a sea-beach and dodged in and out, here and there, to evade the approaching traveller. Everywhere was to be seen white sand. It lay feet deep on the trail, making progress almost impossible. It covered all the vegetation at the roadside, and it filled the air as well. Here for the first time I encountered the type of road that can disappear with the vagaries of the wind. It was easy to imagine that in æons of time this self-same road would help to form some great geological strata deposited in the Gulf of Mexico or elsewhere. The country became hilly and thickly wooded, and sometimes the trail would narrow down to just a few feet in width and then just as quickly open out to fifty or sixty. The trees grew thicker, the sand grew thinner, the trail dodged around boulders and trees, shot up little sandy slopes, and then, all of a sudden, without any warning whatever, stopped at the bank of a great wide silent river.

It was the Illinois River, a tributary of the great Mississippi, which itself was only fifty miles away. About a couple of hundred yards wide,[241] it was navigated by a ferry-boat of unknown antiquity pulled across the river by a cable wound round a drum. Every man, woman, and child, and every vehicle that crosses America by the Pike's Peak Highway, swells the funds of the man who owns that ferry-boat.[242]

"Which is the road now?" I asked him when we eventually reached the other side. I could see no signs of any continuation of the trail. He had better eyes than I, however.

"Go straight ahead; you can't miss it."

There was certainly visible a little pathway that scrambled up the bank and then wound in and out among the trees, and as I could see nothing else, I followed it. Sure enough it led to "Valley City" (population 52), and thence onwards, through "New Salem" and "Barry" towards "Hannibal" on the Mississippi River.

The Mississippi! Long had I conjured up visions of this mighty river of over 4,000 miles total length[243] that cuts through the United States from north to south, and drains nearly 1½ million square miles of land![244] I had imagined its vast breadth and followed in my fancy the great, silent, moving river as it flowed from west to east and north to south through ever-changing scenery and ever-widening banks. And here I was within a few miles of it! The thought was almost absurd.

Just when the sun was about to set the road made one more swerve to the left. The trees and the surrounding country fell away as if by magic, and there was nothing beyond, save a massive bridge of steel.[245] Beneath and from horizon to horizon flowed the majestic river.

The other end of the bridge was probably some 3,000 feet away in the town of Hannibal and the State of Missouri. Hannibal bristles with statues, tablets, posters, placards, and picture-postcards. They all have the same theme for a subject—"Mark Twain." The Hanniballians, if such they are called, are just as bad. I believe it is not possible for a stranger to be in Hannibal for five minutes without being told that Mark Twain was born there.[246] If the "clerk" at the refreshment bar doesn't tell you, the man at the post office does. If the young "fellar" who pumps a couple of gallons of "gas" into your tank forgets to tell you, the old girl at the fruit-shop doesn't. They must have a secret code in Hannibal whereby they arrange these things. And I will guarantee there aren't two out of every dozen picture-postcards on sale in Hannibal that don't show Mark Twain's birthplace or his cave or his statue or his ass or his ox or something that he either did or did not "immortalize."

Seeking a quiet little spot by the river where I could spend the night and fulfil one of my long-cherished hopes—to bathe in the River Mississippi, I turned down a little road that ran along the bank and reconnoitred the country. To my dismay a railway ran between the road and the river, almost at the very water's edge. Nothing daunted, and hoping that it would sooner or later swerve away and leave me in peace with my river, I continued for miles, long after it was dark, but with no success. The road itself was on a ledge high above the railway, and the railway was on a ledge built some six or eight feet above the river. Eventually I left Lizzie at the roadside, camouflaged her with leaves and branches, and scrambled down with my bags over the ledge on to the bank below. I found a comfortable little spot about ten feet from the rails and laid my bed. And oh, what a glorious bathe I had in the river![247]

It was the eve of July 4th, the American "Day of Independence." Sounds of revellers from far away were wafted over the calm, silent waters. Now and then would be heard the faint swish of a canoe as it glided past in the darkness of the night, and soft music crept up the river from time to time, now clear, now faint, as if from its dark and mystic depths.

I tucked myself under the blanket feeling like a good Christian that night, with never a worry in the world—a world was good and kind and comfortable always.

Nevertheless I should have liked to know when a train would be coming past to disturb my slumbers.

Just as I was dozing over, I heard footsteps along the rails. They came closer and closer, but I could see nothing. The night was pitch-dark. As the footsteps came opposite to me, I made out the form of a man against the starlit sky. He did not see me.

"Say, bo, can you tell me how many trains pass here to-night?" I asked.

He jumped as if struck in the back.

"Only a couple, brother," he replied to where the air had spoken, "one of them in about half an hour and the other about one in the morning;—but they won't worry you," he added.[248]

Sure enough in half an hour's time I heard the distant rumble of a train. I began to wonder if I had not rolled any closer to the rails than when I lay down. The earth shook and a red glare appeared in the distance, and with a mighty roar the huge train came thundering through an opening in the trees. Although I knew I was at a safe distance, the feeling of impending annihilation swooped suddenly down upon me. "Don't be an ass," said I, "what's the use of getting the wind up?" And the next second it seemed that the rushing torrent of steel and fire was but an inch from my head.

Clatter bang-thump, clatter-bang-thump, for twenty long seconds, and the intruder was gone. In another minute not a sound broke the silence of the midsummer night.

Thinking what an excellent test of self-control it would be to pitch my bed between the rails, but disinclined to do so on account of the possibility of a cow-catcher being in front of the trains,[249] I rolled over into heavy slumber.

In half an hour I was awake again and the same process was repeated. I deemed then that I should be left in peace for the night. But my friend had not reckoned on the freight trains. Only the passenger trains were of account to him!

Regularly every half-hour they thundered past. At dawn I had counted thirteen in all.[250] I resolved not to sleep on a railway embankment again, even though it be in company with the Mississippi.

CHAPTER 8 NOTES

224. Figure 70 is an example of the horse-drawn road grader C.K. seems to be describing.

Figure 70: Horse-Drawn Road Grader.
Source: US National Park Service.

225. There seems to be no evidence that such statutes existed, but it is possible many farmers were held to this standard by social pressure within their respective communities. As early as 1913, however, Indiana law obligated every township in the state to elect a roads supervisor who had broad power (and obligation) to maintain roads within that township.

226. *"Glacier des Bossons"*: Bossons Glacier (see Figure 71) is one of the larger glaciers of the Mont Blanc massif of the Alps, in the Chamonix valley of Haute-Savoie département, southeastern France.

Figure 71: Postcard of Bossons Glacier at the Mont Blanc Range, Chamonix Valley, France.

227. According to the *Blue Book*, Chrisman, IL is eighty-six miles west of Indianapolis along the route C.K. took. It seems the bad road conditions continued even beyond this point.

228. "Flivver": Early twentieth century American slang for an automobile. It is also a nickname for the Ford Model T.

229. Hume, IL is 10.7 miles past Chrisman, IL, which is eighty-six miles west of Indianapolis. With this in mind, C.K. had bad roads—the "worst patch"—as far west as Hume, 96.7 miles west of Indianapolis.

230. "cwt": A UK "imperial" measurement established in 1835 and derived from the term "centum weight" and later, "hundredweight," and represented 112 pounds. Its use was officially ended in 1985. However, in 1919, "four-cwt" equaled 448 pounds.

231. Throughout the book, C.K. consistently spells *Mohave* with an "H." Today, with the exception of Mohave County in Arizona and its adjacent Mohave Mountains, the modern convention is to spell it with a "j," as in *Mojave*. While no changes to the original text have been made, the notes in this annotated version use the modern conventions (and exceptions).

232. Murdock, IL, is another 12.6 miles past Hume, IL. C.K. suggests that he struggled mightily to get even that much further for "afternoon tea."

233. The story about his visit to a business operated by "Henry T. Hodges" is likely an amalgamation of his recollection of shops he saw on his trip, rather than recitation of an actual name and sign he saw in Murdock or people he met while there. A review of the data from the 1920 US Census revealed no "Hodges" in Murdock. The following Murdock businesspeople were listed in the census: six owners or employers at a grocery store (Dee Cotterman, Grover Craven, Charles Shultz, Thomas Stanford, Hugh Wilson, and William Yocum); two restaurant proprietors (Andrew Vise and Fred Hayes); and two assistant postmasters (Dwight Chilcote and James Parlier). Expanding the search for Hodges to include all of Illinois, there were thirty-three men with the surname Hodges, but no "Henry T. Hodges." All but three were so far off C.K.'s route that it is unlikely he visited any of them. Of the remaining three along C.K.'s route, none reflected occupations consistent with having their name on the front of a general store:

- Walter H Hodges: twenty-two-year-old newspaper office worker in Decatur, IL.

- John T Hodges: forty-eight-year-old farmer on Vandalia Road in Jacksonville, IL.

- Levi T Hodges: sixty-five-year-old retiree in Meredosia (5.5 miles north of Bluffs, IL).

234. If C.K. drove twenty miles past Murdock before stopping for the night, he would have paused and camped after Garrett, which is just short of Atwood,

IL (see Figure 72). Given his preference to camp near rivers, it seems likely he camped west or south of Atwood.

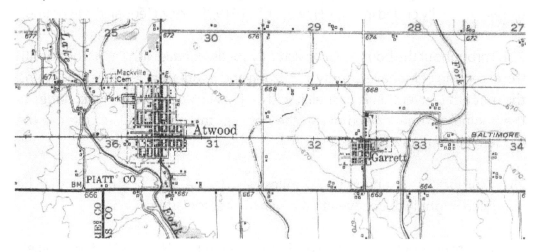

Figure 72: Map of Garrett and Atwood, Illinois.
Source: USGS: *Illinois Tuscola Quadrangle*, 15 Minute Series, 1952.

235. "get-fed-quick": A period term unique to the US that later mutated into to the expression "fast food." As it implies, it refers to a cafeteria-style restaurant where efficient dining is more important than decor. Frederick A. Bisbee, another traveler of the period, characterized the "get fed quick system" in *A California Pilgrimage*, his 1915 book about his first visit to California: "In Los Angeles we were first introduced to a common experience of the 'get fed quick system' locally known as the 'cafeteria.' This system which originated somewhere on the earth— or below—like everything else which is transplanted to California, has grown to mammoth proportions and takes root in curious and most unexpected places."

A review of proximate city directories for Decatur (only 1911 and 1922 were found) indicates that there were two-dozen restaurants in the city during the period. Although it can never be known, the following are the four most likely places C.K. had breakfast that morning because of their name, longevity (the first three were also present in 1911), and location directly on the road and route that C.K. *should* have been on:

- Johnson's Hotel and Café, 139 S. Water Street.

- Singleton's Café, 111 N. Main Street.

- Heady's Café/Café Louvain, 121 E. Main Street.

- Cooper's Cafeteria, 244 N. Water.

236. Although C.K. reports passing tiny two villages in the forty miles after Decatur, it is unclear whether he is saying that he passed *only* two villages in this distance. The populations he provides cannot be verified one hundred years later. If he only passed two villages, then his statement that his route consisted of "more right-angle bends, more losing of the way" takes on new meaning. In fact, there were six towns on the road between Decatur and Springfield—all but one with populations of over 400 in 1910. (Harristown's population is unknown.)

According to *Blue Book* Route 229, there were forty-three miles of road between Decatur and Springfield, IL. This route identifies *six* communities or landmarks and provides elapsed distances toward Springfield: Niantic (13.6), Illiopolis (18.0), Lanesville Station (23.7), Buffalo (26.9), Dawson (29.9), and Riverton (35.5). Although the population data from 1910 reflects numbers for these communities (except for Lanesville Station) as numbering from 620 to 1,911, historic USGS maps of the route indicate the existence of additional smaller communities along the way. For example, Harristown, whose "downtown" area in the 1954 map shown in Figure 73 appears to occupy about one quarter the space of Niantic four miles further down the road, had no population cited in the 1910 US Census.

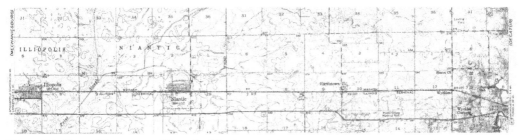

Figure 73: Map of Decatur to Illiopolis, Illinois.
Source: USGS: *Illinois Niantic Quadrangle*, 15 Minute Series, 1954.

The populations of Niantic and Illiopolis in 1910 were 685 and 849, respectively. In the USGS map shown in Figure 74 (next page)—also from 1954—three small places are identified prior to Lanesville. It is not known if these were communities present in 1919 but, in 1910, Buffalo and Dawson had reported populations of 475 and 620, respectively.

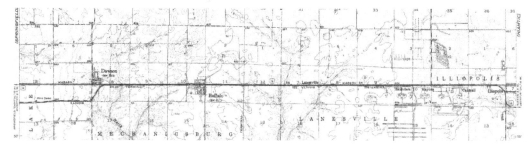

Figure 74: Map of Illiopolis to Dawson, Illinois.
Source: USGS: *Illinois Mechanicsburg Quadrangle,* 15 Minute Series, 1954.

Riverton, a town about seven miles northeast of Springfield, reported that it had a population of 1,911 in 1910. In Figure 75, it can be seen on the right in the 1922 USGS map of the area.

Figure 75: Map of Riverton to Springfield, Illinois.
Source: USGS: *Illinois Springfield Quadrangle,* 15 Minute Series, 1922.

237. If C.K. departed Decatur at 8:00 a.m. after breakfast and arrived in Springfield at 11:00 a.m., it would have taken him three hours to drive the forty-three miles between these cities at an average of 14.3 mph. Alternatively, if he departed Decatur a bit later and took two hours to get to Springfield, he would have averaged 21.5 mph—a figure more consistent with prior reports, bad road conditions notwithstanding.

238. In fact, *only* the Pikes Peak Ocean-to-Ocean Highway passed through Springfield, marked by its red over white bands. There were no highways marked with white over red bands. It seems C.K. simply got lost leaving Springfield because there would have been no other national highways marked on poles.

239. The 1910 US Census reported identical populations for Berlin and New Berlin, but Riddle Hill, Alexander, Orleans, and Arnold are not broken down in the report. Arnold, Illinois is an unincorporated community in Morgan County and is 4.5 miles east-southeast of Jacksonville. Even today, Arnold appears on maps as

nothing more than an intersection. He probably did not pass directly through all of these places from Springfield to Jacksonville, but they were within a few miles of his likely route as described in the *Blue Book*.

240. Some of these communities may have appeared on a map C.K. was using, but *none* were actually on his route.

241. The Illinois River is about 250 yards wide where he crossed, so "a couple hundred yards" is a fair characterization.

242. This was "Philips Ferry," named after Nimrod Philips—a descendant of an early American family who bought the ferry and, with his family, operated it until 1836 when it was sold to Charles Perry, who opened a store and hotel in what later became known as Valley City.

243. The total length of the Mississippi River is actually between 2,320-2,552 miles, depending on who is speaking. Even considering this difference of opinion, it is nowhere near 4,000 miles long.

244. It is difficult to ignore the double-standard implicit here, since C.K. earlier made light of America's penchant for qualifying the greatness or importance of something by reference to its "millions" of whatever. But here, without qualification, he is excitedly boasting about the millions of square miles being drained by the Mississippi River. The "drainage basin" of the Mississippi River covers "only" 1.2 million square miles. However, it includes all or parts of thirty-one US states and two Canadian provinces.

245. C.K. is saying that there was a steel bridge across the Mississippi River that was about 3,000 feet long ending in Hannibal, MO. The bridge across the Mississippi at Hannibal—originally just a railway bridge—was built in 1871 for the Wabash Railroad and was actually only about 1,600 feet long. In 1919, it would have had a pivoting "swing bridge" section that allowed boats to get past. This bridge was used for rail, pedestrian, wagon, and automobile traffic until 1936 when the Mark Twain Memorial Bridge was opened.

246. Celebrated American author and humorist Samuel Langhorne Clemens (pen name Mark Twain) was *not* born in Hannibal. He was born about forty miles

from Hannibal in Florida, MO on November 30, 1835. (A state historic site has been placed there commemorating his birthplace.) Four years later, the Clemens family moved to Hannibal into what is now described as having been Samuel's "boyhood home." It is now a museum located at 120 N Main St., Hannibal, MO 63401. He spent much of his adult life in his home at 351 Farmington Avenue in Hartford, CT (now a historic museum), except when he was away on a national or international lecture tour. He died on April 21, 1910 in Redding, Connecticut—a town I coincidentally called home for ten years beginning in 2002.

247. There are two problems with C.K's story about how he found his bathing and sleeping location short of Hannibal:

   A. The railroad coming out of Hannibal was the Wabash Railroad which, after crossing the Mississippi, continued generally east, ran nearby the river for a mile or so, and then headed due east to Hull. The Chicago, Burlington, and Quincy Railroad (CB&Q) headed northeast of Hannibal after crossing the river and went inland for three-to-five miles before turning north toward Quincy. Although the track of the CB&Q toward Quincy generally paralleled the Mississippi, it was still a mile from the banks of the river at its closest point until reaching Quincy. The topographic map excerpt (Figure 76) is from 1932; the railroad map (Figure 77) is from 1919.

   B. Even where the highway parallels the Wabash tracks for a couple of miles southeast, it is still not located along the riverbanks. It is probably next to the flood plain of the river, but not on the banks.

Figure 76: Map of East Hannibal, Illinois.
Source: USGS: *Illinois-Missouri Hannibal Quadrangle*, 15 Minute Series, 1932.

Figure 77: Wabash Railway Company Map.
Source: USGS: *Poor's Manual of Railroads*, 1919. Page 1592.

It is reasonable to assume that, although C.K. may have driven around looking for a good spot, he doubled back and ended up camping somewhere near where the "d" is in the oddly coincidental "Shepherd" in Figure 76. That spot is about 500 feet south of the current highway, Interstate 72. He may have bathed there, but most probably not in the actual Mississippi River.

248. Available period timetables document three Wabash passenger trains daily traveling east from Hannibal through Hull and onward with the same number heading west. The representation by C.K.'s informant that two passenger trains would pass in the night is plausible.

249. Figure 78 (next page) is a still photograph of comedian Buster Keaton from his 1926 silent film classic *The General* (1926). The image illustrates why C.K. understood that sleeping between the rails was not a good idea. If the train had a cow catcher installed, there were apparently no more than six inches separating the bottom of it from the railroad ties.

Figure 78: Comedian Buster Keaton in his silent film classic, *The General* (1926).
Source: IMDb.

250. The operation of freight-only trains was almost certainly on a more irregular schedule. Although twice an hour might be an exaggeration due to the sleep disruption it caused, it is plausible that a substantial number of trains would have passed C.K.'s camp site throughout the night.

CHAPTER IX

STORMY WEATHER IN MISSOURI

Hannibal is a nice, clean, respectable place; were I an American tourist I would call it a "cute little city."[251]

I found an eating-house with a tempting smell around it, and ordered a hearty breakfast. After polishing off this meal, I mounted Lizzie and started off once more.

We were now in Missouri, the State of the small farmer. Not that the farms are so very small, but they are not on so large a scale as further on in the west, where the hundred-square-mile ranch is the order of the day.

Again the scenery experiences a quick change; the country becomes hilly and rough; one sees maize growing almost everywhere and very often pigs (or hogs as they are termed in the States) turned out to pasture. Nevertheless there is much uncleared and uncultivated land to be seen; the towns and villages are clean, modern, and well laid out, and all give an air of prosperity and plenty. Every farmer has his car, and it is generally a Ford; youngsters of twelve and fourteen can be seen driving them,[252] and generally with as much skill as their parents, if not more.

But for all its hills and vales and the luxuriance of its natural beauty, Missouri has one great drawback. There is a very big fly in the Missouri ointment—RAIN. And when it rains in Missouri, it rains properly, not in tantalizing little showers as it does in England. It is as though the whole sky had burst its water-mains. It falls not in inches but feet; not for hours but for days. Then suddenly the sun breaks out and scorches everything with renewed vigour. If a car is out far from home when the rain comes, it generally has to "stay put." The rain sinks into the road and so does the car. Every car carries a set of chains for its wheels,[253] but although they improve matters slightly, they are often futile in ploughing through the thick slime. Then come the teams of horses at five and ten and twenty dollars a time to drag the unfortunate automobile to some garage where it "lays up" until the rain has gone and the sun has dried the roads sufficiently for further progress.

Sometimes enterprising individuals do not wait for rain to bring in the shekels.[254] I have often heard of perfectly authentic cases of a farmer deliberately flooding

129

likely patches of the road and then waiting patiently with his horses to drag out some unfortunate victim.[255] This seems absurd, but care is always taken to select a spot where it cannot be definitely proved that natural conditions are not entirely responsible for the result!

In the early afternoon, after a hard ride from Hannibal, punctuated at every village with a stop for the consumption of ice-cream,[256] I reached a small town called "Bucklin." No sooner was I there than a huge black cloud appeared suddenly in the sky and a terrific windstorm rose which blew everything that was not fixed to something in all directions. For half an hour it raged. The air was thick with dust, leaves and bits of paper. Then, as suddenly as it had come, the wind subsided, and rain commenced in torrents. So fast did it fall and so heavy were the drops that the surface of the road was beaten into a froth which hovered all the time a few inches above the road itself. Even to walk across it was a test of skill; so slimy was the mud that one's feet slid aimlessly about in any direction but the one desired. For this reason concrete pathways are invariably provided so that pedestrians can move with comparative ease and can leave their homes and visit anyone anywhere in the town without actually touching the mud at all. These concrete pathways naturally have to cross the road in places, and when the road surrounding them is washed away, as very often happens, the result to a passing vehicle can be imagined.

Further progress being out of the question that day, I hied me[257] to the only hotel in the place[258] and prepared to while away the days that were to follow in writing letters, studying an obsolete almanac, and eating bad food.

It rained in a continual deluge all that day, all night and all next morning. At midday it stopped with a bump, the sun came out with another, and the birds began to sing again. At three I ventured forth with Lizzie. I had not gone a dozen yards when the back wheel slipped sideways round to the front and left me reposing in the half-baked mud. Back again for another hour's wait while the broiling sun did its work. Next time I got as far as the outskirts of the town before I decided to turn back. After another hour we started out to do or die, come what might. During the remainder of the day until dark we covered ten miles,[259] going hard all the time. When I was not extricating myself from a spicy bit of quagmire, I was poking semi-hard mud out of the wheels and mudguards.

On one occasion I came to a sudden dip in the road, followed by an equally sudden rise. As usual there was an uninviting "slough of despond"[260] in the hollow.

After trying two or three different ruts in an effort to "get through," giving up each one in turn as hopeless, and pushing back again to where still another rut branched off from the one I was in, I eventually worked my way through. The struggle up the slope on the other side was a formidable one and was being slowly accomplished by a combination of bottom-gear driving, pushing, lifting, and "paddling." Just before the summit was reached I was thrown by a steep furrow into the ditch at the roadside, breathless, exhausted, and extremely bad-tempered.

As I was extracting myself, a young man in shirt-sleeves strolled leisurely over, hands in pockets, from a stationary car a little further on. When I had safely extricated my right leg from under the machine and hauled Lizzie on to her wheels again, the stranger spoke.

"Say, fella, does that front cylinder get hot? I've heard say that's the weak point about them four-cylinder motorsickles."

Here follows a flow of language from self entirely unprintable. The stranger opens his eyes, whistles softly, then adds, as if to turn the subject:

"Where you from?"

He remained with his hands in his pockets staring at my diminishing form. He was still there when I looked over my shoulder half a mile further on. He is probably there now!

As time went on, black clouds appeared in the sky; the sun went in; the wind rose, and a repetition of the events of the day before commenced just as I arrived in the small town of "Wheeling."[261] The only thing to do was to eat ices until the climatic conditions adjusted themselves. This took the best part of two hours. Once again I sallied forth with Lizzie. This time in the short space of five yards I reposed gently but thoroughly in the Missouri mud, much to the amusement of the population, who had all turned out to witness my departure. Again I tried and again I fell. The whole machine seemed to act as though it were made of jelly. I gave it up on the third attempt.

"Try the railway," jeered the village comedian, pointing to a level-crossing in the distance. This amused the onlookers "considerable." For myself, I discerned a glimmer of wisdom in the suggestion.

"Look here, you guys," I retorted, "what about giving me a hand to push this as far as the depot" (I never made the fatal mistake of referring to it as a "station") "instead of looking on and grinning like a lot of schoolboys?"

It had its effect. Three or four volunteered at once. We all pushed; we slithered to right and left; we slipped over each other and ourselves. But we got there.

Riding on the sleepers was hardly humorous, but it was better than the road. They were not filled in and were very irregular. Consequently progress was slow and a trifle disjointed. The "depot" was not far away. The "line-boss" looked at me curiously, as though I were a strange offshoot from some wayward train.

"Many trains coming along this way?" I queried, wishing to know what I should have to meet, as there was only a single track, double tracks being seldom, if ever, laid in the States, and if one was unprepared it might prove embarrassing to meet a train coming in the opposite direction just in the middle of a tunnel or a bridge. American railway bridges are remarkable for their narrowness. Very often the sleepers themselves project into space, and never is there any track beyond them.

"You said it, brother," he replied, "dozens of 'em." "And what's more, there's a couple of long tunnels just a mile away— look, you can see the beginning— and beyond them there's a bridge pretty nigh half a mile long— and trains is mighty funny things to play hide and seek with, y' know!"[262]

I was of that opinion myself. As I looked, I saw a train emerge from the tunnel ahead. I reflected that I should have been just about there by now if I hadn't stopped. I went back to Wheeling.

The next day I covered twenty miles in four hours and found myself back in Wheeling again, but this time by another road. Nothing daunted, I said nothing, clenched my teeth, and polished off another twenty until dark.

The day after I did better. The nett progress at the end of the day's work was twenty-five miles instead of twenty. I arrived at the conclusion that Missouri had one great advantage that I had hitherto overlooked. It was an excellent place to get out of!

On the next day I covered five miles in six hours, and although only forty miles or so from Kansas City, which marks the commencement of the historic Santa Fé Trail leading to the Pacific Coast, I made a solemn vow that I would "ship" everything there by train at the next town. The next town happened to be "Excelsior Springs," twenty miles further on. The road improved considerably, and the comforting thought of civilization at so short a distance urged me on and I broke that solemn vow. I rode into Kansas City late that afternoon, a mass of bruises from head to foot, just as the speedometer showed 1,919 miles from New York.[263] I ferreted out the Henderson agent[264] and left Lizzie in his tender keeping.

Figure 79: Hannibal, Missouri, ca. 1923.
Source: US Library of Congress.

CHAPTER 9 NOTES

251. Figure 79 is a panoramic photo of Hannibal taken in 1923.

252. Laws pertaining to automobiles were in their infancy during this period. Age restrictions typically applied to commercial vehicle operators (chauffeurs or vehicles driven as employees of the employer owning the vehicle) but, in 1919, there wasn't a minimum age driving requirement in Missouri as well as many—if not all—other states.

253. Every volume of the *Blue Book* contained a special orange-bordered section titled "What to Take on the Tour," containing the advice that: "Some sort of emergency tire chains should always be carried, whether your tires are anti-skid or not. For heavy deep mud heavy single chains or mud hooks fastened over the tire and around one spoke of the wheel will insure a prompt getaway from the worst mud hole. It is possible to put on such chains without getting off the running board. In using lighter chains for regular travel over slippery roads it is advisable to use springs to hold them fairly taut—though not too stiff to prevent creeping." Years earlier, in 1916, the National Tire Chain Co. in Grand Rapids, MI promoted their line of tire chains (see Figure 80, next page). These types of chains saw actual use, as depicted in Figure 81 (next page).

Hodges Anti-Skid Chains

The National Tire Chain Co., Grand Rapids, Mich., is putting out a line of anti-skid chains for pleasure and commercial cars.

Hodges Anti-Skid Chains.

Wedge Mud Chains.

The pleasure car types are the ball-bearing anti-skid chains and the wedge mud chains. The main feature of the Hodges anti-skid chains is that the driver is able to remove and replace the cross chains by hand, eliminating the use of any tools whatever.

The spoke lock prohibits the wheel from excessive freedom inside the chains, giving them great gripping power. These chains are said to be simple and easy to adjust under all weather conditions. Prices are $3.50 to $15, according to size. The ball bearing anti-skid chains are made with single unit interchangeable, interlocking hardened steel ball links. These links are claimed to have extra wearing qualities and afford great traction, reducing skidding to a minimum. The cross links are capable of being removed and replaced individually. Wedge mud chains are made with extra large link double cross chains, using extra strong hardened steel forms, which project out on either side of the tire even with but not riding on the tread. This arrangement is claimed to give them gripping power and traction in deep mud, sand and snow. Mud chains range from $.90 to $1.40 in price.

Figure 80: Hodges Anti-Skid Chains.
Source: *Automobile Trade Journal*, Vol. XXI, No. 6, December 1, 1916. Page 151.

Figure 81: Man with Tire Chains.
Source: *Safety* No. 1389, September 22, 1913. US Library of Congress.

254. "shekel": An ancient Hebrew word literally meaning "weight," but it was used as a valuation of currency as far back as 2000 BC. The first use in English was in the translation of the Bible in the Book of Genesis. In this context, C.K. is expressing sarcastic frustration with the alleged practice of farmers increasing their income by flooding the roads so that motorcars would become mired in the mud and could be charged "shekels" to be pulled out by a team of horses.

255. C.K. may have believed the stories he heard as "authentic"—that farmers would deliberately flood roads in order to charge a premium to pull motorists out. However, no examples of these kinds of tactics have been found in available literature.

256. If C.K. stopped at *every* community between Hannibal and Bucklin to have some ice cream, he would have consumed *twelve* bowls of ice cream by the time he reached Bucklin. The *Blue Book* Route 406 reflects the following communities along the 100 miles of road from Hannibal to Bucklin (with distance from Hannibal): Oakwood (2.8), Rensselear (11.8), Huntington (15.6), Hassard (19.4), Monroe City (23.5), Hunnewell (32.6), Lakenan (38.8), Shelbina (45.1), Lentner (51.5), Clarence (58.8), Macon (71.7), Callao (80.3), and Bucklin (100.4).

257. "hie": An English verb common in the nineteenth century to mean "hasten." Used here, C.K. is saying that he proceeded quickly to the hotel.

258. Although it is not known if it was the *only* hotel in Bucklin, the Coen Hotel *was* operating in Bucklin in 1919. It was owned and operated by Cynthia Adeline (Bennett) Coen, with possible assistance from her eighteen-year-old daughter, Ruth "Murr" Coen.

259. Here, C.K. says he stopped and camped ten miles west of Bucklin. This would have been about a mile and a half before reaching Brookfield, perhaps a campsite on West Yellow Creek as identified in Figure 82 (next page).

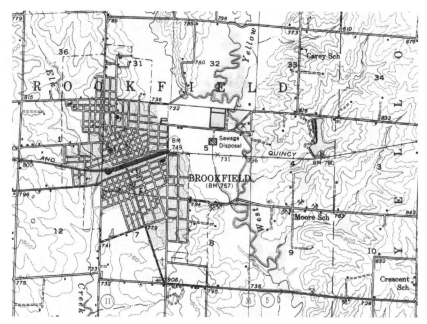

Figure 82: Map of Brookfield, Missouri.
Source: USGS: *Missouri Brookfield Quadrangle,* 15 Minute Series, 1948.

260. The "Slough of Despond" is a fictional bog identified in *The Pilgrim's Progress from This World, to That Which Is to Come* (1678), an allegory by John Bunyan. In this bog, the protagonist, Christian, sinks under the weight of his sins and his sense of guilt for them. Although this is probably the circumstance that C.K. intended to evoke, "Slough of Despond" has also been recorded on maps as a marshy area near the boundary of Dundonald and Symington parishes in South Ayrshire, Scotland, since the mid-nineteenth century.

261. If C.K. camped ten miles west of Bucklin, drove all day, and then stopped for the night in Wheeling, MO, he would only have traveled 18.6 miles that day.

262. Although there may have been a railroad bridge ahead, there seems to have been no tunnel. Wheeling is two miles east of Medicine Creek—a natural tributary of the Grand River—that runs north and south. There was also an artificial canal paralleling Medicine Creek a little over a mile west of Wheeling. The topography in the area is quite flat with the elevation of the creek/canal at 687 feet, while the elevation of Wheeling was 749 feet. The terrain rose gently to the west of Medicine Creek as well but didn't include any hills, necessitating a tunnel. So, while there was certainly an elevated train track/bridge about two miles long across the river flood plain west of Wheeling, there is no indication of

any history of a tunnel (or any terrain necessitating a tunnel) about a mile west of Wheeling where it could be seen departing Wheeling.

263. It seems C.K. is saying the odometer read 1,919 miles when he arrived in Kansas City. The most recently stated odometer reading was 1,000 miles in Springfield, OH. However, the roads of the day along the route C.K. took can only account for 746.9 miles. This indicates that he put an additional 172 miles on the motorcycle at one or more places along his route between Springfield, OH and Kansas City, MO, which is certainly plausible given the number of times he was lost, had to turn back due to poor roads, etc.

264. Excelsior-Henderson Motorcycle Company was located at 211 East 15th St., Kansas City, MO. This may have been a business office address (not a repair shop) because C.K. had the photo (Figure 83) in his photo collection and captioned it "C.K.S. outside Henderson Agency: Kansas City." This photo was actually taken in front of 1421 Grand Avenue (now Blvd.), an address that the 1919 Kansas City Directory (Page 126) said was the *Indian* Motorcycle Sales Company. However, on Page 31 of the May 15, 1919 edition of *Motorcycle and Bicycle Illustrated* a short article states that Arthur Stephens—previously owner of the Indian agency in Kansas City—was now the

Figure 83: C.K. on His Motorcycle in Kansas City.
Source: C.K.'s personal slide collection.

representative for Excelsior-Henderson. Thus, it seems likely that the individual with C.K. in the photo is Arthur Stephens. A similar photo accompanied a full-page article about C.K.'s journey on Page 22 of the July 23, 1919 edition of *MotorCycling and Bicycling*.

CHAPTER X

RESULTS OF A BREAKDOWN

It took three days for me to find that the Kansas City I was in was not the Kansas City I thought I was in. I took it for granted that Kansas City would be in Kansas State. But it was not. *My* Kansas City was in Missouri, but after searching diligently at the post office for mail that wasn't there, I found there was another Kansas City on the other bank of the river. All good citizens of Kansas City, Mo., turn up their noses at the mention of Kansas City, Kan.,—"no connection with the firm opposite" sort of thing.

Of the two, Kansas City, Mo., is by far the more commendable town. It hustles and bustles just as every good American city should do. It is exactly "one hundred per cent American." The advertisements in the papers said so. I believe it, because any city that boasts of being four times larger than it really is must be 100 per cent. American! But I must give Kansas City its due. It represents the essence of keenness and enterprise in business and farming circles. It has that "breezy" air that is so healthy in city life, compared with the dull, gloomy inertness so characteristic of most manufacturing towns, especially here in England. Kansas City has some excellent streets and some magnificent buildings, and has undoubtedly grown at a remarkable rate during the last ten years. Being the last city of really large dimensions that one meets until the Pacific Coast is reached, it is the connecting link between the East and the Far West. Grain and farm produce from the vast States of the West flow unceasingly through its warehouses and stockyards. A network of railways concentrates to a focus at Kansas City, railways bringing in and taking out millions of tons of produce annually.

The next day, when I visited the motor-cycle agency, "Lizzie was standing disconsolately where I had left her the day before. I begged, entreated, exhorted, and threatened that she be given immediate attention. I lied abominably to the manager that I was putting up a record between the coasts and every minute was important.

How could I expect to beat all existing records if they kept my machine in dock for a week? I was promised that it would be started on "right now." That term "right now" has a significance unknown to Europeans. It is subtle and evasive, intangible and incomprehensible. It conveys a sense of such utter obligation on the part of the speaker that one has not the heart to query its exact purport. As far as I can ascertain, or at any rate as far as I have experienced its application, it is more similar to the French "tout de suite"[265] than any other expression I can identify, in that it might imply anything between the immediate present and the indefinite future.

Lizzie required several replacements, including a new set of bearings, a cylinder and two gudgeon pins, these latter being broken in half at the middle. The agent told me that they always were liable to break. If they were put in upside-down, as he always fitted them, so that the oil hole was at the bottom instead of the top, they would not break at all. Further he hinted that my particular machine was turned out while a good fat strike was in progress at the factory.[266]

"Well, you can stick it together so that it will take me to the coast all right?" I queried anxiously.

"Well, yes, I guess I can," was his studied reply.

"Go right ahead then, boss, but do it quick! I'm running short of money and can't afford to stay in your metropolis right here for the benefit of my health."

Being destined then to remain in Kansas City for four or five days more, I found myself with ample leisure in which to collect my thoughts and prepare for the journey through the "wild west" ahead.

One result of my leisure was that I paid a visit to the editor of the *Kansas City Star*. This is one of the most progressive newspapers[267] in the United States, and circulates everywhere in the West. The extent of its circulation and the results of its progressiveness I was, however, still to learn.

The editor was found as usual at his desk in the middle of a large room, surrounded by his myrmidons[268] in typical American style. He greeted me with extreme cordiality. "No need to tell you I'm English, I suppose?" I said.

"See that door over there?" (pointing to the one in the far distance through which I had entered). "Well, I spotted you were an Englishman the minute you came in there."

I explained with complete humiliation that I was travelling across the United States of America on a motor-cycle and wondered, whether his readers would be interested in the point of view of such a despicable object as an English motor cyclist on this great and wonderful country. "Not for the love of the thing, you know," I added, "I don't see why I shouldn't earn a dollar or two on the wayside."

He pointed to a typewriter standing idle at a desk. "Let's have the story right now, and give us something about roads. There's a big movement just started to get good roads, so you can just hand out the straight dope to everybody on the subject. Get me? Something good and snappy."

I explained that while no one was more eminently capable of writing about American roads than myself, I had never graduated as a typist in the course of my business career. I should, therefore, have to retire and push the modest pen.

"What! a business man who can't use a typewriter? I didn't know there was such a thing," was his rejoinder.

I let them have it about roads. I referred also to their commendable system of arresting road-hogs.[269] This with a few pro-American embellishments such as "wonderful country," "indescribable beauty," "inexhaustible wealth," etc. etc., rounded off the theme.

My friend the editor not only rewarded me at the noble rate of a dime a line (5d.),[270] thus assuring the hotel expenses for my stay in the city, but also gave me about an hour of his valuable time in talking about almost everything under the sun—mainly American. It is rather surprising to an Englishman to find that practically any worthy American business man, no matter how busy he may be or how valuable the time lost thereby, will entertain a visitor for an incredible length of time. If the visitor happens to be an Englishman, he is all the more pleased to do so because then he can talk uninterruptedly about America and what a wonderful country it is. All the noted men of Europe, I learned, had been in the office and sat in that same chair. The editor told me so.[271] Lord Northcliffe[272] spent all his leisure hours there while in the States. So also did many other notorieties, some unknown to me. Leastways, so the editor told me. I took his money and bade him farewell.

CHAPTER 10 NOTES

265. *"tout de suite"*: This phrase literally means "immediately; at once." The inference from C.K. is that this concept is not meant to be applied in conversation and misrepresents something as immediate when it is actually expected to take some indefinite time.

266. There *is* evidence that there were one or more strikes at the Excelsior plant in 1919. Some news articles of the day referred to the union strikers as "Communists."

267. In a 1920 article titled "How Much is Two and a Half Million?" in *Advertising & Selling*, the periodical writes that "the progressive newspaper invariably has a progressive following and a progressive following means the young, active, aggressive, thoughtful and successful element of a community. And this is the most valuable clientele for a newspaper and an advertiser."

268. *"myrmidon"*: This word refers to a member of the Thessalian warriors led by Achilles at the siege of Troy. However, in the early twentieth century it was often used to describe a hired ruffian or unscrupulous subordinate.

269. The *Kansas City Star* article was titled "Sees America by Cowpath." It appeared on Page 15 on July 11, 1919. Published in a long single-column, the article (see Figure 84) has been reformatted for this book. The term "road hogs" is not used, but C.K. *does* describe and lament the problems he faced in Maryland when the judge took almost all of his money.

SEES AMERICA BY COWPATH

ENGLISH WARRIOR GETS LITTLE REST TOURING AMERICA BY MOTOR CYCLE.

No Roads Like His Home Land, Capt. C. H. Shepherd, Here Recovering From Bruises, Writes–Impressions of "Speed Cops."

"Roads? What roads? I haven't seen any roads. I have been following a place where cows had been walking."

That is the declaration of an English motor cyclist touring America. He came to America for the tour as a "rest" after serving with the royal air forces in the war. Capt. C. H. Shepherd, Birmingham, England, was in Kansas city today and wrote the following impression of this country's highways:

To attempt to describe any except a minute fraction of my impressions in America in a few hundred words would be folly. Some day, when I find myself back in England, that is, if I survive the American roads, I am going to sit down for three solid months and write a detailed history of my travels and experiences in this wonderful country of yours "across the duck pond." Many a worthy American citizen has predicted that I shall never see England again, and on many an occasion, when for the tenth time that day I have extricated myself and the machine from the ditch and examined myself for bruises and cuts after a "header," I have thought the same way about it!

To be more explicit, I am on my way from coast to coast on a motor cycle–of all things. Now there is a very big difference between motor cycling here in America and in England. In England everyone rides a motor cycle, men and women alike–office boys, journalists, business men, "city" men, millionaires, lords, dukes and princes. In fact motor cycling is now the king of sports in England, and the most popular way of spending a holiday is to tour the country on a motorcycle. But in America it is different. Only the mad brained young "blood" who doesn't mind whether he is graduated for the lunatic asylum or the county hospital with being seriously of risking his neck on a motor cycle tour.

"ROADS? WHAT ROADS?"

When at some town or village on the way I stop to quench a legitimate thirst and I am met with numerous inquiries as to the roads, I respond: "Roads? What roads? I haven't seen any roads. I have been following a place where a cow had been walking." Roads are my only real sore point about America. At present I am recuperating from the effects of them. My starboard leg has to be kept permanently straight until further orders, and a square inch or so of good English epidermis is missing from my forehead as a result of a gigantic hole in the road some ten miles north of Kansas City.

Of course (I hear someone saying), "it is all very well for this Englishman to come to our country and complain to us about our roads. Let him stick to his own country." Quite right. I wouldn't complain, but do you Americans realize what a tremendous lot you're losing through bad roads and how much your commerce is being hampered and your motor car and motor cycle industry is being stinted on account of them?

IMPRESSIONS OF A "SPEED COP."

Another decidedly definite "impression" is the American "speed cop." I thought that England was the only place cursed (or blessed) with them. I succumbed to the energies of a "speed cop" before I had been in the country two days. The kindly old "judge" left me with just twenty-six cents in my pocket wherewithal to buy me food and gasoline for the next four hundred miles. Even that didn't amuse me half so much is the unceremonious way in which it was done. In England, if anyone is unfortunate enough to be arrested for speeding, there is a great fuss made. You receive a summons politely requesting you to be at the assizes, or the high court, or whatever it happened to be, on a certain date, sometimes weeks ahead. When the hour arrives you feel almost proud as you walk up the marble steps of the law courts. In the court, you are made speechless by the constables in their brilliant uniforms, by the reporters who are there as silent recorders of your fate, by the throng of faces in the public gallery come to witness your condemnation, and last but not least, by the awe-inspiring judge who deigns to look upon you. Finally you feel that it was really worth while for the experience when, after much argument, persuasion and deliberation, you are relieved of five shillings and costs.

But not so in America. You have an altogether different way here. You are doing, say, forty-five. A man asks you to stop and leads you to the local judge. He takes your money and out you go on the road again!

How many hundred times I have heard the eternal question, "Where are you from?" Of late I have referred people to the number plate. The other day I had been fighting my way along through endless mud for hours in the full heat of the baking sun. It was real hard work "paddling" that heavy machine along through the ruts, up hill and down dale. I was all but exhausted and soaking in perspiration. Just as I had successfully negotiated a difficult part the road I struck a rut edgewise and the machine landed on top of me in the hedge. A young fellow in a car near by got out, came over, and said, "Say, fella, do you have any trouble with your back cylinder getting hot?"

However, I shall never regret having started on this trip. America is a beautiful country and I have not seen a fraction of its beauty yet. To travel across America has for years been one of my ambitions and undoubtedly one can see more of any country by traveling it by road. Once America has good roads there will be nothing to prevent an American seeing and knowing his own country the same as the Englishman now sees and knows his.

CAPT. C. H. SHEPHERD.
Royal Air Force, Birmingham, England.

Figure 84: "Sees America by Cowpath" Article.
Source: *Kansas City Star*, July 11, 1919. Page 15.

270. The equivalence of a dime (10¢ or $0.10) to five pence (5*d.*) UK is accurate for the period. It is not clear how a "line" was counted, but if C.K. was paid by the line of the article in print (about 140 lines), then he would have been paid fourteen dollars for this one article—certainly enough to pay his expenses in the city with hotels in cities costing approximately three dollars a night. However, if you adjust his fourteen dollars for inflation in the US over one hundred years, it would be worth about $210 dollars, an amount that would not last long in Kansas City today.

271. The city editor at the *Kansas City Star* in July 1919 was George Baker Longan, a gentleman who had held that position for many years. The assistant city editor was C.G. "Pete" Wellington, who succeeded Longan in November 1919. (Longan would go on to become president of the newspaper.)

272. Lord Northcliffe was a British newspaper baron (controlling both the *London Times* and *London Daily Mail*) who had visited Kansas City two years before C.K. and met with representatives of newspapers from Kansas, Missouri, Iowa, Nebraska, Oklahoma, and Arkansas. Lord Northcliffe had arrived in the United States on June 11, 1917 and stayed for several months as head of the British War Mission. His purpose was to exhort media executives in the US to "tell the truth" about the war effort—to learn from England's mistake of "censorship"—so the American people would fully support the war effort at the outset of America's entry into the conflict. The October 26, 1917 edition of the *Kansas City Star* dubbed Lord Northcliffe "the British Kingmaker" and praised him for his "just" criticism of media policies that kept the public in the dark.

CHAPTER XI

THE SANTA FÉ TRAIL

On the fifth day after my arrival in Kansas City all was in readiness for my departure.[273] There was another big bill to meet for Lizzie's overhaul, but I had the satisfaction of knowing that the bearings had all been replaced, as well as a few cylinders and pistons and things, and that there was just a chance of getting to the coast before something else went wrong. Once again I wrote polite letters to the factory at Chicago, paid many dozen "green backs" over the counter, and started off once more, this time with only thirty-five dollars in pocket. Once again fate and the post office had been unkind. Not a suggestion of anything was there at either of the post offices at any of my calls thereon. Amid vague wonderings and oft repeated doubts I promised myself a big cheque at Santa Fé, next stop. I was just beginning to know the ins and outs of the postal service.

The Santa Fé Trail is the oldest and most interesting highway in America. Rather should it be said that the pioneers over what later became known as the Santa Fé Trail were the first to leave permanent marks on routes that have since become "highways" between the Central-Western and the Far-Western States. In the days of the ox team and prairie-schooner,[274] the plains and mountains were crossed by trails, usually along the lines of least resistance, keeping as close as possible to bases of supplies and water. Travel over the Santa Fé Trail began about 1822, starting from Little Rock, Arkansas (pronounced Arkansaw), and following the Arkansas River west. A few years later, this trail was superseded by a more permanent one going west from Kansas City (then called Westport) to "Great Bend," a base situated, as its name implies, on a great bend of the Arkansas River, and thence to Santa Fé by a choice of two routes. An important trade with the Spanish population of the south-west was early developed, reaching its zenith in the '60s.[275] This route, the one which I followed, has now been marked a considerable part of the way by stone monuments erected by the "Daughters of the American Revolution"[276] and constituted the chief inroad from the East to the Far West. Santa Fé itself, next to St. Augustine, Florida,[277] is the most ancient city in America,[278] having been founded in 1605 by Spanish settlers[279] on the site of a "pueblo" or Indian village of far-distant origin. Naturally, therefore, it was the centre of trade for years numbered by hundreds, and traders from afar brought their goods and supplies in boats up the rivers as far as navigable and then in teams across the dreary plains and over the steep Rockies to this one destination.

Later, in the gold-rush to California in 1849,[280] emigrants reached San Francisco, the "Golden Gate,"[281] via this same Santa Fé Trail, undergoing indescribable hardships on the way, and at all times subjected to frequent onslaughts by the hostile Indians.[282]

The first railroads were built across the plains alongside the old trails. The first automobile trips (and I take off my hat to them!) naturally followed the railroads, from the necessity of keeping near to supplies. But the motor-car of to-day frequently makes either short cuts or detours—leading perhaps 100 or 200 miles away from the railroad—in order to visit sections offering unusual attractions, or places of historical interest, even when located in desert regions.

Thus, with Kansas City behind me, the journey begins to be really interesting from an historic, if not from a scenic point of view. The hand of modern civilization at last is seen to relax its grasp. Now, instead of the prosaic,[283] the conventional and the luxurious, are we to find the unique, the heterodox[284] and the primitive. After the tainted breath of huge cities and the seething, crushing, maddening turmoil of wealth and modernism are to follow the pure unbounded atmosphere of the giant plains, the mystic call of the great mountains, the vastness, the fearfulness and the rapture of the scorching deserts. Which shall it be for me?

Before me lie 500 miles of perfectly flat and uninteresting country before I leave the State of Kansas and enter Colorado. Then follow another 200 equally flat, equally drear, to be crossed before the Rockies loom into sight. Seven hundred miles of endless weary prairie, stretching always, everywhere, as far as the eye can see, with never a hill nor a dale nor hardly a tree in sight!—Nothing but boundless, illimitable corn, wheat and prairie.

That night, after an afternoon's run of 120 miles, I rested in a cornfield. The road had ended abruptly. An old bridge had been demolished and a new one was about to be erected. A heap of debris in the middle attracted my attention, and I was fortunate. Here the road ended; there was a little chasm some thirty feet across; beyond was the road again. Nothing for it but to turn back. Turning back is always objectionable. I deemed that it would be less so in the morning. That is why I wrapped myself in my mosquito net behind a hedge in a cornfield and offered up thanksgiving.

The mosquito net—I have not mentioned it before! I purchased three yards of it in a little store back in Missouri while waiting for the road to dry up.[285] I also bought a cap. Having worn no headgear since leaving New York, I soon discarded the cap[286] and later gave it away to a little urchin who looked as though he needed one more than I. But the mosquito net remained for a longer spell. Nightly was it unfolded and wrapped around my unworthy self, and daily was it folded carefully up again and packed into the bag once more.

I shall never forget that mosquito net. It was white. Leastways it was when I bought it. I tried countless ways of enveloping myself in its folds, but never with any great measure of success. The *tout ensemble* when struggles had subsided, with self in pyjamas surrounded by wrappings of white chiffon on a black background (my waterproof groundsheet) must have presented an extraordinary spectacle to the poor birds above. No doubt they mistook me for some miscreant angel served with an ejectment order without notice from the star-lit sky! At first all went well. I breathed the calm midnight air unmolested. "It can't be true," I told myself, "there is a catch in it somewhere." There was. I discovered that whereas it was comparatively difficult for a mosquito to get inside the net, once he did get inside it was an utter impossibility to get him out again. One mosquito inside a mosquito net is worth much more than two outside. He is worth at least forty!

Then I tried various stunts because, when I did get properly wrapped up, I invariably rolled out of it in my sleep. I rigged up poles and sticks and cut little pegs from twigs to hold the net down like a tent. I had it stitched up the sides like a bag and wriggled into it nightly, only to find it wrapped around my feet in the morning and my face and arms a mass of bites. Finally, in the heart of the Rockies I think it was, I gave it up as a bad job and resorted to the Citronella method once again.[287] For aught I know that old mosquito-net is still hanging to the fence of a cow-ranch at the foot of Pike's Peak, Colo.!

Up at dawn in the morning and away. I found another road some three miles back and continued on my way westward rejoicing. Sixty miles were covered before breakfast. The towns and villages became very few and far between, and Council Grove, where I enjoyed my morning repast,[288] was practically the first town to be encountered. I had set my mind on a good day's run and prayed for good roads. On my map, which was said to be the only roadmap of the United States published,[289] and was hopelessly inaccurate and inadequate, there was a huge river, the Arkansas, a couple of hundred miles ahead. I judged it to be about half a mile wide. Verily,[290] thought I, the Arkansas River shall be my resting place to-night, and Great Bend my destination.

After a long day's ride I toiled into Great Bend at sunset. The journey had been monotonous and the road fatiguing. I longed to stretch my weary bones on the banks of yon mighty river and bathe in its refreshing waters. While I was devouring my evening meal, on a little high stool in the one and only café of Great Bend,[291] I was consoling myself with this prospect.

Outside, a little group of men were sitting on the pavement[292] eyeing Lizzie propped up against the kerb. It is the general thing to sit on pavements in the Far West.

They are much higher than those we are accustomed to and afford adequate and comfortable accommodation for the weary population. Often one can see a row of men sitting on the kerb for the whole length of "block" when the sun is in such a direction that the sitters are sheltered by the buildings behind them. I made a mental note: "Another good idea for importation to England." I pictured tired Londoners sitting down in rows on the pavements of the Strand[293] or clustered leisurely around Piccadilly Circus[294] chewing "shag"![295]

My pockets bulged with bottles of "Buckeye,"[296] an imitation root beer sold extensively in the States (since prohibition) and alleged to have "kick" in it. A suspicious swelling elsewhere on my person indicated a tin of pineapple chunks (a delight of my youth). "Goin' far?" inquired one of my scrutineers. "Down to the river to-night. This the right road?" "Right slick in front of your nose half a mile away." I came to a long wooden bridge arrangement, but could find no river. After going two or three miles and finding no Arkansas, I returned to Great Bend to try another road. This time I inquired at the café.

"Straight ahead, you can't miss the bridge."

"Oh, is there a river there? I didn't see one."

Back again to the bridge, but no signs of a river. Instead there was a great stretch of white sand like a sea-beach, but with little trees and shrubs and tufts of grass dotted here and there.

"Well, this is no Arkansas River," said I to myself, "but I'm through. This sand looks pretty comfortable, so here goes."

In amongst the sand dunes I made my bed and never did traveller camp in more delightful surroundings or rest in more peaceful conditions. The stars shone out with unusual brilliancy in the heavens, and the moon rose at the setting of the sun, enveloping all in a magic sheen of silver. A soft cool breeze played gently over the plain and little birds of unknown song and uncounted variety slowly sang themselves to rest. This indeed was no night for sleep; more was it a time for quiet contemplation of all the things that make life good and noble and worthy of the living. How terrible, how awful it would be when I should in the end return to the narrow beaten track of city life, and once again be fettered to "the trivial round, the common task"[297] that knows no magic spell and thrills with no mystic breath. Could it ever be that the duties that bind and numb, the needs that hamper and clog, the tasks that chill and estrange, should once again enshroud me in their toils? Such I suppose are the meditations of everyone who breaks away from home to enjoy for a spell the bounties of nature and whose canopy is the sky.

In the morning I awoke as fresh as the merry sandpipers and waterwagtails[298] that ran and hopped about in dozens. There was no trace of fatigue, no thought but of the glorious day that was opening, no regret but that every day had not brought and would not bring this rapturous dawn.

I learned in the village that I had indeed slept in the middle of the Arkansas River! The summer had been excessively dry and that part of the river which, several hundred miles away, had risen boisterously in the heart of the Rockies and had not been dried up with the heat, had drained through the sandy bed, never to emerge again. This though was one of many rivers that I was to meet with no water in them. Sometimes even, I was to see fences and railways erected across would-be rivers to prevent the cattle straying!

The farther westward I travelled the fewer became the towns. Nevertheless, albeit they were sometimes thirty and forty miles apart, they were all prosperous, new and inviting. Of gasoline there was always an abundant supply at 22 cents (11d.) per gallon.[299] Of garages there were enough and to spare. Indeed, it was surprising what palatial garages were to be found everywhere. Outside each was the familiar "Bowser" pump[300] communicating with a 1,000-gallon tank below the pavement from which anything from half a gallon to six gallons at a time could be pumped up by the garage hand at one turn of the handle. A flexible pipe with a cock at the end leads from the pump, and one's tank can be filled in a few seconds without a drop being spilt. Not once in all my travel through the States have I seen a petrol tin.[301] I do not believe they are used at all because nowhere in the States is it necessary to travel by road with spare petrol on board, provided, of course, that one is careful to fill up regularly at the different towns or stations on the way. Even in the heart of New Mexico and Arizona, even in the terrible "Death Valley" and Mohave Desert of California, stations are found where "gas" and oil can be bought in plenty to carry one well beyond the next to be reached.

At Larned I made a hearty breakfast from canteloupe, coffee and "pie."[302] Now "pie" is one hundred per cent, symbolical of America. In the States they have attained the absolute limit of perfection in the manufacture of pies; indeed I think it must be a "key" industry. Not only can pies of every conceivable kind of fruit (and many inconceivable ones) be obtained, but the cooking thereof is perfection itself.

On the road again, ever westward, ever looking forward to the day when from the dreadful monotony of the plains the Rocky Mountains would loom high and faint upon the horizon.

I passed a few small towns at long intervals, towns with picturesque names such as "Cimarron," "Garden City," "Lamar," and "Las Animas." In every case an approaching town was heralded by an unspeakable stretch of road. With the passage of traffic of all kinds the road was ground up into powder. Every inch of it was loose sand, sometimes a couple or three feet deep, sand that would be impassable to any but horse-drawn traffic. As a saving grace it was generally less deep at the edges of the road than in the middle, and locomotion was just within the range of possibility with frequent assistance by way of "leg-work" and with occasional spills and crashes. The only use I had for these towns lay in the unlimited scope for ice-cream consumption which they all afforded. As time went on, Lizzie showed signs of further disrupture. Gradually little noises and rattles developed and slowly her power fell off by almost imperceptible degrees. Of course I had ample power even at that to cover the country, which, with few exceptions, was level, and the road, where dry, was good. I averaged no more than twenty-five, and as there was hardly any stop to make or traffic to slow down for, this did not mean travelling more than thirty at any time. A good conscientious motorist, I told myself, would stop and examine everything. I had got far beyond that stage. "Let the old crock go on till she busts," I muttered inwardly and opened up to avoid an oncoming thunderstorm.

Thunderstorms travel quickly in U.S.A. They get a hustle on and don't mess about generally. There's never any doubt about it when you see one coming. It means business; there is none of that burbling, gurgling, gloomy overture that hangs around for hours in England and very often comes to nothing at all. No, no. In U.S.A. you see a thundercloud on the horizon and before you've got "George Washington" off your lips it's on you with a crack and a bump and a splash and woe betide any innocent motor-cyclist who is riding in his shirt-sleeves with his jacket strapped on the back.

But that rain was good! Kansas can be hot when it likes and it's mostly liking all the time, so that a shower-bath is a gift from the gods. When it stopped, and fortunately before it had had time to do its foul work on the surface of the dirt road, I arrived in Syracuse, a small town with not much of a population to substantiate its artistic name, and but twenty or thirty miles from the Colorado State Line. Net result 150 odd miles that day and to-morrow with luck I should behold the Rockies. Oh, those Rockies! How I longed to see them!

The rest of the evening I spent adjusting Lizzie's tappets (they had all worked loose, hence the noise) and eating pies and ices at every café in the place.[303] The night was spent in a dirty inhospitable little inn calling itself, I think, the Broadway Temperance Hotel.[304] Heaven help Broadway, and the Devil take all temperance hotels! I shivered as I compared this with the night before.

Westward once more. In an hour I crossed the State Line. Invariably there is a large sign-board denoting this fact. "THIS IS THE STATE OF COLORADO, THE MOST

PICTURESQUE AND FERTILE STATE IN THE UNION,"[305] it read on this occasion. This time there was not such a marked change in the country. It was still flat, still dismally uninteresting. Everything looked dried up.

At times the trail, which hitherto had followed the Arkansas "River," crossed and re-crossed it by long low creaky wooden bridges. There was still no water flowing underneath them. "Water? That was only meant to flow under bridges," says the confirmed toper.[306] The Arkansas River "puts him wise"[307] on that point!

Flagrant mistakes now appeared on the map. Roads and towns which in reality lay on one side of the river were alleged to be on the other. Distances became either grossly exaggerated or hopelessly underestimated, so much so that I only expected to get to a place when I found myself already there. If it turned out to be another place than that I had expected—well, there, that made it all the more exciting.

Later on the trail became very dishevelled and forlorn. Great waves of sand were piled up in ridges and furrows defying all comers. Sometimes a benevolent signpost advised all drivers of automobiles not to risk travelling thereon, but to follow such and such a detour which would lead back to the road ten or fifteen miles farther on. I saw many such notices. At first I scorned them, but the sand grew so thick and deep that it enveloped the frame of the machine and the projecting footboards brought progress to a standstill. For several hours I pushed and heaved and skidded and floundered about on highways and detours and pathways that baffle description. If I averaged ten miles an hour I was content with that. I got through many places that passing pedestrians swore were impassable. In short I was beginning to reduce locomotion over American roads to a science.

At La Junta, the Santa Fé Trail swerves to the southwest towards New Mexico, but another trail continues westward and northward towards Pueblo, Colorado Springs,[308] and Denver, the three "cities" of Colorado State, and Pike's Peak, one of the highest points of the Rockies. I decided to leave the trail for a day or two and go sightseeing in famous Colorado. So I continued westward, scanning the horizon all the time for a vision of a vast and rugged mountain range. The sight of mountains would be as balm to a sore wound; as welcome as a spring of water in the desert; or even as the sight of land to a shipwrecked mariner, so heartily tired was I of the endless plains and the inexhaustible flatness and monotony of the country for the past thousand miles.

Instead of mountains came a cloud. Soon the whole horizon was black. I knew what that meant. It meant "laying up" for a day or two and looking round for a good place to lay up at "right slick."[309] But I was in the midst of nowhere. Not a house or a shack could be seen anywhere. Even as I scanned the country the rain came. The road was not sandy enough for it to soak through. Instead it absorbed it greedily and changed to mud. I rode as far as riding was practicable and then I pushed. In a few miles I came to a little wooden shack at the side of the road near a large dyke already swollen with rain. The shack looked as though it had recently been thrown together with matchboarding and liberal use had been made of tarpaulins as curtains instead of doors. I left Lizzie in the road and went to explore.

CHAPTER 11 NOTES

273. The implication that C.K. departed Kansas City five days after arrival creates a date-related discrepancy that may never be reconciled. He stated he left Cincinnati on July 1, 1919 after having been there for ten or twelve days; the exact number is unclear but might be calculable. C.K. described a total of eight stops between Cincinnati to Kansas City:

- Camp east of Indianapolis.

- Camp about twenty miles west of Murdock.

- Camp on the east bank of Mississippi River.

- Hotel in Bucklin.

- Camp about ten miles west of Bucklin.

- Hotel in Wheeling.

- Camp about twenty miles west of Wheeling.

- Camp another twenty-five miles down the road.

- Arrive in Kansas City.

   If C.K. departed Cincinnati on July 1, 1919 on the aforementioned timeline, he would have arrived in Kansas City on July 9, 1919. This arrival date is consistent with the publication dates of articles he wrote for the *Kansas City Star*. The discrepancy arises through critical examination of *other* newspaper accounts of his trip. Specifically, on Monday, July 14, 1919, The *Santa Fe New Mexican* reported that C.K. was in Kansas City on Friday, July 11, 1919. While he *could* have arrived in Kansas City on July 9, 1919 and stayed five days through July 13, 1919, this presents a conflict with his arrival date in Santa Fe, because he reported a total of *nine* overnight stops from Kansas City before arriving in Santa Fe on the tenth day:

- Camp short of Council Grove.

- Camp in Great Bend.

- Hotel in Syracuse.

- Home in Nepesta.

- Camp west of Pueblo.

- Rooming house in Walsenburg.

- Camp south of Raton.

- Hotel in Las Vegas (NM).

- Rooming house in Pecos.

- Santa Fe.

If C.K. departed Kansas City on July 13, 1919 and the above stops are accurate, then he would have arrived in Santa Fe on July 24, 1919. The discrepancy becomes clear when considering that, on July 22, 1919, the *Santa Fe New Mexican* reported that, "Captain Shepherd, British royal air service veteran, arrived in our fair city yesterday..." That means that C.K. had arrived in Santa Fe by at least Monday, July 21, 1919.

The most likely explanation for this type of discrepancy—there are a few others noted in this book—is that C.K. did not make as many intermediate camp or hotel stops as he wrote about—particularly when these stops were between cities where he remained for several days while his motorcycle was overhauled.

274. The "Prairie Schooner" was often used by emigrants traveling west. (see Figure 85, next page). The schooners were lighter than heavier covered wagons and could be drawn by as few as two oxen or horses.

Figure 85: "Prairie Schooner" Wagon.
Source: Illustration by Harold Cue in *A Prairie-Schooner Princess,* 1920.

275. This is obviously a reference to the 1860s (not the 1960s).

276. The Daughters of the American Revolution (DAR) began their effort to mark the Santa Fe Trail with monuments less than ten years before C.K.'s ride.

277. St. Augustine was officially founded in 1565 and is believed to be the oldest city in the US to be continuously settled by Europeans.

278. While St. Augustine is widely believed to be the oldest city founded by *Europeans*, the oldest *indigenous* settlement in the US is believed by many historians to be the ancient city of Cahokia, settled as many as 3,500 years ago. in Southwestern Illinois Today, Cahokia is home to the Cahokia Mounds State Historic Site.

279. Santa Fe was established in 1607 and is regarded as the second oldest city founded by European colonists in the US (after St. Augustine). However, the foundation of the "De Vargas" house in Santa Fe predates settlement by Europeans, so it seems Santa Fe may legitimately lay claim to the oldest continuously settled city in the US.

280. On January 24, 1848, James W. Marshall found gold at Sutter's Mill in Coloma, CA, officially starting the California Gold Rush. However, California wasn't the first place to see a "gold rush," with gold rushes in North Carolina and Georgia preceding California by several decades. Still, the size and scale of the operations in California were unique. An estimated 300,000 people relocated to California between the years 1848 and 1854 looking for gold.

281. This reference to "Golden Gate" could not be to the famous Golden Gate Bridge, since its construction did not begin until 1933 and lasted over four years. Rather, in this context, "Golden Gate" is a reference to the Golden Gate Strait at the opening of San Francisco Bay that the Bridge now spans, with San Francisco to the South and Marin County to the North. It does not seem that the "Santa Fe Trail" ever went to San Francisco, though it could easily have been part of the route taken by many on their way toward San Francisco.

282. Initially, indigenous Americans primarily targeted traders for their horses and mules.

283. "prosaic": lacking poetic beauty.

284. "heterodox": Not conforming to accepted or orthodox standards or beliefs.

285. The July 21, 1919 advertisement in Figure 86 advertises pink netting rather than the white netting C.K. describes, but it reflects he probably paid about 15¢ a yard or around 45¢ for the three yards of net he purchased in total.

Figure 86: Advertisement for Mosquito Netting.
Source: *St. Louis Post-Dispatch*, July 21, 1919. Page 5.

286. In Figure 83, where C.K is seen photographed with the Henderson agent in Kansas City, he is wearing a cap—likely the one he mentions here. It is not known where he gave it to a "street urchin."

287. It is not clear what "Citronella method" C.K. used, but Figure 87 is an excerpt from a 1914 US War Department bulletin.

> For use, as a temporary measure, a mixture of oil of citronella and vaseline, when smeared upon the skin, is very serviceable and is not unpleasant. If liquid vaseline is used, about one part of oil of citronella should be mixed with six parts of liquid vaseline and applied frequently when exposed to the bites of mosquitoes. If liquid vaseline can not be obtained ordinary vaseline may be used, a teaspoonful of the oil of citronella being mixed with two ounces of vaseline.

Figure 87: The Citronella Method.
Source: *The Prophylaxis of Malaria,* August 1914.

288. The cafés in Council Grove included the Norton Café (run by a Mrs. Norton) and the Arway Café (run by William A. Cripe).

289. Although roadmaps were not common at the time, a number of maps existed, including a 1918 map from AAA which was patterned after railroad maps of the period with lines drawn to connect cities that were marked by circles of differing size depending on the size of the city.

290. "verily": Archaic word meaning in truth; really.

291. There were apparently at least *two* cafés in Great Bend, within two blocks of each other:

- Clink's Café, 1209 Main Street.

- Service Café, 1406 Kansas Avenue.

Of these, Clink's seems like the more established as it was also part of the Manhattan Hotel. However, since C.K. had camped in the dry Arkansas River bed in Great Bend the night before, it seems less likely that he entered a hotel.

292. "pavement": In the UK, the term "pavement" is synonymous to "sidewalk" in the US.

293. This is a reference to the Strand, a major thoroughfare, in the City of Westminster, Central London. It runs just over ¾ mile from Trafalgar Square eastwards to Temple Bar, where the road becomes Fleet Street inside the City of London.

294. Piccadilly Circus is a famous landmark—both a road junction and public space—of London's West End in the City of Westminster. It had originally been built in 1819 to connect Regent Street with Piccadilly. Figure 88, a postcard from 1922, depicts the busy intersection at that time.

Figure 88: Postcard of Piccadilly Circus, *ca.* 1922.
Source: *The Prophylaxis of Malaria,* August 1914.

295. "shag": This slang word for tobacco was used for rolling self-made cigarettes, but C.K. is using it here to describe chewing tobacco.

296. Buckeye was the name of a brewery in Toledo, Ohio that began producing soft drinks after the advent of Prohibition. They patented some of their beverages in 1920, as shown in Figure 89 (next page). Not only was Buckeye Root Beer sold in syrup form for use in fountains, it was also bottled (see Figure 90):

135,619.   GINGER-ALE,   ROOT-BEER,   AND   CIDER.
THE BUCKEYE PRODUCING CO., Toledo, Ohio.
Filed March 22, 1920.   Serial No. 130,018.   PUB-
LISHED JUNE 15, 1920.

Figure 89: Buckeye Beverage Patents, 1920.
Source: *Official Gazette of the US Patent Office,* Vol. 279, October 19, 1920. Page 526.

Figure 90: Advertisement for Bottled Buckeye Root Beer.
Source: *Wilkes-Barre Times Leader,* July 11, 1919. Page 9.

297. "The trivial round, the common task" is an excerpt from a poem in *The Christian Year* (1827) by John Keble.

298. "water wagtail": A colloquial name for a pied wagtail (*Motacilla alba yarrellii*), a small bird of mostly black-and-white plumage. It is the most common wagtail in the UK, but it is rare in southwestern US.

299. Twenty-two cents a gallon in 1919, when adjusted for inflation one hundred years later, is $3.31. Interestingly, gasoline has retained the same relative value in the US, despite the passage of time.

300. This pump is named after Sylvanus Freelove Bowser, an American inventor who is widely credited with having invented the automobile fuel pump (see Figure 91).

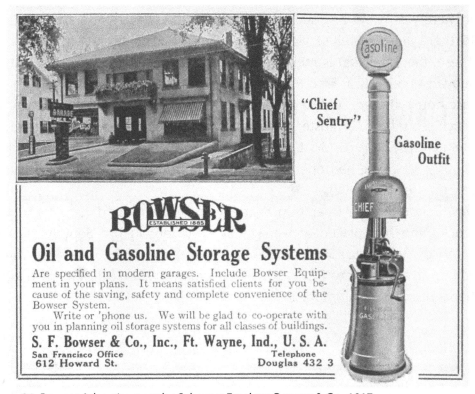

Figure 91: Bowser Advertisement by Sylvanus Freelove Bowser & Co., 1917.
Source: *The Architect and Engineer of California,* Vol. LI, No. 1, October 1917. Page 135.

301. "petrol tin": A gas can.

302. Three cafés were found to exist in Larned:

- Electric Café (and Hotel), John P. Larkin, proprietor (1917-1920).

- Elite Café, located below Arlington Hotel (1917-1920).

- Merchant's Café, located under Landauer's Store (opened October 6, 1917).

303. Three cafés were found to exist in Syracuse:

- Elite Café, J.H. Jeffers, proprietor (1917-1918); Mrs. E.M. Gottman, proprietor (1919+).

• The Rex Café and lunchroom, the Belt Brothers proprietors (1917+).

• The Syracuse Café, first door south of National Bank, B. Van Hall, proprietor (1919+).

304. There was never any such place as the Broadway Temperance Hotel. In 1919, there were two full-service hotels in Syracuse: The Rex and the Sequoyah. Of these, the Rex Hotel is mentioned more in advertising and news, but the Sequoyah Hotel was a "Fred Harvey House" at the rail depot. Both being full-service hotels, it seems unlikely that either were the establishment that earned so much scorn from C.K. Instead, it is more probable that he stayed at the Iowa Rooming House. In 1916, Mrs. L.A. Cole became the proprietor of the Iowa House. Previously, Mrs. Cole had operated an "eating house" in town for at least ten years prior (see Figure 92).

Mrs. Cole took over operation of the Iowa House around 1916 from Harry Peacock, who had placed a display advertisement in the September 1915 *Directory of the Syracuse Telephone Exchange*. (see Figure 93). Mrs. Cole offered beds from twenty-five to fifty cents—a far cry from the $3.00 C.K. paid at the National Hotel in Washington, DC.

Figure 92: Mrs. Cole's Eating House, *ca*. 1906.
Source: Courtesy of the Hamilton County Museum.

Figure 93: Iowa House Advertisement, *ca.* 1915.
Source: *Directory of the Syracuse Telephone Exchange,* September 1915.

It should be noted that Syracuse was the home of the first all-female City Council in 1887. There are indications that they were active in the Women's Christian Temperance Union (WCTU) during the statewide prohibition of liquor sales that existed in Kansas from 1881 to 1948—longer than any other state. By characterizing a place like the Iowa House as a "Temperance Hotel," C.K. was perhaps commenting on a local cultural mindset that he found objectionable.

305. No evidence has been found that this slogan was ever used in print or signage to promote or announce the State of Colorado.

306. "confirmed toper": A chronic/heavy alcohol drinker.

307. "puts him wise": A phrase meaning "to educate him."

308. The *Auto Club Map 26* reflects that the trail heading southwest from La Junta to Trinidad was part of the National Old Trails Road. The *Auto Club Map K* of this series identifies the other road—due west to Pueblo—as the New Santa Fe Trail. For comparison, Route 178 in the *Blue Book* (1918) does not name the road from La Junta to Trinidad but *does* refer to the road from La Junta to Pueblo simply as the Santa Fe Trail (Route 177).

309. The origins of "right slick" are unclear, but it seems to be a variation of "right quick" to mean "extremely urgent."

CHAPTER XII

THE ROYAL GORGE OF ARKANSAS

There were two huts. I drew aside the tarpaulin and peered in one of them. It was stuffy and dark and filled with beds, tables, cupboards and piles of odd furniture and miscellaneous clothing, boots, blankets and mattresses. In a clearing amongst the general debris sat a middle-aged woman on the top of a trunk before a sewing machine.

"Hope I'm not intruding, but is there anywhere I can get out of the rain until it goes off?"

From a heap of assorted oddments under my very nose came a voice, a man's voice.

"Sure; come right in, brother. You're welcome to any shelter we can give you. Guess you've gotten a little wet out there? Jim, go you into the kitchen and bring a chair for this gentleman."

A pile of musty books rocked on its foundations in another corner and a young lad of fifteen or sixteen rose as if from out of the earth.

We talked for an hour, but the storm showed no signs of abating. The wind whistled through the tarpaulin doorway and gloomy blobs of water dropped from the ceiling from time to time on all and sundry.

Strange to say I did not betray my nationality. I presume that by that time I had unconsciously acquired in a small degree the language of the race.

"You're from the East, I suppose?" queried mine hostess after half an hour, the first words I had heard her speak.

"Oh, sure, I'm from the East, the far East—in fact, the VERY Far East!" I replied.

"Boston?"

"You've said it," was my rejoinder. "Ever been to Boston?" I added.

"Yep, I was there I reckon fifteen fall.[310] All I remember now was the railway depot. What do they call it, the South Union?"

"Sure, it's the South Union all right. Why, I was born only a couple of blocks from the South Union depot."[311]

Miserable liar that I am, I have never been in Boston in my life.

"Fine city, Boston," interjected the male voice from below.

"The finest in the world, sir," I effused.

Meanwhile the rain continued, with not the slightest sign of abating.

"You best bring your motor-sickle under shelter and stay the night right here," suggested the man of the house when the shadows deepened and still the rain went on.

"I'm sure that's very good of you, sir, but I'm afraid I'd better not trouble you any more."

"No trouble at all; we're delighted to have you; we can soon make a bed up with a few chairs and some of these blankets."

I was only too pleased to avail myself of their hospitality and agreed.

At supper I had a chance of studying the various members of the family. Apart from the man and his wife, there were two boys, and quite a few more people rolled in afterwards from a source unknown to me. Supper consisted of stewed beans, with plenty of bread and water, and more beans.

That night I slept on four chairs in a row near the door. The two boys were elsewhere in the gloomy darkness within. All through the night I waged war upon mosquitoes and slapped myself vigorously for many hours until the guerrilla warfare grew so tiring that sleep overcame its anxiety. The mosquitoes then nibbled my face to their hearts' content—if they have hearts, which is doubtful.

In the morning breakfast consisted of stewed beans with plenty of bread and water, and more beans.

By lunch-time it was still raining, but slower. I stayed to lunch. It consisted of stewed beans, with plenty of bread and water, and lots more beans.

In the afternoon the sky cleared, the sun opened his eyes with a snap and began his work of drying up the roads. Throughout the day I had employed my time with giving Lizzie an overhaul. I had the cylinders off, examined the bearings, and tightened things generally. Meanwhile I discovered that my friends were building a house on an adjoining field. They were doing the work alone, with the help of a few friends, who no doubt accounted for the other partakers of stewed beans. A pile of timber lay in one corner of the field and the foundations had already been laid and the uprights erected.

It was well seen that the house was for themselves to live in. Never have I seen a house grow so quickly or watched the progress of one so keenly. Moreover the walls were not all out of the vertical or the windows far from square as one generally gets in home-made houses (and very often other kinds too!)

"You'd better stay and have something to eat, brother," said mine host as I was strapping my bag on Lizzie's back in preparation to depart. "We've only got stewed beans, but they're a mighty wholesome food."

But I had visions of apricot pie in Pueblo, thirty miles ahead, and urged my desire to be getting on the road "right now" while the weather lasted.

They were good folks, those house-builders of Nepesta.[312] Not a cent would they accept under any circumstances for their hospitality to me. They worked hard and feared God, and every time they partook of their frugal meals grace was said beforehand and afterwards as well, in thanksgiving for the blessings that rewarded their toils. One could not refrain from comparing the civilization of the West with the sordid life-scramble of the East.

Once on the road again the despondent sort of gloom that seemed to surround everything became a thing of the past, as gradually the Rockies loomed up on the horizon; at first faint and mysterious they gradually deepened in colour and sharpened in outline. What a refreshing and soul-inspiring sight after nearly 1,000 miles of travel across the dusty, dreary, tiring plains!

In the late afternoon a thin cloud of curling black smoke was seen upon the horizon. This is invariably the forerunner of a western town. Long before one actually draws near to one's destination, if that destination be a town, it is discernible sometimes twenty and even thirty miles away by the tufts and clouds of smoke that hang over it. The sight is as that of a huge Atlantic liner no more than a fraction above the horizon. One cannot discern its hidden size or form, but the smoke from its funnels threads upwards into the heavens like a sentinel in the engulfing vastness of the sea.

Thus does one approach a town set in the heart of a bewildering plain. Gradually it is possible to discern here and there a chimney-stack and sometimes the reflection of a solitary window in one of the tallest buildings will scintillate on the distant horizon.

The busy town of Pueblo drew nigh. With a rapidly increasing population of over 50,000 and nearly 300 factories, some of which are among the largest steel-manufacturing plants in the States, Pueblo is known as the "Pittsburgh of the West."[313] But let not the reader be misled by this title into thinking that Pueblo is miserable and gloomy and odoriferous as is the wont of most towns of its character. Its streets are wide, clean and well-lit with electric lamps; its buildings also are clean and of comely architecture; there are no slums or poverty-stricken quarters, and with the giant mountains looming in the distance Pueblo is an ideal manufacturing town in ideal surroundings, besides being the centre of a rich mining district.

From Pueblo, after ministering to the wants of the inner man, I turned again westward towards Canyon City,[314] some forty miles away in the heart of the Colorado

Rockies, in order to visit the famous Royal Gorge, known also as the "Grand Canyon of the Arkansas,"[315] thence to return by a large detour through Colorado Springs, another western city like Pueblo, and with perchance a side-trip up the automobile road that has been cut to the summit of Pike's Peak (the highest highway in the world), to return to the trail to the south into New Mexico.[316]

That rise from Pueblo into the Rockies will linger ever in my memory. Surrounded in all directions but behind with glowering mountain ranges, the road cut across vast rolling plains and prairies that spoke of desolation immense and wonderful. As the sun set behind the mountains they became tinged and fired with every shade of colour, and darkness slowly crept through the valleys and filled the air with vague wonder and glorious contentment. In front and slightly to the right rose Pike's Peak high above its fellows, thrusting its massive splendour 14,000 feet[317] and more into the ruddy[318] heavens. An eerie feeling of intense loneliness crept through my veins as mile after mile was passed through naked prairie in the midst of such awful surroundings, with never a soul to be seen. I travelled thirty miles before the chilly breezes and the growing darkness constrained me to stop.[319] (The headlight was *hors de combat*;[320] only the "dimmer" would work.) In all that distance I saw no living thing save the tufted grass and the black pine-trees peppered over the sides of the foothills.[321]

When progress was no longer possible, I pulled Lizzie to the side of the dusty road, propped up her stand, and unfolded my blanket on the grass of the prairie at her side. Once again I should enjoy the sweet luxury of Nature's bedchamber in the heart of Nature's best.

But Dame Nature's bedchamber is oft a chilly and inhospitable one, and despite the invitations she tenders to all who count themselves her lovers. "Bring your own blankets" is the one stipulation. She will provide the rest. She will bring the magic sleep, the fairy dreams, the golden dawn and the thrills of ecstasy as one wakes again fresh and strong into her lovely world of health and beauty.

From rolling plains we passed to bounding foothills where the road twisted and turned and crossed torrential streams, spanned by picturesque stone bridges, until the delightful little town of Florence was reached. Here came a short stop for breakfast[322] and thence on again towards Canyon City.

From Canyon City to the Royal Gorge has been built a wonderful piece of road,[323] winding and climbing into the very heart of Colorado's rugged bosom. The gradient in places is terrific. Every ounce of power was sometimes necessary to surmount certain stretches, and blind S-bends carved from the solid face of the rocks made travelling a danger as well as a test of skill. At every bend and every turn some new panorama would spring to view and farther and farther away would fade the distant horizon of the east. Whither the road led was impossible to see. Frowning cliffs and wooded crags seemed to be the only goal ahead. After half an hour of heavy toil we reach an opening. There is a turn to the left, a flat plateau and a slight dip down; the trail dies away to nothing and a sign "Royal Gorge" is announced from a bungalow near its end. The gaunt pine-trees also end, there is a huge gap in the earth and the plateau beyond is seen a clear half-mile to the westward.[324] We clamber over the rocks and boulders, carefully and gently, where the ground has suddenly stopped, and peering down from the brink we gaze upon a tremendous cleft in the crust of the earth. Some 3,000 feet below[325] we see a raging torrent like a huge white snake lashing with a sullen roar along its tortuous path, hemmed in by vertical walls of cold relentless granite. The rushing torrent is the Arkansas, a mighty flood although but a few miles from its source, and the same river whose bed 700 miles away towards its mouth had afforded such excellent nocturnal accommodation a week before!

It is as though one is peering into the very bowels of the earth. That this gigantic chasm has been cut out by that river which now is over half a mile below seems almost incredible. As we gaze there is another surprise in store. Like a tiny plaything, a train emerges from a bend in the cliffs and with little infantile puffs of smoke crawls along the rails which one now sees running along the narrow river bank.[326] Clinging close to every twist and turn the train proceeds. There is scarcely sufficient space between the rugged walls and the surging river for the single track. At one point the width of the ledge is but 10 yards and the track has been built out over the water. The river dashes madly through; the engine sways from side to side as it drags its heavy load onward. Down there, it is said that the sky above is but a thread of light and the stars can be seen at midday as in a mine.

One moves one's gaze and scans the rugged boulders that lie heaped and stacked and strewn about as if but a push would suffice to send them hurtling down into the chasm below. Here and there are stunted growths of sage, cactus and prickly pear, or a giant fir-tree springs from a grassy cleft in the rocks.

Retracing the trail, we find ourselves soon descending the precipitous winds and turns that lead back to Canyon City.[327] On the left we pass "The Famous Sky-line Drive,"[328] which announces itself by placards here and there as "The greatest scenic highway wonder of the world." But a little distance from here is also "the one-day trip that bankrupts the English language"[329] and such beauty spots as are suggested by the names "Hell Gate,"[330] "The Frying Pan,"[331] "Roaring Fork,"[332] "The Devil's Thousand-Foot Slide,"[333] "Cripple Creek,"[334] "The Garden of the Gods,"[335] and other similarly euphonious[336] and onomatopœic[337] appellations.[338]

It would be tempting to explore all these places and to see more of Colorado and the immense fund of natural beauty which she displays in endless variety. But impatience draws me again towards Pueblo,[339] so that I can once again strike the trail that leads to California. I am already getting anxious to see the blue sea, though yet only half-way between the oceans!

That afternoon as I paused beneath a "bowser" in Pueblo while Lizzie was filled to the brim, I inquired the condition of the road to Trinidad, some 100 miles to the south on the Santa Fé Trail.

"Trinidad? The worst road in America, sir!—ab-sol-oot-ly the worst road in America, sir."

The prospect was not pleasing. There was certainly an element of interest about it because it would be fascinating almost to see for oneself exactly what Americans did consider a bad road. My formula so far had been that when an American said a road was good, it was bad. When he said it was bad, it was damn bad! But what would the "worst" be like?

As I sped along, the sky deepened and a severe thundershower threatened. Heavy black clouds glowered around the mountain-tops and every moment I expected a sudden outburst from the heavens. On my right the Rockies rose higher and higher. In the distance, but gradually approaching, rose Blanca Peak,[340] a dreadful, ponderous giant amongst its brethren, its gloomy crest piercing the very vaults of the sky and hardly visible in the sombre blackness that so often hangs in the neighbourhood of these western mountain peaks. Now and again a streak of lightning would flash through the heavens, and the dull thud that followed, belated and awe-inspiring, would rumble backwards and forwards along the valleys, reverberating from peak to peak until finally it was lost in the depths of the firmament.

On the left spread the rolling plains as far as the eye could reach, like as the sea stretches up to the shores of Dover whence the cliffs rise sheer and stubborn.[341] In front lay the road, skirting the borderline twixt plains and peaks.

I soon came to the conclusion that that garage hand in Pueblo had been "pulling one over me." The road was just splendid. Laid in hard flat well-made macadam, its surface was excellent, passing all understanding. As I sped on ever quicker to avoid the gathering storm, the non-skid pads of the tyres hummed a merry tune. Could I be on the right road? I asked myself once again. I must be, for in these parts there is only one road to be taken. No others exist. There must be a catch in it somewhere, I told myself.

An hour went by and still the thunder rushed around Blanca Peak the Mighty, now receding from view.[342] An occasional shower just on the edge of the storm would hasten me on my way. Still the road was perfection itself, and still it fringed the chain of minor peaks that runs from north to south, the boundary of the vast plateau of over 1,000,000 square miles that includes, in those unassuming words, "The Rockies."[343] Another hour flew by.

And then it came, like a thief in the night, sudden and unexpected. The smooth grey macadam vanished, as though the magic wand had ceased its power. Instead lay ahead a villainous track in the dark brown soil of the prairie, a track beaten with sorrow and stricken with grief, here battered into ugly patches, there heaped into fearful ridges and seething masses of mud and rock. It had rained. Those words alone express a world of sin and shame, when one speaks of a trail "out West." Here once more were the old agonies, the old discomforts, the old tortures, the old haulings, heavings, pushings, joltings and bruisings. The sky again became overcast. The rain began to fall tormentingly. I had still twenty-five miles to go to the nearest town. The sun sank lower behind the mountain ridge. The rain fell faster; if I did not reach Walsenburg that night I should have to rest among the prairie-dogs in the pelting rain. And what chance was there of reaching Walsenburg before dark with no lights and at an average of six miles an hour "all out," with only a paltry hour before dusk?[344]

I will not attempt to describe that ride. I feel it should not be described. "The ride that bankrupts the English language,"[345] indeed, thought I. Many times I left the road altogether and pursued my course whither I listed over the rough prairie. Strewn with boulders, rocks and ugly stones, carved here and there in fantastic shapes, with mysterious hollows and quaint prairie-dog holes, it was just possible to scramble along. From a distance the "road" I had left looked better and I returned to it, only to find that the prairie still looked more enticing. How I leapt over the smaller stones and skipped round the larger ones always intent on nothing but the few yards that were to follow, I shall never completely remember. Again and again I returned to the road and endured its agony for a spell, and again I swerved away from it, my every bone shaking in its joints and my teeth rocking in their sockets with the vibration.

Let me forget. These things are not good to gloat upon! I remember but one amusing incident, which was but the forerunner of many more to come. I had returned to the road for a spell. I came to a slight dip. It was like a lake full of fluid mud where a wayward stream had swollen with the rains and encroached upon the sanctity of the road. "Not negotiable" was the unspoken verdict. Strange to say, the prairie was now fenced off from the road boundary, so there was no avoiding the coming struggle. "It's got to be done, so here goes"; slowly I dived into the yellow mass. Just half-way the back wheel turned to jelly and seemed to crumple up to nothing. With one big splosh the whole five hundred-weight of us[346] flopped gaily over into the mire. Pinned down by the weight of the machine, the mud had ample time to soak through all my clothing, into my pockets and down my neck. Lizzie's submersion would have been entire instead of partial had I not intervened. . . . After a short struggle I ultimately succeeded in extricating my right foot from between the brake-pedal and the engine, and heaved the bulky mass from its repose. No sooner was this done than we slithered once more and fell over *en bloc*[347] on the opposite side.

Oh, the joys of motor-cycling in Yankeeland!

I did get to Walsenburg that night. As luck would have it, the two hotels were full.[348] At least the desk-clerks avowed by the bones of their saintly grandmothers that there wasn't a room left. Probably they were moved to anxiety lest their worthy name should be soiled by this mud-covered intruder!

I found a room after a long search at a fifth-rate "doss-house"[349] devoid of furniture, where the landlady demanded my money in advance before giving me the key to my room.

Thus passed another day.

CHAPTER 12 NOTES

310. "Fifteen fall" is most likely an informal variation of "fifteen falls ago," a term used to describe something that happened fifteen years ago. It may also associate the anniversary to a particular season (fall, as opposed to winter, spring, or summer) as a farmer might, but in this instance it seems to be used only as an expression meaning "fifteen years ago."

311. This station in Boston has always been called "South Union Station." In Chapter 9 of this book, C.K. wrote that he "never made the fatal mistake of referring to it as a 'station,'" implying that he had been instructed to refer to train stations as *depots* when traveling in the US. Thus, C.K. apparently defaulted to calling it South Union *depot*. But if his hosts had been more aware, they would have detected his bluff as to where he was from because no one who was actually from Boston would have ever referred to it as "South Union depot."

312. The first wagon bridge across the Arkansas River between La Junta and Pueblo was at Nepesta, which was built in 1886.

313. Pueblo's slogan was "Steel City of the West." Terre Haute, in Indiana, had been called the "Pittsburgh of the West" (apparently back when Indiana was still "the west").

314. In most publications of the period, as today, "Canyon City" was spelled "Cañon City."

315. In *Titan of Chasms: The Grand Canyon of Arizona* (1905), Royal Gorge is described as follows: "The Grand Canyon of the Arkansas, in Colorado, is a noble little slit in the mountains."

316. Although C.K.'s original plan may have been to take his motorcycle up Pikes Peak (a challenging ride even today) and then descend through Colorado Springs before heading south, he did not do that. Instead, he backtracked through Cañon City and Pueblo.

317. Although Pikes Peak is about forty-five miles northwest of Pueblo—and C.K. may have caught glimpses of it on his way toward Cañon City—driving up Pikes Peak from Cañon City would have been a lengthy excursion. According to the *Blue Book* (1920), C.K. would have had to cover 157.9 miles to get back to Pueblo via Pikes Peak and Colorado Springs (87.6 miles from Cañon City to the top of Pikes Peak; 27.7 miles from Pikes Peak to Colorado Springs; and then 42.6 miles from Colorado Springs to Pueblo). Compared to the 44.1 miles from Cañon City back to Pueblo, the difference would have been 113.8 miles in extremely mountainous terrain, representing at least one extra day of driving.

318. "ruddy": red/pink.

319. According to the *Blue Book* (1920), Route 249 from Pueblo to Cañon City is noted as being a section of the "Rainbow route." The town of Florence is 35.2 miles of road west of Pueblo toward Cañon City.

320. "hors de combat": A French term literally meaning "out of the fight," but generally used to mean "out of action due to injury or damage" or—as in this case—simply inoperative.

321. Much as C.K. indicates, Florence is the first community he reached west of Pueblo. He is effectively saying that he camped about five miles short of Florence, just after crossing over the Arkansas River (again), near where "Portland" is located on this 1959 USGS map (Figure 94).

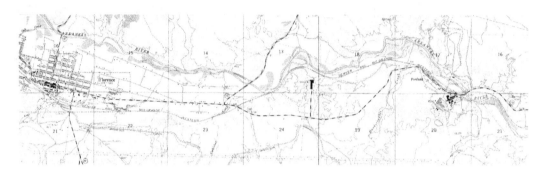

Figure 94: Arkansas River Near Portland, en Route to Florence, Colorado.
Source: USGS: *Colorado Florence Quadrangle*, 7.5 Minute Series, 1959.

322. Although insufficient detail is included to identify exactly where he ate breakfast in Florence, there were three restaurants listed on Page 128 of the *Florence City Directory 1905-1906*:

• Chile Parlor, 105 E Main Street.

• Idlewild, 113 S Pikes Peak Avenue.

• The Royal, 103 S Pikes Peak Avenue.

323. The road from Cañon City to the Royal Gorge that was used in 1919 is no longer passable. Route 269 in the *Blue Book* (1920) describes it, while the 1920 US Forest Service map (Figure 95) illustrates it and Figure 96 depicts one section of road through Priest's Canyon. It opened in 1911 through Priest's Canyon and was built using "convict labor." (The actual canyon name is Ohio Canyon; a man named Priest was a local landowner, and so the road was named after him.)

Figure 95: Map of the Route to Royal Gorge from Cañon City, *ca.* 1920. **Source:** US Forest Service.

Figure 96: One Section of the Road through Priest's Canyon. **Source:** *Motor Age,* Vol. XXI, No. 17, April 25, 1912. Page 9.

324. The photo in Figure 97 shows people in an auto that is parked within twenty feet of the edge at the summit of the Royal Gorge.

Figure 97: Top of the Royal Gorge.
Original caption reads, "After traversing the Skyline Drive the traveler may turn to the west and climb to the summit of the mountain in which the Royal Gorge is cut."
Source: *Guidebook of the Western United States, Part E,* 1922. Plate 34.A.

325. The photo in Figure 98 shows the view looking down into the Royal Gorge and Figure 99 is a photo C.K. took at the top of the gorge.

Figure 98: View Looking Down into Royal Gorge.
Original caption reads, "When one stands on the rim above the old station of Gorge and looks down into this great chasm the railroad looks like a thread stretched beside the foaming stream."
Source: *Guidebook of the Western United States, Part E,* 1922. Plate 37.

Figure 99: C.K.'s Photo of the Top of Royal Gorge.
Note the mountain silhouette in the distance. It is the same range shown in Figure 97 from the USGS indicating C.K. took this photo at nearly the same place. Also note the scaffolding and railing erected under the tree and connected to the rocks. Apparently, they were placed there to provide a better—and safer—view of the gorge below.
Source: C.K.'s personal slide collection.

326. Figures 100 and 101 (next page) depict the track at the bottom of the Gorge. In the distance of both, the unique "hanging bridge" can be seen. This structure was used to support the tracks where the river was too narrow to lay tracks on the ground, so the tracks were hung out over the river. This structure has been maintained and is still in use today.

Figure 100: Upper End of the Royal Gorge—
With Train.
Source: *Guidebook of the Western United
States, Part E*, 1922. Plate 39.

Figure 101: Hanging Bridge, Royal Gorge.
Original caption reads, "The Hanging Bridge, in
the narrowest part of the canyon, is a striking
feature. When the road was built there was not
room at this point for both river and railroad side
by side, so a bridge was necessary."
Source: *Guidebook of the Western United States,
Part E*, 1922. Plate 38.

327. Here C.K. implicitly explains that he had made the decision not to attempt
to climb Pikes Peak or travel back through Colorado Springs.

328. Figure 102 is a photograph of Skyline Drive from the USGS. This roadway was built using "convict labor" from the prison in Cañon City.

Figure 102: Photograph of Skyline Drive, Cañon City.
Source: *Guidebook of the Western United States, Part E*, 1922. Plate 35.

329. This sign advertising such a "one day trip" was almost certainly referring to the train ride from Colorado Springs to Cripple Creek (which is located about fifty miles northeast of Cañon City by modern road). The identification of that trip as one that "bankrupts the English language" (a phrase repeated by C.K. as discussed in Note 345) was widely attributed—perhaps with some creative license by the press—to Vice President Theodore Roosevelt who had visited Cripple Creek in 1901. He had been asked by journalists how he enjoyed his trip on the "Short Line" railroad between Colorado Springs and Cripple Creek (now a popular hiking trail called the Gold Camp Road). Roosevelt's reported answer referred to the exhaustion of words available to describe the scenic beauty of the trip.

330. Hell Gate is a narrow section along Hagerman Pass Road (FSR #105) to Hell Gap, where the valley drops far below and the road winds along a ledge rising above Ivanhoe Creek. It is about one hundred miles (as the crow flies) northwest of Cañon City.

331. The Frying Pan River, a tributary of the Roaring Fork River, is approximately forty-two miles long, and begins in the mountains about one hundred miles northwest of Cañon City.

332. The Roaring Fork River, a tributary of the Colorado River, is approximately seventy miles long and joins the Colorado River about 150 miles northwest of Cañon City.

333. This is an apparent reference to Devil's Slide, a peak about forty miles northeast of Cañon City (see Figure 103).

Figure 103: Devil's Slide, *ca.* 1901.
Source: US Library of Congress.

334. Cripple Creek, Colorado is a former gold-mining camp about twenty-five miles north of Cañon City.

335. The Garden of the Gods was designated as a National Natural Landmark in 1971 and is a public park about five miles west of Colorado Springs and about forty miles northeast of Cañon City.

336. "euphonious": Pleasing to the ear.

337. "onomatopœic": The naming of a thing or action by a vocal imitation of the sound associated with it (such as *ping* or *gong*).

338. "appellations": Names.

339. Once again C.K. implicitly abandons his plan to travel up Pikes Peak or to Colorado Springs.

340. Blanca Peak was about forty-five miles due west of his route at his closest point, in Walsenburg, which was still twenty miles ahead. It is clear that he misidentified this mountain, because he later says that it faded from view before he reached Walsenburg (even though it would be closest to him when he arrived at Walsenburg). It was probably Greenhorn Mountain, 12,352 feet in elevation and only ten miles west from this road at his closest point, with twenty miles still to go to reach Walsenburg. The photo of Greenhorn Mountain shown in Figure 104 was taken in October 2018 along the same road C.K. was on, about ten miles east, while heading south to Walsenburg.

Figure 104: Greenhorn Mountain.
Source: Photograph by Jay Gannett.

341. C.K. is referring to the world-famous cliffs at Dover (see Figure 105), which are located on the southeast coast of England where the English Channel between England and France is at its narrowest point.

Figure 105: The Cliffs at Dover.
Source: Photographer Greetz Jeecee. Used with permission.

342. Similar to Note 340, it was probably not Blanca Peak that receded from view, but rather, Greenhorn Mountain—which was twenty-two miles behind him to the right when he reached Walsenburg.

343. As point of fact, the Rocky Mountains "only" covers about 300,000-400,000 square miles (including land in Canada), depending on which resource is cited.

344. If heavy rain began when he was twenty-five miles north of Walsenburg—which would have been five miles before he was closest to Greenhorn Mountain—and he was averaging six miles per hour in the rain in the evening with no operable lights, he would have arrived in Walsenburg after driving in the dark for at least two hours with no lights.

345. C.K.'s use of the phrase "bankrupts the English language" is a sarcastic reference to the sign he saw coming down from the Royal Gorge—one that advertised the beauty of the train ride between Colorado Springs and Cripple Creek (as had been described by Theodore Roosevelt). C.K. was essentially observing that he had bankrupted the English language cursing the bad road upon which he was riding.

346. This would have been the aforementioned four hundredweight of Lizzie plus his own "hundredweight."

347. "en bloc": A French term meaning "all at the same time."

348. Today it is not possible to determine precisely where he stayed in Walsenburg. The 1915-1916 Biennial Report of the Colorado Bureau of Labor Statistics listed all hotels and boarding houses in Walsenburg. A number of these were evidently boarding houses operated by local mining companies primarily to house employees. The table shown in Figure 106 describes them sorted by number of employees but with hotels listed first.

Lodging Establishment	Nature of Establishment	Employees
The Klein Hotel	Hotel	18
St. John Café & Hotel	Hotel	8
The Southern Hotel	Hotel	2
The Oxford Hotel	Hotel	1
Ideal Mine Boarding House	Boarding House	5
The Morris House	Rooms	3
Victoria Rooms	Furnished Rooms	3
Walsen Co. Boarding House	Boarding House	3
J.H. Ryan Mutual Coal Co.	Board and Room	-

The Klein Hotel is the only establishment listed in the nationwide 1917 Official Hotel Red Book and Directory (on the "European Plan," for $1 and up).

Figure 106: Hotels in Walsenburg, Colorado.
Source: 1915-1916 Biennial Report, Colorado Bureau of Labor Statistics.

349. "doss house": A cheap lodging house, especially for homeless people and tramps. It seems most likely that, given his description, C.K. stayed at the Ideal Mine Boarding House, Morris House, or Walsen Co. Boarding House.

CHAPTER XIII

IN SOUTHERN COLORADO

There is only one road in the States as bad as that from Walsenburg to Trinidad. I refer to the road from Trinidad to Walsenburg.[350]

In spite of that it was a good road; I got through. It took endless patience, perseverance and a morning of time to do those fifty weary miles. The scenery was strange, almost to the point of weirdness. From the surrounding flatness would rise sudden plateaus, with dead vertical sides and perfectly flat tops. Even the hills and mountains where they occurred (save in the distant Rockies) were modelled on the same plan, rising abruptly from the plain and ascending in two, three or more sudden steps. The effect was just as though the land architecture had been entrusted to some aspiring cubist or futurist instead of to the well-disciplined laws of Nature.

I do not profess to have attained much learning in the science of geology, and speak, therefore, as one without authority. But it seemed to me on many occasions that to study the geology of the Far West, the English scientist would have to forget all he had ever learnt about physical geography and start all over again in Southern Colorado.

At first I was puzzled in the extreme to see how the mountains rose suddenly out of the great plains, without any warning almost, and without the customary foothills and valleys that one would expect to see clustering around a mountain range of several thousands of feet in height. Afterwards I became accustomed to this unusual formation, when I found that mountains always grow that way in the Far West, and particularly farther on in New Mexico and Arizona. All their ranges seemed like elongated "Wrekins"[351] set in a plain of gigantic dimensions.

At Aguilar,[352] half-way on the road to Trinidad, I met the first really Mexican town. It will be remembered that all the south-western States once belonged to Mexico and one by one they have been ceded or bought or otherwise appropriated until Mexico now is only a shadow of its former self. Nevertheless a large proportion of the population is still Mexican, in spite of the continued influx of American settlers, and consequently Mexican is spoken[353] almost universally in addition to English as the national tongue.

Trinidad styles itself "The industrial and commercial centre of S.E. Colorado."[354] With a population of something in the region of 14,000, it stands at the base of Fisher's Peak[355] (10,000 feet),[356] and it is an admirable example of the inextricable mixtures of Old Mexico and New America in the cities of the West. I took its picture[357] and left its shining well-paved streets to track down my old friend, the Santa Fé Trail.

I got one mile away from the town and then struck. The trail climbed rapidly, skirting the Peak all the time in preparation for the Raton Pass soon to follow, which cuts right over the Rocky Mountains into New Mexico. That in itself was nothing. I am always game for a good hill-climb. But I had thought better of the Santa Fé Trail. After climbing 1,000 feet in just over a mile, it changed into the most absurd hotch-potch of ruts and mud-heaps that ever eye witnessed,[358] and this for as far as one could see. The condition of the road strained my credulity to breaking point. Getting through the far-off mud-hole at Hume in Indiana was a child's tea-party compared with this. In half an hour I did just 100 yards and then, after resolutely determining to return to Trinidad and take the train, I found that to go back was as much out of the question as to go forward. It simply couldn't be done single-handed. To turn Lizzie round would require nothing less than a sky-hook[359] and pulley-blocks.

I left her standing in a huge rut in the middle of the road and reconnoitred to see how far this appalling state of affairs continued.

Fortunately a Flivver appeared round a bend in the road ahead, coming in the opposite direction. It heaved and swayed and bumped and side-slipped and hiccoughed its way along. I watched it until it finally reached the spot where Lizzie blocked the way. Then something had to be done. The car had two occupants, both hefty-looking men, whom I enlisted to my aid. Together we lifted and pulled and heaved and pushed until the worst was past, and then I struggled on alone.

Farther into the mountains we travelled; higher and higher we climbed. In places the trail was hewn out of the rugged mountain sides, and except in a few places there was hardly room for more than one vehicle to pass. Occasionally a "washout" would be encountered where a mountain stream had encroached on the road and washed it away altogether. Then would come a short detour over a gap in the bank, with the grassy slope strewn with branches and small tree-trunks to prevent the unfortunate vehicle sinking in and thus permanently blocking all progress that way.

The ascent of the Raton Mountains by the Raton Pass is made amongst some of the most beautiful scenery imaginable. The trail is only visible a few yards ahead and is lost in sudden twists and turns as gradually the mountain slopes are devoured. On the right, almost behind, are still to be seen the famous Spanish Peaks towering like twins in solitude above the rest of the Sangre de Cristo range, some forty miles away.[360] Soon we shall be leaving Colorado State behind us—Colorado the Glorious, the Beautiful, the Great.

It is said that "amongst all the mountain kingdoms, Colorado seems to stand easily first in physical adornment: not even Switzerland and her Alps offering more than a fair comparison."[361] Mont Blanc, the highest peak in the Alps, is 15,784 feet high,[362] while Colorado has many peaks lacking little of this height. The lowest depths of some of Colorado's famous parks are higher than the average height of the Alpine Chain.

Upward we climb, amid thickly-wooded mountain tops, round thrilling bends and tortuous precipices and over the rockiest of roads. The end is in sight. A depression in the sky-line ahead shows where the Raton Pass (7,620 feet to be exact)[363] reaches its highest point and gazes forwards into the heart of New Mexico and behind into the vastnesses of Colorado.

A gradual bend, a sudden swerve, and then—the summit is reached. Colorado is passed. Before us lies a great and thickly-wooded valley, broad and deep and beautiful.[364] Beyond lie the great plains of New Mexico, plains so vast that in their utter defiance of limit and dimension they beggar description. The eye could not follow the great expanse. So immense were the distances that the earth merged indefinitely into the sky at the horizon. Dotted and strewn here and there were hills and mountain ranges that seemed to have sprung up so suddenly out of the plateau to have really no connection with them.

Here I stood at the gate of another world. Before me lay a land of mystery and romance, a land of health for body and soul; a land of desert and sage-bush, of cactus and strange vegetation; a land of antiquity unparalleled by any other in the world. Here at my feet lay New Mexico and beyond, Arizona, the two States that at the same time are the oldest and the youngest in America. Although only admitted to the Union in 1912, their history dates from remote ages when they were peopled by a race unknown to-day[365] but nevertheless well advanced on the road to civilization, a race that built cities while Babylon was as yet unknown,[366] and laid down irrigation systems that puzzle the engineers of the present day.[367]

Arizona and New Mexico, you are the pearls of great price that no human being has ever yet valued at your true worth. When the day shall come that man can say of you, "I have seen you in all your moods and have discovered all your secrets," then this old earth will be a lifeless, soulless, aimless globe, its purpose fulfilled, its course completed.

A five mile descent through the scented pine-trees brought me to Raton, another half-Mexican, half-American town, small but modern and well-arranged. "No more 'rooming-houses' for me," I resolved and turned my gaze to the far-distant plains where the darkness was slowly gathering.

Even in New Mexico, one need never go without a meal. The way to an Englishman's heart is through his stomach (this applies also to Americans and most human beings in general!). My heart was greatly touched by Raton in this manner,[368] and shortly before dusk I was speeding on my way southwards towards Santa Fé.

Ten miles out the trail crossed a river. It must have been the Canadian River,[369] a tributary of the Arkansas, which it joins several hundred miles to the east. The surrounding country was desolation and solitude itself. Half prairie, half waste, almost desert, it was a country of new sensations. Just to the west, from horizon to horizon, stretched the gaunt and rugged Sangre de Cristo range,[370] dark and threatening always in their aspect. Not a living thing was in sight, not even a suggestion of life. I ran Lizzie off the road to the brink of the river and laid down my bed in the silver rays of the rising moon.[371]

At 6.30 in the morning the sky was ruddy and the air pure with the fresh breezes of the dawn. From minute to minute the myriad colours of the mountains changed their tints as the sun rose higher in the Mexican sky. I continued on my way.

The road was broad and good, but a surprise was in store. After a few miles there appeared a dilapidated signpost where a bedraggled pathway joined the broad highway through a gap in the fence which now ran alongside.[372] It bore the legend "To Santa Fé" and pointed through the fence to the left. My first impression was that some small boy had been playing pranks. It was inconceivable that these two ruts but a few inches wide in the coarse green grass should lead to Santa Fé while there, straight on, was a good broad highroad that led nowhere. It ran clear ahead and was lost over the brow of a hill. I never found where that road went. I have never seen it on any map and have made many inquiries since.[373] Some travellers, like myself, had seen that road and wavered, but not one had gone that way and could enlighten me.

New Mexico is not a nice country in which to lose oneself. Towns are very few, and often one can go a hundred miles without seeing a village or meeting a soul. So in spite of the temptation I swerved to the left and entered the field that was without corn or pasture, following those two ruts that cut deep into the prairie soil and were not visible more than 50 or 100 yards ahead at the most. In places the two ruts had become too deep for further use and another pair had been started at the side, running parallel with the original ones. When these had worn too far another pair had sprung up, and in many places I counted eight distinct pairs of ruts running side by side across the prairie, each representing a distinct phase in the evolution of the Santa Fé Trail. At any point, if one looks far and long enough, one can find the original tracks that centuries ago were formed by the old prairie-schooners as they journeyed westward across the plains to Santa Fé.[374]

The next town lay far across the plains beyond the horizon. I should have to hurry if I were to get any breakfast, but the riding was rough. Tufts of coarse grass and sharp stones covered the prairie and held back the speed; here and there were the holes of prairie-dogs, who respect no one in their choice of a site.[375] If it pleases them to build their front-door entrance where your favourite inter-rut strip happens to be, well, they build it there. Their holes are generally about six inches in diameter, the mouth being funnel-shaped. Passing vehicles smash them in until the opening is sometimes two or three feet across. Our friend the prairie-dog doesn't mind in the least. He continues to live there in spite of the traffic and never a curse escapes his lips. He is a dear little animal. One cannot help loving him. In stature these animals have the characteristic of both a squirrel and a rabbit, and are about a foot in length. They sit on their fat little haunches like a squirrel, but have only a little bobbed tail like a rabbit. I believe they are the most friendly rodents in existence, and have the reputation of dwelling in friendship even with rattlesnakes, who never harm them! If you surprise one when he is away from home, he watches you, motionless, to see if he has been seen, if only a few feet from the intruder. And when he sees that you have seen, away he runs with his head well down and his little tail well up until he reaches his burrow in the flat prairie. This done, he considers himself safe, turns round, sits on his haunches and stares inquiringly at you. But if you dare come too close he disappears in a second and is seen no more.

One cannot help laughing at the antics of these amusing little animals as they scamper off like month-old puppy dogs. Ofttimes I have chased one to his hole in the road and watched the anxious look on his face as for a brief moment he turns his head before flashing into the ground below your front wheel. No true traveller could harm one of these innocent little beasts; they are often his only companions for hundreds of miles.

Ten, twenty, thirty miles I travelled over the almost trackless prairie. Occasional mud-pools barred the way, but when the trail was unfenced, these were easily avoided. Later on fences appeared, limiting the road from some neighbouring ranch. I judged I was getting near to Springer.

An old shack of a two-seater car hove[376] in sight, coming in the opposite direction; I had an opportunity of studying it in detail as it came close up. Naturally we both stopped. All travellers are friends in the Far West, where distances are great and people are few.

"Guess you'd better follow us if you want to get to Springer this week," essayed the driver.

"Why, is there any mud about?"

"Mud? There's a hole down there outside the town that we've been trying to get either in or out of these two-and-a-half hours. Had to get some hosses to pull us backwards out of it in the end. Gosh, I've never seen a mud-hole like it in all my days. We kin get around another way though, I'm told. Where you headin' for, stranger?"

"Santa Fé."

"Oh, we was expectin' to get to Santa Fé this mornin'. We're bound for El Paso, and must get there by tomorrow."[377]

I reflected that El Paso was in Texas on the Mexican border, some 500 miles to the south![378] "Well, if you don't mind, I'll come along to Santa Fé with you, so then we can each help dig each other out of any holes that happen along."

"Righto, glad to have your company, but we're not speed merchants like I guess you are with that 'oss there."

"Don't make any mistake, brother. I passed the speed craze a thousand miles back. It doesn't pay."

So we retraced our tracks, the car leading. It was shorn entirely of mudwings and footboards to save the wheels becoming clogged or the running boards fouling the road.[379] On the back was strapped a large trunk. This I found is the usual way of travel by "auto" in the West. Seldom does one see wings on a car that is driven for any distance from home. Running boards, if present, are generally of an improvised variety made by planks suspended and fastened in place by ropes around the body work. Thus the road clearance is increased and the necessity for constant cleaning removed. By far the most popular "machine" is the Ford. You can buy one cheap and sell it as scrap when the journey, if a long one, is finished. Owners of large expensive touring cars very often have a Ford as well for emergencies and for long distance travelling. In New Mexico and Arizona I have seen scores of huge touring cars stuck helplessly in the road and often abandoned altogether until the seasons permit of their removal.

I followed my friends from Texas along little pathways and rough tracks strewn with boulders, through gaps in fences, across fields and back gardens, all, to my mind, at an alarming pace. It was only with difficulty that I kept up with them at all, owing to the many ruts and rocks and other obstructions that are far more hindering to two wheels than four.

Arrived eventually in Springer, I resolved to postpone the promised meal until later in the day.

We passed many ranches and crossed many mud-holes, some of alarming width across. In most I managed to fall off at least once and wallowed in the mud. Sometimes the car got so far ahead as to be lost altogether, but after each encounter with a mud-lake I managed to make up the lost time.

Thus passed nearly thirty miles in which I realized the utter absurdity of two wheels compared with four. At one place I lost so much time that I began to give up as hopeless the attempt to keep up with the car ahead. After all, what was the use? Once out of the mire, however, the trail became better and turned into loose sand for many miles.

Over this sand I made good progress. It was now nearly midday, and I had visions of a meal in Wagonmound,[380] a small village some twenty miles away. The appetite was there all right, and as I trimmed off mile after mile at good speed I forgot all about mud-holes and the like.

All at once the engine burst into a wild roar and Lizzie began to slow down.[381] What new trouble was this? A broken chain, or something worse? I stopped as quickly as I could and proceeded to an examination of the transmission. The chain was all right, but the engine sprocket had almost come right off the driving shaft. The key and nut, where were they?

For an hour I searched up and down in the sand and in the grass at the roadside for the missing parts, but without success. The sun was almost vertically above and its rays poured down unmercifully from a cloudless sky. There was not a sign of water or of any living thing in any direction.

I returned to another examination to discover whether I could remove a nut from any other part of the machine to replace the defaulter. Not a nut was there anywhere that at all approached either the size or the thread required. I searched once more, wondering in how many days' time another vehicle would pass that way, and half resolved to walk the next twenty miles.

What! Leave Lizzie and walk! NEVER!

Another hour elapsed. I had explored all the ruts and searched every inch of the road for half a mile back. I stopped, and wondered where I could find water to drink. Water would be even more acceptable than the nut and key now. I scanned the sun-baked prairie in all directions. From horizon to horizon there was nothing but the solitary distant mountains, and here and there a lonely parched-up hill. Truly a nice outlook! Henceforth I would carry a water-bag with me.

I decided to return to Lizzie, push her off the road and try walking. But just to think of coming 3,000 miles in her constant company, and then having to forsake her! "Poor old Lizzie, she's a dear old crock," I murmured to myself.

What was that? I stooped down to see, and there hidden in a crack in the hard mud was the missing key. That put a different aspect on matters altogether. The nut would in all probability not be far away. I set out to explore every stone and every rut and every crack. Sure enough I found it not very far away.

In a few minutes the midsummer air was whistling past my ears once again.

In ten minutes I found myself surveying the biggest thing in mud-lakes that it has ever been my misfortune to negotiate. The road was fenced in, naturally. There was a ranch on either side of it. The lake of mud extended sideways to the very borders of the road, ninety feet wide. The distance across was about fifty yards. I estimated that the mud and water were waist-deep in the middle. Ridges and furrows of harder mud, where passing cars had churned it up, in a desperate attempt to get through, led into the sickly mass and then were lost.

"This requires a scientist, not a motor-cyclist, to cross," I averred, and, propping Lizzie upon her stand, went to reconnoitre.

I then created a precedent in the art of crossing mud-holes by which I benefited on all future occasions. I was wearing water-tight field boots[382] which came up to my knees. The *modus operandi* was this: I would select a likely-looking rut and walk along it as far as I could without the water coming over the top of my boots. If it came over I went back and tried another one. This process was repeated until I had a good idea how the land lay. If I could possibly get through without the mud reaching my knees, I knew I could get Lizzie through all right. This manner of prospecting in advance I found indispensable and at the same time perfectly successful.

I got through somehow, but prayed that I should never meet another like THAT.

I rolled into Wagonmound about three in the afternoon a very weary and mud-stained traveller. When I got there, it started to rain; it naturally would.

There is but one restaurant in Wagonmound,[383] which enjoys a population of 200 or so Mexican-Americans.[384] Here I learnt that there had been a "cloud-burst" near Santa Fé but a few days back; also that the oldest inhabitants of New Mexico had never known so much rain to fall as this summer; also that the roads ahead were almost impassable; also that at one place on the other side of Santa Fé and at a distance of fifty miles between two towns there were one hundred cars stranded in the mud and abandoned![385] I was proof against it all, however. I considered that by now I could get through anywhere. I was not to be daunted by fancy yarns and sceptical reports. Time was when I cursed the Americans for being optimistic about their roads. That stage had long since been passed. Now I was proof against even their pessimisms and discouragements.

The rain stopped and I proceeded once more, determined to make a big effort to reach Santa Fé that night, though still ninety miles away.

At Wagonmound there was a station of the Santa Fé Railway,[386] which for a good distance ran close to the trail. I inquired at the "Depot" what were the chances of travelling on the track. I did not want to try conclusions with any trans-continental trains if avoidable.

"What! Ride in the track!" ejaculated the line-master. "You can't do that!"

"Oh, I guess I can if I'm careful," was my response.

"Waal, I jest guess you *can't*, my friend," was his rejoinder. "I'll have you arrested if you try to work that stunt."

Argument was useless. "D'ye think I want to damage your bloomin' old track?" I asked him heatedly after much discussion. We settled the matter finally by my tendering the information that I would ride up and down his track all day long if I wanted to (not much fear of such a desire developing!) and if he liked he could "write to *John Bull* about it"![387]

The humour of the situation was lost upon him.

"You'll get shot," was his reply, whereat we parted.

CHAPTER 13 NOTES

350. Figure 107 is a photograph taken by C.K. on his ride. A route scouting survey in 2018 established that he took the photo three miles south of Walsenburg, thirty-two miles north of Trinidad, at N37°34′50.3″, W104°45′38.2″. The two formations appearing to be rectangular are identified on topographical maps of the period as "Castle Rocks."

Figure 107: The Road to Trinidad, Colorado.
Source: C.K.'s personal slide collection.

351. The Wrekin (pronounced REE-KIN) is a hill in East Shropshire, England. It is located some five miles west of Telford. Rising to a height of 1,335 feet above the Shropshire Plain, it is a prominent and well-known landmark.

352. Aguilar was first settled in 1861, at which time it was known as "San Antonio Plaza." Seven years later, it was renamed in recognition of José Ramón Aguilar—a local cattleman, pioneer, and legislator who incorporated the town in 1894.

353. It is interesting that someone who was apparently well schooled and spoke French would characterize Spanish as Mexican. Perhaps C.K. believed the Spanish dialect spoken by Mexicans was distinct enough that he did not think it proper to call it Spanish.

354. I couldn't find any record of Trinidad styling itself as an "industrial and commercial center." In an 1891 article in the *Magazine of Western History Illustrated*, Trinidad was characterized as the "trade and money center for an immense territory, including portions of northern Texas, southern Colorado, and northern New Mexico." In *Colorado, the Queen Jewel of the Rockies* (1918), Pueblo was the industrial and commercial center: "Today, Pueblo is well along toward being the industrial and commercial center of the region between the Missouri River and the Pacific Coast."

355. Fisher's Peak is just five miles southeast of downtown Trinidad. Figure 108, a photograph from 1907, shows Trinidad in the foreground and Fisher's Peak rising to the southeast.

Figure 108: Trinidad and Fisher's Peak.
Source: Photograph by Arthur Russell Allen.

356. According to an 1897 USGS map, elevation on Fisher's Peak is 9,583 feet. Today, however, elevation is set at 9,633 feet.

357. The photograph of Commercial Street in Trinidad in Figure 109 (next page) was published in September 1919 and thus is certainly representative of the "shining well-paved streets" that C.K. wrote about seeing just two months earlier.

Figure 109: Commercial Street in Trinidad, Colorado, ca. 1919.
Source: *Colorado Highways Bulletin*, Vol. II, No. 9, September 1919. Page 7.

358. Because this is grammatically improper, this phrase could be a typographical error or malapropism from a handwritten original manuscript. C.K. may have intended to state, "mud-heaps that ever *an* eye witnessed" or "mud-heaps that ever *I* witnessed."

359. The term "sky hook" was apparently often used in this period to describe a magical hook that was connected to an imaginary lifting device in the sky (not a crane), well before helicopters were built that could actually do such things.

360. The Spanish Peaks (West Spanish Peak, 13,626 ft, and East Spanish Peak, 12,683 ft) are east of, and separate from, the Culebra Range of the Sangre de Cristo Mountains and would have been about thirty-six miles behind and to the right of C.K. at this point of his journey. However, the Culebra Range of the Sangre de Cristo Mountains includes two peaks that may have been what he saw as the "twins": Vermejo Peak (13,723 ft) and Culebra Peak (14,047 ft). These are about forty miles due west of Raton Pass, were likely visible from the summit of the Pass, and would have passed behind him as he headed south over it.

361. It is accurate for him to have claimed "it is said that…" because there are numerous examples of this characterization found in literature for at least fifteen years prior to C.K.'s journey, such as the excerpt below from *The Burlington's Number One* (1904), the obvious source of his perceptions:

"Among all the mountain kingdoms Colorado seems to stand as easily first in material wealth as in physical adornment. This is saying a very great deal, for, scenically, Colorado is without a peer, not even Switzerland and her Alps offering more than a fair comparison. […] Its crowning peak, Mont Blanc, is 15,784 feet high, is the world's most famous and most often name of the mountains of the modern world. […] Some of the beautiful and famous parks of Colorado have their lowest depths higher than the average height of the Alpine chain."

362. Although C.K. drew his elevation data from the railroad brochure, the recorded elevation of Mont Blanc has varied over time. The most widely reported elevation of Mont Blanc is 15,781, a figure published as early as 1918. But there were other elevations published earlier, such as one in 1915, which cited the elevation as being 15,974 feet. C.K.'s use of 15,784 is further indication of an unattributed railroad brochure being used as a source for some of the particulars he included in his book.

363. It appears C.K.'s citation of 7,620 feet as the elevation at the top of Raton Pass also came from railroad literature. This elevation was used in numerous period publications, and reflected the highest elevation of the railroad tunnel. The road up over Raton Pass was at least 225 feet higher. The USGS *New Mexico-Colorado Brilliant Quadrangle* 15 Minute Series, 1915, depicts the highest elevation on the road over Raton Pass as being 7,889 feet. The USGS *New Mexico Tin Pan Canyon Quadrangle* 7.5 Minute Series, 1971, depicts the elevation at the border at exactly 7,845 feet. The fifty-four-foot difference may be due to the fact that the *Brilliant* elevation is marked about 1,000 feet south of the Colorado/New Mexico border (the highest point on the road), whereas *Tin Pan* is marked on the road at the border.

364. C.K. snapped the photograph depicted in Figure 110 (next page) at the top of Raton Pass looking into New Mexico.

Figure 110: The Top of Raton Pass.
Source: C.K.'s personal slide collection.

365. In 1919, the nature of the first human inhabitants of New Mexico was unknown, but a series of discoveries in the 1930s revealed human presence near Clovis, New Mexico some 12,000 years earlier.

366. Babylon was a key kingdom in ancient Mesopotamia from around 1800-600 BC.

367. Although the Hohokam and the Anasazi peoples did perfect large-scale irrigation methods in Arizona and New Mexico, the consensus today seems to be that these irrigation systems were developed at least 1,200 years after Babylon was a "going concern." For example:

- The Hohokam in Arizona began building canals in the area around 600 AD. By 1100 to 1450, they had built 500 miles of canals irrigating 110,000 acres to provide food for up to 80,000 people. Their descendants survive as members of the Tohono O'odham Nation.

- The Anasazi (the Navajo word for "the Ancients") lived in cliff dwellings in the Chaco Canyon area in northwestern New Mexico, an area with limited surface water running through washes and arroyos and then evaporating.

Around 900 AD, they began diverting water from the upper mesa into canals about fifteen feet wide and four feet deep, with the water then being directed by a series of gates and locks into fields, ponds, and small reservoirs. By 1300, however, a series of droughts caused famine and migration from the area and their culture was assimilated by the Hopi, Zuni, and Pueblo societies.

368. The establishment in Raton where C.K. had dinner cannot be identified. In the *1913-1914 New Mexico State Business Directory* (the closest year readily available), six restaurants or restaurateurs are listed in Raton, in addition to three hotels.

369. The bridge over the Canadian River on the road C.K. took was 8.25 miles south of Raton, so his estimate of ten miles is reasonable. The Canadian River originates from watershed northwest of Raton in Colorado and is the longest tributary of the Arkansas River (906 miles) running through New Mexico, Texas, and Oklahoma.

370. Today, the convention is that the Sangre de Cristo *Range* is entirely within Colorado. However, the Sangre de Cristo *Mountains* form a shallow arc from the area of Salida in Colorado (forty miles west of Cañon City) to the area between Santa Fe and Las Vegas in New Mexico.

371. On July 17, 1919 (the calculated date of this stop), sunset in the area was at about 8:15 p.m. and the half-moon rose at 10:47 p.m., so there would have been some moonlight in the area.

372. It appears that this "break in the fence" was about fifteen miles southwest of Raton and was the north end of the road that tracked due South toward Maxwell, a road that is now identified as New Mexico State Road 445.

373. This "mystery road" from Raton that C.K. observed continuing straight continues along the base of the Sangre de Cristo Mountains toward Taos. However, it first reaches Cimarron—about forty-one miles southwest of Raton—before heading into the mountains, and is now part of US Route 64.

374. The wagon ruts for the old Santa Fe Trail remain visible in some places even today. The photo of parallel tracks (Figure 111) was taken in approximately 1939 near C.K.'s route, about twenty miles southwest of Wagon Mound, NM.

Figure 111: Santa Fe Trail Wagon Ruts Near Fort Union, New Mexico.
Source: Courtesy Palace of the Governors Photo Archives (NMHM/DCA), Negative Number HP.2007.20.105. Photograph by David Wyatt.

375. The *Cynomys ludovicianus* species of prairie dogs, known as the black-tailed prairie dog (Figure 112), is native to the Pacific Southwest of the United States where C.K. saw them.

Figure 112: Prairie Dogs.
Source: US Fish & Wildlife Service. Photograph by Curtis J. Carley.

376. "hove": An old English word used meaning "heave." In this context, it means that C.K. felt the car had "to make an effort to raise or lift oneself; to struggle, lift with difficulty."

377. Santa Fe was about 135 miles of driving from Springer, New Mexico. El Paso, TX, is another 300 miles south of Santa Fe.

378. El Paso, Texas, is less than 300 miles—as the crow flies—from Springer, NM. Even taking the roads of the day through Santa Fe, it would have only been 435 miles of road.

379. The terms "wings" and "mudwings" appear to be interchangeable with "mud-guards" and, in England, these terms referred to what Americans called "fenders" or "fender extensions." Here C.K. is describing a car without fenders and running boards.

380. Wagon Mound gets its name from the unusual shape of a nearby butte that looked like a covered wagon, and so it became a landmark for those traveling on the Santa Fe Trail in the mid-19th Century. The photograph in Figure 113 was taken around 1887 and shows the railroad, several depot buildings, and the beginnings of the community of Wagon Mound. The photo is taken looking southeast with its namesake a mile distant.

Figure 113: The Town of Wagon Mound, *ca*. 1887.
Source: Courtesy Palace of the Governors Photo Archives (NMHM/DCA), Negative Number 057104. Photograph by J.R. Riddle.

381. If C.K. was twenty miles outside of Wagon Mound when the nut and key fell of his drive sprocket, he was about ten miles south of Springer on a road that ran close to the railroad tracks. In another two and a half miles, C.K. would pass through a settlement called Colmor, still seventeen and a half miles north of Wagon Mound.

382. There are two photographs in this book of C.K. wearing his knee-high water-tight boots: one is Figure 83, taken on Grand Ave., Kansas City; the other is Figure 194 taken on the front steps of the Lowell Observatory visitor center in Flagstaff.

383. Although it is possible that one of the restaurants closed after 1907, the community profile in *The Spanish American* stated there were *two* restaurants.

384. There were at least three times as many "Mexican-Americans" living in the village of Wagon Mound than the two hundred C.K. reported. The 1920 US census data reflects a total of 875 residents. The data also suggests that about 85% of the residents were born in New Mexico and spoke Spanish as their first language.

385. This news may have reached Wagon Mound due to a report on the front page of the *Albuquerque Journal* on July 19, 1919 (see Figure 114). These events occurred *very* far west of Santa Fe—in Arizona, actually—between Williams and Seligman.

100 MOTOR TOURISTS STRANDED IN ARIZONA

[BY MORNING JOURNAL SPECIAL LEASED WIRE]

Flagstaff, Ariz., July 18.—Approximately 100 automobile parties principally eastern tourists en route to California, are reported stranded in the mud between Williams and Seligman, Ariz., on the national old trails highway as a result of the recent heavy rains.

A heavy shower here late today brought the total precipitation for the past two weeks to 6.50 inches. The normal rainfall for July and August is 5.09 inches.

Figure 114: "100 Motor Tourists Stranded in Arizona" Article.
Source: *Albuquerque Journal*, July 19, 1919. Page 1.

386. Figure 115 is a photograph C.K. took approaching Wagon Mound. The southbound road into Wagon Mound approaches from the east and the namesake butte is about one mile southeast of the settlement, which is why the butte is out of view to the left.

Figure 115: Approaching Wagon Mound.
Source: C.K.'s personal slide collection.

387. This reference to *John Bull* is noteworthy. During WWI, "write to *John Bull*" was something that British soldiers would say to one another in much the same way C.K. used it here. ("I'm doing this and, if you don't like it, you can write to *John Bull* about it!"). At the time, *John Bull* was a periodical weekly publication in England. The frequent suggestions being made to write to *John Bull* caused so many random complaints to be sent to *John Bull* that the publication's mailbox was often overwhelmed. Ironically, *John Bull* was published by Odham's Press—the same publisher that published C.K.'s *Mammoth Book of Working Models* around 1940.

CHAPTER XIV

NEW MEXICO

I set out from Wagonmound with a light heart and a heavy stomach.

The road ran parallel with the rail for a mile, then crossed over by a level crossing and continued parallel on the other side. I did not get far. No doubt there had been unusual rain; great fields were now lakes with the grass bottom not always visible; little streams, normally no more than the size of a small spring, were now swollen rivers. These crossed the road in places. The road was fenced in. And thereby hangs a tale.

After precisely half an hour I found myself just three miles advanced,[388] and in the midst of a hopeless chaos of sun-dried emaciated mud. I had "explored every avenue" of the road, but found none possible of negotiation. Bit by bit I dragged Lizzie back and returned to the level-crossing. Come what may I would try the track. Even if the sleepers[389] shook my very bones to powder it would be better than eternally forging through the mud of New Mexico.

On each side of the road where it crossed the rails the track was guarded by a satanic device in the form of spikes and knife-edges skilfully arranged and extending to a distance of several yards.[390] The function of these was evidently to prevent cattle and other animals straying on the line. Traversing these was no easy task. If one did not ride on top of the spikes, one's tyres wedged in between the knives. Once past, the rest seemed easy. But things are not what they seem, especially on railroad tracks. The sleepers were not ballasted and were anything but level. There was no room outside the track, for it was steeply banked, and the sleepers projected beyond the rails into space. At every few hundred yards the track ran over a brick bridge spanning a bog or a stream. The bridge was just the width of the rails apart. But when it came to riding—ugh! As every sleeper was passed, the wheels fell momentarily into the intervening space between it and the next, and a series of sudden, sharp shocks was hammered through Lizzie's poor frame as each sleeper in turn was struck by the front wheel. The faster I went the quicker and smaller were the shocks, and above a certain speed it was quite tolerable running.

I was just getting up a comfortable speed when I imagined I heard the whistle of a locomotive behind. This was discouraging and certainly unexpected. I stopped quickly and looked back. Sure enough there was a train coming, but it was easily half a mile away. To go forward in the hope of out-pacing it would be useless. There was not even room to get off the track, for once I got down the steep bank, I knew it would be next to impossible to get back again, or to get anywhere, for that matter.

Neither was there room to turn round and go back.

More than ever before did it appear to me that discretion was better than valour.

So I commenced to push Lizzie backwards to the level crossing, prepared to roll sideways over the bank if I found the train got there first.

I was just beginning to feel sure about winning the race, and judged that I should get there with a good hundred yards to spare. I reached the crossing, but as naturally as one would expect, the back wheel wedged tight between the knives of the cow-guard.

Would she budge? No.

As I struggled and heaved (I could not look on and see Lizzie go west in such an absurd fashion), the "California Limited" bore down upon me.[391] Fortunately American trains do not always go so fast as they might; at any rate, not so fast as one thinks they should when one is travelling in them.

With a final desperate lunge, Lizzie yielded to my efforts and came unstuck. No time was lost in getting out of the way. Fifteen seconds afterwards the train rolled by at a modest thirty. She had evidently not got properly under way since her stop at Wagonmound.

I returned to the mud-hole like a smacked puppy with its tail between its legs, and reflected on what might have been.

But it was no use. I stuck again.

This time I was well armed with refreshments. I had bought six bottles of a ginger-pop concoction from the last village.[392] I carried one in each pocket and the other two as reserves, only to be used in case of great emergency, enveloped in the blanket strapped on the carrier.

I drank one bottle at the close of every engagement with the road. But after an hour I was still no farther ahead. I reclined on the bank and waited for something to turn up.

Fact revealed itself stranger than fiction once more. Something turned up very speedily. It came in the form of "Marmon" touring car,[393] bearing a Californian number-plate. I had taken the precaution, of course, to leave Lizzie in the right spot, so that no disinclined passer-by could get through if he wanted to. After all, one musn't RELY on everyone playing the Good Samaritan.

The two occupants of the car were courtesy itself. They not only assisted me in lifting Lizzie over the *pièce de résistance*,[394] but also showed considerable interest in me. Out here, where friendship between motorists is much more marked (almost as a matter of necessity), there is seldom any need for anxiety, and it is remarkable how potent a thing is this roadside courtesy. Practically every town I stopped at afterwards had heard of the strange traveller who was coming along on a 10 h.p. motor-cycle,[395] and awaited my arrival with interest.

"Had a fella in here on his way to California told us about you," said one garage hand, in the heart of Arizona. "Said you'd be here sooner or later."

"Oh yes? And how long ago was that?" I queried.

"Um—guess well over a couple of weeks ago." (The word "fortnight"[396] is unknown in America.)[397]

Such little incidents happened many times, and these, coupled with the amazing reports that had been circulated by the Western Press about me[398] since that inflammatory article on "Roads," etc., in the *Kansas City Star*, had generally managed to achieve for me quite a notorious reputation in most towns long before I ever rattled into their midst.

It was now nearly fifty miles to the next town.[399] I pushed ahead as fast as I could to reach it before dark. Progress, however, was slow. In places where the road was not fenced, I rode upon the rocky prairie. It was, for the most part, a considerable improvement, and one could ride around the bogs and mud-holes instead of crossing them.

Never had I been in such wild and barren country. It was quite beyond hope of cultivation in most places, being strewn with rough stones, rocks, and boulders, and only sparsely covered with meagre-looking grass which, in its efforts to keep alive at all, had to arrange itself in small tufts dotted here and there in order to derive the maximum nutriment from the scanty, unfruitful soil. The country itself changed from flat to hilly as the Sangre de Cristo range once more drew nearer,[400] When it became hilly, great rocks projected through the surface of the trail, which seldom or never swerved to avoid them.

The trail itself resolved itself later on into no more than a mere medley of ruts and grass-bare strips of all widths, running and crossing each other at all angles and in all directions. There was no time to look around and enjoy the wild scenery or study the ever-changing sky-line; it was "eyes on the road" all the time. It was quite impossible to dodge more than a fraction of the rocks and boulders, and one was always abruptly brought back to stern reality, if for an instant one's thoughts diverged to other things, by a sudden shock from one's front wheel, or a sickening crash on the bottom or side of the crank-case.

It was a slow job, and travelling was more in the line of a mountain goat than a motor-cycle. I was ultimately satisfied if I could average eight or ten miles an hour.

After thirty miles of this, I was surprised to discern ahead something which looked like a caravan.[401] There were two vehicles, apparently joined together, but with no visible means of locomotion. Nevertheless they moved slowly. I judged that some enthusiast of the "See America first" order had converted a Ford into a travelling home, or maybe a wandering tribe of gipsies had become sufficiently modernized to appreciate the benefits of auto v. horse transport.

I caught them up and stopped to have a chat. Both sides seemed curious at the other's means of locomotion, and wanted to know the why and the wherefore.

The team, I found, consisted as I had surmised of a Ford chassis, on which had been skilfully built a caravan body. Behind was a trailer, on two wheels, and of construction similar to, but smaller than, the other. Evidently one was the parlour, kitchen, and store-room, and the other the bedroom.

The driver stopped his engine and jumped down.

"Good day, sir; how do?" I inquired.

"Very fit, thanks; you the same? How in Heavens'n earth d'you manage to get along on THAT?"

"Mostly by plenty of bad language and good driving," I returned." And what in the world are you doing in this benighted place with THAT?"

"Oh, I'm goin' west. . . ."

"Shouldn't be at all surprised at that!"

"I'm bound for somewhere in Arizona. Come from Chicago. Fed up with the life there, so I'm out for a change. Looking for a likely spot to settle down where there's plenty of fresh air."

"What! You've come all the way from Chicago on THAT?" I inquired incredulously.

"Sure enough."

"How long has it taken you?" (I was already becoming sufficiently Americanized, the reader will observe.)

"Best part of three months."

"How many with you?"

"Wife and two children. Here they are."

"Well, I wish you luck, brother; but it doesn't strike me that the roads are ideal from a furniture-removing point of view, so to speak."

"Roads?" (Here he waxed furious: I had touched a sore spot.) "Don't talk to me about roads. The gor-dem Government oughta a' bin shot that provided roads like this. Just think that across a civilized country like America there isn't a dem road fit to drive a cow on to!"

"Ah, I've thought that way myself; but there's a fallacy in the observation, old man."

"What d'ya mean?"

"Just this—who told you America was a civilized country?"

Long pause.

"Aye, you've said it," and he relapsed into a stony silence.

I bade him farewell, and left him scrambling slowly over the rocks and mounds, while the caravan rocked from side to side and jerked its weary way along. I reflected also that, after all, THAT was the way to see the country.

At dark I was but a few miles from Las Vegas.[402] Once, again heavy clouds rolled over the sky. Rain began to fall. My spirits did likewise. I wondered whether it was a habit. But what cared I for rain or mud? By now surely I was proof against them. I struggled on. And ultimately I got there.

Las Vegas is a fair-sized town.[403] In order of merit it is the second largest in New Mexico. The first is Albuquerque and the third is the capital, Santa Fé.[404] There are no more towns of any size in New Mexico.[405] Including native Indian villages there are, in addition, in the whole of New Mexico, some seventy or eighty small towns and very small villages, making the total population of the whole State about 50,000.[406] When it is understood that New Mexico is about four times the area of England, the reader will be able to form an idea of the sparsity of its people.

Now most people would have predicted that immediately on my arrival in Las Vegas I would have sought out the best hotel and consumed a big square meal. I did no such thing. I went to the movies instead.[407]

Then I returned and went to bed, half wondering whether to standardize the one-meal-per-day experiment for future requirements.[408]

In the morning it was not raining, but all the time until midday it showed signs of just commencing.

At midday I became impatient and started out for Santa Fé. I had just left the outskirts of the town when it did finally and irrevocably decide to rain after all. I continued for five miles,[409] when a Ford car hove in sight. "Here goes for a chat and some straight dope on the subject of roads to come," said I to myself and stopped. The Ford stopped also. It had two occupants, a man and his wife. They both looked bored, so we made a merry party.

"What's the road like back there?" I inquired.

"Mighty rough—mighty rough. They get better the further east we come."

"Do you think I shall be able to get through to the coast?"

"Well, it's mighty hard riding, but I guess you ought to be able to get through. Oh, but stay a minute, there's a big wash-out before you get to Santa Fé—big stone bridge washed clean away with the floods, not a trace of it left. I don't know much about motor-cycles, but I guess you could get across the river all right. You'll want to be careful though. There was a whole cartload of people washed down the river last week, so they say; all of 'em went west, horse and cart and all!"[410]

"Ah well, that'll add a bit of excitement to the trip. I'm good at crossing rivers."

"Ugh! Guess you'll not be looking out for any excitement time you've gotten to Santa Fé!"

I was particularly interested in these people's domestic arrangements. Without a doubt I have never seen an ordinary touring car, much less a Ford, equipped and arranged in such excellent style. They carried with them a portable stove on which could be cooked any dish they required. They carried ample supplies of vegetables, fruits, eggs, butter, bacon, bread and tinned goods, and even tanks of fresh water for culinary and drinking purposes. This is certainly a wise precaution, because it is never safe to drink water from even the most tempting of rivers in the West. Furthermore, they had two collapsible beds, which could be laid upon the top of the seats from back to front, and which were fully equipped with feather mattresses and blankets! One would think that all this paraphernalia would have taken up an enormous amount of room. Not so. Apart from the fact that the back part of the car was neatly covered in, there was not the slightest sign that the car was anything but an ordinary Ford with a lot of luggage in the back.

I bade them farewell only on the strict condition that if the rain continued I should return and share their supper. They would not be far away, they told me. The *plat du jour*[411] was salmon and Mayonnaise sauce, above all things!

Still, it is a habit of mine never to go back, however tempting the circumstances. At intervals I passed a few Mexicans driving teams of horses, and once more I was alone with Lizzie. As a compensation for the drizzling rain, the scenery was perfect. The trail had now swerved into rugged, mountainous scenery, thickly wooded, wild and picturesque in the extreme. It was almost ridiculous to watch how the narrow trail dodged in and out of the trees, cutting across small forests of cedar, aspen, and pine, curving to right and left round some awkward prominence, now dipping down suddenly into a little valley, and then darting up over hilly slopes all strewn with loose rocks and broken with jutting crags.

We were approaching the Pecos,[412] the haunts of the bear and mountain-lion, and the headquarters of numerous tourists and campers attracted thither by the fine fishing, shooting, riding, and mountain-climbing.

Occasionally, as one took a sudden swerve around the face of a projecting hill, one would see, away there in the valley beyond, a Mexican village set back from the road, and would marvel at the strange sight of the square mud buildings, congregated together in such unique and regular formation. The brick-red hue of the houses was so near to that of the surrounding country as almost to hide the village altogether from view, even though it was right "under one's nose."

My first impression of a Mexican village was one of amazement. To think that several hundred people can live together in those single-storied mud huts in peace and comfort, with ne'er a sheet of glass in the windows and seldom a door within the door-posts—well, it was absurd! But my second impression absorbed the first entirely, and was one of appreciation for the primitive beauty of these native dwellings. It is a beauty that lingers in one's memory, a beauty that lies in natural flowing forms, defying the unrelenting sharp corners of modern architecture. And I have seen many "adobe" houses in New Mexico that would be far more comfortable to live in than many that have sheltered my bones in Europe!

I was meditating thus when the sound of rushing waters reached my ears. Sure enough, the road ended abruptly, like a cliff, and continued in like fashion on the opposite side. Between, and several feet below, swirled the River Pecos.[413] It was still swollen with rain from the mountains, although it had evidently been much higher recently.

Not a soul was about. There was a solitary Mexican house on a hill to one side. I contemplated the river in silence, save for the sound of its waters as they swirled over the rocky bed and now and then dislodged a weighty boulder.

To the right two rickety planks had been erected, supported partly by ropes and partly by vertical props from rocks in the river, for pedestrians to cross. I wondered what pedestrian would find himself in these parts!

To the left, a detour had somehow been dug at an angle of about 20 degrees to the water's edge. In the opposite bank a similar detour had been dug, but at an angle of about 30 degrees. Evidently several cars had already passed through the river that way. But a car is not a motor-cycle. I meditated. A car on four wheels could not only hold its own better in the middle of the torrent, but could also get up the opposite bank easier. One thing was quite certain—even if I got through the river all right, it would require a superhuman effort to push the machine up the steep, greasy incline on the opposite side.

I reconnoitred up and down the river bank in the hope of finding a better place to cross, but the quest was in vain. The banks grew steeper and higher and the river-bed wider and rougher than ever. I returned to Lizzie and said a prayer for her. Then I took off my tunic and removed the bag and blanket from the carrier.

I judged that it would be expedient to rely upon momentum as far as possible, as the engine would certainly not run for long under water, so, starting the engine once more, I put in the bottom gear and charged down the greasy slope into the river.

There was a tremendous hiss, and a cloud of steam went heavenwards. The engine stopped long before I reached the middle, and the smooth nature of the loose rocks that formed the river-bed was treacherous for two wheels. There was nothing for it when the engine stopped but to dismount quickly and push. When I reached the middle, the water was up to my waist, and it took most of my strength to keep the machine upright and hold it against the force of the river, which swirled around the cylinders and washed up against the tank. I managed to avoid being washed away, however, thanks to the great weight of the machine, and got her to the opposite bank.

It was a relief to be out of the water, but the task still remained of climbing up the bank. I exerted all my strength, but the slope was so greasy that neither my feet nor the wheels would grip on anything. Twice or thrice I got it half-way up, only to slither down to the river again *tout ensemble*. Then I tried the expedient of wedging a huge stone under the back wheel and pushing an inch or two at a time. But it was no use. The grease was impossible. I laboured with it for a quarter of an hour.

I was just on the point of giving it up after we had all slid down to the bottom once again, when a huge Mexican appeared on the scene. He was evidently the owner of the house on the opposite bank, and looked hefty enough to lift a tram.

We pushed with our united effort. We slipped and slithered and wallowed about, but we got to the top. I breathed a sigh of relief, rewarded the Mexican liberally, and walked across the plank to bring my tunic and luggage.

Lizzie had never been so clean since the day she came out of the crate. Every speck of mud and dirt had been washed clean away, and her pristine beauty was revealed once again. It was an hour's task to dry the carburettor and the magneto and get the engine running. It was getting dark when I got going again. The rain had stopped, but the mud was terrible. Every half-mile I had to stop and poke it out of the mud-guards with a screwdriver.

Eventually, just before dark, I reached the tiny Mexican village of Pecos,[414] called after the river in the locality. It consisted mainly of a general store and "rooming-house" for the benefit of stranded travellers. A rooming-house, by the way, is a kind of boarding-house but with no accommodation for meals.[415]

At Pecos I was surprised to see an Indian motor-cycle and side-car "parked" on a strip of green, which in generations to come would be the plaza or square. Examination revealed it to be a most remarkable machine. It was equipped with tool-boxes galore at every available place and, strange to remark, there was a small emery wheel mounted skilfully on the top tube and driven by a round belt from a pulley on the engine shaft[416] There was also a small hand-vice clipped to the frame, and numerous other small tools and fitments, which, to say the least, were not usually found in the equipment of a motor-cycle.

"Well," I said to myself, "if all this paraphernalia is required to get a motor-cycle across to the coast, I'm in for a rough time."

But I was relieved to find that it was the property of a tinsmith who, out for a holiday, combined business with pleasure, and repaired people's tanks and pots and pans wherever he went! In this way he not only defrayed his travelling expenses, but made a far better income than he used to get in his home-town in Ohio.

He was a tall, burly-looking chap, and greeted me with effusion. In like manner did I welcome him. The sight of another motor-cyclist removed my worst apprehensions.

"Strike me pink!" quoth I, "I thought I was the only madman in this part of the world!"

He glanced at my number-plate.

"Gee, brother, put it right there. I wuz beginnin' to think I'd never see another motorsickle agin; you goin' to the coast?"

"That's where I'm heading for, but of late I'm not so sure about getting there as I was when I left New York."

"Oh, boy, yew'll git there all right if yew've come this far—I said it; but say, there's some smart bits o' travellin' to do ahead on yer!"

"What? Is it worse than what I've passed?"

"Waal, I've bin there an' got back—travellin' with the missus here—an' I tell you, the road gets better the further east I come. And what's more'n that, brother, yew've got some mighty warm times ahead before you see California—like goin' through Hell, it is. Wait till you find yourself in the middle o' the Mohave Desert with the sun beatin' down at 130 in the shade, and no shade—no nothin' except prickly pears and funny-lookin' cactuses and a bit of sage-bush here and there. Say, boy, wait till you see piles o' bones and carcasses by the score lyin' at the side o' the road, an' yew'll begin to think it's warm, all right. Whatever you do, boy, take water with yer. Yew'll drink GALLONS of it!"

"How long have you been here, then?" I asked.

"Nigh on a couple o' weeks, brother. We've bin waitin' fer the rain to clear off."

Truly a bright prospect.

I slept well that night, in spite of the fact that my day's mileage was only thirty,[417] and awoke to find the sky clear and promising.

I spent the morning in tuning Lizzie and making minor adjustments and preparation. I commissioned my tinsmith friend to make me a new accumulator box,[418] my own having become entirely disintegrated with the vibration. For 1,000 miles it had been held together with straps fastened tightly round it to the frame.

The distance to Santa Fé was only twenty-five miles, so I judged I should be able to reach it that day.[419]

Those twenty-five miles took four hours. I will not attempt to describe those four hours. They were filled to the brim with mud, rain, wash-outs, and bridgeless rivers. In many places there were great "washes" of sand brought down from the hill-sides that nearly completely obliterated the trail as it struggled across the mountains.[420]

It was a very weary motor-cyclist indeed who rattled into Santa Fé at 5.30 that afternoon.[421] And that motor-cyclist had quite made up his mind to have a few days' rest before anything else happened his way.

With a deep sigh of relief I leant Lizzie up against the pavement opposite the "Montezuma Hotel."[422] With heavy, aching limbs and sodden, mud-stained clothes, I walked towards the door.

It opened ahead of me.

"Ah! how do you do, Captain Shepherd? We've been expecting you for over a week. Come right in. We know ALL about you. Here, James, take Captain Shepherd up to his room at once. No, don't bother to say anything. Just go and have a good hot bath."

It was the voice of an angel that spoke!

CHAPTER 14 NOTES

388. C.K. would not have passed through any communities in the three miles he drove south of Wagon Mound in a half an hour (therefore averaging six mph). The road ran alongside the railroad tracks for several miles south of Wagon Mound and crossed it in numerous places. C.K. decided to go back to the last crossing to get off the tracks. Bond Siding, a railroad stop, was 4.8 miles south of Wagon Mound, but C.K. returned to the auto road before reaching it.

389. "sleeper": A primarily British term, referring in the US to the wood railroad ties that lay in the gravel bed below the steel rails.

390. Figure 116 is from a patent for a railroad crossing cattle guard dated 1897.

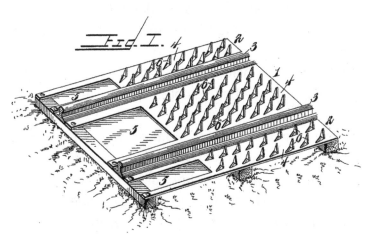

Z. WIGGS.
RAILWAY CATTLE GUARD.

No. 594,050.   Patented Nov. 23, 1897.

Figure 116: Z. Wiggs' Railway Cattle Guard, Patented November 23, 1897.
Source: US Patent and Trademark Office.

391. The No. 3, known as the California Limited, ran daily from Chicago to San Francisco via La Junta, over Raton Pass, to Albuquerque and beyond. However, the #3 was an express train and did not normally stop in Wagon Mound. Examination of timetables and newspaper clippings from 1907, 1918, and 1921

indicate that four trains ran westbound through Wagon Mound on the Atchison, Topeka & Santa Fe Railway (ATSF). Only two stopped at Wagon Mound:

- No. 1, "The Scout" (1921): Stopped at Wagon Mound at 12:16 p.m. (1907) and passed through Lamy, NM, at 5:40 p.m. (1907) or 4:50 p.m. (1921).

- No. 7, "Fargo Fast" (1918): Stopped at Wagon Mound at 4:00 p.m. (1907).

Since C.K. reported the train had passed him at slow speed—and because he believed it had stopped in Wagon Mound—it seems most likely that this train was the ATSF No. 1, known as Scout, not the No. 3 (California Limited). The 1907 timetable indicates that the California Limited would have rolled through Wagon Mound at 5:30 a.m., yet this encounter occurred at about 12:20 p.m.—so it was most likely the No. 1, the Scout, if it was on schedule.

392. The "last village" where he purchased his ginger pop soft drinks was presumably Wagon Mound. It is possible, however, that he was referring to a village *prior* to Wagon Mound, such as Nolan or Colmor. The first community south of Wagon Mound was Watrous. It was about twenty-three miles south of Wagon Mound, but still twenty-two miles from Las Vegas (which he later reports having reached in the evening, as it grew dark). Ginger pop and sarsaparilla became popular during Prohibition because they did not contain any alcohol but had strong flavor or "bite." In the second edition of *The American Language* (1921), author H.L. Mencken included a footnote regarding "ginger pop" and its meaning on both sides of the Atlantic (italics in original):

> "An English correspondent writes: 'Did the Americans invent *ginger-ale* and *ginger-pop*? Then why don't they make some that is drinkable? Do you know of a decent unimported dry ginger? *Ginger-pop*, in England, is *ginger-beer*, an article rarely seen in America. *Stone-ginger* is the only temperance drink worth a damn, perhaps because, properly made, it contains a certain amount of alcohol. It is brewed, not charged with CO. Where in America can I buy *stone-ginger*; that is to say, *ginger-beer* from a brewery, sold in stone bottles? We say *pop* in England, but not *ginger-pop*.'"

393. The Marmon Touring Car of 1916 had a dark blue body, black running gear, and cream-colored wheels. It was powered by a six-cylinder 33.75 horsepower

engine. Marmon made a five-passenger model and a seven-passenger model (Figure 117), with the extra two seats costing only fifty dollars more.

Marmon Model 34, 7-pass. Touring Car, $2950. Also 5-pass. Touring Car, $2900; 4-pass. Roadster, $2950; 7-pass. Limousine, $4200-$5250; 5-pass. Sedan, $3950; Town Car, $4500-$5350. Made by Nordyke & Marmon Co.

Figure 117: 1916 Marmon Model 34 Touring Car.
Source: "Seventeenth Annual Complete Car Review" in *Automobile Trade Journal,* Vol. XXI, No. 6, December 1916. Page 186.

394. *"pièce de résistance"*: A French term with the literal meaning "piece which has staying power." Most often it is used linguistically to characterize the most important, or remarkable, add-on feature to conclude something (such as a fancy dessert after an exquisite entrée).

395. The advertised power rating for the 1919 Henderson was 14.2 horsepower, not ten.

396. "fortnight": A unit of time equal to fourteen days. It derives from the old English *fēowertyne niht*, meaning "fourteen nights."

397. Even accounting for correcting irregularities in the chronology of C.K.'s journey, it had been no more than eight days since he had left Kansas City—although apparently it seemed much longer to him.

398. C.K.'s writings on road conditions in the *Kansas City Star* were referenced in an article in the *Santa Fe New Mexican* prior to his arrival. This is the only advance notice that has been discovered to date, but it seems likely there were others.

399. The next town of any size after Wagon Mound was Las Vegas. However, the latter was only forty-five miles from the former, so this statement that he was "nearly fifty miles to the next town" does not make any sense. It could be that this encounter occurred at some other point during C.K.'s trip; or, it could be that his estimate of miles remaining to Las Vegas was an exaggeration.

400. This is a generally a correct reference because he turned mostly south of the Sangre de Cristo Mountains after Raton, but the route began curving west toward Santa Fe after Wagon Mound.

401. "caravan": This word is used in England, Australia, and New Zealand to refer to a furnished vehicle used as a dwelling. Back in 1919, this was typically a trailer towed behind an automobile, but now it would also include motorized recreational vehicles. C.K. describes a customized Ford pulling a trailer with both vehicles providing different housing functions.

402. Although it was dark, the road paralleled the railroad tracks in that area. He would have crossed the Onava rail station about eleven miles north of Las Vegas, which was likely the last type of settlement of any kind until reaching Las Vegas.

403. Although the *Official Hotel Red Book and Directory* (1920) reported that the population of Las Vegas, NM was 10,000, the *Abstract of the Fourteenth Census of the United States* of the same year reflected a Las Vegas population of 3,902. The *Abstract* listed another 4,304 people in the area using a Las Vegas Post Office address for a total of 8,206, which is an 18% increase over the 6,934 people recorded for 1910.

404. It is not clear what C.K. means by ordering them by "merit," but the populations of Albuquerque and Santa Fe according to the 1920 census were 15,157 and 7,236, respectively. (This is substantially different from the round numbers listed in the *Official Hotel Red Book and Directory* of the same year: 11,020 and 10,000, respectively.) If population was the measure of merit, he was probably correct.

405. C.K.'s assertion that there weren't "towns of any size" in New Mexico is not quite correct. According to the 1920 census, there were quite a few. The round and often inconsistent numbers in the *Official Hotel Red Book and Directory* from the same year suggest that the population numbers in the 1920 census are more representative of actual populations (Figure 118).

City	Population
Albuquerque	15,157
Las Vegas (including East Las Vegas P.O.)	8,208
Santa Fe	7,236
Roswell	7,033
Raton	5,544
Clovis	4,904
Las Cruces	3,969
Gallup	3,920
Deming	3,212
Tucumcari	3,117
Silver City	2,662

Figure 118: Populations of Towns in New Mexico in 1920.
Source: US Census Bureau.

406. In 1919, the population of New Mexico was well in excess of 50,000 people. The 1920 *Abstract of the Fourteenth Census of the United States* reflects a statewide population of over seven times that amount: 360,350. Even ten years earlier, the population reported by the census was 327,301.

407. C.K. probably spent the night in Las Vegas on or about Friday, July 18, 1919. According to IMDb, a total of 2,339 motion pictures were released that year. Without any newspaper or other records, it is unlikely that the film C.K. watched will ever be determined.

408. C.K. does not indicate where he stayed in Las Vegas, but he implies that it was not the best hotel in town. The following hotels were in operation in 1919, with nightly prices for American Plan (A.P.) with meals or European Plan (E.P.) without meals:

- Plaza Hotel: (E. P.) $1 up. Byron T. Mills, prop. Opened in 1882, the Plaza remains in operation. It is currently run by the same people who own the Castañeda.

- The Castañeda—A Fred Harvey Hotel: (A. P.) $4.50 up. 44 rooms. This hotel is being restored with hope of being ready for occupancy in the spring of 2019. Fred Harvey hotels were generally high-end, probably not where C.K. stayed in July 1919.

- La Pension Hotel: (E. P.) $1 up. W.V. Woods, prop. Still operating in 1930, current status unknown.

- The Troy Hotel: (E. P.) $1. M.A. Hagest, prop. Although in operation at least from 1915 through 1920, it is no longer in operation.

- Eldorado Hotel: (E.P) $1 and up. Twenty rooms. By 1972, it had been converted into offices and senior citizen center and, although the building is still standing at 514 Grand Avenue, it appears to be vacant.

409. The *Blue Book* (1918) Route 729 from Las Vegas to Santa Fe was seventy-three miles, so it was reasonable for C.K. to believe he could delay departure until later on and still reach Santa Fe the same day. If it took C.K. two miles to clear town—and then he drove five more miles before it started raining when he came upon the Ford heading in the opposite direction—he would have just passed a small community called Romero with slightly larger Tecolote still about five miles ahead.

410. Something like this did occur on Sunday, July 20, 1919, but it is highly unlikely that C.K. heard about it from fellow travelers on the road south of Las Vegas. Since it can be calculated that C.K. left Las Vegas on or about July 19, 1919, C.K. could not have heard about this tragic event because it had not yet occurred. In fact, an article about this tragedy appeared on the front page of *Santa Fe New Mexican* on July 21, 1919 (see Figure 119), the day after C.K. arrived. It seems more than coincidental that an article about C.K. being interviewed the

evening before appears on page three of this same issue. In terms of the incident being discussed, it occurred on July 20, 1919, nine miles west of Silver City, New Mexico (about 350 miles southwest of Las Vegas, NM). A family's wagon was overcome by water while trying to cross a swollen stream. Candelaria Galvan and her nine children were all washed downstream and died, but the husband/father lived to tell the tale.

411. *"plat du jour"*: A French term meaning a dish specially prepared by a restaurant on a particular day, in addition to the usual menu; also commonly known as the "daily special."

412. This is a reference to the Pecos River, not the town of Pecos.

413. If this was the Pecos River, the location would have been less than ½ mile north of San Jose, NM, which was a small town even in 1919.

414. The 1920 census data for Pecos, NM reflects a population of 692—almost all of whom were farmers and their families.

415. No records of boarding or rooming houses in Pecos have been discovered that might identify where C.K. might have spent the night. The search for such establishments was hampered by the lack of newspapers in the town in 1919. Additionally, rooming houses were the cheapest form of accommodation. Guests most likely heard about the rooming houses by word of mouth or a flyer at the general store.

FAMILY OF 10 ARE DROWNED

Hurley Mother And Her Nine Children Die in Flood

TORRENT WHIRLS WAGON AWAY

(By Leased Wire to New Mexican.)
Silver City, N. M., July 21.—Her 3-year-old infant clasped in her arms, Mrs. Candelaria Galvan, 36 year sold, of Hurley, N. M., and nine children were drowned nine miles east of here late yesterday when a wagon in which they were riding was swept away in a swollen stream. Five of the children, whose ages ranged from 2 to 15 years, were those of Mrs. Galvan.

Ramon Galvan, the woman's husband, had started on a trip to a nearby ranch to spend the day, accompanied by his family and the children of some friends. After crossing the creek, the team stalled on the grade and backed into the water. A torrent four feet high struck the wagon, lifting off the bed and overturning it. Galvan and his wife succeeded in extricating themselves from the wagon and both then tried to save the children, five of whom were rescued. In the effort, however, Mrs. Galvan was drowned.

The names of the nine children who perished, are Marcos Galvan, 3; Basllie Galvan, 5; Marie Galvan, 12; Sabas Galvan, 4; Caleria Galvan, 11; Calvador Gonales, 2; Galvan Gonales, 15; Thomas Gonales, 8; Lila Allison, 6.

Figure 119: "Family of Ten Drowned" Article.
Source: *Santa Fe New Mexican*, July 21, 1919. Page 1.

416. Although the motorcycle shown in Figure 120 appears to be a 1913 Reading Standard (not an Indian motorcycle as C.K. describes), it has been customized for much the same purpose, with an emery wheel on the rear rack and even a drive pulley to power the mechanic's shop grinder.

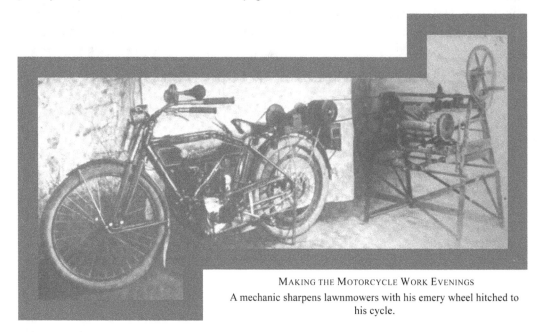

MAKING THE MOTORCYCLE WORK EVENINGS
A mechanic sharpens lawnmowers with his emery wheel hitched to
his cycle.

Figure 120: Making the Motorcycle Work Evenings.
Source: *Technical World Magazine,* Vol. 20, No. 5, January 1914. Page 748.

417. Although C.K. writes that his day's mileage was thirty miles, the *Blue Book* (1918) Route 729 reflects a distance of 47.6 miles from Las Vegas to Pecos.

418. This is most likely a reference to the "battery box" in front of the rear wheel that housed the battery and light switches. It was the term used in for such enclosures in period publications in England.

419. C.K.'s cited distance of twenty-five miles to Santa Fe was valid. The *Blue Book* (1918) Route 729 reflects a distance of 25.4 miles from Pecos to Santa Fe.

420. The photo in Figure 121 of the road conditions, including what appears to be a complete washout about a mile or two southwest of Pecos, looking southwest toward Santa Fe.

Figure 121: Photograph of Road Near Pecos Toward Santa Fe Taken by C.K.
Source: C.K.'s personal slide collection.

421. Considering the July 21, 1919 report in the *Santa Fe New Mexican*—as well as other known details—there is evidence that C.K. took the photo in Figure 122 as he arrived on the outskirts of Santa Fe on July 20, 1919 at about 5:30 p.m.

Figure 122: Photograph of Entering Santa Fe, New Mexico Taken by C.K.
Source: C.K.'s personal slide collection.

422. The Montezuma Hotel, built in stages beginning prior to 1883, was the only hotel in Santa Fe that advertised in the *Blue Book* (1918). The Montezuma is also the only hotel listed for Santa Fe in the 1920 *Official Hotel Red Book and Directory*; the rates on the American Plan were $3-$4 per night (up from $2.50 to $3.50 in the same publication in 1917). The photo of the hotel in Figure 123 is estimated to have been taken between 1900-1910. The building has been remodeled several times since then and its bottom floor currently houses a number of retail shops.

Figure 123: Montezuma Hotel, Water Street and Galisteo Street, Santa Fe, New Mexico.
Source: Courtesy Palace of the Governors Photo Archives (NMHM/DCA), Negative Number 014034.

CHAPTER XV

SANTA FÉ

Santa Fé is the most delightful of places. It has a charm all its own. It is small, quaint, and intensely old. It is far removed from other American towns—just as far as west is from east. It represents the quintessence of New Mexico, and at the same time—so it is alleged—sets the standard of art in America.

The first words of a mediocre Easterner when he enters the *plaza*[423] of Santa Fé are "Heavens'n earth! what kind of a hole have I struck now?" But if he has a soul underlying that eastern veneer of his, if he has an appreciation for art and beauty in architecture unimpaired by familiarity with gigantic skyscrapers, he will repent those words. His disdainful grin as he first catches sight of the Art Museum[424] and sees an edifice of mud with ne'er a corner that could be called sharp, will fade slowly from his face, and once he has recovered from the shock of the "sudden uniqueness" of everything, his look will turn to one of wonder and admiration.

Santa Fé is small. It contains no more than 6,000 inhabitants—a curious mixture of Mexicans, Indians, and Americans.[425] Its population, moreover, is at a standstill. As the capital of a State of 160,000 square miles, it seems ludicrous, until one reflects that there are but 50,000 people in the whole country. Of Spanish origin, it is laid out in Spanish style, with the *plaza* or public square in the centre. Around the *plaza* are arranged most of the more important buildings. These, with few exceptions, follow closely the "adobe" architecture of the "Pueblo" Indians, combined with the architecture of the later "Franciscan" Missions that were instituted by the Spanish Friars, who in the early days of colonization penetrated far into the continent.

In the forefront of every march and every exploration there was always the brown-robed Franciscan, bearing along with his crucifix the trowel and the book. To convert, to build, and to teach—these were the self-imposed tasks to which he consecrated his life.[426] Especially do we honour him as a builder. Living among a passionate people, who resented the intrusion of strange gods among their own, often surrounded by cruel and relentless foes, the type of his structures was determined by the conditions of his existence. There must be a church in which to preach the new religion, a convent in which to live, and along with these, a school in which he might give instruction. These must be connected and compactly placed to serve as a fortress against present enemies; and they must be massive, to withstand the ravages of time. There were eleven such churches in New Mexico alone prior to the landing of the *Mayflower*[427]—and more than fifty others were established during the century which followed.[428]

This is the only type of architecture that can be referred to as truly "American," saving perhaps the unenvied skyscraper of the East. This latter, however, belongs to no school and knows no creed; it is not indigenous to the soil or produced by environment, native material, or climate. Instead, it defiles the heavens and cuts the landscape into futuristic nightmares of edge and angle.

THE ART MUSEUM AT SANTA FÉ.

By far the choicest flower of this renaissance style is the New Art Museum at Santa Fé. Recently completed, it is admired by all, architects and laymen alike. It embodies the designs of six of the ancient Spanish Missions, three centuries old, some of which have now disappeared. The others are fast decaying with the ravages of time. The outlines of the Museum are plastic, smooth, and flowing, rising in curves and terraces, without stiffness, sharpness, or repetition. There is a noticeable lack of symmetry, contrasting so much with the style of the Californian Missions. Consequently, there is a different composition and an added charm with every new position or change of aspect. Inside are paintings and sketches of Indian, Mexican, and desert life and scenes, specimens of native handiwork, and an exhaustive library.

Across the road, on the opposite corner, is the Governor's Palace, the oldest governmental building in the States.[429] Its appearance would in modern eyes hardly justify the term "Palace." It is a very unimposing building of native architecture but contains relics, trophies, and works of art brought from all corners of the Western world. Within its adobe walls are housed prehistoric remains of the extinct civilization that thousands of years ago thrived in Western America.

But not only the public buildings of Santa Fé are of Pueblo construction. Many of the latest private edifices, both residential and commercial, are of this strange architecture. The offices and works of the "Santa Fé Water and Light Company"[430] give one the impression of its unique application to business buildings. But for sheer delight give me the private dwellings. It is beyond my power to convey an adequate impression of the soft beauty of one of these exquisitely-designed houses, with its smooth-flowing profiles, its shady "patio," open-air bathing pools and well-planned garden. One must go and see to understand and feel the charm of it all.

But from the Mexican houses as residences Heaven preserve me! Seldom do they boast more than one story; the roof is flat, and very often grass and weeds are found thriving thereon. The "adobe" walls are recovered from year to year throughout the ages as the hand of Time and the ravages of weather work their destructive way. It can almost be said that a Mexican house never grows old. The sun-baked mud that forms its walls withstands the weather to an extraordinary extent. There is a little house in a little street in the outskirts of Santa Fé, now uninhabited, from whose roof rises a notice-board: "This is the oldest house in America," it reads. It was supposed to have been built over 250 years ago.[431]

THE OLDEST HOUSE IN AMERICA, AT SANTA FÉ.

The citizens of Santa Fé are not progressive.[432] The climate is against them. They do not run any risk of over-exertion; a considerable time is spent in eating ices, drinking cold concoctions, and lounging about the *plaza* in the early hours of the afternoon.[433] Here it was that I developed this Western habit. In almost every Western town there is a central square shaded with many trees, or palms in the hottest places. The good citizen and the weary traveller alike are welcome here. They lie about on the grass, or sit on their toes as only a Westerner knows how. Thus pass the blazing hours. It is a treat to find oneself away from the eternal hustle and bustle of city life and in the midst of languid, easy-going freedom. I had several photographs that I took to the drug-store to be developed and printed.[434]

"Shall I call in to-night for them?" I said.

"To-night? Why, we won't be able to get them through for four days," he replied, amazed at my ridiculous presumption.

"But in New York they develop and print in one day only. Surely You're not behind New York?"

"Oh, we don't do things like that in this part of the country, friend; you've made a big mistake. Nobody hurries in New Mexico!"

By dint of special pleadings, I got the photographs in three days. They were nearly all ruined with having been hurried!

For three days I created quite a furore in Santa Fé. The news of my doings and misdoings was published daily in the *Santa Fé New Mexican* during my stay.[435] I evidently afforded just the right kind of newspaper fodder that New Mexico wanted. My fame had spread all the way from Kansas City long before I actually fell upon the anxious population. My article on Roads, etc., was reproduced immediately after its publication in Kansas, together with several caustic editorial comments.[436] Here is one example:—

"SEES AMERICA BY COW-PATH."

English Warrior gets little rest touring America by Motor-cycle.

"Roads? What roads? I haven't seen any roads. I have been following a place where cows had been walking. . . ."[437]

Here is another heading to a two-column "article":—

"COW-PATHS"—and not roads in America: —Verdict of British Royal Airman here on Motor-cycle.

And again (this headed a quarter-page "Report").

"BALLOON"—Only way to get over New Mexico roads, declares British Aviator.[438]

I was pounced upon immediately after my arrival. No sooner was I settled down in a good steaming hot bath (oh, joy untold!) than the telephone bell in my room rang. I let it go on ringing for two or three minutes. It would not stop. I jumped out and lifted the receiver.

"A reporter is here to see you, sir."

"Och, Hell! Tell him I'm having a bath," and I banged the receiver down and plunged again into the tub.

In a minute there was a knock at the door. "No use trying to shake off an American reporter," I told myself. . . . "Come in!"

The result appeared in next morning's paper[439] not the result of MY observations, be it noted, however. Amongst other statements the following was laid to my charge:—

"In my opinion the old Prairie-Schooner is far superior to a motor-car (for travelling in New Mexico). If you can't get a schooner, try horse-back travel. I really believe some horses could get through the mud and dodge the boulders. (It was almost funny there!)... But the ideal form of transportation over these United States is a big dirigible, say 700 ft. in length, modelled on Great Britain's R.34. (It had just recently crossed the Atlantic, hence the introduction.)[440] ... I might have suggested the use of an aeroplane, but I have been told two aviators got stuck in Santa Fé last winter[441] owing to the deep snow in the environs. So then, after seeing your roads, I should recommend the R.34 type of machine in which to travel. . . ."

Suffice it to say that I never mentioned Prairie-Schooners, dirigibles, or aeroplanes! We talked (or rather our friend the reporter did) about the many notorieties that had passed through Santa Fé of recent years, and the Lowell Observatory[442] at Flagstaff some 500 miles away.[443]

Every day during my stay our friend the reporter called in at my hotel. Every day appeared in the press a lengthy report of an alleged interview.

What an interminable worry it must be to newspaper editors of the West to provide adequate copy for their hungering readers!

CHAPTER 15 NOTES

423. *"plaza"*: A Spanish word literally meaning "place," but commonly used to describe a public park or square in an urban setting

424. C.K. took the photo of the Art Museum included in the original book (see The Art Museum at Santa Fé), but kept a higher-resolution copy in his slide collection. This annotated book replaces the book's photo with the image from C.K.'s slide collection.

425. The 1920 census for reflected that 7,236 people in Santa Fe, 20% more than the highest number C.K. believed lived there. The 1917 *Official Hotel Red Book and Directory* estimated the Santa Fe population at 10,000. However, the *Blue Book* (1918) reported a Santa Fe population of 6,000—just as C.K. believed— so it seems likely the *Blue Book's* source was also his source for the number. In any case, as previously noted, Santa Fe was the third-largest city in New Mexico, coming in after #1 Albuquerque and #2 Las Vegas.

426. These two sentences appear *verbatim* in the address of the Honorable Frank Springer (who was president of the Santa Fe Society of the Archaeological Institute, scientist, and attorney) at the dedication of the New Museum in Santa Fe on November 24, 1917, almost two years before C.K.'s trip. The text of Mr. Springer's address was immediately published in *El Palacio*.

427. The *Mayflower* landed on Cape Cod in Massachusetts Colony on November 9, 1620. Because this assertion was actually the statement of Mr. Springer, not C.K., no effort was undertaken for this book to test the veracity of the claim that eleven major Franciscan mission churches existed in New Mexico before November 9, 1620.

428. The rest of this paragraph is also virtually verbatim from Springer's address, *Id.*, Page 15.

429. Figure 124 is a photograph of the Governor's Palace and edge of the plaza in Santa Fe taken by C.K.

Figure 124: Palace and Plaza Santa Fe New Mexico, *ca.* July 1919.
Source: C.K.'s personal slide collection.

430. C.K. was apparently fooled by the façade applied a few years earlier to the front of the Santa Fe Power and Light buildings, photographed prior to 1919 as shown in Figure 125. This building was at the intersection of Don Gaspar Avenue and Water Street. This intersection was also home to the Montezuma Hotel, on the diagonal opposite corner. The main entrance of the Montezuma was on the corner, so C.K. could not have missed seeing this building as he came and went from the Montezuma. Although this building gives the *appearance* of a similar building style to the Art Museum, it was actually a façade that had been applied—around 1914— in front of a more conventional industrial building, the blockhouse and rooftop of which can be seen above the roofline and in front of the tall smokestacks.

Figure 125: Santa Fe Power and Light, Don Gaspar and Water Street, Santa Fe, New Mexico, *ca.* 1915.
Source: Courtesy Palace of the Governors Photo Archives (NMHM/DCA), Negative Number 054394.

431. The "De Vargas Street House" is located at 215 East De Vargas Street on the eastern side of Old Santa Fe Trail in Santa Fe, New Mexico within the Barrio De Analco Historic District. It rests on part of the foundation of an ancient pueblo dating from around 1200 AD. The source photo that C.K. included in Chapter 15 of the book (see The Oldest House in America, at Santa Fé), was kept in his slide collection. This annotated book replaces a scan of the book photo with the better quality image from C.K.'s slide collection.

432. The word "progressive" as used here implies that C.K. was suggesting only the people lacked energy, a much narrower characterization of "progressive" people as being the "young, active, aggressive, thoughtful and successful element of a community" (see Chapter 10, Note 267).

433. In 1919, the plaza at the center of Santa Fe was largely unchanged from how it appeared in 1912, shown in Figure 129.

Figure 126: People Sitting on the Plaza, Santa Fe, New Mexico, *ca.* 1912.
Source: Courtesy Palace of the Governors Photo Archives (NMHM/DCA), Negative Number 011263. Photograph by Jesse Nusbaum.

434. In 1919, two drug stores in Santa Fe sold Kodak products. One directly advertised film processing; the other may have offered this service, but did not advertise it. Of the two drug stores, it seems most likely C.K. asked Zook's Pharmacy to process his film.

- Zook's Pharmacy: 56 E San Francisco Street, the southwest corner of the city plaza, only one block away from the Montezuma Hotel. However, a 1920 New Mexico business directory provides a 232 San Francisco Street address, still only a little over two blocks from the Montezuma Hotel. In any case, Zook's was actively advertising film processing when C.K. arrived at the Montezuma. See their advertisement in Figure 127.

- Weltmer & Burrows Drug Co.: 108 Lincoln Avenue, on the west side of the city plaza, just over one block away from the Montezuma Hotel. In 1919, Weltmer & Burrows also advertised books, stationery, ice cream, candies, and Kodak products, which may have included film processing as shown in Figure 128.

Figure 127: Zook's Pharmacy Advertisement.
Source: *The Santa Fe New Mexican,* July 18, 1919, Page 7.

Figure 128: Weltmer & Burrows Advertisement.
Source: *The Santa Fe New Mexican,* December 22, 1919, Page 3.

435. The *Santa Fe New Mexican* published several articles before, during, and after his visit, including:

- "Captain Shepherd of Royal Air Force is Touring on Motorcycle," July 14, 1919, Page 5.

- "COW PATHS, And Not Roads In America–Verdict of British Royal Airman Here on Motorcycle," July 15, 1919, Page 2.

- "BALLOON, Only Way to Get Over New Mexico Roads Declares British Aviator," July 21, 1919, Page 3.

- "Don't Mention It," July 22, 1919, Page 4.

- "Briton Says Britain Leads World in Conquest of Air," July 22, 1919, Page 5.

- "Personal Gossip Of the Old Town," July 23, 1919, Page 8.

436. C.K. indicates his article in the *Kansas City Star* on July 11, 1919 (see Chapter 10, Note 269, Figure 84) was republished in other cities. This was certainly the case with respect to Santa Fe but no other examples have been located. On July 14, 1919, the *Santa Fe New Mexican* did republish C.K.'s *Star* article, but they assigned it the "verdict" headline cited by C.K. and also added their own three-paragraph introduction, as can be seen in Figure 130 (on page 234). At the end of the article, the *New Mexican* editor added, "California alone probably has as many practically perfect miles of road as all of England."

Captain Shepherd of Royal Air Force is Touring on Motorcycle

Captain C.K. Shepherd of the Royal Air Force of England is expected to arrive here in a few days and an English valise, packed with $100 worth of things, has arrived at the Montezuma hotel ahead of him with instruction to hold until called for.

The visit of Captain Shepherd here would not cause so much interest were it not for the fact that the captain is performing an unusual feat in the way of taking a rest. He is traveling from the Atlantic to the Pacific ocean on a motorcycle, and his tour is to carry out an ambition to see America and also to have a much needed vacation.

Captain Shepherd was in Kansas City Friday and there he gave an interview describing the trip he is making. He said:

"I am on my way from coast to coast on a motorcycle—of all things. Now, there is a big difference between motor cycling here in America and in England. In England everyone rides a motorcycle, men and women alike—office boys, journalists, business men, 'city' men, millionaires, lords, dukes and princes. In fact motor cycling is now the king of sports in England, and the most popular way of spending a holiday is to tour the country on a motorcycle.

"But in America it is different. Only the mad-brained young 'blood' who doesn't mind whether he is a graduate from the lunatic asylum or the county hospital, would think seriously of risking his neck on a motorcycle tour."

The forthcoming visit of this Englishman to Santa Fe on a motorcycle recalls the visit paid by Lady Auckland and her son, the Hon. F.G. Eaton, several years ago when they traveled from Denver to Los Angeles on a motorcycle, Lady Auckland riding in the side car.

Figure 129: "Captain Shepherd of Royal Air Force Is Touring on Motorcycle" Article.
Source: *Santa Fe New Mexican,* July 14, 1919, Page 5.

COW PATHS

And Not Roads in America Verdict of British Royal Airman Here on Motorcycle.

"Are there good roads in America?"

This is the question asked Captain C.K. Shepherd, British aviator, who is now on his way from New York to California, traveling on a motor cycle, and he replies that he hasn't seen any roads. He is expected to arrive in Santa Fe in a few days although the heavy rains may make his trip slower than he expected. He was in Kansas City Friday.

Captain Shepherd declares that in answer to the query concerning America's roads he must say that he hasn't seen any roads so far, but mere cow paths. He predicts that when America gets roads such as England has, then America's beauties will be known to the American just as England is familiar to most Englishmen.

Captain Shepherd's views on America as he has seen it from the seat on a motor cycle are decidedly interesting and amusing. He has written the following article which appeared in the Kansas City Star last week and when he arrives here he may have more information on roads, especially if he visits the Pecos:

To attempt to describe any except a minute fraction of my impressions in America in a few hundred words would be folly. Some day, when I find myself back in England, that is, if I survive the American roads, I am going to sit down for three solid months and write a detailed history of my travels and experiences in this wonderful country of yours "across the duck pond." Many a worthy American citizen has predicted that I shall never see England again, and on many occasions, when for the tenth time that day I have extricated myself and the machine from the ditch and examined myself for bruises and cuts after a "header," I have thought the same way about it!

To be more explicit, I am on my way from coast to coast on a motor cycle—of all things. Now there is a very big difference between motor cycling here in America and in England. In England everyone rides a motorcycle, men and women alike—office boys, journalists, business men, "city" men, millionaires, lords, dukes and princes. In fact motor cycling is now the king of sports in England, and the most popular way of spending a holiday is to tour the country on a motor cycle. But in America it is different. Only the mad-brained young "blood" who doesn't mind whether he is graduated for the lunatic asylum or the county hospital, would think seriously of risking his neck on a motor cycle tour.

"Roads? What Roads?"

When at some town or village on the way I stop to quench a legitimate thirst and I am met with numerous inquiries as to the roads, I respond: "Roads? What roads? I haven't seen any roads. I have been following a place where a cow had been walking." Roads are my only sore point about America. At present I am recuperating from the effects of them. My starboard leg has to be kept permanently straight until further orders, and a square inch or so of good English epidermis is missing from my forehead as a result of a gigantic hole in the road some ten miles north of Kansas City.

"Of course (I hear some one saying) it is all very well for this Englishman to come to our country and complain about the roads. Let him stick to his own country." Quite right. I shouldn't complain, but do you Americans realize what a tremendous lot you're losing through bad roads and how much your commerce is being hampered and your motor car and motor cycle industry is being stinted on account of them?

Impressions of a "Speed Cop"

Another decidedly definite "impression" is the American "speed cop." I thought that England was the only place cursed (or blessed) with them. I succumbed to the energies of a "speed cop" before I had been in the country two days. The kindly old "judge" left me with just 26 cents in my pocket wherewithal to buy me food and gasoline for the next 400 miles. Even that didn't amuse me half so much as the unceremonious way in which it was done. In England, if any one is unfortunate enough to be arrested for speeding, there is a great fuss made.

You receive a summons politely requesting you to be at the assizes, or the high court, or whatever it happened to be, on a certain date, sometimes weeks ahead. When the hour arrives you feel almost proud as you walk up the marble steps of the law courts. In the court you are made speechless by the constables in their brilliant uniforms, by the reporters who are there as silent recorders of your fate, by the throng of faces in the public gallery come to witness your condemnation, and last but not least, by the awe-inspiring judge who deigns to look upon you. Finally you feel it was really worth while for the experience when, after much argument, persuasion and deliberation, you are relieved of five shillings and costs!

But not so in America. You have an altogether different way here. You are doing, say, 45. A man asks you to stop and leads you to the local judge. He takes your money and out you go onto the road again!

How many hundred times have I heard the eternal question "Where are you from?" Of late I have referred people to the number plate. The other day I had been fighting my way along through endless mud for hours in the full heat of the baking sun. It was real hard work, "paddling" that heavy machine along through the ruts, up hill and down dale. I was all but exhausted and soaking in perspiration. Just as I had successfully negotiated a difficult part of the road I struck a rut edgewise and the machine landed on top of me in the hedge. A young fellow in a car near by got out, came over, and said, "Say, fella, do you have any trouble with your back cylinder getting hot?"

However, I shall never regret having started on this trip. America is a beautiful country and I have not seen a fraction of its beauty yet. To travel across America has for years been one of my ambitions and undoubtedly one can see more of any country by traveling it by road. Once America has good roads there will be nothing to prevent an American seeing and knowing his own country the same as the Englishman now sees and knows his.

CAPT. C.K. SHEPHERD,
Royal Air Force, Birmingham, Eng.

(Editorial Note:—California alone probably has as many practically perfect miles of road as all England.)

Figure 130: "COW PATHS, And Not Roads In America" Article.
Source: *Santa Fe New Mexican,* July 15, 1919, Page 2.

437. The article to which C.K. refers was published on Page 15 in the *Kansas City Star* on July 11, 1919. See this article referenced in Chapter 10, Note 269, Figure 84.

BALLOON

Only Way to Get Over New Mexico Roads Declares British Aviator

Captain C.K. Shepherd, British aviator now doing a 10,000 mile tour on a motor cycle through the United States, arrived here last night on his way to San Francisco, and as he was dressing in his room at the Montezuma Hotel this morning he made a few remarks on the best way to "See America First." He said in part:

"I have traveled 3,000 miles over your roads since June 14 and I am constrained to say that a motorcycle is not the best machine to trust your locomotion to at this time. I do not think a motor car is the best machine either, although it might prove about as good as a motor cycle with a side car attached. In my opinion the old Prairie schooner, which formerly travelled over the Santa Fe trail, is far superior. If you can't get a schooner, try horseback travel. I really believe some horses could get through the mud and dodge the boulders.

"But the ideal form of transportation over these United States is a big dirigible, say 700 feet in length, modelled on Great Britain's R-34. I am an aviator and I might have suggested the use of an aeroplane, but I have been told two aviators got stuck in Santa Fe last winter owing to the deep snow in the environs. So then, after seeing your roads, I should recommend the R-34 type of machine in which to travel."

Captain Shepherd said the worst road he has encountered so far, since he left New York, is between Las Vegas and Santa Fe. "You may have had an exceptionally wet month," he remarked, "I do not know as to that. But I do know that there is more mud between Las Vegas and Santa Fe than I have encountered elsewhere and more boulders carved out of it.

"It may not be polite for a foreigner to come to America and criticise the roads, but I think it is fair to say that when Americans talk of this or that road being 'good,' the foreigner accustomed to roads in England or on the Continent has a thrill in store for him when he realizes just what the adjective 'good' means. We should call some of your 'good' roads 'wicked.' About the wickedest piece of road was from Pueblo to Santa Fe, with special emphasis on the stretch from Las Vegas to this city."

Captain Shepherd is traveling on a four cylinder Henderson motorcycle, an American machine, and he averaged 200 miles a day in some parts of the country but recently he has done much less. He carried a small English leather valise on his machine but he is going to ship it by express tomorrow as he says all the glass fittings inside for tooth and nail brushes and for soap have been reduced to powder.

The captain will return to New York via Salt Lake City, Yellowstone Park, Bismarck and Duluth, and he expects to get back by September 8. He is an inventor and has business in various American cities.

"I am going to stay in Santa Fe a day or more; until the pain leaves the muscles of my arms and legs," he said laughing.

Figure 131: "BALLOON, Only Way to Get Over New Mexico Roads" Article.
Source: *Santa Fe New Mexican*, July 21, 1919, Page 2.

438. The "BALLOON" article was published in the *Santa Fe New Mexican* on July 21, 1919, the day after C.K. arrived and gave his interview. C.K. claimed the article covered ¼ of the page, but it actually took up far less space. (The article occupied less than 9% of the available space on the page.) The article can be seen in Figure 131.

Don't Mention It

Captain Shepherd, British royal air service veteran, arrived in our fair city yesterday on a motorcycle and By Jove he finds our blighted roads simply execrable. In fact, he has found nothing but cowpaths, he says, all over the country, and believes the only way to cross the country is by airplane or balloon. Nothing like the good old roads in blooming England, what?

As a matter of fact the mileage of perfect roads in America would make the total linear measurements of all the highways in England, good, bad and indifferent, look like a mere suggestion. England, if we recall our geography aright, is about as large as Alabama. There are 1,000 miles of paved roads in Los Angeles county alone, and you can go from Indianapolis or Augusta to Portland, Maine, without getting off brick, concrete or asphalt. The gentleman from Britain is quite right in whatever aspersions he casts on the roads of New Mexico at this time. Despite the record breaking wet season which would paralyze almost any roads that could be built in this section, the fact remains that New Mexico has merely begin to construct what may properly be called permanent roads.

However, if the conditions were reversed, and we came over from England and found stretches of impassable highway we should reply courteously that although we had discovered some pieces of road that were hardly all that could be desired, we admired the general progress in highway building and appreciated the monumental achievements of the country along this line and would make a few constructive suggestions to aid this wonderful country, which makes England look like a fly speck on a window pane, in building roads more rapidly and efficiently. We should also be inclined to say that while we were disappointed in the particular roads which we had traversed, owing to the immensity of the country and the vast areas which we had not traveled over, we should not attempt to pass any general verdict on the highway system of the country as a whole. We should be chary and wary of any such sweeping condemnation as to state that America's roads were none of them better than cowpaths, for fear we might be astonishingly inaccurate and destroy the effect of our reasonable criticism by wild-eyed exaggeration.

Otherwise we might apprehend that some one might politely inform us that it was a matter of wonderment that, with such fine roads in Britain, one should deliberately leave them to flounder and boggle around in the unspeakable roads of this country.

And all that sort of bally rot, what?

Figure 132: "Don't Mention It" Article.
Source: *Santa Fe New Mexican,* July 22, 1919, Page 4.

439. This was the "BALLOON" article published on July 21, 1919, the day after C.K.'s arrival in Santa Fe. The article titled "Don't Mention It" (Figure 132) is a biting editorial commentary on the views C.K. expressed regarding road conditions in the US. It is most likely the chief example of the "caustic comments" C.K. complained about. An additional two articles are shown in Figures 133 (facing page) and 134 (on page 238).

Briton Says Britain Leads World in Conquest of Air

Great Britain led the world in the conquest of the air at the end of the great war, according to Captain C.K. Shepherd, British aviator and inventor, who arrived here on a 10,000 mile motorcycle tour of the United States.

Captain Shepherd admitted that the attempt of Harry Hawker to cross the ocean in an airplane had shown that the British government had not taken as much interest in such a daring feat as it might have, but he said that the trip of the R-34, the mammoth dirigible, has shown the world that Great Britain had solved a problem which had long baffled mankind.

"At the beginning of the great war," the captain continued, "the British fliers used French airplanes, because they were considered superior. But before the end of the war the British as well as the French were flying in British planes, showing the advancement made by the British."

There had been talk of the Germans having gigantic Zeppelins which would cross the ocean, but Captain Shepherd said that undoubtedly the R-34 is larger than any Zeppelin yet seen.

During the war Captain Shepherd, who is an engineer by profession, had charge of the repairing of airplanes, and he served many months in France in close touch with the activities of the aerial combatants.

Captain Shepherd has invented several parts of machines to simplify transportation by motorcar, motorcycle and airplane, and he has with him at his hotel here a carburetor the interior of which can be seen through glass sides. "As every motorist knows, the carburetor gives lots of trouble at times," he said, "and I have been at work on a new type which will permit inspection at a glance. If there is the lack of oil it is at once apparent with this device."

The captain has invented various improved spark plugs as well as several kinds of carburetors, and he has made arrangements on his present tour to have several American companies manufacture them in this country.

"My present trip across country in a motorcycle was designed as a rest after the strain of the past war," he said, "but so muddy are the roads I find the vacation rather exhausting."

FINDS HOTEL CLERK

ALSO AN AVIATOR

Captain Shepherd was surprised and pleased today to ascertain that the day clerk of his hotel is an aviator—or was until he took an 800-foot drop and broke 23 bones.

"I have been informed that Mr. Monell who formerly demonstrated for the Curtiss company in this country has done 3,000 hours of flying," said the British aviator. "I have met men who have done 2,000 hours of flying but never a man in England or France who had done 3,000. When an aviator has done 1,000 hours there is a bust up—you call it banquet or big feed—and a drinking party. When he has done 2,000 there is a celebration which makes him think the world is coming to an end. But 3,000 hours is wonderful. I myself have flown a bit, but my time in the air can be measured by a few hundred hours. It is evident that to do 3,000 hours a man has to fly daily for years. It is a tremendous accomplishment."

Captain Shepherd is preparing to leave for Flagstaff tomorrow morning. He intends to stop in Flagstaff to call at the Lowell observatory as he is greatly interested in books the late Prof. Lowell wrote on Mars. He will ask permission to peep through the monster telescope there, as he says he has cherished this ambition for years.

Scores of Santa Feans and visitors this morning inspected the motorcycle this daring air man from across the seas is using to tour America. The captain explained that it is the same type of machine on which the transcontinental record was made a few weeks ago. The machine fully equipped cost $550. At times it makes as much noise as an average aeroplane in action, according to its owner.

Figure 133: "Briton Says Britain Leads World in Conquest of Air" Article.
Source: *Santa Fe New Mexican,* July 22, 1919, Page 5.

"Briton Says Britain Leads World in Conquest of Air" (see Figure 133) is informative on several levels because it describes—purportedly, in C.K.'s own words—the additional business purpose of his journey, to find manufacturers for his inventions. It is also interesting because it indicates that people (including reporters) assumed that an officer of the Royal Air Force was a pilot. In other articles, C.K. was described as an "aviator"—but this article goes further. It seems that C.K. did little to correct people's assumptions and perhaps even contributed to them. For starters, in the photograph of C.K. in the front of this book, he is wearing an aviator's jacket with his RAF uniform hat. But C.K. was not a pilot then or any time after that. The "flight of fancy" extends even further, as C.K. is quoted in a reflection of his flying time: "I myself have flown a bit, but my time in the air can be measured by a few hundred hours." In fact, except for a single flight experience that C.K. recounted later in his life—in which a test pilot took him up on one test flight during World War I in France and performed some acrobatics, frightening C.K. and causing him to abandon his aviation dreams—there is no indication that C.K. ever logged *any* time as a pilot, much less "a few hundred hours." Of course, it is quite possible this content only reflected the imagination of an impressionable reporter. According to C.K., he never even mentioned airplanes to this journalist. If this is true, then many of the words attributed to C.K. are fabrications.

> **PERSONAL GOSSIP**
> **Of the Old Town**
>
> ...
>
> Captain C.K. Shepherd, of the British air forces, who arrived here two days ago on a motor cycle from New York, left this morning for Flagstaff, Ariz.
>
> ...

The final "sendoff" announcement was included in the "Personal Gossip" column on July 23, 1919, an excerpt of which appears as Figure 134.

Figure 134: "Personal Gossip Of the Old Town" Article.
Source: *Santa Fe New Mexican*, July 23, 1919, Page 8.

440. The British R34 airship had—just two weeks earlier—completed an historic transatlantic journey at Mineola, NY on July 6, 1919 after a 108-hour non-stop flight. It was the first westbound aircraft to cross the Atlantic non-stop. See Figure 135, which shows R34 after its arrival in Mineola.

Figure 135: R34 Airship at Mineola, New York, on July 6, 1919.
Source: US Library of Congress.

441. On January 3, 1919, the *Santa Fe New Mexican* reported that two military pilots had to disassemble their aircraft and ship them east due to heavy snow. On the front page of the same edition, it was noted that the entire country was hit with a cold wave and that it was -10ºF in Santa Fe that day.

442. In Chapter 18, C.K. provides detailed information about his visit to the Lowell Observatory. Several additional photos taken by C.K. while he was there have been included in this book.

443. C.K. was not far off with his 500-mile estimate for Santa Fe to Flagstaff. In a series of five separate route instructions, the *Blue Book* (1918) description of how to get from Santa Fe to Flagstaff totals 516.7 miles. Today it is about 384 miles from Santa Fe to Flagstaff.

CHAPTER XVI

THE RIO GRANDE VALLEY

My stay in Santa Fé was a pleasant one. At the Post Office[444] I found a few letters and some money, the former forwarded from Cincinnati,[445] and the latter from Washington (it had been cabled there two months before[446]). On the morning of the fourth day my weary frame was sufficiently rested to warrant my continuing once more. I bought a two-gallon water-bag[447] in preparation for the 700-mile desert journey ahead, and once more set out westward. A crowd of interested citizens witnessed my preparations outside the hotel, plied me with questions as to how far I was going, how long it would take, and how old I was, and finally bade me farewell as Lizzie burst into a roar, and we moved sadly, if noisily, away.

The next town was Albuquerque, some sixty or seventy miles ahead.[448] The road in between lay over a barren wilderness of sand and prairie. The blazing sun poured down upon it fierce and unrelenting; nowhere was there a sign of any living thing. Hardly a hill or a swelling relieved the monotonous flatness of the trail. In the distance, on my right, rose rugged mountain ranges suddenly out of the trackless plains.

After twenty miles appeared La Bajada Hill, crossing the trail at right angles. There was not much climbing to be done, but going down the other side was a different matter. It seemed that a great "fault" or outcrop had appeared in the plain,[449] making it much lower on the one side than the other. No less than thirty-two acute hairpin bends conducted the trail[450] down the precipitous slope. The gradient in places was terrific. At the bottom was a cemetery![451]

Here and there we crossed the sandy wash of a one-time river, leaping over bumps and boulders and picking the road as well as possible. Occasionally a wooden shack was passed, with a few dirty-looking Indians hanging around: Indians dressed not in native garb but in pseudo-modern style. The only things that betrayed them were their faces and lank dark hair. He that goes to the West and expects to see the landscape decorated with Indians dressed in multicoloured garbs of picturesque pattern, is doomed to disappointment. The first impression of a modernized native is disheartening if one has lingering thoughts in one's mind left from childhood's days when one read with ceaseless delight of stalwart Indians with huge muscles and painted bodies galloping along, bow and arrow in hand, on a fiery white mustang in pursuit of an unfortunate "pale-face."

Ah, no!—*Nous avons changé tout cela!*[452] The Indian as a rule is not stalwart, and decidedly not picturesque. Having had the gentle arts of civilization thrust upon him, and being naturally of a lazy disposition, he is content to loaf around chewing shag and disfiguring the landscape generally with his presence.[453]

As Albuquerque was approached, things looked more flourishing. The land was cultivated where possible, and in places corn and wheat appeared.

It is very strange to find a prospering city in the midst of such desolate surroundings as Albuquerque has. It came as a pleasant surprise to me to see the electric trams,[454] the wide streets and the clean modern buildings. I was puzzled to know just what it was that kept the place going. Albuquerque, however, although the largest town in the State, has only 10,000 or so inhabitants, and is the nucleus of a very extensive ranching district which undoubtedly largely constitutes its *raison d'être*. I left it rather sadly, because, with the exception of Flagstaff some 500 miles away, I should not meet another town of anywhere near its size until I reached the Pacific Coast.

Shortly after leaving Albuquerque the trail crossed a very wide shallow muddy river—the famous Rio Grande. It was spanned by a low wooden bridge which creaked and rattled in its planks as we rumbled across it.[455] We saw quite a lot of the Rio Grande and got to look upon it as a friendly sort of river. That is not to be wondered at, because in a wilderness that is next to being called a desert one can become attached to anything that has life or movement, even if it be a muddy stream! Probably in consideration of the feelings of weary travellers, but for no other apparent purpose, the trail from time to time crossed and re-crossed the same old river with the same old friendly wooden bridges until finally, eighty miles farther on, it was left to wander southward unmolested through the plains and deserts of New Mexico and Texas into the Gulf of Mexico.

At Isleta there was a surprise in store. Isleta is a charming Indian pueblo,[456] built wholly of "adobe" mud and populated entirely by native Indians. So unique, so bewitchingly attractive are these pueblos, that I must digress awhile to describe their nature and origin.

The history of the American Indians since the advent of the White Man is an unsatisfactory one from all points of view. Different authorities on the subject have widely different opinions as to the eventual outcome of the American domination, which from generation to generation has vacillated in its policy and, sometimes with bloodshed, sometimes with bribery, has gradually reduced the red man to subjection, occupied his country and enforced an unwilling civilization upon him.[457] But all are agreed that the Indian of to-day is in a far lower stage of civilization than when the early settlers first drove him from his rightful property.

There are, however, a few tribes which advanced much farther along the road to civilization than the others. Moreover theirs was a civilization quite their own, not acquired through contact with the whites. Chief among them are the Pueblo (pueblo-building) Indians, and the Moqui Indians,[458] the town-building natives of New Mexico and Arizona.

The "Pueblo" Indians include several different tribes, each speaking a different language.[459] Each tribe, with only one exception, comprises a number of separate "pueblos" or villages, generally built on the "community dwelling" basis, that is, the houses are in a large and solid mass, several stories in height, each one receding from the one below and approached by ladders. In these houses, which look like great pyramids, live a number of families. In some pueblos most of the houses are on this plan and as many as 1,600 people have been known to live in one house. The houses are built of adobe, and sometimes of stones cemented together with adobe.[460]

Several of these Indian villages are clustered together in the vicinity of Santa Fé, often on the banks of the Rio Grande. Each has its own customs and makes its own laws.[461] All are centres of interest. Artists flock to them from all parts of the Continent to paint and sketch them.[462]

PUEBLO OF TAOS.

By permission of Dr. F. Rolt-Wheeler.

Travellers tramp for miles to see the Indians in their native costumes and conditions. Some make jewels; some make vases, ornaments, idols, and all manner of earthenware goods; some work in silver, while others make blankets and rugs. With hardly an exception they all make an excellent living out of the things they make and sell.

Each of the pueblos has its own feast-days, or "fiestas," when, for a time varying from a day to over a week, the whole population devotes its time to feasting, dancing and games. The religious rites that are performed and the strange customs that prevail at these feasts and dances form in themselves a vast and interesting study.

THE RIO GRANDE, NEW MEXICO.

By permission of Dr. F. Rolt-Wheeler.

At Isleta the road again crossed the Rio Grande. This done, it found itself in a dry sandy wilderness, with the Manzano Range running from north to south in the distance.[463] In patches the ground was white with sandhills, and the trail became two straggling white lines, where the wheels of passing vehicles had left their imprint in the soft white sand. These two white ruts were my only guides. All around was desolation. Nothing was to be seen anywhere, save those two thin white lines straggling aimlessly ahead, the sun-scorched desert with its ragged stones and evil, scanty, tenacious vegetation, and on the horizon that fiery stretch of mountain range, whose peaks rose rugged and defiant and glistened with red as if roused to anger by the eternally raging sun. I had never before realized the great depth of feeling that a mountain range is capable of evoking. The Alps are majestic beyond description. They awe the observer to a sense of his own utter insignificance as he gazes upon that glistening majestic sky-line, and feels the overwhelming influence of those mighty mountains upon him.

But if it is an overwhelming influence, it is a friendly one at least I have found it so. Although there is an instinct in me, as in most people, impelling me to guard and protect myself against anything that is tremendous—a relic, I suppose, of prehistoric days—I feel towards the Alps always like a little boy feels towards his "big brother." The same feeling is seen reflected in the "Sierra Madre" (Mother Mountains) of California.[464]

But in New Mexico I have seen huge ranges that one could truthfully call nothing else but "wicked." They seem to gaze and glower with a cruel, terrifying gleam upon the wanderer who defies their hateful solitude.

The hours of travel that followed were hours of weary monotony. A brief lapse every thirty miles or so when a tiny Mexican village on the Rio Grande was passed, and once more the two white ruts came into view, the stones and cactus, and again the evil mountains.

Later, the sand turned to rocks. The trail began to climb the mountains, and the sun sank low in the sky. If ever there was a place to starve to death, thought I, it is here. I reflected upon what the consequences would be if I ran out of petrol or had a bad smash.

I didn't run out of petrol and I didn't have a smash. Instead of that, after about eighty miles from Isleta, the trail descended the mountain pass, re-crossed the Rio Grande for the last time, and swerved at right angles, to continue its course westward. Shortly before sunset I arrived at a little Mexican town called Socorro, where both man and machine were rested, while the man that kept the "C'fay"[465] in the *plaza* got busy with some "eats" for weary me.[466]

After dinner away once again we go. The sun is setting. We must find a resting-place before dark sets in, for in these countries where the air is clear and mountain ranges hem in every horizon the darkness comes quickly and the sinking of the sun below the sky-line means almost the final close of day.

There is another range to climb: it lies right ahead of us. As we approach, it looms its massive bulk like a wall before us. The trail bends and turns as if hesitating before it tackles this difficult feat; up there in front is a great gap. The road cuts through it, and is seen no more. Beyond are much greater heights to climb. Shall we attempt it now or leave it till the morrow?

The smell of petrol, which the last few minutes was a suggestion, became a reality. I look down in the fading light and find the precious fluid spurting out from the carburettor union. Evidently the pipe has broken away with the vibration. So I swerve off the road (almost easier done than said) and stop at the flattest patch of earth that I reach.

Oh, the joys of the open life once again! Never shall I forget that night in the desert past Socorro.[467] The sun as it set behind the range that I had commenced to climb plunged everything around into gloomy blackness. Across the valley, from north to south, stretched the Manzano Range that I had already crossed. It shone like fire throughout the whole of its length. Gradually the rugged shadow of the range behind me crept farther and farther away, crossing the river and mounting up the opposite side of the valley. Slowly, slowly it mounted up, higher and higher as if a great black cloak were being drawn by an unseen hand over that fiery ridge that glistened in its evil splendour. In five short minutes there were but a few of the highest peaks remaining above the inky shadow. They enjoyed their splendour for a few brief moments and then were gone, as though wiped suddenly out of existence. All was blackness: silent, heavy blackness. The stars appeared, one by one.

I prepared my bed for the night.

What was that? A faint tinkle reached my ears. It sounded like the noise of a cow-bell, such as one hears in the Swiss valleys. Yes, there it was again. It must be a cow! But what was a cow to live on here? No doubt there was a well near by. I felt then that nothing in the world would taste better than a drink of pure fresh milk. The heat of the day had been intense, and one can always drink in New Mexico.

I slipped into my field-boots, took a collapsible cup from my bag and set out in search of the cow. I was quite determined to milk that cow, come what may.

I stumbled over the rough stones, picked my way between the cactus plants and sage-brush. I arrived at a fence. The tinkle, tinkle seemed to come from just the other side. Cup in hand, I climbed over, very gingerly so as not to tear my pyjamas. Pyjamas in a desert, think of it!

"Now, where are you?" Ahead I saw dimly a large black form.

"Come along, girlie, come and be milked," quoth I in my most bewitching manner. She moved not. I advanced slowly, trying to discern which was the business end. Meanwhile I pictured the cow asking herself, "Wot's the big idea milking me in py's at this time o' night?"

I drew closer and looked. . . .

It was a bull!

I returned hurriedly to my bed, and cursed when a prickly pear[468] caught me on the left shin!

CHAPTER 16 NOTES

444. The post office in Santa Fe in 1919 was a 2,100 square-foot rental at 106 Palace Avenue with just twenty-five feet of storefront. It was a half block southeast of the plaza, with a mortuary next door as shown in Figure 136. Construction on a new post office began in 1920. Part of it was built on the vacant lot seen next to the mortuary (the lot the two women are walking across). But the new post office's front door was around the corner, with 180 feet of frontage on Cathedral Place and covered 16,200 square feet, almost eight times the footprint of 106 Palace Avenue. Although the post office shared this new building with other federal agencies, it is conceivable that, in 1922, the post office suddenly had three-to-four times the amount of working space compared to what it had in 1919. Figure 137 (next page) is a photo of the post office that opened in 1922, and Figure 138 (next page) is a new diagram that shows where the post office was in 1919 in relation to the location in 1922.

Figure 136: Santa Fe Post Office at 106 Palace Avenue, August 9, 1917.
The post office is the smaller storefront with the flag on the far end.
Source: Courtesy Palace of the Governors Photo Archives (NMHM/DCA), Negative Number 149884.
Credit: Robert H. Williams.

Figure 137: New Santa Fe Post Office, *ca.* 1930.
Source: Courtesy of the Vogt Family. Credit: Evon Z. Vogt, Sr.

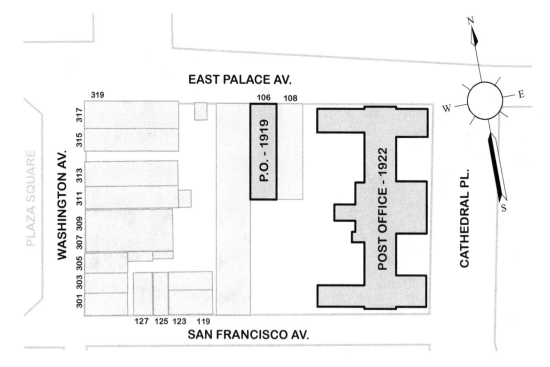

Figure 138: Santa Fe Post Office Locations—1919 and 1922.
This diagram shows the location of the post office at 106 Palace Avenue in 1913, where it
remained until the new building was opened round the corner in 1922.
Source: *Sanborn Fire Insurance Maps of Santa Fe*, 1913 and 1921. Diagram by Mark L. Hunnibell.

445. It is not clear if the letters from Cincinnati were forwarded by the Cincinnati Post Office directly, or if they were letters that had been sent to 3450 Clifton Avenue but arrived after C.K. departed, and Steve then forwarded them to Santa Fe as C.K. had requested. It seems most likely that the letters were forwarded in a single package by Steve.

446. Here C.K. reports that he finally received money on July 21, 1919, funds that he had cabled to Washington, DC two months before (and had not arrived when he went to the post office to receive it). Taken literally, C.K. would have originally cabled this money to Washington, DC himself on May 21, 1919, just two days before he sailed from Liverpool on May 23, 1919.

447. The photo of C.K.'s motorcycle on the beach in California (see Chapter 21, Note 686, Figure 232) shows a canvas water bag on the handlebars. It is not clear if the bag in the photo is of the two-gallon variety, but a number of makes and sizes—up to five gallon—were certainly available, as represented in Figure 139 (below) and Figures 140 and 141 (next page).

SELF-COOLING WATER BAG

Travelers in the tropics and in arid regions need cool water to drink. This can be had by using a linen duck water bag, which exudes a slight amount of water which evaporates in the hot sun, and this evaporation cools the contents. When hung up and swung in the air greater evaporation takes place and consequently cold water is had. Invaluable for explorers, miners, prospectors, herdsmen, etc.

2½ gallon size weighs 1 lb......Price $2.00

5 gallon size weighs 1½ lbs.....Price 3.00

Figure 139: Appell's South African Water Bag.
Source: *Catalogue and Price List of Complete Outfits for Explorers, Campers, Prospectors, Hunters.* Manufactured by Abercrombie & Fitch Co. New York, 1907. Page 75.

Egyptian water bag (T32)

The Whitaker Mfg. Co., 409-15 S. Green Street, Chicago, Ill. The Egyptian open top water bag has a detachable spout, an opening the full width of the bag which is sealed by a wire holder and a tubular steel sliding clamp which also secures the spout and the tie rings. Made of imported flax fabric and holds from one to five gailons. Prices are from $1 to $2.50.

Figure 140: Whitaker Egyptian Water Bag. **Source:** *The Horseless Age,* April 1, 1917. Page 42.

African Water Bags.

Made of a specially constructed heavy flax canvas, which has the peculiar property of holding water and exuding just enough to the surface to keep up a continual evaporation. The bag is fitted with a porcelain mouthpiece and has a good cork attached. A rope handle, which can be adjusted to any size. Water bags are practical and are becoming more popular every year.

6H5932—Size, 1 gallon. Shipping weight, 12 ounces. Price, each....................**35c**
6H5933—Size, 2 gallons. Shipping weight, 1 pound. Price, each...**$1.15**
6H5935—Size, 5 gallons. Shipping weight, 1½ pounds.

Figure 141: African Water Bag. **Source:** Sears, Roebuck and Co. Catalogue, 1922. Page 782.

448. C.K.'s characterization that it was sixty or seventy miles from Santa Fe to Albuquerque is accurate. The *Blue Book* (1918) puts it at 66.6 miles.

449. "Escarpment": A term that describes the geologic nature of La Bajada Hill, though it is often informally used to identify the top edge of La Bajada Hill.

450. *"La Bajada"* means "the Descent." The remains of roads down La Bajada Hill that are still visible include the "original alignment," which C.K. would have used and was first constructed around 1909 with labor from the local Cochiti community. The "southern alignment" that became U.S. Route 66 was built around 1926, but both roads continued to be used concurrently for some time after. The "original alignment" has about eleven "switchbacks" before merging with the "southern alignment." Figure 142 shows the family of Evon Z. Vogt, Sr.

heading down the hill near the top of the original alignment in approximately 1930; this was the very same road and view that C.K. wrote about.

Figure 142: Evon Z. Vogt, Jr., Shirley Bergman Vogt, and Barbara Vogt Driving down La Bajada Hill, New Mexico.
Source: Courtesy Palace of the Governors Photo Archives (NMHM/DCA), Negative Number 008231. Credit: Evon Z. Vogt, Sr.

Although the upper part of both "alignments" are on US Forest Service land, the common lower portion of the road after the merge is on what is now understood to be the tribal lands of the Pueblo de Cochiti. They have since fenced it off to prevent further damage to areas they deem culturally and archeologically significant. The land upon which the "original" and "southern" alignment roads were built remains within the Santa Fe National Forest administered by the US Department of the Interior. In 2008, the National Park Service undertook a project to chart the history of roads and trails at La Bajada, including the road that C.K. drove down on Wednesday, July 23, 1919 (see Figure 143, next page).

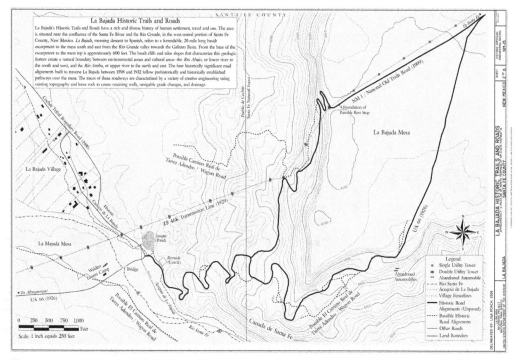

Figure 143: La Bajada Historic Trails and Roads.
Source: US Department of the Interior, 2008. Credit: Lisa Roach.

451. There is a small cemetery in the village of La Bajada at the bottom of the hill. Figure 144 is an excerpt from *Auto Club Map 21* that shows the route with twists and turns coming down the hill, and then turning right through the village (presumably past the cemetery) over a couple railroads to pass through Domingo about six miles away.

Figure 144: La Bajada Hill Map, *ca.* 1915.
Source: *Auto Club Map 21.*

452. *"Nous avons changé tout cela"*: A French phrase meaning "we changed it all."

453. This sentence seems inexplicably incongruous with views C.K. expresses elsewhere (see Note 457) where he portrays appreciation for the heritage of Native Americans and what became of them.

454. The streetcar in Figure 145 was photographed in Albuquerque in approximately 1917.

Figure 145: Electric Streetcar in Albuquerque, 1917.
Source: Albuquerque Museum, Milner Studio/Crouch collection, 1980.101.005. Credit: Alabama Milner.

455. A photo of one the bridges over the Rio Grande near Albuquerque is shown in Figure 146 (next page).

Figure 146: Bridge over Rio Grande Near Albuquerque, New Mexico, *ca.* 1935.
Source: Courtesy Palace of the Governors Photo Archives (NMHM/DCA), Negative Number 051466. Credit: T. Harmon Parkhurst.

456. The photo of Isleta Pueblo (Figure 147) was taken in about 1908.

Figure 147: Isleta Pueblo Showing Mission Church, New Mexico, *ca.* 1908.
Source: Courtesy Palace of the Governors Photo Archives (NMHM/DCA), Negative Number 036248.

457. This is a compassionate characterization that contrasts with his "lazy disposition" remarks observed in Note 453.

458. It is true that the Pueblo and Moqui peoples were the main building cultures in Arizona and New Mexico. In *Children of the Sun* (1883), American writer William Eleroy Curtis wrote of the building history of Moqui (or Hopi) and how it relates to the Pueblo, who he termed "the permanent Indians":

> "The Moquis, who live in Arizona, seventy miles northwest of Zuni, have a legend that the earth was once a small island, inhabited by one man, whose father was the sun, and whose mother was the moon; that the gods sent a wife to him to cheer his loneliness, and that the earth grew as their family multiplied. The children became dissatisfied and restless after years, began to wander, and built up towns. Visits between them became infrequent, and finally ceased, until in generations their common ancestry was forgotten. Centuries ago a war broke out between the Pueblo, or permanent Indians, and the wandering tribes, and the former were driven to the rocks and caves, where they built nests like wrens and swallows, erected fortifications and watch towers, dug reservoirs in the rocks to catch the rainfall, and held their enemies at bay. The besiegers were beaten back, but the hollows in the rocks were filled with blood, and it poured in torrents through the canyons. It was such a victory that they dare not try again, and when the fight was over they wandered to the southward, and in the deserts of Arizona, on isolated, impregnable bluffs, they built new towns, and their descendants, the Moquis, live in them to this day."

459. This statement is true. The Pueblo speak six different languages: Hopi, Keres, Tewa, Tiwa, Towa/Jemez, and Zuñi. In their 1998 article, "Pueblo Indian Languages," Laura Redish and Orrin Lewis wrote:

> "The Pueblo people are linguistically diverse, speaking languages from four unrelated language families: the Acoma, Cochiti, Laguna, San Felipe, Santa Ana, Santo Domingo, and Zia Pueblos speak Keresan languages; the Isleta, Jemez, Nambe, Picuris, Pojoaque, Sandia, San Ildefonso, San Juan, Santa Clara, Taos, Tesuque, and Tigua/Ysleta del Sur Pueblos speak Kiowa-Tanoan languages; the Zuni speak their own language which is

not known to be related to any other; and the Hopi, furthest west, speak a Uto-Aztecan language distantly related to Nahuatl."

460. An adobe brick is typically made of dirt mixed with water and an organic material, such as straw or dung, to form a composite brick.

461. There are nineteen different pueblos in New Mexico today, each recognized by the US government as "domestic, dependent nations." The legal landscape in which such nations exist within the borders of the United States has changed over hundreds of years, but it was true in 1919—and remains so today—that each pueblo has broad authority to regulate its own affairs according to the nation's own individual laws. Six of those nineteen pueblos are southwest of Santa Fe, on the Rio Grande along the route C.K. took. In order, these are the pueblos C.K. would have seen after coming down La Bajada Hill until reaching Socorro:

- Cochiti.

- Kewa (Santo Domingo).

- San Felipe.

- Santa Ana.

- Sandia.

- Isleta.

462. There was indeed a thriving artist's colony in Taos in 1919. Although Taos is about fifty-three miles due north of Santa Fe near the headwater of the Rio Pueblo de Taos—a tributary feeding the Rio Grande—C.K. did not make it there. However, he knew someone who had travelled to Taos ("*more anon*"). The closest C.K. got to Taos was about 75 miles southwest near the Kewa Pueblo on the Rio Grande. Still, the Taos Society of Artists—an organization of visual artists that existed from 1915-1927—changed Taos into an international art center to which artists flocked in order to paint Native Americans in New Mexico. Joseph Henry Sharp (1859-1953) was one such artist.

463. The mountains of the Sandia-Manzano Range begin rising up about fifteen miles east of the bridge after Isleta and generally parallel the Rio Grande southward, maintaining that fifteen-mile distance.

464. The Sierra Madre Mountains are generally on a northwest-southeast line, north of the San Rafael Mountains and southeast of the Santa Lucia Range. They are bound on the north and west by the Cuyama River and Cuyama Valley, on the east by Santa Barbara Canyon, and on the south by the Sisquoc River. Although C.K. did not pass through these mountains, they rose about twenty miles to his east as he passed through Los Olivos in California. C.K. would have been able to see them, which is probably why he mentioned them in the context of his view of the Sandia-Manzano Range (situated fifteen miles east of him in New Mexico).

465. *"C'fay"*: This seems to be C.K.'s attempt to phonetically describe the local pronunciation of "café," beginning with just a short "hard "K" sound and greater emphasis on the "FAY" (as opposed to common modern English use, more like \ka-'fā).

466. The *New Mexico State Business Directory* (1920) has separate listings for only two cafés in Socorro. There were six hotels listed, some of which—such as the Chambon Hotel and Café—had restaurants. Whether the Chambon was adjacent to the Socorro plaza is not known, but it had its own plaza around which the rooms were located. The café was on the end of the building at the street, so C.K. could have eaten there and felt he was on the plaza.

467. The lack of roads and signage, as well as the rather nondescript landscape on display (see Figure 148) makes determining the location of this photo from C.K.'s collection impossible. It was probably taken in the morning of Thursday, July 24, 1919 after C.K. woke up but before he started driving again, since he says he stopped for the night when it was already dark and he was just west of Socorro.

Figure 148: Desert Near Socorro, *ca.* July 1919.
Source: C.K.'s personal slide collection.

468. "prickly pear": The common English name for about a dozen species of the *Opuntia* genus of *Cactaceae* in the North American deserts. As shown in Figure 148, they typically have flat, fleshy pads that look like large leaves.

Figure 149: *Optunia* Examples.
Source: *The Cactaceae*, 1919. Plate XXXIV.

CHAPTER XVII

THE PETRIFIED FOREST OF ARIZONA

In the morning I patched up the broken petrol pipe as well as I could with insulation tape,[469] and started again on my way. I had to do forty miles before I should see a soul—forty miles before breakfast could be thought of.

It was as well that I had stopped where I did the night before. The road twisted around precipitous bends and climbed up rough rocky slopes into the mountains. Down on the other side we found ourselves in a great sandy plain, stretching due west and bounded by parallel ranges of rugged mountains.[470] There were frequent washouts and frequent spills. In places the little streamlets that flowed from the mountain sides cut great chasms across the road, sufficient to crush one's wheels if one leapt into them at too great a speed.

Magdalena is a typical cow-boy town.[471] In the heart of ranching country and hundreds of miles from anything but a few similar towns, it was in the early days (before prohibition) one of the "warmest" places in the West. Cow-boy outfits are seen advertised at all of the few "Stores," but there has been one big change—the notorious saloons are no longer. New Mexico adopted prohibition several years before its universal approval. Consequently Magdalena had had ample time to settle down by the time of my arrival.

I was directed to a "C'fay" that had the reputation of providing the best meal in the town.[472] I pushed open its swing doors and beheld a picture of cleanliness and tidiness. The tables were all spick and span in their clean white tablecloths and not a vestige of dirt was visible anywhere.

The small boys of the town displayed a lively interest in me as I disported myself[473] with my camera at the expense of their public buildings (to be exact, one wooden church).[474] "Look at 'is boots, Jem," said one. "Looks like as though he's a gor-dem buck-jumper."[475] "Aye, but 'is pants don't look ter be the right stuff, Joe."

I left them wondering and fell upon the trail once more. A few miles out I came to a "round-up" of steers. There were ten or twelve cow-boys on horseback, and some 5,000 or 6,000 steers grouped together in a large dense mass, blocking the road altogether. "Tough guys, those cow-boys," I remarked to myself and pretended to ignore them. But I couldn't help thinking what MIGHT happen if I barged into one of their animals or if for any reason they didn't like the look of my face![476]

Slowly, very slowly, the great mass of cattle moved, like a tide sweeping over the plain. Carefully I picked my way along and felt relieved when I left them right behind. I opened out and prepared for a long weary jaunt. The next town of any kind was ninety miles away.[477]

The first thirty were dead flat but hard going. There had evidently been considerable rain recently. Emaciated mud-holes were now rock-hard contortions in the road. Often I rode on the prairie in preference.

Another thing was evident. There had been a great drought the previous year.[478] Ranching is impossible without water, and even now, in spite of the recent rains, could be seen here and there a great lake-bed completely dried up. Nothing remained but a great mass of sun-baked hoof-marked mud, and here and there a skeleton lying upon it. The ranches of New Mexico are of huge size and cover enormous areas. True, a few good years mean a fortune to the rancher, but one bad one means ruin. Hundreds of ranches had been ruined the previous year, I found, and several thousand head of cattle had died from the drought.[479] As I passed along, their skeletons lay strewn at the roadside, sometimes singly, sometimes in groups of a dozen or more.[480] Hardly a refreshing sight for a poor innocent motor-cyclist!

At the end of the thirty mile stretch we entered hilly, thickly-wooded country.[481] The scenery was wild and rough. I met no one and saw no one. After another fifteen miles was a shack at the side of the road.[482] The occupation of the owner was selling petrol and oil to passing travellers. I opined that this was probably not an enviable vocation from a financial point of view. I filled up, and found to my dismay that the price, instead of being twenty-five cents per gallon, was seventy-five. It was 100 miles from the railway, and all supplies had to be brought by road, hence the trebled cost.

I have never been through wilder country than that which followed for 100 miles. Hilly, densely-wooded, and fertile, it was most difficult to believe that it was so thinly populated. Strange rock-formations appeared. Grotesque boulders of leviathan size lay strewn and standing in grass-covered openings. Wild pigeons by the score darted in and out amongst the trees. Merry squirrels scampered up the pine trees and eyed me from above. Huge "Jack Rabbits"[483] and young antelopes bounded here and there, and, seeing the intruder, disappeared. It all seemed such a change from the desert journey of the day before.

At Quemado, about ninety miles from Magdalena,[484] I felt hungry. Quemado consists of a wooden shack of an "hotel," and one "general merchandise" store.[485] I stopped at the "hotel" and fed. Meanwhile it commenced to rain. My spirits sank with the barometer.

The rain stopped three hours afterwards.

I set out full of energy and perseverance an hour after that. We slipped and slithered and slid in the miry road. Ten miles was enough.[486] All the energy and perseverance had flown to the winds. I rode up on to a hill-side to a spot on the fringe of a forest of cedar and yew.[487] Propping Lizzie up on her stand, I went in search of fuel. I had decided on the luxury of a camp fire.

Fuel there was in abundance. Withered trunks and broken boughs lay strewn about the hill-side. I soon had a roaring fire and passed away an hour or two before dark in writing letters and ruminating on the delights of a camp fire.

As the sun sank down in the valley, I slipped under the old blanket and watched the flames as they leapt from the burning embers. Just ahead, almost in sight from where I lay, was the western borderline of New Mexico.[488] Just beyond there, where the golden sun was slowly sinking in the valley, was Arizona; the Arizona that I longed so much to see. I had heard much of Arizona; its wonderful climate, its ancient, unknown ruins, its extinct volcanoes, its stupendous gorges, its great thirsty deserts. What would Arizona have in store for me? I wondered. And the fragrant smell of the burning cedarwood wove a magic charm about my thoughts as they slowly drifted into the mystic realm of the unconscious world.[489]

Morning brought a smiling dawn. I rose early and returned to the trail.

In ten minutes I was in Arizona.[490] A large signboard indicated the fact.[491] The road grew wider and better. Even the scenery seemed to change perceptibly. I somehow felt at home in Arizona.

At Springerville[492] I breakfasted and bought picture postcards. When travelling the latter operation is equally as important as the former.

Here the road makes a sudden turn to the north, bearing afterwards to the north-west. After twenty miles of riding, the country became flatter; it seemed as though it were now an immense plateau. After another twenty, I reached a little town known as St. John.[493] Here I filled a half-hour in the commendable process of consuming ices.[494] I had now to traverse some difficult country, as the great desert of Arizona was approached. There were more mountains to climb, but when the summit was reached there was little or no decline on the opposite side, the altitude grew higher and higher, and as it did so, strange as it may seem, the earth grew flatter and flatter.

There is but one ridge ahead to climb. The rocky trail bends and twists as it slowly swallows up the gradient that connects us to the horizon. A final swerve, and we commence a slight descent. There is a gap in the hills; the trail skirts around one side, and behold, a vast, unbounded plain lies before us, stretching to left and right as far as the eye can see.[495]

But what is this strange sight? On our right, barely a half of a mile from the road, is a gigantic mound.[496] Its presence there, rising abruptly out of the mathematical flatness of the plain, seems ridiculous, absurd, uncanny. It gives the impression of having been just dropped from the sky. It is a mud volcano—an uncommon sight,[497] and formed by the ejection of sand under pressure from below the surface of the earth.[498] All around, the plain is of distinctly volcanic formation. Indeed, we have now entered a vast volcanic region, extending for several thousands of square miles. Many of the mountains that we shall see, some of them giant peaks, and some only little hills, are extinct volcanoes of other ages. They were young and active while man was in his barbaric infancy on this weary globe, perhaps even before that.[499]

But soon is to appear a far more wondrous sight. In a few miles we enter a country of strange shapes and magic colours—the Petrified Forest of Arizona.[500] The first signs of approach are chains of little lava hills of grey and white. They also have an air of abruptness. One wonders how they came to be there at all. Flowing down to the flat plain in graceful, mathematical curves, they look like mounds of chalk, although they are softer still. Composed of soft, fine lava-dust, they weather rapidly away. Now all the plain is lava-dust and a tuft of lean grass here and there has found a spot wherein to make a home. Further on one notices great blocks of stone, like pillars of marble, lying strewn about the plain, some half buried, some barely projecting, and some perfectly naked. Here is one, there is another—they are everywhere, in every direction, of all shades of colour and varying in size from fragments an inch in diameter to pillars twenty or thirty feet in girth and over 100 feet in length. Every fragment, every massive block of marble once formed part of a great forest that spread for hundreds of square miles. The trees of this great forest were huge leviathans, unlike anything we know of in the Old World and similar only to the giant Sequoias of California[501] (but a few hundred miles away[502]), that send their mighty trunks hundreds of feet into the air—the relics of a bygone race.

A Petrified Leviathan.

This great forest of Arizona was at its prime. The stately pine trees rose towering into the sky. Birds of wonderful plumage lived in those mighty branches, and wild animals roamed amongst its undergrowth. Then something happened; no one knows exactly what—this great forest was enveloped in volcanic dust that in time buried it completely.[503] To the eye, if eye there was to witness the scene, the forest was no longer visible; it lay buried in the bowels of the earth; it had passed away; as a mighty, living forest it would exist no more. But those monster trees remained awhile, preserved by the all-surrounding lava. What happened then took thousands of years to achieve, though it can be recited in a few brief words. The trees in substance disappeared, but their forms remained in the hardened lava, like huge moulds waiting to be cast, their every crack and wrinkle preserved with inexorable accuracy. In time, it may have been æons, the moulds were cast, by some inexplicable phenomenon, and where once were timber and vegetable tissues came fluid marble rock that filled the hollows and cracks and wrinkles and reproduced the forms that ages before had been so suddenly arrested in their growth. Further ages passed, and gradually the soft lava was removed by the action of wind and rain and other causes. Gradually the harder material was laid bare, and the giant trees once more saw the light of day, but this time they were trunks of solid marble instead of pine wood. The work of denudation continued. The marble pillars, unsupported, fell to earth.[504] Some broke into huge blocks, while others remained more or less intact through the whole of their length, and unless one examined them at close quarters and saw the nature of their texture, they could not be distinguished from a tree that had been recently felled.

There are hundreds of these marble pine and spruce tree trunks,[505] whose cross-sections, revealed where they have broken, glisten with every colour of the rainbow. In places, where they lie tumbled and heaped together, it is as though a whole quarry of onyx had been dynamited out. In one place a fallen trunk of marble, nearly 200 feet in length, has spanned a gorge and formed a natural log bridge that all who dare can walk across.[506]

Such is the fairy tale that scientists tell.[507] The traveller whose privilege it is to journey across the Petrified Forest of Arizona will be lost in amazement at this fact which is so much stranger than any fiction.

"Lizzie" in the Petrfied Forest, Arizona.

I left the wonderful scene behind me with a feeling that I was bidding farewell to one of the prime mysteries of the world. Trunks and fragments of trunks could be seen projecting even from the surface of the road over which I passed, and a few blades of fine grass, with here and there a stunted cactus plant, were the only sign of life in any direction. I passed out as suddenly as I had entered. A double S-bend, where strange contorted rocks lay piled up in confusion on either side—and the Petrified Forest was left behind.

The sun was nearly setting when a couple of hours later I set out from Holbrook, well fed and well refreshed.[508] From my map I judged I should be able to reach the Little Colorado River, on whose banks I could spend the night.[509] But in Arizona the sun sets quickly. It can almost be said to get dark with a bump. The result was that in half an hour I was completely lost in the outskirts of the Great Arizona Desert. The trail had somehow disappeared, I knew not where, and but for my headlight, I should undoubtedly have ended in difficulties amid the inky blackness. Loth to turn back, I continued over the almost trackless waste of rock, sand, and prairie. I arrived at the rocky bed of a small stream. There were a few inches of water here and there, but it was not perceptibly moving. It could not possibly be the Little Colorado. I walked across to the other side. There I found a large ditch, more like an artificial dyke, that I knew I could never get Lizzie across. There was grass growing near, however, so I laid down my bed for the night, resolving to leave further investigations till daylight.

I should have known better than to camp by an almost stagnant stream, but I was so utterly tired that I defied the counsel of my own experience. Mosquitoes literally filled the air. Never have I known them so thick and so tenacious. The vibration of millions of wings kept the air in a constant shriek—a wild yell that never abated. I could only obtain relief from their attacks by enveloping my face completely with the thick blanket, and breathing through it. Then everything became so hot—the night itself was very sultry—that sleep was next to impossible. I snatched an hour or two of rest, but was a mass of bites and itching lumps next day.

In the morning, I returned to Holbrook, had breakfast,[510] and searched for information about the road. It appeared that a bridge had collapsed somewhere, so a new trail had been formed to circumvent it. I had missed the turning the night before. At the garage where I made these inquiries,[511] I took the opportunity of removing Lizzie's wheels, and of cleaning and adjusting the spindles. I packed them with new grease in preparation for the sandy journey to come, and removed and re-aligned the chain sprockets; I wanted no breakdowns or searches for missing parts in the baking, sandy desert. It was as well that I had taken precautions. I found the lock ring of one chain wheel missing altogether, and the sprocket half-way unscrewed from its shaft.[512] The only item for regret was the charge of one dollar for the use of the garage! Having already had experience of American garage mechanics, I resolved not to allow any more to learn their trade at Lizzie's expense.

I had no difficulty in picking up the trail in the full light of day. Once again I set out to cross the great Desert of Arizona.[513] The next town, a kind of oasis, was Winslow, about forty miles away.[514] The barren prairie soon gave way to bare limestone rocks and shifting sand; vegetation disappeared altogether, save for occasional clumps of greeny-grey sage brush dotted here and there over the rocky waste that ever met the eye. The air was hot but clear. On an elevation one could see for tremendous distances. The little tuft of black smoke that hung over Winslow looked clear enough to be a mile or two away. It was thirty;[515] in the distance was a great silver line, threading its way intermittently across the plain. I knew it to be the Little Colorado,[516] which, like its mother, the Great Colorado, flows nearly the whole of its length in a canyon and seems deliberately to choose the path of greatest resistance, cutting through rocks and gorges of limestone and granite with ne'er a murmur.

As Winslow drew near, the narrow sandy track gave way to a broad concrete highway. I had not seen a made road of any description for many days. The appearance of concrete here in the middle of a desert seemed ridiculous. I would enjoy it to the full. Lizzie's throttle jumped open unexpectedly and away we sailed through the breeze. "There's a catch in this somewhere," I told myself. There was! It nearly meant grief. The city architect had foreseen the goading lure of that cold flat stretch of concrete and made up his mind that speeding should not exist thereon. So he made several dips therein at intervals, each dip about five or ten feet below the normal level of the road. Any attempt to travel at more than twenty would mean damage to the vehicle when it hit the opposite side.[517] Unfortunately these obstructions were absolutely invisible until but a few feet ahead. Sometimes there was a warning. More often there was not. The first I came to quite unawares and at a high speed. The machine with its momentum nearly leapt clean across the space, and had I been going much slower it would have struck the opposite side lower down and inevitably have caused a serious crash. I went warily after that and wondered what ingeniously contrived anti-speeding devices I should meet next.

Arrived at Winslow, I ate heartily of ices.[518] The busy modern town seemed a most remarkable contrast to the sandy wastes that surrounded it.

I now had a long journey ahead. Flagstaff, the next town, was over eighty miles away,[519] and the trail ran across some of the most arid country of Arizona. For mile upon mile there was nothing to be seen but yellow sand and, on the horizon, a rugged range of hills. Ahead, nearly a hundred miles away, loomed up the San Francisco Peaks, dark and threatening.[520] Overhead the sun beat down with unrelenting fury. One could see the shimmer of the air above the baking sand as the tremendous heat oozed out of it into the atmosphere. Here and there, one could see spirals of sand hundreds of feet high whisked up by some strange whirling motion of the air,[521] and carried for hundreds of yards across the wilderness, gathering in volume and height as they moved, only to collapse again and give birth to others. Not a sign of life or vegetation was visible anywhere. What a place to be stranded in without water! But

I had plenty with me. I stopped to drink from the bag on my handlebar every few miles. The heat and the glare were awful.

A few miles out of Winslow one cylinder ceased to fire. I had been wondering when the next instalment of misfortune was to arrive. Like a true pessimist, I expected it would come in a place like this. So I was not disheartened.

I stopped two or three times to change plugs and examine the engine. It was of no avail, and the heat grew so intense when I was not moving that it was impossible to stop for longer than a few minutes at a time. There was no shade, not even a rock to hide me from the fiery sun. The frame of the machine seemed red-hot, and even the tools in the tool-box were too hot to handle unprotected.

"Another overhaul at Flagstaff," I told myself, and continued again on three cylinders. Ploughing through the loose sand absorbed much of the power of the engine, but I was content, so long as we kept moving. Slowly the metal sign-posts of the "Touring Club of California"[522] that marked the miles were passed. They were the only items of interest in this barren country. Many times they were missing altogether. Often they lay prone upon the ground, the strong, eight-feet-long steel tubing of the post bent in strange forms. They had been uprooted by some unfortunate traveller and used as levers or crowbars to extricate a car that had left the beaten track and sunk in the loose sand of the desert. Some even bore conflicting particulars, and it was quite usual to notice the distances increase instead of decrease the nearer one drew to one's destination! Often the signs themselves had been riddled with bullet-holes "just for fun" by some blasé traveller with a taste for shooting.[523] Splendid amusement, to shoot at a sign-post put there at enormous expense by a private club for the benefit of all!

Slowly the hours went by and, as they did, a huge thunder-storm could be seen brewing over the San Francisco Peaks, now only forty miles away.[524] The whole sky became dull and overcast. The loose yellow sand gave place to rocks and shingle, and gradually the desert was left behind. As the altitude increased—we were climbing slowly all the time—signs of life appeared. Lean grass, parched with thirst and brown with the heat, was seen once more, and later a few sheep were noticed sheltering behind rocks and boulders.

I pushed forward with all haste. Flagstaff was at the foot of the San Francisco Peaks and there would certainly be a deluge very shortly. The road was abominable. In most places it was so rocky and the gradient so steep that it was like riding up great flights of rugged steps. The sharp rocks dug in the tyres down to the rims, and the vibration shook the very sockets of one's bones.

On the left, barely a mile from the trail, we passed the "Meteor Mountain."[525] This is a most remarkable sight. Situated in the midst of comparatively flat or rolling country, it looks at first sight like the crater of a great volcano. But its origin is not volcanic. It gives the impression of having been formed by artificial and not by natural means. The crater is half a mile across[526] and the interior of the crater is saucer-shaped. An air of mystery envelops its origin, and many theories have been put forward to explain it. But the theories have either been disproved or have never been definitely accepted.[527]

"Meteor Mountain" remains to this day a mystery of geology. In its crater is a ranch-house and hundreds of sheep graze in its vicinity.[528]

A dozen miles farther on the trail led on to a magnificent steel bridge spanning the "Diablo Canyon"[529]—a wonderful gorge in the limestone rocks. Far, far below ran a little stream of clear water.

The sky grew blacker still. We continued climbing over the sharp, rocky trail. The mighty peaks ahead were almost lost in a sea of blackness. Distant thunder rumbled and groaned across the desolate waste. Sharp flashes of lightning lit up the heavens for a moment and revealed the sharp, lurid outlines of the three giants around whose peaks centred the fury of the skies. Slowly the storm abated. I thanked Heaven for that.

Then we came to the fringe of a wonderful forest that covers the plateau and clothes the mountain sides almost to the summit of their peaks. The sight of the trees, the sound of the breezes as they rustled through the branches bearing with them the magic scent of the pines, was like passing from death to life. It was a new world, a world of new sensations and pleasant forms. The broiling wastes, the dazzling yellow sand, the strange and sometimes ugly shapes, the grotesque, the mysterious, the incredible: these were left behind—for a while.

The storm had almost passed. Much rain had fallen, but fortunately the trail lay through a stretch of volcanic dust. The rain when it fell did not dissolve it, but soaked through as quickly as it fell, leaving the surface almost as hard and dry as it was before. I thanked Heaven again for that. Closer, closer, ever we climbed, until often the mountains were hardly to be seen; we were amongst them, climbing them, in them. Here and there the clustering trees grew thinner and fields of wild flowers, mauve and purple-coloured, would burst into view, clothing the valleys and the slopes like a great carpet.

Then a glade would appear of fresh green grass—grass so fresh and so green that it would seem to have been meant more for a child's fairy-book than for a real live world. Then a beautiful mountain would appear through the trees, its sides and its angles glistening with every colour of the rainbow and changing with every new aspect. This would be an extinct volcanic cone and the colours would be reflected from the loose cinders that formed its whole. Then amongst the lofty pine trees the traveller would see—as a last remnant of the grotesque—vast fields of lava, great beds of solid cinder, thrown up into monstrous shapes with strange, sinister outlines.[530]

And onwards, ever onwards, ever nearer to Flagstaff we went, the wheels gliding noiselessly over the smooth lava-track that wound its way in and out of the pine trees and up and over the foothills and valleys towards the West. We enter a large valley, from which a wonderful view of the San Francisco Peaks delights the traveller. They are barely a half-dozen miles away now;[531] their great volcanic cones, over a couple of miles in height above the sea, can be seen as sharply and as clearly as though they were but 100 yards away. So mighty are they, and so pure is the air of Arizona, that on a clear day they can be seen for 200 miles in any direction.[532]

At last the small town of Flagstaff is reached.[533] It is clean, modern, and laid out in pretentious square blocks, some with only a few bungalows built thereon.[534] Evening was drawing on. Not having had a meal for over twelve hours, I hied me to a restaurant[535] where puffed cereals[536] and apricot pies and mugs of good coffee effected a miraculous disappearance. Thereafter I followed the scent of a comfortable hotel, where once more I slept the sleep of the righteous.

CHAPTER 17 NOTES

469. Figures 150 and 151 describe how to use insulation tape to repair leaking fuel lines.

The use of insulation tape for emergency repairs is in many instances invaluable. One of the purposes for which it is often called into use is shown in Fig. 5, where a quick repair to a leaky gasoline line is depicted. A leak in the line itself is rare, most of the troubles which develop in this direction taking place in the joints in the piping. The joints can be repaired just as well as any other part of the piping with winding of this nature. Insulation tape has been used with success to repair even greater troubles than these. A case which was noticed some time ago in which a rapid repair was made with insulating tape may prove of interest.

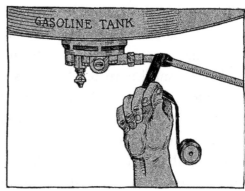

Fig. 5—Tape is successfully used for stopping gasoline leaks

Figure 150 and Figure 151: The Use of Insulation Tape for Emergency Repairs.
Source: *Automobile,* May 30, 1912, Pages 1242-1243.

470. The "great sandy plain" that C.K. describes is called the Plains of San Agustin. On its western edge is the southern end of the Crosby Mountains which rise west of Datil, about thirty-seven miles west of Magdalena. On the eastern edge of the Plains of San Agustin—C.K.'s vantage point when reporting this visage—are the Magdalena Mountains, which run south from Magdalena. The Plains of San Agustin are so large and flat that, in 1973, construction began to build the Very Large Array ("VLA"). The VLA consists of multiple radio telescope dishes to listen to some of the oldest "sounds" in the universe. The dishes are positioned along three diverging sets of ultra-heavy-duty steel rails—each of which radiate out thirteen miles from the center compound about fifty miles west of Socorro.

471. The 1920 census reported 1,869 people living in Magdalena in January 1920. *The Official Hotel Red Book and Directory* (1920) cites a Magdalena population of 2,500, a round number that may have included people living in the surrounding desert. The photos in Figures 152 and 153 were taken a few years before 1919, but it is easy to envision C.K. riding west on the highway (left-to-right on 1st Street at the flag pole seen in Figure 152) and turning onto Main Street to park his Henderson at the Magdalena Cafe or the Hotel Aragon for a full breakfast.

472. C.K. wrote that he ate at the café that he had been told served the best food in town. He describes the entrance something like an old saloon ("swing doors"), but with nice dining inside. The Hotel Aragon was a full service hotel, was listed in AAA guides and the *Blue Book* (1918), and reportedly had a restaurant, barber, and beauty salon. However, the Magdalena Cafe and Hotel was virtually across the street (and had the name "cafe" before "hotel," implying it was more café than hotel). It is unlikely we will ever know where he breakfasted, but the evidence seems to tip toward the Magdalena Cafe and Hotel.

473. "disport": Archaic English: "to enjoy oneself unrestrainedly or frolic."

474. The photograph(s) of this "wooden church" do not survive in C.K.'s collection. He was probably referring to the Community Church on the southwest corner of Main and 4th Streets, across the street and only a block and a half south of the Magdalena Cafe. The spire of this church is visible in the photo in Figure 152, in the distance just to the right of the flagpole in the foreground. The Community Church was built in 1907 and remains in use as a church today.

Figure 152: Looking South on Main Street in Magdalena, *ca.* 1915.
This photo captures the full length of Main Street in Magdalena from the railroad tracks to 10th Street, which is three-quarters of a mile away. At right is the railroad warehouse of Becker-Mactavich Co. The Hotel Aragon is located before the Becker-Mactavich offices at 1st Street (Now US Route 60). Two signs for the Magdalena Cafe and Hotel are visible attached to buildings on the left, on the block between 1st and 2nd Streets.
Source: US Library of Congress. Photograph by Adolph Wittemann.

Figure 153: Looking North on Main Street in Magdalena, *ca*. 1915.
This photograph shows the view north on Main Street from the perspective of standing in the middle of 1st Street (now US Route 60). The Magdalena Cafe and Hotel is out of view directly behind the photographer. Across the street—in order—are: the Becker-Mactavich store; Beagle drug store; R.W.D. Pool Hall (with Budweiser signs in the window, so this photo was taken before Magdalena "settled down" following New Mexico's enactment of Prohibition in 1917); Hotel Aragon; two small shops; the Becker-Mactavich railroad warehouse; a freight train car on the tracks; and a larger warehouse across the tracks.
Source: US Library of Congress. Photograph by Adolph Wittemann.

475. "gor-dem": This is C.K.'s phonetic attempt to represent how the locals said, "God damned." "Buck-jumper," in this context, means a cowboy who rides bucking broncos in rodeo contests.

476. C.K. was riding in a section of what was locally called "Hoof Highway" (the official name was Magdalena Livestock Driveway), a route across the desert west of Magdalena used to drive cattle to the railroad head at Magdalena from as many as 125 miles west in Springerville, Arizona.

477. C.K.'s estimate of the next town being "90 miles away" is reasonable. Quemado is the next main town west of Magdalena. The *Blue Book* (1918) provides a distance of 82.7 miles from Magdalena to Quemado, although C.K. would have passed through tiny Datil 36.9 miles west of Magdalena; this means it was probably closer to eighty miles from the herd to Quemado.

478. There was a serious two-year drought in New Mexico beginning in 1916 until it finally broke in the summer of 1918. In an article, "New Mexico is Hard Hit by Drouth," appearing on Page 8 of the January 4, 1918 edition of the *Western Liberal* (in Lordsburg, New Mexico, just a few miles east of the Arizona border), the newspaper reported on the drought's persistance:

> "How wide and persistent the drought in New Mexico is, can be gathered from the report by the United States weather bureau. During November, the report says, practically one-half of the state, from the Rio Grande westward, was without precipitation, or had but a mere trace...the drought remains unbroken, completing the thirteenth month of light precipitation for the state, during which period the total average amount has been only ten inches."

479. Although no news reports have been found documenting the demise of thousands of cattle during this drought, it seems most likely that C.K. heard the stories from the ranchers and cowboys directly. News reports of the period did mention that some ranchers would send younger cattle to market, even though they were not full grown and went for lower prices. Apparently they had concluded that a young steer at the slaughterhouse was still worth more than a dead steer in the desert.

480. The viewing of roadside cattle skeletons was a common theme amongst motorcyclists who reported about their trips. For example, during the same period that C.K. was heading west, Herbert Charles "Hap" Scherer began and finished an eastbound coast-to-coast "tour" on a Harley-Davidson Sport and reported seeing skeletons of cattle in eastern Arizona. Scherer, who was not on one of his many speed-record-setting trips, spent five luxurious weeks on the road, leaving eastbound from Los Angeles on July 3, 1919 (when C.K. was heading west at the Mississippi River) and arriving in New York about August 9, 1919 (before C.K. had left Los Angeles for San Francisco). Scherer had passed eastbound through Kansas City on July 12, 1919, the day after C.K. had departed on westbound on the National Old Trails Road—the same "highway" that Scherer had taken eastbound. In the second in a series of three articles Scherer contributed to *Motorcycling and Bicycling* on September 10, 1919, Scherer wrote that ranchers had told him most of the remains of cattle he had seen had died in the recent extremely hard winter (apparently the same

season that stopped the pilots in Santa Fe with four feet of snow and -10°F temperatures):

> "Going from St. Johns to Springerville I noticed, in gradually increasing numbers, the carcasses and, in most case skeletons, of cattle lying in the fields, and often near the road. The weirdest sight of all was when I later saw the remains of what apparently was a whole herd of cattle lying in the field near the road. It was explained to me by a rancher in Springerville that the loss of all these cattle was due to an unusually hard winter; in fact, the most severe winter that section had experienced in 35 years."

481. Assuming that the beginning of the "thirty-mile stretch" was when C.K. got past the herd of cattle, he would have been about thirty-five miles from Magdalena. The *Blue Book* (1918) Route 835 reflects 36.9 miles between Magdalena and Datil. Just as C.K. indicated, it is approaching Datil that the plains end and the Datil Mountains begin, and the road heads up into White House Canyon. The map underlying Figure 154 is a topographical map of the area from 1954, after the road (identified by 1954 as US 60) had been straightened a bit. Dashed range rings reflect five-statute-mile distances from Magdalena (reflecting an "as the crow flies" distance between Magdalena and Datil of about thirty-four miles). The problem is that C.K. would have driven through Datil before entering "hilly, thickly-wooded country," so it is difficult to reconcile his statement that he saw no one for fifteen miles, unless he means fifteen miles after Datil.

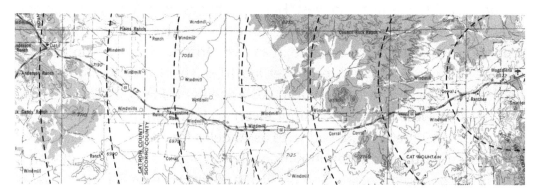

Figure 154: Distances from Magdalena Toward Datil.
Source: USGS: *New Mexico Socorro* (1:250,000), 1958.

482. There wasn't much of anything fifteen miles past Datil. There was a fork in the road about 13.6 miles west, but there is no community indicated on any maps of the period or since. It is likely that C.K. was more than fifteen miles past Datil. Although it was not called Pie Town until the late 1920s, in 1919 there was a small settlement about twenty-one miles west of Datil that may have existed as little more than an intersection of two roads. It seems most likely that the settlement that is today called Pie Town is where C.K. stopped and bought gas.

483. Figures 155 and 156 depict a jackrabbit and "antelope" that are native to New Mexico.

Figure 155: Black-tailed Jackrabbit (Lepus californicus).
Also known as the American desert hare, this is the largest jackrabbit native to New Mexico. Its size is about two feet in length and up to six pounds.
Source: Photograph by Jessie Eastland. Reproduced with permission.

Figure 156: Pronghorn (Antilocapra americana).
The pronghorn is not actually an antelope, but it has been colloquially referred to as an antelope since Europeans arrived. The pronghorn is the second-fastest land animal on earth (after the cheetah), capable of sustained speed of sixty mph.
Source: US Department of Agriculture. Photograph by Jack Dykinga.

484. It was not quite ninety miles from Magdalena to Quemado. The *Blue Book* (1918) Route 835 reflects that Quemado is 82.7 miles west of Magdalena. *Quemado* is a Spanish word meaning "burned" or "burnt."

485. The 1920 census data reflects that Quemado had a population of 568. The *New Mexico State Business Directory* (1920) reports a population of Quemado of 350, with the difference likely being the latter's reliance on old information and estimates or focused on just the main community. The *Business Directory* lists only fifteen individuals and businesses in Quemado. Since C.K. wrote there was only one hotel and that he ate dinner there, he probably met one or more of the following people listed in the *Business Directory* (those identified with "B" below) and/or the census data (identified as "C" below):

- Fannie E. Graham, Hotel Proprietor (B)(C).

- O.D. and Lola Collins, Hotel (B)(C).

- Maggie and Bessie Wyche, Hotel Waiters (C).

- Anecito and Teodoria Carry, Restaurant Cooks (C).

- A.E. Underwood, Restaurant (B).

486. C.K. reports that he camped for the night about ten miles west of Quemado. However, based upon what he said he did the next morning, he must have instead driven about thirty miles west of Quemado before he camped for the night.

487. The "yew" (*Taxus baccata*) is not native to the wilds in North America. It is a conifer native to western, central, and southern Europe, northwest Africa, and southwest Asia, so it seems C.K. was describing a tree *like* a yew that he had seen earlier in his life.

488. If C.K. stopped about ten miles west of Quemado, he would have been twenty-four miles from the New Mexico/Arizona border and would not have been able to imagine seeing it—even in the dark. On the other hand, if he stopped thirty miles west of Quemado, he would have camped four miles from the border, certainly close enough to imagine seeing it.

489. C.K.'s characterization of falling asleep as "drifting into the mystic realm of the unconscious world" seems of prescient relevance given C.K.'s activities related to spiritualism later in his life.

490. If C.K. had camped ten miles west of Quemado and was still twenty-four miles from Arizona when he awoke, he would have needed to average 144 mph from his campsite to reach the border in ten minutes. That did not happen. He was more likely just four or five miles from the border when he awoke, which would mean that he had driven and stopped thirty miles west of Quemado the night before—not ten.

491. C.K. took the photo in Figure 157 (next page) on the morning of Friday, July 25, 1919 at the Arizona state line. Today, the road does not go around the hill to the right; it is cut through the saddle between the hills, approximately behind the sign that C.K. mentions (enlarged and inset Figure 158, next page). The sign was evidently sponsored by Becker's Transcontinental Garage, a few miles ahead in Springerville. Becker's Garage also purchased a display advertisement in the *Blue Book* (1918), as shown in Figure 159 (next page). Becker's Garage was owned by Gustav Becker—a German immigrant, pioneer merchant, and businessman who was an advocate of highway construction in Arizona and a charter member of the Arizona Good Roads Association. He also owned multiple businesses in Arizona, New Mexico and as far east as El Paso, TX, including Becker-Mactavich Company in Magdalena, NM, whose store and railroad warehouse can be seen in the photographs in Note 471, Figures 152 and 153. Additionally, C.K. stopped at Becker's Garage and signed on line 2110 of the logbook (Figure 160, next page), noting that he was from Birmingham, England, on a Henderson motorcycle, and bound for California.

Figure 157: Arizona State Line, July 25, 1919.
Source: C.K.'s personal slide collection.

Figure 158: Arizona Border Sign (Close Up of Portion of Figure 157).
Source: C.K.'s personal slide collection.

Figure 159: Advertisement for Becker's Transcontinental Garage.
Source: *Blue Book,* Vol. 7, 1918. Page 846.

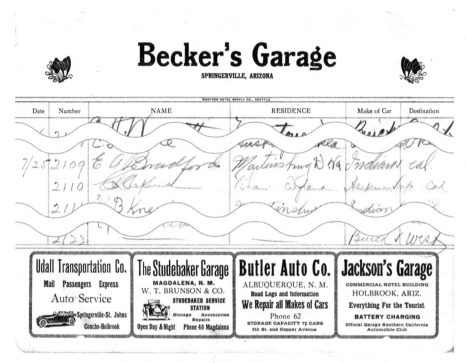

Figure 160: Excerpt from Becker's Garage Log, July 25, 1919.
Source: Becker Garage Log, Becker Family Papers, MS 65, Box 23, Folder 257.
Courtesy of Arizona Historical Society, Tucson, Arizona.

492. The 1920 census population of Springerville was 479. In addition to Gustav Becker's Transcontinental Garage, which sold gasoline that C.K. almost certainly needed to buy, Becker also owned an adjacent hotel and a general store catering to travelers. While one of these two establishments seems the most likely place for a hungry motorcyclist to eat breakfast, there may have been other restaurants in town.

493. Although C.K. says he rode forty miles in total from Springerville to St. Johns, directions from the day consistently reflect it as a thirty-two mile leg. The terrain in the area is generally flat and all of the original road may be lost to time. However, the instructions in the *Blue Book* (1920) Route 616 include, "**Caution** for sharp turns downgrade 19.1 [miles]" (**bold** emphasis is in the original). This notation is consistent with *Auto Club Map 16*, 1915, which depicts a "summit" that is north of a "wide valley" and is shown in Figure 161, a location nineteen miles from Springerville and thirteen miles (circled) from St. Johns; a "Summit." The "10%-12% Up Grade" reflects the southbound road prior to the summit, so it would be a 10%-12% descent for C.K. as he drove north down into the valley.

The above depiction of the road is consistent with the topographic map of the area from 1971 that still shows the general route of the old road—with a three-hundred foot drop into a canyon—as the excerpt in Figure 162 shows, allowing the location of C.K.'s view to be estimated as being at N34°21'19", W109°24'50"—a site that appears on some contemporary maps as being on Arizona Route 4365.

Figure 161: Excerpt of *Auto Club Map 16* from Springerville to St. Johns.
Source: *Auto Club Map 16.*

494. It is not certain where C.K. would have had ice cream or such frozen delights in St. Johns. On the front page of the October 16, 1919 edition of *The St. Johns Herald* (Vol. 36, No. 8), the weekly newspaper proudly announced that: "St. Johns is surely growing. She now supports three restaurants." Several hotels and restaurants have been identified, although it has not been ascertained which one C.K. selected. These are two restaurants known to have existed in July 1919:

- Gibbons & Dawson, previously owned by E. Dawson; however, he may have moved away by 1919.

- Whiting Restaurant, believed to have been operated by Ralph E. Whiting and his family.

495. It seems most likely that C.K. took in this view of the wide open plains and a key area of the Little Colorado River watershed when he reached the northwest side of Potter Mesa, at approximately N34°43'19.79", W109°45'43.16", around thirty-five miles on the old road from St. Johns.

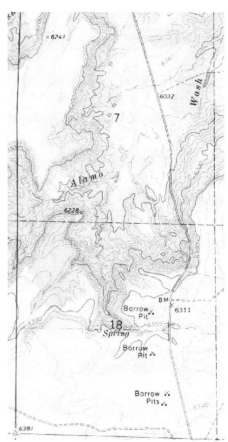

Figure 162: Three-Hundred Foot Drop Into Canyon.
Source: *USGS: Arizona Lyman Lake SW Quadrangle, 7.5 Minute Series, 1971.*

496. Figure 163 is a photograph that C.K. took of a mud volcano as he drew closer to the Petrified Forest.

Figure 163: Mud Volcano Formation Near Petrified Forest.
Source: Auto Club Map 16.

497. Mud volcanoes may not be common in England, but they are quite common all over the world.

498. This is a generally accurate description of how mud volcanoes or mud domes are formed. In truth, they are not actually volcanoes because they do not emit molten rock or lava.

499. The Sunset Crater volcano, about twenty miles northeast of Flagstaff, Arizona, last erupted about between AD 1080 and AD 1150, a period during which numerous human communities were active in the area, so they would have witnessed the eruption. "Clovis Man" is believed to have been in the area as early as 9000 BC. Maize (corn) was introduced around 4500 BC and irrigation systems began around 1500 BC.

500. President Theodore Roosevelt designated this area as Petrified Forest National Monument in 1906. It was renamed Petrified Forest National Park in 1962. C.K. would have arrived in the area of what is now the south entrance, but all of the roads were different then and C.K. may not have driven all the way north through

the current park boundary at the north entrance. Figure 164 is an excerpt from a modern map of the park.

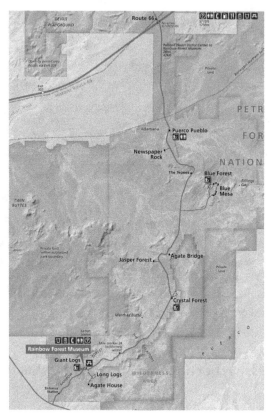

Figure 164: Petrified Forest National Park, 2018.
Source: US National Park Service.

501. In 1919, most of the trees in the Petrified Forest were believed to be related to the Norfolk Island pine (*Araucaria excelsa*), but that is not the current prevailing theory. Most scientists now believe that most were a *type* of pine tree (*Araucaria*) that grew 200 feet tall, but are no longer found in the Northern Hemisphere.

502. Sequoia National Forest is 500 miles west of the Petrified Forest.

503. Even in 1919, the scientific consensus was that the trees had grown to full height, but that heavy rains had caused them to fall down and become swept from floods into basins where they were covered deep underground for millions of years. In *Guidebook of the Western United States, Part C* (1915), the USGS described the genesis of the logs in the Petrified Forest:

"The logs are the remains of trees that grew in Triassic time... Doubtless they grew in a near-by region and, after falling, drifted down a watercourse and lodged in some eddy or a sand bank. Later they were buried by sand and clay, finally to a depth of several thousand feet. The conversion to stone was effected by gradual replacement of the woody material by silica in the form called chalcedony, deposited by underground water."

The Triassic period lasted about fifty million years beginning about 250 million years ago at the time of the "Permian-Triassic extinction event" that killed about 80% of every living thing on earth, so it is not surprising that these huge trees did not survive.

504. C.K. believed the trees were turned to stone while standing vertically and then broke apart after being exposed to the elements. This is not true. If it were, there would be at least one example of the remnants of a tree trunk still standing vertical—with its rocky roots going into the earth—even if the tree's main trunk had broken off and fallen over.

505. Current scientific consensus is that most were a type of pine tree (Araucaria) that grew 200 feet tall, but they are no longer living in the Northern Hemisphere.

506. The famous petrified "Agate Bridge" is actually only 110 feet long. Although it was almost certainly found intact, reinforcement pillars were added to make it safe to walk upon without breaking. Figure 165 is made from two 1908 photos to create a panorama and depict the original pillars. However, in 1917, these pillars were replaced with a single steel-reinforced concrete beam supporting the entire span, a configuration that remains today.

Figure 165: Petrified Bridge, Petrified Forest of Arizona, *ca.* 1908.
Source: Haines Photo Co., Conneaut, Ohio. US Library of Congress.

507. C.K. seems to be dismissing the scientific consensus, preferring to contemplate a magical creation rather than the "fairy tales" recited by scientists.

508. The *Arizona Business Directory* (1920) from the Gazetteer Publishing & Printing Co. in Denver contained almost three pages of business listings for Holbrook, people in business, and the businesses in the community. It is not an all-inclusive listing, since two additional establishments were advertising in the newspaper in 1919 and they are not in this 1920 directory. Except for the numerous hotels listed—many of which may have had a restaurant—only one establishment stands out as a possibility for C.K.'s dining spot: Rees Bros. Café (James R. & Frank B. Rees). Figures 166 and 167 are advertisements for two additional establishments, the Palace Café and the Navajo Café.

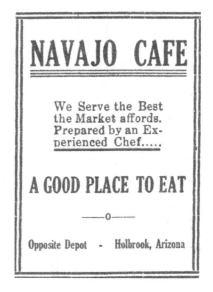

Figure 166: Palace Cafe Advertisement.
Source: *Holbrook News*, July 18, 1919. Page 5.

Figure 167: Navajo Cafe Advertisement.
Source: *Holbrook News*, July 18, 1919. Page 6.

509. The Little Colorado River actually flows from east to west less than a half a mile south of Holbrook. C.K. would have crossed that river arriving in Holbrook, so it is not clear why he would characterize it as being a challenge to reach before darkness leaving Holbrook near sunset.

510. Since C.K. did not describe a bad experience with the prior day's meal, he probably ate at the same café.

511. There were at least four garages in Holbrook in 1919. The *Arizona Business Directory* (1920) listed them, as well as the individuals who worked there:

- The Jackson Garage, C.H. Edmunds, proprietor. In addition to being a Cadillac dealer, Jackson's provided auto repair, storage, welding, and battery service. This garage was also prominently advertised at the bottom of the log book that C.K. signed at Becker's Garage in Springerville (see Note 491, Figure 160).

- Freeman H. Hawthorn, Auto Repairs.

- Jennings Automobile Co., C.H. Jennings, president. Primarily a Ford dealer, Jennings was also listing as providing general auto and machine repairs.

- Navajo Garage, W.D. Bradley and W.F. Williams. "The nearest point to the Hopi Indian Villages, and the best road to Petrified and Painted Desert" (*Santa Fe* magazine, October 1920).

For several reasons, it seems most likely that Jackson's Garage was the place where C.K. would have pursued maintenance workspace for a short period.

512. This is a reference to parts of the speedometer system C.K. had on his bike, not the main drive train. The drive sprocket on the engine is held on by a nut (which had previously fallen off), while the sprocket on the rear wheel held in place by a large "nut ring" which, even if it somehow got loose, would still be on the axle.

513. Figure 168 (next page) is a photo from C.K.'s collection that may depict the road ahead after leaving Holbrook (the second time).

Figure 168: Arizona Desert—River Colorado in the Distance.
Source: C.K.'s personal slide collection.

514. The *Blue Book* (1918) Route 836 provides a distance of 36.8 miles from Holbrook to Winslow, so "about forty miles" is a reasonable estimate.

515. C.K. was probably less than thirty miles away when he first saw Winslow. The distance between Holbrook and Winslow "as the crow flies" is less than thirty-two miles, and that would mean he was just two miles out of Holbrook. It seems more likely he was fifteen—or perhaps twenty—miles away at this point.

516. In fact, the roads C.K. traveled on since entering Arizona had *paralleled* the Little Colorado River. The Little Colorado originates around Greer, Arizona, about ten miles southwest of Springerville. However, after reaching Winslow, the Little Colorado does run north. Clear Creek feeds into the Little Colorado at Winslow, so C.K. may have observed these two rivers as being a single river "across the plain" as he approached Winslow.

517. These dips in the road do not appear to be related to speed control, but rather were strategically installed to allow water to "drain" (pass over the road) during periods of heavy rain.

518. Central Drug Co., Dr. Ross G. Bazel, proprietor, was the only establishment listed as having a soda fountain in the *Arizona State Business Directory* (1920). In 1919, its name was Kelly Drug store, reflecting the name of Dr. Bazel's business partner when the store opened in 1916. Thus, Kelly Drug store was the most

likely establishment where C.K. consumed "ices" (a period term that seems to have been used interchangeably for ice cream and crushed-ice drinks).

519. The *Blue Book* (1918) Route 837 provides a distance of 64.7 miles from Winslow to Flagstaff, so "over eighty miles" is a rather high estimate.

520. The San Francisco Peaks are much fewer than one hundred miles from Winslow. They are actually less than sixty miles away from Winslow.

521. Figure 169 is a modern photo of a "dust devil."

Figure 169: Dust Devil in Arizona.
Source: NASA.

522. The Touring Club of California is probably C.K's literary amalgamation of two clubs that actually did exist:

- The Automobile Club of Southern California was founded in 1910 and became one of the largest affiliates of the American Automobile Association (AAA).

- In June 1917, the National Touring Club of America, Inc. was announced to be operated—in national scope—to "further good roads, just and equitable motoring laws, and to promote the interests of motoring in general." However, within five years at least one of the organizers had been sentenced to five years in federal prison for fraud because the organization had collected membership dues from nearly 10,000 people, but used the funds for not much more than the enrichment of the organizers. They almost certainly did not place any road signs in Arizona.

523. Although the photo in Figure 170 was taken eighty-two miles west of Laramie, Wyoming, on the Lincoln Highway, it indicates that shooting at road signs was a real problem—especially on the open road. The photo depicts an official from the Engineering Department of the Automobile Club of Southern California inspecting a damaged sign put up by his club. Not only does this image illustrate the damage caused by vandals, it also provides clear evidence that the Automobile Club of Southern California had placed signs all over the country and established a department to maintain them.

SIGN-SHOOTING ON THE LINCOLN HIGHWAY
OPEN SEASON, JANUARY 1st TO DECEMBER 31st EVERY YEAR

Figure 170: Sign Shooting on the Lincoln Highway, *ca.* 1920.
Source: *See America First,* Vol. 7, No. 2, Jan-Feb 1921. Page 54.

524. Because C.K. had not yet reached "Meteor Mountain" (which is about forty-two miles from the San Francisco Peaks), it is more likely that the San Francisco Peaks were still fifty miles away—not forty.

525. The old road that C.K. was on in 1919 came within a mile north of what is now called Meteor Crater. Today, the crater can be reached via a six-mile access road from Exit 233 on I-40.

526. The crater is more than a half a mile across. Because it is not perfectly round, it varies between 0.7 and 0.8 miles across at the rim.

527. By 1903, the crater had been bought by a geologist named Daniel Barringer, who first published his theory of "impact" as being the origin. He believed there were ten million tons of iron buried in the crater left by the meteor. However, in 1929, astronomer Forest Ray Moulton calculated that the meteor had vaporized upon impact. Daniel Barringer's impact theory (but not his belief in iron deposits) was finally proven correct in 1960 when Eugene M. Shoemaker discovered the presence of minerals that were known to only exist after severe shock and overpressure. The age of the crater has since been established as approximately 49,000 years old, a time when wooly mammoths roamed the region. Still, by the time C.K. came through in 1919, scientists had accepted its extra-terrestrial origin albeit erroneous as to its relative size, as described in a 1915 article titled "A Mine in a Meteor-Made Crater" by Arthur Chapman published in *Scientific American* (Vol. CXII, No. 3, January 16, 1915, Page 70):

> "This is not a volcanic crater, but was formed by the fall of a tremendous meteor in some past age. Scientists who have examined the crater are of the opinion that the meteor which struck the earth there must have been of almost incalculable size and weight. In fact, there is no indication anywhere else of the alighting of a meteor approximating the size of this Arizona visitor."

In 1915, limited exploration and lack of satellite imagery hindered accurate classification of the size of meteor craters around the world. Today, only a hundred years later, Meteor Crater is not even considered among the top ten largest craters on earth—if even among the top fifty. Figure 171 (next page) is an illustration of the crater by Daniel Barringer published in 1914 by the Proceedings of the Academy of Natural Sciences of Philadelphia.

PROC. ACAD. NAT. SCI. PHILA. 1914.

PLATE XXII.

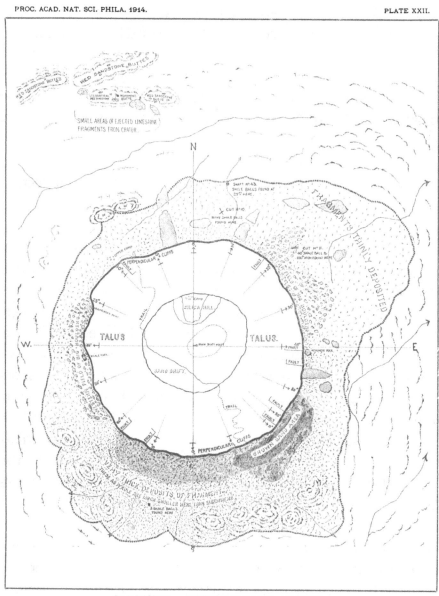

BARRINGER: METEOR CRATER, ARIZONA.
Scale, 1290 feet = 1 inch.

Figure 171: Meteor Crater.
Source: "Further Notes on Meteor Crater, Arizona" in *Proceedings of the Academy of Natural Sciences of Philadelphia*, September 1914. Plate XXII.

528. To this day, the crater is owned by descendants of Daniel Barringer. Daniel Barringer was also known to Carl Lampland, an astronomer at Lowell Observatory with whom C.K. had spent considerable time during his stays in Flagstaff. Barringer and Lampland exchanged substantial correspondence about the origins of Meteor Crater, among other things, from 1928-1933.

529. The Canon Diablo bridge was actually only eight miles west of the short road to "Meteor Mountain" and, although very impressive, was made mostly of concrete (not steel), as shown in Figure 172.

Figure 172: Bridge at Diablo Canyon.
Source: *The Cement Era*, Vol. XV, No. 8, August 1917. Page 40.

530. Although the recent photo of Bonito lava flow in Figure 173 was taken near Sunset Crater (which is visible in the background) and not along the roadside approaching Flagstaff, as C.K. describes, it seems representative of what he is describing. It should also be noted that C.K. hiked this area on August 3, 1919, so he could have been remembering this kind of scenery.

Figure 173: Lone Pine Tree Amidst the Bonito Lava Flow—View Towards Sunset Crater.
Source: Photograph by John Crossley, americansouthwest.net. Used with permission.

531. The San Francisco Peaks are about nine miles north of Flagstaff. Elden Mountain is about five miles southeast of the San Francisco Peaks. They can be seen about seventy-five miles away coming from the east.

532. The visibility is not the only limiting factor. The terrain approaching these mountains is uneven, and it seems unlikely that these peaks could be seen two hundred miles away no matter how clear and unpolluted the air might have been.

533. Analysis of events prior, during, and subsequent to C.K.'s stay in the Flagstaff area indicates that C.K. arrived in Flagstaff on Saturday, July 26, 1919.

534. A bungalow is a type of house, originally developed in the Bengal region in South Asia, but with various uses in many countries. In England, the first bungalows were built around 1870 and were prefabricated single-story buildings used as seaside holiday homes.

535. Below are the two best possibilities for the restaurant where C.K. had his "dinner" of puffed cereals frequently advertised in the *Coconino Sun* in 1919. A third, the Commercial Hotel Cafe, also advertised, but it seems unlikely C.K. ate there.

> • Coconino Restaurant and Lunch Room; No. 10 Front Street; "The Oldest in Town"; Woo-Yen, proprietor: This establishment was next door to the Commercial Hotel, less than 200 feet from the corner door of the Bank Hotel, where it is believed C.K. stayed.

> • White House Cafe: "Good Food and Good Cooking; Large helpings–low prices; Open Day and Night; Jos. Bender, proprietor": The location of this establishment has not been determined.

536. "Puffed cereals" would have included only wheat and rice, since no other cereals of this type were made in the period.

CHAPTER XVIII

THE GRAND CANYON

I woke up next morning feeling very groggy, for no reason accountable to myself. It was Sunday. My first endeavour would be to fulfil one of the desires of my boyhood. It lay at my very door.[537]

The Lowell Observatory at Flagstaff[538] is known throughout the whole of the civilized world. Years ago, hundreds and thousands of people read with unabated interest of the theories and discoveries of Professor Lowell[539] concerning the planet Mars. In his book, *Mars and its Canals*,[540] he recorded the researches of a lifetime on this most interesting of planets. He announced his conviction that civilized life of a very high order was present and flourishing on Mars, and supported his theory with exhaustive data and series of beautiful photographs of the planet at different times and under different aspects—the result of the work carried out at the Lowell Observatory which he himself had founded, built, and maintained at his own expense.

In my boyhood's days that book read like a wonderful fairy story, illustrated with photographs that were far more wonderful and far more strange than the merely pretty pictures of fancy.[541] Some day, I promised myself, I would see the Lowell Observatory, and look through the giant telescope that revealed to the human eye, millions of miles away, so much of the mysterious and the unknown.

SAN FRANCISCO PEAKS FROM FLAGSTAFF.

THE LOWELL OBSERVATORY, FLAGSTAFF. [542]

And here I stood, at the door of the hotel, but a few hundred yards from that same Observatory.[543] Looking up the main street I could plainly see the white dome, perched on the summit of a hill overlooking the town, surrounded, but unobscured, by the tall pine trees that clustered thickly on its slopes.[544]

An hour later I was standing inside the great dome. The dream had come true.

The astronomers of "Mars Hill" treated me, like all visitors, with the utmost hospitality.[545] My wishes to see this and that and the other thing had only to be expressed, and they were granted. I was shown the result of years upon years of tireless, ceaseless research. In the library, a magnificently designed and equipped building, I found myself in a veritable Monte Cristo's cave.[546] Arranged around the walls, and lit from behind by a wonderful system of electric lights, were treasures of far more value than would appear to the casual, disinterested sightseer.[547] There were transparent photographs of planets, star clusters, nebulæ, and comets by the hundred, some but a fraction of an inch in diameter, and others several feet across. There were volumes of records and reports of every Observatory, besides astronomical and other scientific works of all classes, sizes, and tongues.

Hours afterwards I slowly descended the path that wound down the hill-side through the pine trees, wrapped in thought and proudly conscious of having at last achieved something that for so long had been but a vague vision of the imagination.

Unfortunately my indisposition of the morning did not disappear. It increased. I surmised that somewhere or other I had drunk some poisoned water—an easy thing to do—and must suffer the consequences.

The consequences I suffered were those of ptomaine poisoning.[548] The next day was spent in the throes of it. I crept out of bed for an hour or two, with just enough courage to visit the garage to whose charge I had confined Lizzie for an overhaul.[549] Finding her once again in pieces, but with no parts broken, I returned, with a sigh of relief and a body full of pains, to bed. I had discovered that many patrons of a certain restaurant—the one which I had so heartily greeted upon my arrival—had also suffered from ptomaine poisoning.[550] I reflected that this was an ailment that often proved fatal. But I determined that it would not be so in my case, at any rate not until Lizzie and I had gazed down on the deep blue waters of the Pacific Ocean. That accomplished, anything could happen!

The next day found things much brighter. The sickness was fast disappearing, and I was consoled towards midday by the sight of Lizzie erected, tested, and passed O.K. I was, however, sceptical of the youth to whom, in my indisposition, I had entrusted her delicate body. He had sworn that he had overhauled Hendersons until he could do them blindfold. With characteristic American modesty he claimed to be the only man between Kansas City and Los Angeles who knew anything at all about the breed. That made me a trifle suspicious at the outset. Furthermore, he had agreed to turn in on Sunday and commence operations, but when Sunday came he was hardly conspicuous by his presence— the garage door was locked.

However, I paid over the required quota of dollars with Spartan stoicism[551] and took Lizzie once more unto my bosom. Being naturally of a lazy disposition and a firm believer in the futility of walking whenever there is the remotest opportunity of some form of mechanical transit being available, I had deferred an extensive survey of the town until I could execute it in comfort.

Originally a stores depot on the early trail through the West, Flagstaff soon became a ranching centre and a kind of "Mecca"[552] for cow-boys, globe-trotters, wasters, drifters, Indians, Mexicans, and, of late years, speculators and East-weary business men. Although boasting only a few thousand inhabitants, the town is growing fast, and naturally where towns grow fast—a thing known only in the west of America and the Colonies—the "real estate" agents flourish in their legions. The people of Flagstaff are "boosters," and so do all they can to encourage and quicken the growth of their neat little town. Many come there, buy a plot of land in one of the outlying blocks, build a bungalow and settle down for good, charmed with the climate, the atmosphere, the surroundings, the great pine forests, and the view to the north of the mighty Peaks that are almost always capped with snow and seem to look down and protect the little town that lies scattered at their feet.

Next morning[553] I had concluded all preparations for the fulfilment of another life-long desire. My next ambition was to see the Grand Canyon of the Colorado,[554] of which I had read much in school-books in my childhood.

THE TRAIL TO THE GRAND CANYON.

In and out through the pine trees we swung once again, darting down sudden dips in the road and skipping up little hills all fresh with grass and thick wild flowers. In ten or fifteen miles of exquisite woodland scenery we had come once more to the fringe of the forest.[555] Ahead lay plain, prairie, and desert, with never a town or a village or a house to be seen until the Canyon was reached seventy odd miles to the north.[556] On the left rose the great San Francisco Peaks, clothed in green and white. On the right lay Sunset Mountain,[557] a volcanic cinder cone of ruddy-brown hue, that glistened in the morning sunlight.

Slowly they were left behind as we hopped, skipped, and jumped over the rough trail that swerved and twisted untiringly through the strangest country imaginable. Here it would be broad and sandy; there it would narrow down almost to nothing; further on, it would make a sudden bend and dip across a "wash" or some waterless river that had never known a bridge; then it would enter a beautiful valley all aglow with golden flowers that crowded thickly up its sides—there were yellow flowers everywhere, in each direction as far as the eye could see, and at the same time so close that they were swept aside by the machine as it passed. Then that picture passed away and there remained just two deep undulating ruts that struggled persistently across a wilderness of sand, rock, and boulder. We passed on either side the remains of ancient volcanoes,[558] now but solitary hills rising abruptly from the desert around. Then appeared giant heaps of stone clustered strangely together, the ruins of ancient towns for many a thousand years deserted.[559] Then for miles and miles was nothing but barren, arid waste that tired one's patience and cut one's tyres and shook one's limbs, while thousands upon thousands of prairie-dogs were ever running, hurrying, scurrying away from the intruder upon their solitude. Their holes were everywhere, even in the ruts of the trail that stretched always like a forgotten, lifeless thing through this land of scorching loneliness.

Four hours and a half we had now been travelling, and not a soul, not even a sign of a living being had we seen, save the merry little vermin that scurried off at the sound and the sight of us. For the first time in the whole of the trip I felt a great sense of loneliness creeping over me. The solitude, the peace of the great barren distances at last made itself known—it was a solitude and a peace that I had never felt before. It took time for me to appreciate its worth. I amused myself by bursting suddenly into song. All the old familiar refrains came to my aid, were they hymn tunes or ridiculous rag-time airs.

Feeling absurd—even positively ridiculous—in my efforts to remain cheerful at all costs, but comforted by the thought that there was no one to witness my insanity, I continued thus until my voice rebelled and I relapsed once again into stony—very stony—silence!

Once again the trail entered a great forest; huge pine trees and cedar trees closed densely around and the trail branched and split here and there to avoid them. The vegetation grew thicker. It seemed wonderful how it could possibly thrive in such a country. Not a drop of water had I seen for eighty miles, when suddenly a most beautiful vista appeared directly ahead of me. There was a wonderful lake bordered with giant pine trees, its waters still and flat like a great jewel. At its edge a few horses were drinking. It was such a magnificent sight that I was forced to stop to admire it to the full. I breathed a prayer that my little pocket camera would do it justice, and convey, if only a fraction, some of that entrancing charm that hung over its glassy waters.[560]

On once again we rode, through avenues of pine and cedar; the further we went, the thicker the forest grew and the greater the stately trees became. It was possible only to see a few yards ahead in some places. . . . "But say, we must be getting near the Canyon soon! How can all this be?" I asked myself.

Swerving now to the right, now to the left, to avoid some obstacle, now leaving the trail altogether to ride on the soft green grass at the side, when a boulder or a fallen branch blocked the way, it was like exploring one of those magic forests where fairies . . .

The thought was never finished.

It seemed as if the whole earth had suddenly stopped dead. There, in front, the great tree trunks stood silhouetted against space itself. It was as though something dreadful had happened. Beyond was tremendous, awful nothingness that made the observer catch his breath and sent a shiver throughout his frame. But see, there, on the distant horizon, like a dimly-coloured shadow, lies the opposite side of the gigantic rift, ten, twenty—aye, in places thirty miles away.[561] It is a sight to enjoy in silence, with reverence and with fear. Once seen, it is never to be forgotten, that first glimpse of the greatest of all natural wonders—the Grand Canyon of the Colorado.

The trail made a sudden swerve to the left and followed close to its brink. There were some wooden railings; beyond, a varying strip of broken, rocky moorland; and then, space. Leaving Lizzie, I clambered down a narrow pathway carved in the rocks that led to a jutting prominence known as "Grand View Point."[563] Seated on a huge lump of limestone that reared like a lofty pinnacle thousands of feet above the chasm below, I surveyed in mute bewilderment the overpowering, awe-inspiring sight.

The Grand Canyon has never been described. It is too immense, too sublime, too unearthly for mere words to convey one iota of its might and majesty. One struggles with the futility of mere expression by words where such a spectacle is concerned and finds that all the known phrases and well-used artifices of speech are useless to convey to another the sense of infinite grandeur that only sight can appreciate—and that so feebly!

The Canyon is a titanic rift in the earth, over 200 miles in length.[564] The Colorado River, hardly ever seen from its brinks, lies 6,000 feet below[565] the surface of the plain through which it has cut. Æons of time have been taken in the making of it, and it is yet but young, its progress still continuing. That sinister river, to reach which takes a seven-mile walk down the trail[566] that leads to its waters, has cut down through strata of rock that took untold millions of years to be deposited, has cut lower and lower until it has come to the very beginning, the foundation of the earth, and then it has carved its way even through the granite, the very crust of the earth, to a depth of almost 1,000 feet. Eternal erosion by water, winds, and frost has helped it to play its part, and now nigh on 2,000 cubic miles[567] of limestone, sandstone, and granite have disappeared entirely—all carried as sediment into the Pacific Ocean by the river that for ever swirls and rages in its bosom.

The actual settlement that goes by the name of the Grand Canyon is twenty miles further on.[568] The trail follows closely the rim of the Canyon, cutting through the fringe of the "Coconino National Forest," with its stately pine trees that crowd up to the very edge of the plateau.[569]

When the end of the trail is reached, it is as though the traveller had arrived at the edge of the world. On the right is a luxurious, low-built hotel all but toppling over the edge;[570] on the left is a railway station;[571] and that is all. The road almost doubles back on itself, swerving due south towards the Continental Trail eighty miles away.[572] I do not mean to imply that at the end of this world there will be either a luxurious hotel or a railway station at the service of the weary traveller, but the appearance of finality of all things is complete when one is faced with that terrible chasm ahead.

For three days and three nights I sojourned at the Canyon,[573] content to gaze upon its ever-changing colours, and to marvel at the wealth of beauty and variation of spectacle that lay in its mighty bosom, always changing, always fresh, always more wonderful than before. One day after breakfast I began strolling down the narrow "Bright Angel Trail" that leads from the summit to the river. Between two and three feet wide in most places, it is wonderfully built and kept in excellent repair for the mule-back parties of tourists that daily descend its seven tortuous miles[574] in the morning and ascend them again in the evening. In places it is like a spiral pathway down an almost perpendicular wall. One looks over and sees it doubling and folding and twisting on itself like a thin white line until it is lost behind some prominence thousands of feet below.

I did not mean to walk down. Walking is not my forte; I only set out to take a few photographs. I have the best of reasons for believing that people never walk down the Canyon. Instead they bulge upon diminutive mules in strings of twenty or thirty or more and make the descent slowly, nervously, solemnly, and more or less in comfort. True, there are places where the trail is so precipitous that they have to dismount for safety's sake, but to walk the whole way would be absurd.

Perhaps that was the reason I found myself tramping down the long, steep trail. The more photographs I took, the further down I went to take another. One view followed another with endless change. At every turn there was some new sensation, some fresh vista that just cried out for remembrance. In this way I gradually found myself descending into the depths of the Canyon. Truly it is the most wonderful walk I have ever had.

It was as though the traveller were entering a new world of a new climate, new scenery, and new sensations. Up on the plateau at the top the altitude was 8,000 feet above sea level, and the heat there had been intense. But as I descended thousand after thousand of feet into the bowels of the earth, the air became more dense and the heat more intense until at the bottom, over 6,000 feet below, the climate was almost tropical. Further, the great "temples"—the fragments of the plateau where the erosion had left isolated mountains remaining within the gorge—took on a far different aspect when viewed from below. From above one saw them as one would see hills and valleys from an aeroplane—with hardly any relief. But from below they loomed up sharp against the sky, each one a mighty mountain in itself. What seemed from the brink to be a mere blotch of green mould on the bare rocks below proved on closer acquaintance to be a luxurious coppice, dense with trees and shrubs and tall, thick grass. Minute specks of black scattered broadcast on the slope turned out to be trees that eked out a scanty but sufficient livelihood on the crevices and the crags. A brown, inconspicuous carpet from above developed into a huge tropical plateau several miles across. So clear is the atmosphere and so great are the distances that magnitudes are ridiculed and illusions raised to the point of absurdity.

THE BOTTOM OF THE GRAND CANYON.   *By permission of Dr. F. Rolt-Wheeler.*

It was well after midday when I reached the bottom and watched the roaring, rushing Colorado,[575] like a great yellow flood, lashing its angry way between the steep walls of the granite gorge. Above, it had been invisible, unknown, and whisperless.

The walk back developed into a tiring, eternal struggle up an interminable staircase that had no stairs. Sometimes I half decided to rest until next day. At intervals I grasped my knees in my hands and helped to lift the heavy, tired feet one above the other. I abused myself heartily for not having furnished myself with reserve refreshments before starting, and then remembered that I had only set out to take a few pictures; I had quenched my thirst at a little creek six hours before, but felt that a meal of some kind would be acceptable.

I arrived at the top about 5.30. The mule-party had overtaken me a quarter of an hour before. They had only stopped half an hour at the bottom for lunch.

"Waal, I've done some walkin' in my time, boss, but I guess you've gotten the best pair o' legs that ever MY optics did see," was the remark of one heavily-spectacled American who beamed from his mule upon me as he passed.

"Aye, that's so," echoed others in the long file with undisguised approbation.

So the reader will observe that I am already becoming Americanized, even in true modesty!

My stay at the Canyon was longer than I had anticipated. Considerable rain had fallen on the second day, and a report came through that the road in places had been washed clean away.[576] Just what that meant I did not know, but I did not fear it in the slightest. My experience of the roads in Arizona was that they were much better away than present. But I had no taste for mud, so I waited for the sun to do its work before starting back again.

I left the Grand Canyon with regret. Everything was so wonderful and I just seemed to have begun to make friends with it. At first it all seemed so great, so awful, so grotesque as to give one the impression of anything but friendliness. I had begun to overcome that feeling, as everyone does in time. The truth is that it takes a long acquaintanceship with the giant wonders of the world to form anything approaching a true idea of them.

Mud there was in plenty on the way back. In the forest going was bad and slow, for the sun had not had its due quota of time to play upon the damp earth. But in the open there was a marked improvement. The only evidence of the heavy rains was an occasional pool of water between the tracks of the road that had not yet been completely dried up, and this remained as a pool of muddy water within a ring of soft, dark-brown mud.

I was glad that progress was not so bad as I had expected. I was tired of making slow progress, low averages, and big delays, so whenever I had the chance I gave

Lizzie her reins and with many bursts of speed where the condition of the road permitted, and occasional hold-ups where it did not, we made pretty good progress for a couple of hours.

Until . . .

We were about half-way between the Canyon and Flagstaff. The country was bare and rocky—almost on the fringe of the "Painted Desert."[577] I was riding on the narrow but level track between the two large ruts that formed the road. I was furthermore enjoying a little burst of speed, my eyes glued on the little strip below me, for if I but once missed it and allowed Lizzie to slip into either of those deep, treacherous ruts that bordered it, there would be a nasty smash.

I must have been too careful, for I had not noticed a fairly large and deep mud-pool dead in the centre of the track and only a few yards ahead of me. There were just about three or four inches between either side of it and those terrible ruts. If I banged into it, it would mean a nasty jar to the machine and possible damage. I judged I could steer round all right without fouling the rut.

The front wheel went through splendidly. The back one, approaching at an angle as I swerved, did not. It just skimmed the greasy edge of the pool and commenced momentarily to side-slip down into the hollow. That was the beginning of the end. I was going fast, and the equilibrium of the machine had been suddenly upset. The nightmare known as a "speed-wobble"[578] ensued.

I did my utmost to check it, but it got worse and worse. From one side to the other the machine swayed, like a great pendulum, swinging faster and faster and each time through a greater distance. For some time I managed to keep the swerves within the limits of the track without fouling the ruts and the rocks at the side, but it was no use; I saw a fearful crash coming.

The wobble developed at an alarming speed; no doubt the heavy baggage on the carrier helped. At the end of each oscillation the machine was at a still greater, a still more ridiculous angle to the ground. The front wheel caught something. It had to come sooner or later. With a wild lurch we crashed down on the loose rocks and boulders that bordered the trail. Our momentum was soon absorbed owing to the rough nature of the rocks and boulders aforesaid.

"Here endeth the trip to the coast. Farewell, Lizzie; it might have happened sooner, you know, old girl." That's what I was saying to myself as I struggled from underneath her remains!

CHAPTER 18 NOTES

537. Because C.K. said he walked out of the hotel and looked up the street and saw the observatory, he most likely stayed at the Bank Hotel, where Leroux meets Santa Fe. Figure 174 shows the building in 1900 with a carriage waiting in front to take hotel guests to the Grand Canyon.

Figure 174: The Bank Hotel, *ca.* 1900.
Source: Courtesy of Arizona Historical Society, Flagstaff.

538. Lowell Observatory was established in 1894, but the first telescope—a 24-inch Alvan Clark telescope made in Boston and shipped by train—was installed there in 1896. Figure 175 is a photo of the "dome" holding this telescope that C.K. took during his visit to the observatory.

Figure 175: Clark Telescope at Lowell Observatory.
Source: C.K.'s personal slide collection.

539. Percival Lawrence Lowell was a member of the wealthy Lowell family of Boston, Massachusetts. Lowell was a businessman, author, mathematician, and astronomer. He was born on March 13, 1855 and died November 12, 1916, just under three years before C.K.'s visit.

540. *Mars and Its Canals* was Lowell's second of three related books: *Mars* (1895), *Mars and Its Canals* (1906), and *Mars As the Abode of Life* (1908).

541. Figure 176 is a 1905 drawing of Mars by Percival Lowell.

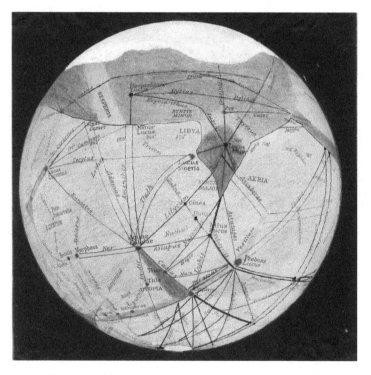

Figure 176: Drawing of Mars, by Percival Lowell, 1905.
Source: Lowell Observatory Archives.

542. Although this building was designed to look like a telescope dome, it was the new administration building for the observatory, which was completed in 1916. The rotunda under the dome served as the library for the observatory and adjacent rooms provided offices for staff. This book contains photographs of both C.K. and one of the astronomers on the steps of this building, as well as interior photographs of this building taken by C.K. and observatory staff.

543. The front door of the Bank Hotel is about 1,500 yards—line of sight—to the Clark Dome. It would be about a mile and a half up the hill to walk from the Bank Hotel to the Clark Dome, which would take perhaps forty-five minutes.

544. The "Clark Dome" is still viewable from downtown Flagstaff today in the same manner described.

545. This hospitality included time with astronomers Carl Otto Lampland and George Hall Hamilton. Mr. Lampland wrote the following in his personal diary on Tuesday, July 29, 1919: "Captain Shepherd of R.A.F. here." This indicates that C.K. had definitely arrived in Flagstaff by then.

546. *The Count of Monte Cristo* is an 1844 adventure novel by French author Alexandre Dumas. "Monte Cristo's cave" is apparently a reference to a chapter in the book where the main character, Edmond Dantès, finds a cavern filled with treasures.

547. C.K. took the photo in Figure 177 inside the rotunda of the new administration building that was only three years old at the time. Seventy years later, in 1989, the building was dedicated to astronomers Vesto Melvin Slipher and Earl Charles Slipher, who had both spent many years working as astronomers at Lowell Observatory and would have been present during C.K.'s visit. Vesto Slipher spent his entire professional life at the observatory—from 1901 until 1954—while his brother, Earl, arrived at the observatory in 1908 and stayed in Flagstaff until he died in 1964, having been involved

Figure 177: View of the Fireplace in the Slipher Building. **Source:** C.K.'s personal slide collection.

in local politics. (Earl Charles Slipher was the mayor of Flagstaff in 1919 when C.K. visited.) Figures 178 and 179 (next page) are photos from the Lowell Observatory archives that provide wider views of inside the rotunda.

Figure 178: Wider View of the Library Fireplace in the Slipher Building from the Balcony, July 7, 1933. **Source:** Lowell Observatory Archives.

Figure 179: Library in the Rotunda at Lowell Observatory, *ca.* 1947.
This is the view of the library looking back toward the front door from approximately the same location where C.K. took his photo (Figure 177) in 1919.
Source: Lowell Observatory Archives.

548. "ptomaine poisoning": An archaic term for food poisoning. This malady was once thought to be caused by ingesting ptomaines—any of a group of amine compounds of unpleasant taste and odor formed in putrefying animal and vegetable matter.

549. There were at least six automobile repair garages in Flagstaff in 1919, but none stand out as the obvious choice where the work on C.K.'s motorcycle was done.

550. In spite of food poisoning by a local restaurant affecting many people, news of the event only spread by word of mouth because no newspaper accounts have been located.

551. "Spartan stoicism": Stoicism is a school of philosophy created by Zeno of Citium *ca.* 300 BC in Athens. According to its followers, stoicism involved "living in the moment" and not allowing oneself to be ruled by raw feelings and emotions, such as pleasure, fear, and pain. Although the Spartans were neighboring enemies of the Athenians, they are widely believed to have served as the model for the ideal Stoic society. Today, the word "stoic" has come to refer to the ability to withstand pain without showing emotion. C.K. was doing his best to portray that he was unaffected by the pain from the price he was being forced to pay.

552. In this instance, Mecca is used to characterize Flagstaff as a place that draws many people of like mind. Mecca was the birthplace of Muhammad. A pilgrimage there—known as the Hajj—is obligatory for all able Muslims at least once in their lives.

553. If his motorcycle was not being serviced on the Sunday after his arrival, then the earliest it could have been completed and paid up was on Monday, July 28, 1919. However, it seems more likely that he picked it up on Tuesday, July 29, 1919, and drove it around town a bit with the "next morning" being Wednesday, July 30, 1919.

554. For years, the name "Grand Canyon of the Colorado" was used to refer to the location. Grand Canyon National Park was officially commissioned on February 26, 1919.

555. The *Blue Book* Route 441 describes the eastern route C.K. took between Flagstaff and the Grand Canyon, including a "winding road thru timber" and then—19.9 miles from Flagstaff—a "left-hand diagonal road." The description in the *Blue Book* regarding the route after that is conspicuously sparse, but the way to the Grand Canyon was marked by numerous signposts placed there by the Automobile Club of Southern California. The *Auto Club Map 12b* in Figure 180 reflects their version of left turn onto the open plains just north of an area noted as being "Extinct Volcanos."

556. The *Auto Club Map 12b* (Figure 180) provides a distance of seventy-one miles from Flagstaff to the Grandview Point, whereas the *Blue Book* Route 441 specifies that it is 72.6 miles from Flagstaff to Grandview Point and 84.9 miles to the village of Grand Canyon. Therefore, if he had already traveled fifteen miles getting ready to head out over the open terrain, "seventy odd miles" is a reasonable characterization accounting for variations in the starting point.

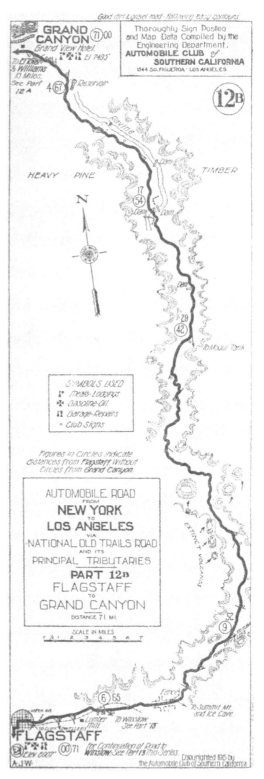

Figure 180: Flagstaff to Grand Canyon Route 12b.
Source: *Auto Club Map 12b.*

557. Figure 181 is a modern mid-day photograph of Sunset Crater from the approximate distance of where C.K. was on his way to the Grand Canyon.

Figure 181: Sunset Crater.
Source: US National Park Service.

558. Although a single photograph is unlikely to provide this description justice, it should be noted that the *Auto Club Map 12b* (Figure 180) depicts locations of extinct volcanoes both left and right of the road to the Grand Canyon.

559. It is possible that C.K. saw the abandoned ruins of the stagecoach rest stops and thought they were older, but recent archeological excavations at Sinagua (*Sin ah' wa*) village—several miles northeast of Flagstaff at the modern Elden Pueblo—indicate that village was inhabited from about AD 1070 to 1275, so it is plausible that remains of other ancient communities were visible further north.

560. Figure 182 (next page) is the photo of this scene that C.K. took on July 30, 1919.

561. The Grand Canyon's maximum width is not thirty miles; it is eighteen miles.

562. Not used.

Figure 182: A Tank (Watering Hole) in Coconino Forest Near Grand Canyon.
Source: C.K.'s personal slide collection.

563. The photo in Figure 183, from C.K.'s collection, is annotated as being taken at Grandview Point.

Figure 183: Grandview Point.
Source: C.K.'s personal slide collection.

564. The Grand Canyon is currently described as being 277 miles long.

565. The maximum depth of the Grand Canyon is currently measured at 6,093 feet.

566. It is possible that Bright Angel Trail has been altered since 1919, but it is presently documented to be an eight-mile hike one way to the bottom.

567. The volume of the Grand Canyon is currently estimated to be 5.45 trillion cubic yards—which is exactly 1,000 cubic miles—but some estimates in 1919 *did* cite 2,000 cubic miles as a possible displacement.

568. The *Blue Book* Route 441 indicates that it was 12.3 miles (not twenty) from Grandview Point to the village of Grand Canyon, although other maps cite the number at fourteen miles.

569. Prior to 1910, Coconino National Forest may have run all the way up to the edge of the Grand Canyon but, on July 1, 1910, Tusayan National Forest was created from the northern part of the Coconino National Forest. It included at least the south rim of the Grand Canyon but, when the Grand Canyon National Park was commissioned in 1919, the National Park took over much of Tusayan National Forest, and on October 22, 1934, the remnants of Tusayan National Forest were transferred to Prescott National Forest.

570. As shown in Figure 184 (next page) the El Tovar Hotel is *near* the edge of the canyon, but not quite "toppling over the edge."

Figure 184: El Tovar Hotel on the Edge of the Canyon, *ca*. 1930.
Source: US National Park Service. Photograph by George A. Grant.

571. Figure 185 is the Santa Fe Railroad station at the Grand Canyon in 1925.

Figure 185: Santa Fe Station at Grand Canyon.
Source: Courtesy of Northern Arizona University, Cline Library. Credit: Eddie Newman.

572. This would be the "west" road south to Williams, Arizona, a path that the 1919 ABB says is actually 63.4 miles from the village at Grand Canyon. However, it is not clear what he meant by "Continental Trail." There is a "Continental Divide Trail," but that is well east near the border of New Mexico and Arizona. There was a "National Park to Park Highway" that tied together most of the National Parks in the western states, but the main road he was on (and passed through Williams) was the "National Old Trails Road," not the "Continental Trail." It seems possible that the National Old Trails Road was colloquially called the "Transcontinental Highway" or something to that effect.

573. The best evidence indicates that C.K. arrived at the El Tovar Hotel on Wednesday, July 30, 1919 and was back in Flagstaff on Saturday, August 2, 1919, which means he stayed at the Grand Canyon for three nights. Figures 186-191 (next page) are some photos he took while at the Grand Canyon.

574. See previous Note 566 reflecting a published one-way distance of eight miles in 1919.

575. The photograph of the bottom of the Grand Canyon that C.K. included in Chapter 18, like several others in this book, is noted as being included *"By permission of Dr. F. Rolt-Wheeler."* Rolt-Wheeler was a traveler and prolific author of adventure and history books, but none of the photos that C.K. included in his book have been found in other books by Rolt-Wheeler.

576. Although historic weather information for the village of Grand Canyon is not easily accessible, the *Arizona Republican*, a daily newspaper in Phoenix, included weather reports reflecting increasing rain in Flagstaff. The *Arizona Republican* reported that it was partly cloudy—but no rain—in Flagstaff on Wednesday, July 30, 1919. However, they reported 0.34 inches of rain on Thursday, July 31, 1919. The following day (C.K.'s second full day at the Grand Canyon), Friday, August 1, 1919, the *Arizona Republican* reported that 1.38 inches of rain fell in Flagstaff, so there was clearly rain in the area, but apparently not prolonged heavy rain. Whether that much rain is enough to cause road washouts seems doubtful, but C.K. was reporting what he had heard from others; it does not seem that he encountered any washed out roads on his way back to Flagstaff on Sunday.

Figure 186–Figure 191: Grand Canyon of the Colorado.
Source: C.K.'s personal slide collection.

577. The Painted Desert refers to the "badlands" running from near the east end of the Grand Canyon National Park southeast into the Petrified Forest National Park.

578. "speed wobble": A term used to describe a quick (four to ten cycles per second) oscillation of the steerable wheel of a vehicle.

CHAPTER XIX

THE MOHAVE DESERT

I have often thought there must be a guardian angel watching over mad motor-cyclists. Certainly in my case some theory of that sort is necessary to account for the almost entire immunity from personal damage that I have always experienced when fate has led me into crashes of all kinds. At one time and another I have performed wonderful acrobatic feats after a bad skid or a sudden encounter in the dark with a stray horse or a flock of sheep. By all the laws of nature and common sense, I should long since have ceased to labour on this earthly plane. Instead of that, I continue to flourish like the green bay tree,[579] the terror of the country I inhabit, and the bane of the Company that has the misfortune to insure my machines!

Thus it happened that when I extricated myself from the debris, I found myself still sound in wind and limb. Apart from one finger having been crushed between the handle and the final boulder, and the absence of one or two square inches of good epidermis here and there, I had nothing whatever to complain of.

Lizzie, however, wore a forlorn look. Her left handlebar was badly bent and most of the controls and projections on her starboard side were either bent backwards or swept clean away. The stand, a heavy steel structure strong enough to make a suspension bridge, had broken away altogether, and had not the footboard been of the collapsing type, it would undoubtedly have shared the same fate.

An hour of doctoring, with frequent applications of wire and insulation tape, and Lizzie was going again. I was relieved in the extreme to find that after all there was a chance of continuing to the coast under her own power. My forefinger pained a trifle, and I could not bear to bend it. I believe always in leaving Nature to carry out her own repairs—it saves a lot of time and bother and generally gets the job finished much quicker in the end, so I spent no time in doctoring it.

We got back to Flagstaff all right that evening and, accepting the hospitality of one of the astronomers at Mars Hill,[580] I spent the night at his bungalow up amongst the pine trees.[581] It was nearly a month before I regained the use of my finger and over three months before the sense of feeling came back to it. Evidently it had been broken at or near the joint.

Two days afterwards I made an unwilling exit from Flagstaff.[582] I was so enamoured with the spirit of the West and the cordiality of its people, as well as the scenery and the climate, that it seemed a shame to move away. But how could I do otherwise when in three days' good running I should be enjoying the reality of the deep blue Pacific washing up against the fringe of some golden Californian valley?

From Flagstaff to Williams, a thirty-mile jaunt,[583] the road traversed the edges of the Coconino Forest. In places it was almost impassable. Stretches of rock-hard mud, that had been cut up into fantastic shapes, hindered progress for hundreds of yards at a stretch. I had often to resort to the old expedient of chipping the edges of the ruts away in advance to enable Lizzie's cradle frame to get through. Then for miles there were stretches of incredible roughness where often I left the road and scrambled over the rough prairie at the side, leaping over gullies, mounds, cracks, and rocks in preference to the treacherous trail. But the wild scenery compensated for everything. It was exquisite.

Town after town slowly but surely went by, and as they did so, the country grew wilder and the climate hotter. The trail wound through great gorges with towering cliffs that obscured most of the sky. Mad rivers would come rushing down from mountain sides and seldom were there bridges with which to cross them. Vegetation became less plentiful and here and there were stretches of barren prairie land with great boulders and masses of rock spread indiscriminately about them.

Past Ashforks, some sixty miles from Flagstaff, I came upon a Ford car by a wide, rough-bedded, unbridged river.[584] The owner, dressed in blue combination overalls (the standard garment of the West) was playing round it with a "monkey-wrench."

"Want anything, brother?" I asked.

"No thanks, nothing wrong," he replied, eyeing Lizzie and me curiously up and down. "Gee! What the ..." (his eye caught the number plate)—"Well, I'll be gol-darned!"

"How's the road ahead?" I asked, ignoring his evident amazement at one so young having come so far!

"Pretty tough in places. You've got a fairly good run for a hundred miles, but you've got to keep your eyes skinned for washouts. There's a big one about ten miles further on, just before you come to Pineveta.[585] You can't miss it. It's just beyond a big cliff on the left side where it says 'REPENT YOUR SINS, THE END IS AT HAND.' And by G—, you'd better repent 'em quick in case anything does happen!"

Washouts there were, good and plentiful. Great gullies had been cut across the roads by the rains. Many were not visible much before they were felt. On the whole it was exciting running.

Pineveta was a most "movie-looking" town.[586] I could easily have imagined myself a Gaumont operator[587] on several occasions. Every building, whether a house, the village church or the town hall, was of wood and of the simplest construction possible. Everything seemed loose, ramshackle and toppling. It was a good home for the tough guys of the West, where towns spring up in a night, prosper awhile and then fade into insignificance.

After Seligman, another twenty miles further on,[588] the trail showed signs of nervous prostration. It led into a great canyon whose grey walls towered high on either side. Then it seemed to say to the traveller, "See here, Boss, you can go on if you like, I'm staying right here; had enough of this." It had already dwindled down to a couple of ruts in the sandy bed of the canyon and now it was besieged on all sides with dense growths of grey scrub, like sage-brush. Even the ruts were barely visible and now appeared only in white patchy blotches through the scrub that grew a foot or a couple of feet high in dense, clustered tufts. It seemed as though something would have to be done about it soon.

Finally we came to a wooden fence, rudely but effectively constructed and barring the way entirely. Behind the fence was a railway track. Evidently it was necessary to cross the track somewhere but not the slightest opportunity did there appear of doing so. I explored awhile.

On the left, where the trail had ended, the fence showed signs of having been pulled down and ruts in the ground bore witness to traffic having gone that way at some time or another more or less remote. But stay, what is this? A large post had been torn down from the fence and laid right across the track of the apparent detour. In the middle of it, and fastened on by a piece of wire, was a scrap of paper bearing the following anonymous inscription in scrawled handwriting—"DOANT GO THIS RODE CANT GET THRU."

Now wasn't this kind of some one? I began to wonder if I would have gone to the same trouble if I had struggled through a fence on an old Ford car (I was sure from the writing that it was a Ford)[589] and after proceeding half a mile or so over interminable boulders and gullies had found it necessary to come back again. I came to the conclusion that I WOULD, at any rate, if I was in the West, and thus consoled, I proceeded to search for another outlet.

Yes, here were a pair of ruts leading off backwards at a tangent. Where they went was not possible to see, for they were overgrown with scrub. I started Lizzie once again, put her front wheel into the deeper of the ruts and set off whither it should take me. It was faithful and true. Brushing the bushes sideways with the machine as we passed, we arrived in half a mile at a gate where a good wide road appeared. It was the entrance to the "city" of Nelson, consisting of a few shacks, a ranch-house and a railway station.[590] After opening a few more gates we crossed the rails at a level crossing and were going once again swiftly westwards.

"Dinner in Peach Springs," I told myself. Peach Springs on my AAA Map was a fair-sized town fifteen miles ahead.[591] Evening was drawing on and there would not be much light left for travelling, but where dinner was concerned it was another matter. Proceed we must, until fodder hove in sight.

Slowly the canyon was left behind. The country opened out and became flatter. Vast rolling plains appeared, with cedar woods creeping down their slopes. The air was sultry, hardly a breeze stirred in the trees; wild pigeons in hundreds flew hither and thither; occasionally a young antelope or a great jack rabbit leaped across the plains. I hardly gave them a thought. My mind dwelt upon an imaginary tin of pineapple chunks somewhere in the distance!

Peach Springs showed no trace of materializing when required. There was no sign of it anywhere where it should have been. I stopped at a wooden shack near the roadside. There was a Bowser pump outside the door.[592]

An old man with a goat's beard appeared at the door.

"A couple of gallons of gas, please," I shouted, and while he pumped it in I surveyed the surroundings; there was another little shack not far away and two dirty-looking Mexican women were sitting down outside. Here and there, round about, lay rubbish, pieces of timber, tin cans and other débris.

"Guess you get mighty lonesome here, dad?"

"Aw, dunno," he replied. "Bin here nigh on forty years. Guess I got purty well accustomed to it now."[593]

"Forty years! I should say so! . . . Thanks. Say, how far's Peach Springs from here?"

"Peach Springs? This is Peach Springs. You're in it right here," and he pointed to his shack.

"*This* Peach Springs? I thought it was a big town with umpteen thousand people in it."

"And so it was, till they moved it."

"Moved it?" I stood aghast at the thought of such a horrible thing.

"Aye, I mind the time when there was over 40,000 people in Peach Springs.[594] They'd all come in a heluva sweat lookin' for gold, and what's more, they found it.

Then the gold begun to give out until in the end there warn't none at all, an' when the gold went the people went with it. I'm the only one as didn't go and I guess I'm not much concerned about it neither. Provisions and gas and oil are better'n grubbin' after gold all yer life."

"Provisions?" I queried. "Got any pineapple chunks?"

"Sure thing. Got everything."

Overcome with emotion, I filled my pockets with tinned fruit and biscuits.

That night my camp fire burned in a glorious spot sheltered by high cliffs. Fuel was scarce, there were just a few dried-up bushes to burn, but it was splendid, camping there with the beautiful clear sky above, the stars shining as I had never known them shine before.

On again we went at dawn. This time it was to leave behind the cedar forests and the towering canyons. We were getting near the fringe of the great arid desert that stretches for nearly 300 miles to the heart of California. Gradually the ground became flat, almost as flat as the proverbial pancake. On it grew no vegetation at all, save the scanty sage-brush that can flourish where all other things die. Miles away, but clear enough to be only a few hundred yards, rose ranges of saw-toothed, evil-looking mountains, as barren as barrenness could be. Ahead lies the trail stretching beyond the traveller's vision to the horizon. On the left runs a fence. Beyond the fence is the Santa Fé Railway. The telegraph poles and the distant mountains are the only objects that break the interminable flatness. The sky is cloudless and the heat of the sun intense. At every five or ten miles a stop is made to drink water from the bag on the handlebar. One has a glorious thirst in these parts.

Mile after mile goes by, and hour after hour. The sun grows higher in the heavens, its rays pour down upon my back with unrelenting fury. When shall we get to anywhere? The inner man grows weary of fasting in this infernal heat. A massive rock, lying all alone in the vast plain on the right, asks: "Why will ye not repent?" Oh, the irony of it! The man who painted that rock was a fanatic, but he knew what he was about.

Kingman at last! Kingman meant breakfast.[595] Breakfast meant water melons and coffee and pies and other good—nay, beautiful—things. Kingman meant drinks and ices and sundries[596] to one's heart's content, and one's pocket's contents.

On again I pursue my way, feeling like a new man. Next stop Yucca, thirty miles.[597] Gee! the sun is hot. Nearly eleven. My stars, what will it be like at one? Everything is sand now—underneath, around, everywhere. The wheels tear it up in clouds as they skim through. Sometimes they slip sideways in it and flounder about, trying to grip on to something firm. Sometimes we slither over altogether but the sand is soft and spills do not disturb one much. But the sun—I wish it would stop working a bit!

Vegetation appears once again, but of a very strange kind. It is a vegetation that is different from any we know in Europe. It is at the same time grotesque, mysterious, ridiculous, wonderful and luxurious. It is desert vegetation. You have always thought of deserts as devoid of every sign of vegetation? It is not so in the great deserts of America. Life abounds but, as if in recompense for the privilege of living, it has to take strange forms. Yet, if they are strange, it is only in comparison with the vegetation to which in temperate climes we are accustomed. The unnumbered varieties of cactus plants and trees are in reality beautiful and strange beyond description. They are always green, always fresh and always beautiful. It is a kind of "Futurist" beauty that adorns them. The cactus trees, for instance, have their leafless branches projecting almost at right angles to the trunk,[598] and they in turn branch out in a similar manner, presenting a grotesque appearance. The tall and beautiful Ocatilla[599]—one can almost refer to it as a desert "shrub"—springs directly from the ground like several long waving feelers bunched together below and spread apart above. The prickly-pear, with its needle-covered fleshy leaves, each one joined on to another without stem or stalk, presents a most weird aspect.[600] Even the modest and unassuming sage-brush,[601] the poor downtrodden "John Citizen" of every desert, seems to have been arranged on the barren plain in regular rectangles and rows, spaced at mathematical distances apart.

The secret is that each one has to think of only one thing—water. Each cactus plant or tree is provided in itself with the means of storing a reserve of water. Moisture is the one great thing that dominates them all. That being so, the constitution of desert vegetation has to be altogether different from that of humid climates just as our constitutions would have to be entirely different if we lived on Mars, where there is hardly any water at all.[602]

This was truly a world of wild fancy. It would be ridiculous—I thought—to try to explain a scene like this to people who had never seen anything but ordinary trees and plants and flowers. They would laugh in scorn when I tried to describe to them that strange conglomeration of fanciful shapes, those mad-looking cactus trees with every joint dislocated, those weird Ocatilla waving their long slender arms twenty and thirty feet above the ground. And look at that great organ-pipe cactus over there, nothing but a huge light-green fleshy trunk, with two or three other trunks all perfectly straight and perfectly vertical on top of it! How could one possibly describe things like that?

"With a Watch-Pocket Carbine,[603] of course. What else?" I mused and stopped to take out my camera from the toolbox.[604] It was not so easily done as said. The toolbox lid seemed red-hot to my fingers. I could not bear my hand on the top of the tank even.

Oh, water, water: how beautiful thou art! Even when imbibed under hand-pressure from a smelly canvas water-bag!

Could it EVER get any hotter than this? The only way was to keep going, the faster the better. Then the heat, with frequent drinks, was just tolerable. When I stopped, it was like being plunged suddenly into a great furnace. Never mind; there would be ice-creams at Yucca.[605] On again, as fast as we can, leaping over gullies, ploughing through the loose white sand. Lower and lower we get as we travel. The gradient is not noticeable, for there are ups and downs all the way, and ridges of hills here and there. All the same, we are making a steady descent. In a couple of dozen miles we shall cross the River Colorado. That morning we were over a mile high above it.[606] Now we are at its level. That explains the increasing heat the further we go, and further on for hundreds of miles the road lies but a few feet above the level of the sea; in places it is actually below it.[607]

In the distance appear trees—poplars, eucalyptus[608] and cedars. They denote the small ramshackle town of Yucca, like an island in the plain. The trail widens into a road. Living beings are seen, horses, carts and motor cars. It is the civilized world once again. What Yucca does for a living I am at a loss to know. It cannot certainly be a ranching town. Probably there is a little gold in the vicinity and it is a small trading centre. Probably it is more important as a thirst-quenching centre!

A short stop and on we went again into the desert, leaving behind us the little oasis, and plunging ahead into a still hotter region. The strange cactus trees and desert plants gathered round once more. Rougher and rougher the road became. The sand gave place to sharp loose grit interspersed with rocks and jutting boulders. As it did so, gradually the luxurious vegetation of the desert grew thinner and the dull miserable sage-brush took its place. The trail divided up into two deep and solitary ruts and in between them lay loose shale and grit that absolutely defied progress. The wheels would sink in freely and churn the road up aimlessly. It was necessary then to ride in one of the ruts. Where they were broad this was not difficult, but when they narrowed and deepened a spill was almost bound to occur if one wobbled but a fraction of an inch from the dead centre of the rut. Negotiating a road of this nature was something new in the sport of motor-cycling, but it was exasperating.[609] I was to find later that riding continuously in a rut was like riding on a greasy road, in that the more carefully one went and the more timid one grew, the more dangerous did the riding become. Time and time again I was thrown off by fouling the side of the rut and plunged headlong over the handlebars into the road. The slower I went the more often was I thrown. If I travelled about ten or twelve miles an hour I could maintain my balance by using my feet where necessary. Riding at that speed, however, was out of the question. It was better to go faster and risk the frequent spills than to be roasted alive. So I went faster. The faster I went the easier was it to maintain balance naturally, because the steering became more sensitive and only a very small movement of the handlebars within the limits of the rut would suffice to correct any deviation from perfect balance. I found that at between thirty-five and forty miles an hour it was moderately easy to follow the rut through the swerves in its course. But even then, occasionally there would be a nasty spill, a few bent levers and some scratches. (I learned a week or so later from "Cannonball Baker," the famous American racer, that he travels in these same ruts at between fifty and sixty!)[610]

Here and there the trail would cross a "wash" or a dried-up lake bed and then the sand régime would reappear. And ever did death speak from all around—desolation in bewildering intensity almost cried aloud from the fire-swept waste that lay all about me. Often I passed the remains of derelict cars left at the side of the road; sometimes it was a mudguard or a spring, a tyre or a broken wheel; sometimes it was a complete chassis, stripped of everything that could be taken away. For what could be done in a region like this if the breakdown were too large? Nothing but to push the car off the road and leave it to its fate. Almost without exception the remains were of Ford cars. That shows the wisdom of travelling in a machine that bears no great loss if it is damaged or forsaken!

Occasionally I passed a gigantic heap of small tins all rusty and forlorn. I was puzzled at first. How did they get there? And why had they been heaped up if they were the discarded food-tins of passing travellers? But no. They are the sole remains of a "mushroom" town of the West.[611] In them one can picture the sudden growth and the almost equally sudden decay of a settlement that thrived while there was gold to be found in the vicinity.

Here and there, too, were little heaps of bones, bleached white as snow—the remains of a horse or a cow that had strayed. To lose oneself, be it man or animal, is sure death in the Mohave Desert.[612]

It is just mid-day. The sun is vertically above. It beats down on my shoulders and dries up the skin of my hands. My hair, over which I had never worn a hat since I left New York, is bleached to a light yellow colour and stands erect, stiff and brittle. The alkali sand and dust have absorbed all the moisture from my fingers and gradually cracks and cuts are developing in my finger tips and at the joints. I find it easier to grasp the handlebars with the palms of my hands alone. My clothes are saturated with dust and my trench boots are cut and scratched, with the seams broken away;[613] the right sole has pulled away and threatens to come off altogether unless carefully used. I feel that the sooner I get out of the Mohave Desert the better it will be for me.

But the heat! It seems to know no shame, no pity. It is terrific. Every five miles I stop and drink from the water bag. There is just enough to carry me to the next stop. For the first time I begin to long for shelter from the burning rays. There is none around anywhere—not as far as the horizon. I must push on quickly. . . . The rut suddenly breaks and swerves away. . . . CRASH! . . . Up again, lose no time. On once more; what matter if the footbrake doesn't work? A motor-cycle is made to go, not to stop!

In front, to the left, rise pinnacles of purple granite. They stick up sharply into the sky like the teeth of a great monster grinning over its prey. They are the "Needles,"[614] and they fringe the Colorado River. What a glorious sight it will be to see a river again, with water flowing in it.

Now on the horizon appears a blotch of green. Its beauty in that yellow wilderness is beyond description. It is the green of the stately poplar trees that surround the railway station of Topock.[615] That is where the road and the railway and the river all meet, and where we leave Arizona and enter the State of California. Thank Heaven it is not far away. The pinnacles rise higher and higher, the little oasis grows bigger and bigger, and the trees greener and taller.

At last! Lizzie's rattle is silent. We come to rest under a great shelter thatched with straw that has been erected by the roadside opposite the restaurant the only building in the town beside the railway station.[616] A few yards further on was a massive steel bridge 400 yards long that spanned the Colorado.[617] Beyond lay California, but I was satisfied with Arizona and the straw-thatched shelter for an hour or two.

* * * * *

At two we crossed the great bridge. What good fortune would California bring, I wondered. It brought even worse roads than I had seen in Arizona. There still remained over 200 miles of desert to be crossed. The trail was very rough, like a mountain track at the start, full of ups and downs and swerves and washes. Twelve miles further on I arrived at the town of Needles,[618] so tired and hot that I decided to abandon travel until the evening. Then I would ride out into the desert and make my bed under the steel-blue sky. I was too enamoured of the wonderful sunsets and the glorious sunrises of the open plain to allow them to pass unseen in a musty, stuffy hotel bedroom.

Needles, I was surprised to find, was very much bigger than I had expected. It is now a good-sized town and its main street a bustle of activity. After disposing of a steak at a Chinese restaurant,[619] I bought a book and retired to the square. There I took off my tunic, rolled up my shirt sleeves and lay on the grass beneath the tall, thick palm trees and whiled away the hot afternoon hours.[620]

At evening as the setting sun was drawing a magic cloak over the tropical sky, I stole out of Needles along the lonesome trail that I had learnt to love. Except for low-lying mountains all around, there was nothing but the everlasting sand and sage-brush. Behind lay the gigantic plain and across it, like a silver snake, crept the great silent river. It was the most impressive scene that I have ever beheld from my bedroom window. My mattress was the sand with a waterproof sheet laid upon it. Never did Monte Cristo with all his wealth sleep in such luxury as that.[621]

IN THE MOHAVE DESERT.

He who all his life has associated the dawn with the soft greetings of birds and the mellow noises of awakening nature, is struck at once with the vast difference of desert countries. I have read that in unexplored Africa and South America, the dawn is heralded by a mighty tumult of millions of voices, a great chorus of every soul in the great populace that lives in forest and jungle. In the Mohave Desert the majesty of the dawn unfolds itself in deathly silence. The entire absence of sound of any kind is awe-inspiring, almost weird, and the observer can but watch and wonder at it as he sees the whole firmament set ablaze with colours and shades that he never imagined existed, and gradually the silent grandeur of the spectacle is revealed.

It was with just such feelings that from my bed I watched the unfolding of another day from the depths of the great silent plain which lay beyond that thread of silver in the distance.

CACTUS TREES NEAR SAN BERNARDINO, CALIFORNIA. [622]

And then, on again. There was a low range of mountains ahead to be crossed. It was slow work and very tiring. The constant looseness of the surface, the need for everlastingly keeping one's eyes glued to the trail, and the terrible monotony of it all for mile after mile, made me long all the more for a sight of the orange groves and the blue sea beyond that to-morrow I might, if nothing unforeseen happened, enjoy. Thus went fifteen, twenty, thirty miles. The first halt was reached. It was only a railway station, a "hotel," a garage and two or three houses, but it meant breakfast,[623] and a good one at that, for the journey that was ahead. Feeding over, out we went once more to brave the ruts and the rocks and the sand, for miles and miles unending. The morning sun grows slowly into a midday sun.

We have been climbing a little. Low-lying ranges of absolutely bare, purple-brown jagged hills seem to hem us in. Soon we shall be across them. Beyond there will be—what? More, perhaps. The road here has been "oiled," that is, the sand has been levelled and then crude mineral oil poured on. This hardens the crust and prevents the road from blowing away, giving to the uninitiated the impression of well-laid macadam. It is a relief after the loose sand, and it looks so strange for a black, broad highway to be going across a desert! It does not last long, but comes and goes in patches. Where it does appear it is often lumpy and cut into grooves and slices. Nevertheless it is welcome. . . . The road turns when it reaches the crest, continues for a few yards, and then . . . .

A marvellous sight has suddenly appeared,[624] viewed from the meagre height at which we stand. A great plain lies beneath and before us, greater and flatter and more desolate than my imagination could ever have conceived. All around it are mighty saw-toothed ranges of mountains pressing close upon the horizon and fading away into nothingness. In it is nothing, not a prominence of any kind, save the omnipresent sage-brush that seems to stretch in streaky uniformity like a great purple-brown veil above the cream-white sand. It is impossible to go on—to do anything but stop and wonder that over so great an area nature can be so desolate. It is wonderful, mystifying in its intensity.

Did I say there was no prominence? What are those two minute specks away over there in the heart of the plain? They must be a tremendous distance away, but in their very minuteness they are conspicuous. It is obvious that they are not there by the design of Nature. ... As I look, a tiny white speck appears further still to the left, as though it emerged from behind the range of mountains that I have just crossed. Look! There is a short black tail behind it. It is a train!

Slowly, almost imperceptibly, it moves across the great wilderness. The black specks then are stations, small man-made oases where water has been brought to the surface. Yes, it is true. Ten minutes elapse, and the little white speck merges into the little black speck. Thus are sizes and speeds dwarfed into insignificance when Nature has the mood to show her magnitude!

On again we go, spinning smoothly awhile over the smooth, oiled road. It stops in a mile or two and leaves nothing but the old heart-rending, twisting, wayward ruts and sand to guide us. Hours go by. They are hours of wild effort, maddening heat, and interminable boredom. Generally, every fifteen or twenty miles, there was a railway station and a restaurant where one could stop for drinks, ices, and petrol.[625]

Four o'clock saw me in Ludlow, a small town, larger than the other stops. I was dead tired. Come what may, I was not going to work myself to death. I had done 200 miles since daybreak.[626] That was enough for anyone in a country like this.

At eight o'clock I set out with Lizzie in the deepening twilight to find a resting-place for the night. The road was oiled, but in most places the sand of the desert had blown over it, covering it for several inches in depth, and sometimes obliterating it from view for many hundred yards.

"I will sleep at the foot of yonder hill," quoth I, and saw visions of concrete roads and orange groves beyond the horizon.

CHAPTER 19 NOTES

579. This is a reference to the evergreen bay tree (*Laurus nobilis*), but it is not clear why it is being characterized in such a manner. C.K. implies that it is an invasive species and resistant to eradication, when neither is the case.

580. It seems likely his host was Professor George Hall Hamilton, pictured in Figure 192, a photo that C.K. apparently took on Sunday, August 3, 1919.

581. After C.K. arrived back in Flagstaff following his nasty fall coming back from the Grand Canyon, he went back to stay with his new friends at the Lowell Observatory. On Sunday, August 3, 1919, he hiked up Sunset Crater with them. From the diary of Carl Otto Lampland of Sunday, August 3, 1919: "A beautiful day. Captain Shepherd from England here. He, with Miss [Elizabeth Langdon] Williams, Mr. [George Hall] Hamilton, Verna [Lampland], and myself went out to Sunset and climbed the mountain. Verna did not go to the top." Astronomers George Hamilton and Elizabeth Williams married in 1922. While on this hike and after reaching at the top of Sunset Crater, about twenty miles northeast of Flagstaff, C.K. snapped the photo in Figure 193 (next page), which was at over 8,000 feet in elevation and located approximately N35°21'56.0", W111°30'02.7". The photo was taken facing north-northwest and features O'Leary Peak in the distance. Closer to the camera, in front of O'Leary Peak, is Darton Dome.

Figure 192: Professor George Hall Hamilton on the Steps of Lowell Observatory.
Source: C.K.'s personal slide collection.

Figure 193: O'Leary Peak and Darton Dome from the Top of Sunset Crater, August 3, 1919.
Source: C.K.'s personal slide collection.

The companion photo (Figure 194) of C.K. was almost certainly taken by Professor Hamilton contemporaneously to his own photo being taken. In the photo inset (Figure 195), you can see that C.K's left index finger is bandaged, dating this photo after his accident returning from the Grand Canyon.

582. C.K. reports here that he departed two days after arriving back in Flagstaff. If C.K. arrived on Saturday,

Figure 194 and Figure 195: C.K. on the Steps of Lowell Observatory.
Source: C.K.'s personal slide collection.

August 2, 1919 and hiked up to the top of Sunset Crater on Sunday, August 3, 1919, he would have left Flagstaff on Monday, August 4, 1919.

583. It was a bit more than thirty miles from Flagstaff to Williams. The *Blue Book* Route 602 describes the distance as 36.6 miles.

584. From Flagstaff to Ash Fork, the *Blue Book* Route 602 describes the distance as being fifty-six miles. If C.K.'s sixty-mile distance was measured from Flagstaff, this encounter with the Ford occurred four miles past Ash Fork. Partridge Creek is about three miles past Ash Fork, so it seems most likely that C.K.'s "wide, rough-bedded, unbridged river" was Partridge Creek.

585. Eight Mile Creek was only about four miles further, in Pineveta Canyon followed by Pineveta Wash, and then another two miles further until the ATSF Pineveta railroad station appeared off on the right. It seems most likely that C.K. met the Ford near Partridge Creek and that the reportedly big washout was at Eight Mile Creek, "just before you come to Pineveta" Station.

586. Pineveta Station was just a railroad stop, the first one west of Ash Fork. C.K. may have misidentified a "movie set town" that he had encountered elsewhere, because there is little indication there was anything at Pineveta but a railroad section house. Pineveta is not even identified by name on the Flagstaff to Kingman route in the *Blue Book*.

587. "Gaumont operator": Used in this context, this means "motion picture camera operator." The name derives from Gaumont—a European cinematic film studio founded by the engineer-turned-inventor Léon Gaumont, which began operation in 1895 (the year C.K. was born). Gaumont Film Company remains in operation today.

588. Twenty miles for Ash Fork to Seligman is a reasonable estimate; the *Blue Book* Route 602 provides a distance of 27.2 miles. Pineveta Station was about nine miles west of Ash Fork, so it is generally accurate to say that Seligman was about twenty miles past Pineveta.

589. The implication is that C.K. felt that owners of Fords were prone to making many spelling errors.

590. C.K.'s description of Nelson is accurate. The *Arizona Business Directory* (1920) described Nelson as a "Postoffice in Yavapai county and station on the Atchison,

Topeka & Santa Fe Railway, 66 miles northeast of Kingman, the nearest banking point. Lime manufacturing the industry. Population about 200. Altitude 5,200 feet." One hundred years after C.K. passed through, Nelson continues to support substantial mining operations.

591. It was seven—not fifteen—miles from Nelson to Peach Springs. The excerpt from *Auto Club Map 10* in Figure 196 illustrates this fact.

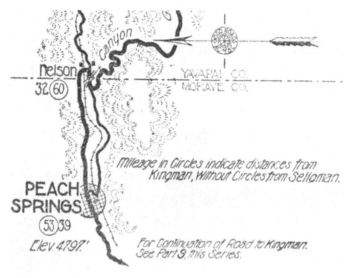

Figure 196: Map of the Route from Nelson to Peach Springs, Arizona.
Source: *Auto Club Map 10.*

592. C.K. pulled into the Peach Springs Trading Post, which had been built only two years earlier in 1917 by Everett H. Carpenter. The building, a trading post on the Hualapai Indian Reservation, was used by the Hualapai Tribe to sell their goods to passers-by. It is depicted in Figure 197 in a postcard photo from about 1918. Figure 198 is an advertisement from the *Mohave County Miner* newspaper on August 3, 1918.

In 1921, four years after startup, Carpenter made his friend, Ancel Early Taylor, an equal partner. Within three years, Taylor bought all remaining interest from Carpenter and, in about 1926, Taylor demolished the old Trading Post and constructed a new one from concrete and stone at the same location. Around 1950, the Hualapai Tribe acquired the building. It is now listed in the National Register Historic Places and is the office for the Hualapai Tribal Forestry Department.

Figure 197: Postcard of Peach Springs Trading Post, *ca.* 1918.

Figure 198: Peach Springs Trading Post Advertisement.
Source: *Mohave County Miner,* August 3, 1918. Page 2.

593. Everett Carpenter was fifty-eight years old in August 1919. He had come to Arizona around 1885 in search of a "strike" in the copper mines in Jerome. However, he failed there and moved west to settle in Peach Springs. After selling his interest in the Trading Post to Ancel Early Taylor, Carpenter remarried and entered the grocery business in Phoenix, where he died at the age of seventy-three on July 14, 1934.

594. The claim that over 40,000 people ever lived in Peach Springs is an extreme exaggeration. The US census summaries beginning in 1860 do not include a breakdown for Peach Springs within Mohave County, but the numbers in Figure 199 reflect Mohave County and Arizona in general for the years indicated and—when separately reported—for Peach Springs.

Year	Peach Springs	Mohave County	Arizona
1860	-	-	6,482
1870	-	179	9,658
1880	-	1,190	35,100
1890	-	1,444	59,620
1900	71†	3,426	122,931
1910	-	3,773	204,354
1920	61†	5,259	334,162

† = Totals from individual census sheets.

Figure 199: Peach Springs and Mohave County Populations.
Source: US census sheets and reports.

595. It seems most likely that C.K. ate his breakfast at Taylor's Cafe. Although records of a Mint Cafe in Kingman in 1919 were found, there was greater prominence and advertising devoted to Taylor's Café (see Figure 200).

TAYLOR'S CAFE

Clean, Cool, Comfortable
Good Food Well Served.

Next to Arizona Central Bank.
SHORT ORDERS 6 a.m to 8 p.m.

Figure 200: Taylor's Cafe Advertisement.
Source: *Mohave County Miner and Our Mineral Wealth*, August 2, 1919. Page 2

596. There were at least two general merchandise stores in Kingman in 1919—Arizona Stores Co. and Central Commercial Co.—but there is no additional record suggesting which one C.K. was more likely to have visited.

597. According to the *Blue Book* Route 603, it is 23.9 miles from Kingman to Yucca—not thirty.

598. C.K. was apparently describing the saguaro cactus (*Carnegiea gigantea*), which can grow to be over forty feet tall and is native to Arizona (see Figure 201).

Figure 201: Saguaro Cactus (*Carnegiea gigantea*).
Source: "Ansel Adams Photographs of National Parks and Monuments," compiled from 1941-1942.
Photograph by Ansel Adams.

599. Ocatilla is a spelling variation of the more common word ocotillo (*Fouquieria splendens*), which can grow as high as thirty-three feet. Figure 202 (next page) was published in 1906 in a book from George Wharton James, an English-born lecturer, photographer, and journalist.

Figure 202: The Ocatilla in Leaf.
Source: *The Wonders of the Colorado Desert*, George Wharton James. 1906.

600. See Chapter 16, Note 468, Figure 149 for a description and illustration of the prickly pear.

601. Sagebrush is the common name of several woody and herbaceous species of plants in the genus *Artemisia*. The best known is *Artemisia tridentata* shown in Figure 203.

Figure 203: Sagebrush (*Artemisia tridentate*).
Source: USDA-NRCS Plants Database.

602. C.K's characterization that "there is hardly any water at all" on Mars reflects his confidence in the theories of Percival Lowell and his progeny, who believed they saw signs of canals on Mars. Although scientists have recently proven the existence of ice on Mars—and there is some evidence of terrain erosion on Mars believed to be caused by water—the concept of *any* water existing on Mars was only hypothetical in 1922 and, even then, often based on erroneous assumptions.

603. A Watch-Pocket Carbine was a popular portable camera with a collapsible baffle that used 2¼ x 2¼ inch film and was originally made by W. Butcher & Son, a British camera maker, from 1903-1930. Figure 204 is a photo of Mark Hunnibell's Watch-Pocket Carbine No. 4. This model was available since 1915 and could easily be the model C.K. used on his trip.

Figure 204: Butcher's Watch-Pocket Carbine No. 4.
Source: Photograph by Mark L. Hunnibell.

604. C.K. snapped the photo in Figure 205 (next page) in the desert near Yucca showing both ocatilla and sagebrush, although no saguaro is evident.

605. As previously reported in Note 597, it was 23.9 miles from Kingman to Yucca. C.K. was probably looking forward to ice cream on the latter half of this leg. However, he may have only imagined he would find ice cream in Yucca. In 1919, Yucca was even smaller than Nelson. It is reflected as nothing more than an intersection in the *Blue Book*. The *Arizona Business Directory* (1920) reports that Yucca was a "Post-office and station on the Atchison, Topeka & Santa Fe Railway, in Mohave county, 24 miles east of Kingman, the county seat and nearest banking point. Mining and stock raising are the principle industries. Population 75. Altitude 1,800 feet." The same directory lists only four businesses there, including the Highway Hotel—where "Mrs. M. Leonard" is listed as proprietor. Thus, if C.K. had some ice cream in Yucca, it was probably not something to which he would have looked forward, but instead was discovered as a most welcome commodity at the Highway Hotel.

Figure 205: Desert Road Near Yucca Arizona.
Source: C.K.'s personal slide collection.

606. C.K. makes this descent sound rather extreme. However, C.K. apparently camped west of Peach Springs, elevation 4,780 feet, so he would have started riding that day not quite a mile above sea level. But Topock, on the Arizona side of the Colorado River, has an elevation of 492 feet so, while he may have descended 4,000 feet over one hundred miles, this averages about 0.75% grade over the distance—not very extreme.

607. Although all of the roads that C.K. travelled on for "hundreds of miles" between Yucca and Los Angeles were *all* above sea level, he did pass one hundred miles south of Death Valley which is 275 feet below sea level in places. He also traveled one hundred miles north of Salton Sink, which is 200 feet below sea level in places.

608. Eucalyptus trees are native to Australia. They were brought to California by Australians in the 1850s during the California Gold Rush. It was thought they would be a good renewable source of timber for construction, furniture making, and railroad ties. By the early 1900s, the State of California encouraged planting of thousands of acres of eucalyptus, but the trees did not produce wood that was as useful as hoped, and they were largely abandoned and allowed to grow wild. It seems unlikely that they would have spread naturally to Yucca in Arizona by 1919. If eucalyptus trees existed there, they were probably brought there by humans and perhaps thrived in conditions similar to their native Australia.

609. C.K.'s description of the difficult road conditions in this area is implied in the characterization of the road from Yucca to Topock in the *Blue Book*: "From Yucca to Topock the road is very winding and crosses numerous sandy washes, making fast time impossible." There is a more grim description of this section of road in a later *Blue Book* (1920): "Good graded, gravelly dirt to Yucca, fair to poor road to Topock... 31 miles fair to poor natural desert road... naturally slows travel, owing to many cross washes and, in places, very poor road."

610. C.K. seems to be saying that he actually *met* Cannonball Baker a week after reaching the California border. If so, that encounter would have occurred on or about August 10, 1919 when C.K. was in Los Angeles and Baker was in town. On June 23, 1919, Baker had arrived in Los Angeles after abandoning a westbound transcontinental speed record attempt coming over Raton Pass into New Mexico. Figure 206 (next page) shows the planned route.

Although Baker left New York a few days after C.K., Baker was "ahead" of C.K. within twenty-four hours of Baker's departure and, when Baker raced west from Kansas City on June 18, 1919, C.K. was still visiting with Steve and his family back in Cincinnati.

In an article in the June 26, 1919 edition of *Motorcycle and Bicycle Illustrated*—the magazine that reported on Baker's unsuccessful record attempt—quoted Baker blaming the worst weather he had seen in thirty-eight previous transcontinental crossings. This lends credence to C.K.'s views on the condition of American roads, especially given that both men covered nearly identical routes after Kansas City. Baker is quoted as telegraphing from Raton: "Rain stops transcontinental trip. Roads impassable. Rode over 1,000 miles of mud from Illinois to New Mexico." Later, after reaching Los Angeles, Baker again telegraphed: "Rains have robbed us of the transcontinental record this time... I was forced to abandon the trip at Raton, New Mexico... Three cloudbursts and rain every day after my first night." It was reported in a shorter story on the same page that Baker learned from the locals in Raton that it had "rained daily for two months between there and Las Vegas [NM]." Despite Baker's woes, he still reached Los Angeles within a day of abandoning his attempt in Raton. The article also mentions that, while he faced difficult roads in places, he covered substantial distances riding on railroad tracks for several legs of his journey west.

C.K. was probably unaware of these things when he spoke with Baker, so he was in no position to challenge Baker's claims of riding over ruts at sixty mph or

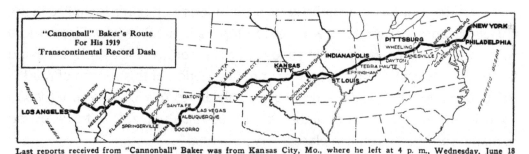

Last reports received from "Cannonball" Baker was from Kansas City, Mo., where he left at 4 p. m., Wednesday, June 18

Figure 206: "Cannon Ball" Baker's Route for His 1919 Transcontinental Record Dash.
Source: *Motorcycle and Bicycle Illustrated,* June 19, 1919. Page 12.

share notes about riding on the railroads. Analysis of Baker's riding history after June 23, 1919 reveals that he was almost certainly in Los Angeles at the same time C.K. was there, resting between the two events:

- On July 11, 1919, Baker arrived in Tijuana, Mexico, setting a new "Three Flags" speed record riding down from the Canadian border to Mexico in less than sixty hours.

- On August 17, 1919, Baker departed from Los Angeles toward New York on another transcontinental speed record attempt, but had to abandon it the next day due to heavy rains west of Flagstaff.

611. There is ample record of "gold rush" towns being characterized as "mushroom towns." In addition, in *The Great Plains* (1907), author Randall Parrish explained the term was also used to describe communities that sprang up to support the construction of railroads:

"An interesting phenomenon of Plains settlement, perhaps without parallel elsewhere, were those strange towns which sprang up in a night wherever the advancing railway paused, and which passed away as suddenly with the further extension of the rails, leaving scarcely a trace behind. The peculiarity of the conditions under which these earliest overland roads were constructed made such mushroom towns inevitable, and the nature of their population served to render them sufficiently picturesque."

612. Although people often identify California as the location of the Mojave Desert, it spreads a bit further east into Nevada and Arizona. So when C.K.

lamented about the heat and conditions around Yucca as being reflective of the Mojave Desert, he was being accurate. But the Mojave Desert runs all of the way across southern California until it reaches the foothills of the San Bernardino Mountains at Hesperia, some 200 miles from Yucca. In other words, C.K. had just entered the Mojave Desert and was a long way from leaving it.

613. The term "trench boots" was used during World War I to reflect boots intended to provide better foot protection in the trenches. As shown in the close-up in Figure 207 (a section of the photo in Figure 194), taken just a few days earlier in Flagstaff, his boots seem to be well worn but serviceable.

Figure 207: C.K.'s Trench Boots.
Source: C.K.'s personal slide collection.

614. The Needles to which C.K. refers are a range of peaks after which the city of Needles in California is named. Although there are other geological features in the United States that share the name, these Needles are a distinctive group of rock pinnacles adjacent to Topock Gorge and the Colorado River on the northwestern extreme of the Mohave Mountains in Arizona (see Figure 208, next page). They range from 1,200 to over 1,600 feet in elevation. According to the USGS, the Needles are located at N34°40'34", W114°26'16" and are classified as Pillars, under the USGS Geographic Names Information System as being "vertical, standing, often spire-shaped, natural rock formation (chimney, monument, pinnacle, pohaku, rock tower)."

Figure 208: The Needles, Arizona, *ca*. 2006.
View of Colorado River from Topock looking downstream towards the Needles at Topock Gorge.
Source: Photograph by Spl553.

615. In 1919, Topock was an extremely small community that was little more than a station on the Atchison, Topeka & Santa Fe Railway.

616. The data sheets for the census visit on January 30, 1920 reflect only fifty-four people living in Topock with occupations consistent the presence of a garage, a store, and a tavern/hotel (see Figure 209). This indicates there was more to the community than a restaurant and train station.

617. C.K. is describing the Trails Arch Bridge, a single-lane bridge built specially for automobiles that was eight hundred feet long and completed in February, 1916. Before its construction, automobiles shared the railroad bridge, riding on planks installed between the railroad ties. The Trails Arch Bridge still stands, serving as a natural gas and utility conduit. Figure 210 is a photo of the Trails Arch Bridge looking south with buildings in Topock on the left and the landing in California on the right.

The Topock Tavern

TOPOCK, ARIZONA

HOME COOKED MEALS

INDIVIDUAL ROOMS

CHICKEN DINNER

Every Sunday

D A N C I N G

Figure 209: Topock Tavern Advertisement, 1920.
Source: *Mohave County Miner and Our Mineral Wealth*, October 23, 1920. Page 2.

618. The estimate of twelve miles from Topock to Needles is low, since the *Blue Book* establishes the distance as being sixteen miles. The Trails Arch Bridge is 800 feet long, so it was still over fifteen miles to Needles after crossing the Colorado River.

Figure 210: Trails Arch Bridge, December 1, 1919.
Source: WaterArchives.org.

619. It is unlikely we will ever know the name of the Chinese restaurant where C.K. ate his steak because no city directories for the period exist. However, by cross-referencing data from the 1920 census forms and *Bradstreet's Book of Commercial Ratings* (1921), one might reasonably conclude that he dined at Ahkin Yee's restaurant. Yee and others of Chinese ancestry operated restaurants on Front Street. Front Street, as its name implies, is parallel to the railroad tracks and near the square where C.K. enjoyed an afternoon siesta on the city side of the sprawling El Garces (Harvey House) Hotel.

620. Figure 211 is a photo of the public square on the city side of the El Garces Hotel. The "front" of the hotel faced the railroad tracks.

Figure 211: Needles Public Square, *ca.* 1919.
Source: Courtesy of the Needles Museum.

621. C.K. does not say how many miles he rode out of Needles before stopping for the night, but it was probably not more than ten miles because of what he wrote of his travels the following day.

622. Although not legible in the image in Chapter 19 of the book (see Cactus Trees Near San Bernardino, California), the original photo from C.K.'s slide collection contains sufficient detail to see there is a sign advertising Hotel Georgia attached to the first cactus. The Hotel Georgia was in Los Angeles at the corner of Pico and Georgia Streets. It is not listed in the main hotel directories of the period, implying

that it was not used for short-term stays by travelers. Figure 212 is a close-up of the Hotel Georgia sign.

Figure 212: Hotel Georgia Sign on desert Cactus.
Source: C.K.'s personal slide collection.

623. It may not be possible to determine the location of this rail stop. C.K. says he rode "fifteen, twenty, thirty miles" after waking up, perhaps already ten miles out of Needles. Since he described it as not much more than a rail station but had a "hotel," one likely spot was Goffs, which, according to the *Blue Book* Route 607, was located 30.4 miles from Needles. Goffs is reflected as being thirty miles from Needles and as having accommodations and gasoline and oil on the *Auto Club Map 7* (see Figure 213). The *Blue Book* route reflects 40.2 miles to Fenner, but neither company portrays any accommodations at Fenner. However, the *Blue Book* says that Danby was 56.4 miles from Needles and *Auto Club Map 7* shows they had accommodations, meals/lodging, and even auto repairs available. The determination as to whether C.K. was referring to Goffs or Danby may never be known because it is dependent on how far out of Needles he rode the night before.

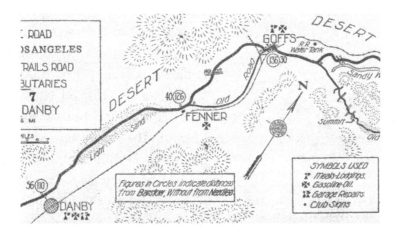

Figure 213: Map of Goffs to Danby.
Source: *Auto Club Map 7.*

624. The photo in Figure 214 seems to be comparable to the one C.K. included in Chapter 19 of the book (see IN THE MOHAVE DESERT) and may have been taken at the same time looking a different direction. The landscape in the distance in either photo is insufficient on its own to establish the location, but it could be where he started out after camping west of Needles.

Figure 214: Mojave Desert, California.
Source: C.K.'s personal slide collection.

625. C.K. was generally accurate when he wrote that there were places every fifteen or twenty miles, but not all of them were documented to have services to provide "drinks, ices, and petrol." Goffs, thirty miles from Needles, had both food and fuel. Danby, twenty-six miles further, also had food and fuel. There was fuel and a small store at Amboy, another twenty-six miles past Danby and 80.5 miles from Needles. It was another twenty-nine miles to Ludlow—a total of 109.6 miles from Needles—where there were apparently a number of choices for

such goods and services. The Murphy Brothers owned key businesses in Ludlow, including a garage, a general store (Figure 215), an eating place, a hotel, a boarding house, and a saloon (though the latter would have been closed by Prohibition). Although there is a gas station today at the Ludlow exit (Exit 50) on I-40, the original Ludlow is a ghost town.

Figure 215: Murphy Bros. General Merchandise Store, Ludlow, California, *ca.* 1913.
Source: *Illustrated Road Maps and Tour Book,* Arizona Good Roads Association, 1913. Page 122.

626. C.K. did not ride 200 miles that day. The *Blue Book* Route 607 reports that it is 109.6 miles from Needles to Ludlow. This means that if C.K. camped ten miles west of Needles, he had not travelled even one hundred miles upon reaching Ludlow and resting for four hours.

CHAPTER XX

I REACH THE PACIFIC COAST

I saw something else on the horizon too. It started as a little black speck on the road, seeming to swerve now and then from one side to another. It emitted a strange noise that at first was scarcely to be heard, but increased until it reverberated indefinitely from the bare angular mountain ranges.

It was a motor-cycle!

An inexpressible feeling of sympathy and comradeship surged through me, as I realized that here was another fool starting to do what one fool had already almost done. I wondered vaguely whether he knew what he was doing.

We both stopped, dismounted, and looked at each other for a few moments before either spoke. The sight of another motor-cycle seemed to take both of us by surprise. The stranger, a young man of twenty-four or so, had an old twin-cylinder Excelsior that looked very much as if it had seen better days.[627] I led off the conversation.

"Where do you reckon you're going on that?"

"New York."

"Ever done it before?"

"Nope."

"Insured?"

"Nope."

"Pleasure or business?"

"Both." Here he fumbled around a huge bruise on his forehead.

"Leastways, that was the idea. I'm writing it up for the *Adventure Magazine*[628] when I'm through"—and he added guardedly, "That is, if I don't kill meself with a few more headers like this."

"How'd you get that?"

"Oh, Boy, I came such a crash on a bit of oiled roadway back there by that salt-lake bed. Don't remember anything of it except being chucked clean over the grips about fifty. My Gad, it was some crash! I came round about half an hour after. Say,

345

Boy, you look out for them ruts; ride plumb in the middle of the road, and you may miss 'em, cause they're filled in and blown over with sand. Jest the right width of your wheel, they are."

"Sure, I've made their acquaintance already; kind of keep a man fit, don't they? But, say, you've got many more like that coming between here and New York. Take my tip, old man. If you've got anyone depending on you for a living and you don't want to knock the 'X' and yourself to little pieces, you had better go back home right now and tootle up and down the Californian coast for a holiday. And if you still want to get to New York—well, all I can say is, there's a dem fine train service, and you'll find a depot right there in Ludlow."

"Don't you worry, Boy; I've done a heap of motor-cycling in my days and I guess I don't get scared at a header or two, and s'long as I can fix anything that happens along, I guess I'll git to Lil Ole Noo York before a couple of weeks is gone."

"Young man," said I in a fatherly tone, "you don't know what you're saying. You're talking blasphemy—sheer heresy. Your crash has turned your wits a little."

"Thanks, but I've made up my mind to go by road, and go by road I will."

"That's the spirit, but just a few more words of advice. Sell it and buy a Ford. Then you'll be able to take some one with you."

"I'm taking some one already, Boy. He's back at Ludlow. Shipped him on from Barstow, the road was so dog-gone bad and he got scared at the desert."

"What! You're taking him on the carrier?" I cried aghast.

"Sure enough. What's against it?"

I was speechless. His youth and innocence held me spellbound for a moment. Then I burst forth:

"Man, you're mad! ABSOLUTELY MAD! Here, c'mon, Lizzie, before it gets too dark and before this lunatic gets unsafe." I kicked her into a roar. "Cheerio, old man! Give my love to the Angels tomorrow!"

Then his open exhaust burst into a clatter and I saw him no more. I often thought about him, though, and wondered how, when, and where he ended up.

Next morning I shook the desert sand from my blanket for the last time. By hook or by crook I should be sailing through the streets of Los Angeles before nightfall. I judged I looked pretty fierce on the whole. I had no looking-glass,[629] having left my suit-case to be shipped on back at Santa Fé,[630] but I had the best part of a week's growth on my chin and I had not known the joy of a wash for four days. My hair, my boots, my clothes, my everything, were saturated with sand and dust. My tunic, which in its earlier days had been a green tweed, was now white at the back, bleached almost colourless with the sun and then soaked with alkali dust. In the front and below the sleeves it maintained something approaching its original colour. My boots? Well, they had not been off for four days, and the right sole, which had been threatening revolution, had so many times nearly tripped me up by doubling underfoot, that I had removed it near the instep with my pen-knife!

And Lizzie was in no better condition. Externally she was a mass of string, wire, insulation-tape, mud, oil, and sand. Internally she was a bundle of rattles and strange noises. Everything was loose and worn; the sand had invaded her at every point and had multiplied wear a thousandfold. Latterly the tappet rods had had to be cleaned and adjusted over a sixteenth of an inch every day until there was no more adjustment possible. The valve rockers were worn half-way through, some more than that. One had worn right through until it had broken in the middle. I began to be afraid that the engine would not hold out even for the 200 odd miles to come.[631] By handling her carefully and giving her ample oil, I hoped to "deliver the goods" and get across the remaining half of the great desert tract that borders on the Sierra Madre Range running parallel with the coast from north to south. Once across that range, everything, I told myself, would change abruptly, the roads, the scenery, and the climate.

Mile after mile of rock and sand went by with the sweating hours. Often little patches of oiled road appeared, stayed awhile, and then miraculously disappeared below the white, loose surface. Nearly always there were two ruts, beautifully sharp and well cut, sunk three or four inches below the rest of the surface, caused by the fierce rays of the midday sun converting the oiled surface into a plastic condition easily moulded by passing cars which, once given the lead, follow blindly in the others' "footsteps." Many a bad swerve and an occasional spill did I have when my front wheel found such as this. But the major portion of the road was just the bare, loose sand and gravel of the desert.

I had by now become so used to my own company that the sense of loneliness almost disappeared, and I felt as perfectly at ease here as anywhere else. I felt that the great wastes had a charm, nay, even a lure, that eclipsed all past sensations and gave a mental satisfaction that no other phase of Nature could ever reveal. I cannot describe the ineffable something which made me love the great solitude and the mighty spaces, but it is there nevertheless, and, like the greatest of passions, it gives extremes. After one has lived but a few days in the desert, either he loves it passionately or he loathes it. There is nothing in between.

On the right there lies the great "Death Valley"[632] that stretches a hundred miles to the north between the Armagosa and the Paramint Mountains.[633] Its name is suggestive of the many people who have miserably perished of thirst in its clutches.

It is the remains of a long-since dried-up inland lake and parts of it are 150 feet below the level of the sea.[634] There is nothing in it save bare rock and shifting alkali sand, with here and there a cactus or a little sage. The heat is tremendous and the thermometer sometimes rises to 140°.[635] In all, not a pleasant place either to live in or to die. But there are those who in the search for gold live here for months at a stretch.

Confound it! There goes No. 1 cylinder again. Why doesn't she fire? Am I to start overhauling the engine in this terrible place? I stop to change a plug. . . . Nothing doing. . . . Try another. . . . Still no result. For ten minutes I tinker with red-hot tools. Gee! the blessed machine will be melting soon if we don't move quick. In disgust I go on again with only three cylinders working. Past memories crowd into my mind, but the eternal battle with the loose sand suffices to keep them out.

It was too bad, to start playing pranks like this within a few hours of the coast. The sand of the road absorbed most of the power I now had left and often I had to change down to bottom gear to get along at all. It was wonderful what a difference just that one cylinder made, and it was most annoying that it should happen just here, where the earth was nothing more than a confused mass of rocks and sand, and the sun stood vertically above in the sky. "Thank Heaven, I've some water left, if anything happens," thought I.

"What in the world is that thing?" I asked myself. Closer acquaintance proved it to be a motor lorry, dressed up as a caravan and minus a back axle—a most remarkable sight in most remarkable surroundings. From the numerous loop-tracks that swerved around it, it had evidently stood there many days. Its owner was lying underneath on his back.

"Pretty place to change a back axle, old man," I remarked intelligently.

"Yep. Not the kind o' thing a feller does for the fun of it, either," he retorted, scrambling out from his resting-place in the sand.

"Well, is there anything I can do for you, anyway? I don't quite like to see a chap stranded in a blankety-blank country like this on blankety-blank roads like these." I forget just the adjectives I used, but I know they were hardly of the drawing-room variety. Imagine my surprise when a feminine voice from inside chirped out:

"Yes, that's just about got 'em sized up! I've never heard such a mighty cute description of 'em."

Five days they had been there. The back axle had broken under the huge strain of dragging the load through the deep, loose sand. A passing car had taken it to San Bernardino to be repaired, and other passing cars had kept them well supplied with water. They expected to have the axle back the next day and then had nothing to fear.

As I could do nothing for them, I propped Lizzie up against the side of the lorry and tried once more to persuade No. 1 cylinder to join hands with the rest.

After half an hour of useless toil, I bade farewell to the caravan and its occupants. "Quite sure I can't do anything?"

"Plumb sure, thanks. Mebbe we shall be there before you, y'know,"—with a wicked twinkle in his eye.

Then followed hours and hours of ceaseless toil. We climbed hills and crossed great lake-beds that glistened white with a dazzling glare. In some of these there was nothing to be seen in the vast stretch of alkali deposit where once, thousands of years ago, rested the briny waters of lakes and inland seas—nothing, not even a plucky bush of sage-brush, clinging valiantly to its life-hold.

We came to Barstow, a growing settlement, a railway centre and with great alkali factories. Here, after nearly 100 miles' running,[636] I had a substantial breakfast-lunch-dinner meal and filled my water-bag for the last time.[637] We were nearing the end of the Mohave Desert.

Here the trail turns sharply to the south to "San Berdoo," the colloquial abbreviation of San Bernardino. At one time the trail had crossed the desert by a different route altogether, in places almost 100 miles from the railway line. So many souls had perished with the heat and lack of water—perchance through some breakdown or through losing their way—that later a new road was "constructed" following closely the track of the railway so that travellers by road need never be in difficulties for long. It is an unwritten law in any of the American deserts that anyone can hold up a train anywhere if he needs water or supplies or other help.[638] It is willingly given, whether it be a freight train or the "California Limited" express from New York to San Francisco![639]

The San Gabriel Mountains[640] now rose high on the horizon. They had but to be crossed, and then all our troubles would be over.

So I thought.

At Victorville, a growing town at the north base of the range, the desert had almost disappeared.[641] Eucalyptus trees became strangely intermixed with cactus trees, and the aroma of their long, grey-green leaves filled the air with a new sensation. It was the approach of civilization once again.

And then followed the long, winding climb up to the Cajon Pass. In the thick sand and with only three cylinders, it was hard work and slow work.[642] I thought we should never get to the top. Looking back, I beheld a wonderful panorama of desert plain, and a glistening sea of sand; looking forward, I saw just a gap in the great black wall and a rocky pathway winding through it.[643]

Are we NEVER going to reach the summit? We must have climbed nearly a mile high already,[644] I argued with myself, when, of a sudden, the twisting, rocky trail ceased to exist. It vanished like magic, and instead there was before us a magnificent, broad highway of smooth, flat concrete that made me yell with delight.[645] It was wonderful. I laughed and sang with childish glee to think that after 4,000 miles of mud and sand and soil and rock and rut and unspeakable goat-track, I was at last on a concrete road once again, with a surface like a billiard table. I swerved madly from side to side to make sure those two haunting ruts had really disappeared, and laughed again when I found I was not thrown off. It was just glorious.

One more turn, and a great valley lay at my feet. It was green with grass and the mountain sides were clothed in pine trees. Pine trees! How beautiful they looked! It was surely a dream, a vision, a trick of the imagination. There was a long, winding gradient down into the valley. I shut the engine off and we coasted down the smooth concrete without even a whisper or a jar of any kind. It was like a sudden entry into heaven—and almost as silent.

There were now seventy miles of concrete leading between avenues of eucalyptus and groves of orange trees into Los Angeles.[646] Further, the road was almost perfectly flat, although bordered by the San Gabriel range, and, with a few right-angle bends here and there, cut straight across from east to west, with hardly a swerve from the straight line.

Truly it was like a new world, this fruit garden of California. For miles unbroken save by little avenues, one passed row upon row of orange trees laid out in perfect symmetry and exactitude in the rich flat soil.[647] A narrow ditch, dug parallel with each row and having small branches to each individual tree, communicated with larger ditches along which flowed a constant stream of fresh water led from the mountain sides.

Interspersed would be groves of prunes, peaches, and apples, then a plantation of water-melons and cantaloupes of all shapes and sizes.

And then, as if to snatch away the enjoyment of all these pleasant things, a great clatter arose from the engine. Something had broken at last, and it seemed that the whole was a revolving mass of loose pieces all knocking up against each other. Then, before I had been able to slow down—it all happened in a few seconds—there was a metallic thud, the back wheel locked dead, and the machine dry-skidded itself to rest. Once again Fate had decreed against me, angry that I should have got so far in spite of all her efforts.

Well, well! There was plenty of time to spare now; no need to hurry. I sat down on the grass at the roadside in the shade of an orange tree, ate two oranges—from the tool-box—and smoked a pipe. Feeling refreshed in every sense, I then proceeded to take the engine to pieces.

No. 1 piston had broken in fragments and a large piece had jammed between the big end of one of the connecting rods and the crank-case. It was strange that it had not punched a hole through it.

It was far too long a job to take off the sump at the roadside—it would have meant taking the whole engine out of the frame—nearly a day's work—so I removed as many of the pieces of piston as I could get at through the inspection window. The piston-head was floating loose like a flat disc above the small end. This I removed and packed the two halves of the broken gudgeon pin apart, so as to guide the small end up and down in the cylinder. It was impossible to remove the connecting rod entirely, even with the cylinder off, without removing the whole engine from the frame and taking off the sump.[648]

In a couple of hours I was going again, but very very gingerly, lest another piece of piston should be caught up and cause another jamb. The noise of the rattle too was terrific, and I could hear the warning of passing cars (of which there were now several) only when they were right behind me. Sometimes it would get suddenly worse and a further disrupture would appear imminent, and then it would go suddenly back again to its normal. Thus we toiled for thirty miles, at an average speed of twelve miles an hour.

At Ontario[649]—the towns were as numerous as they were prosperous—I feared another and final episode. A Ford car that was passing slowed down to offer me assistance, and putting Lizzie in "free engine"[650] I hung on to his hoodstays with my right arm as a tow-rope. This lasted for ten miles, but I could stand it no longer; my arms were stiff and aching with the uneven strain. I thanked my benefactor and let go.[651]

The remaining twenty miles into Los Angeles were endured and accomplished under our own power at about eight miles an hour. The attention I attracted was considerable. Hundreds upon hundreds of cars, buses, and motor-cycles passed, hurrying here and there, their tyres making a continuous low hum on the concrete road. Luxury, wealth, and happiness abounded on every hand. No greater antithesis to the aching void of the desert back behind the mountains could be imagined.

Every house was a picture, a model of cleanliness and homeliness. The art of building bungalows is reduced in California to the irreducible. It is amazing to see the variety of design and the characteristic beauty of them all. They made the modern English bungalows of my memory seem like enlarged dog-kennels by comparison.

At five o'clock in the afternoon we rattled into Los Angeles, the New York of the Far West. Lizzie's clatter rose above the noise of the trolley cars that thronged the busy streets. Here at last was the long-sought-for goal—the goal that for nearly three months had urged me westward! And my steed? Poor Lizzie, she cried aloud for a respite from the long, weary journey!

Had I known where the Henderson Agency was I could not have found my way there quicker.[652] It seemed as if Lizzie's instincts had taken her there just as a lost cat, transported hundreds of miles from home, slowly, painfully and perseveringly drags its tired body back again.

A quarter of an hour later I was sailing in a side-car towards the "Clark Hotel." That was where my hotel at Santa Fé had recommended me to go and had forwarded my baggage.[653]

We drew up at the door of a palatial establishment—the "posh" hotel of Los Angeles. Once again, after many a long day, my knees began to quake. Brushing by the magnificent door-porter, I swung into the luxurious lounge. Afternoon tea was just finishing. I strolled across to the reception desk, trying hard to maintain an air of complete innocence as regards my personal appearance. I endeavoured to assume an attitude of perfect congruity with my surroundings.

To say the least, I was lamentably unsuccessful! Little groups of people chatting together stopped and gazed at the dishevelled intruder. Imperfectly disguised smirks were evident on all sides. Pages, bell-boys, and porters quickly brought their grinning faces to attention as I glowered upon them in turn. At last I reached the desk.

"You've got some baggage for me, I believe—a couple of grips[654]—sent from the 'Montezuma' at Santa Fé.[655] Shepherd is my name."

Meanwhile the manager appeared on the scene. Resting himself with both hands on the desk as if to steady himself against any possible shock that he might receive from the contemplation of so strange a spectacle, he gazed at me in silence. Then, below his breath, he found words to convey his astonishment:

"My Gad!" he said, and paused deliberately. Then he continued explosively, "I've seen some sunburnt faces in my time, but never, NEVER, NEVER have I seen a man anywhere with a face like yours!"

"It's nice of you to say so," I retorted.

"Heavens, man!" he continued, ignoring the interruption, "your hair's nearly white and your chest is nearly black. Where in hell have you been?"

"Oh, I didn't stay there long," I replied, "no longer than was necessary to get here from New York."

"New York!" (I was quite expecting him to say "Whar's that?" but evidently its existence was known in well-informed circles in Los Angeles). "Have you walked it or swum it or what?"

"Only motor-cycled it, Old Bean!"

"Well, now, if that's not. . . . Here; I'll give you your key. Go and have a good bath RIGHT NOW."

I thanked him. A porter had got my bags and stood waiting. His face was the essence of staid immobility when I looked at him. Together we went in the elevator to the *n*th floor. Eager to see what I really did look like, my first indulgence was to look at myself in the glass, a thing I had not done for many a day.

It certainly was a shock. I could barely recognize myself. I really was the most remarkable creature I had ever seen. I could not refrain from bursting into uncontrollable laughter. The hitherto straight-faced porter did likewise, and we both felt the better for it.

A hot bath! Wonder of wonders! I tumbled into it and the past was forgotten in the inexpressible ecstasy of the present.

CHAPTER 20 NOTES

627. Figure 216 is an advertisement for the 1912 Excelsior twin. The advertisement states that Excelsior's first *twin* was sold to the public on July 20, 1910, so C.K.'s characterization of the motorcycle as "old" probably had more to do with his assessment of its condition than its age, because it couldn't have been older than nine years.

628. There were a number of "adventure" magazines at the time and C.K. probably did not recall the full or exact name of this one. Without the name of the magazine, a thorough search for any articles by this unnamed motorcyclist was unsuccessful. It is also possible that, even if the motorcyclist wrote a story for such a magazine, it was never published.

Figure 216: Excelsior Advertisement. **Source:** *Motorcycle Illustrated*, Vol. 7, No. 14, July 11, 1912. Page 9.

629. "looking glass": An old-fashioned term for mirror. It is not known when this term was first used, but the 14th century witnessed the development of wall-mounted crystal (not glass) mirrors, so some theorize that "looking glass" was used to describe them to distinguish them from earlier highly-polished bronze reflective devices.

630. On July 14, 1919, prior to C.K.'s arrival in Santa Fe, the *Santa Fe New Mexican* reported that his "English valise" had arrived at the Montezuma Hotel in Santa Fe, having been shipped ahead by C.K. In the first chapter, he had written that his practice was to send his extra bag ahead by train to his "predetermined stops across the country." It is most likely that C.K. shipped his bag direct from Kansas City to Santa Fe because it had arrived there within three days of when he had left Kansas City.

631. The *Blue Book* mileage total from Ludlow to Los Angeles was 200.4 miles, so C.K.'s forecast that he had 200 miles ahead of him that day is extremely accurate. It also suggests he did not go very far past Ludlow before camping for the night.

632. Death Valley is about 3,000 square miles in eastern California. It is well north of the road C.K. was on. The route C.K. took gets no closer than ninety miles south of Death Valley. It might have been fair to say that it *began* one hundred miles to the north, but it was not just "on the right" side of the road, as is implied.

633. The Amargosa Range is a north-south mountain range in Inyo County in California and Nye County in Nevada about one hundred miles west of Las Vegas, NM. The 110-mile-long range brackets the east side of Death Valley in California, separating it from Nevada's Amargosa Desert. The mountains of the Panamint Range are on the west side of Death Valley and separate Death Valley from the Panamint Valley further west.

634. Death Valley's Badwater Basin is the point of the lowest elevation in North America, presently measured at 282 feet below sea level. In the early 1900s, the elevation was reported in various publications as being between 270 and 280 feel below sea level.

635. The highest temperature ever recorded in Death Valley was 134°F on July 10, 1913, at Furnace Creek.

636. The *Blue Book* distance from Ludlow to Barstow was fifty-five miles. Since C.K. had reported camping after passing Ludlow, "nearly 100 miles" is an exaggeration.

637. In 1919, the main dining establishment in Barstow was the restaurant within Casa del Desierto, the Harvey House at the rail station completed in 1910 (see Figure 217).

Casa del Desierto, Barstow, Cal.

Figure 217: Postcard of Casa del Desierto, Barstow, Cal., *ca.* 1910.

638. There was a time when it was actual law (not just unwritten law) in Nevada (and probably other western states) that trains were required to stop to provide water for people flagging them down in the desert. In "Pioneer Motor Travelers Faced Trying Ordeals," an article by L. Burr Belden appearing on Page 40 of the October 10, 1954 edition of the *San Bernardino County Sun*, Belden recalled the difficulties that motorists had getting across the Mohave Desert in the 1915-1920 time period. The article's content supports C.K.'s claim that it was unwritten law that a train must stop for anyone needing water: "Motorists were urged, in the case of breakdown, to hail either the first car or the first train. The train would stop as would the auto. That was an unwritten rule of the desert. Over in nearby Nevada it was even a state law, that requirement for a train to stop when hailed on the desert and to furnish water to anyone in need."

Additionally, in "The Uncharted Valley," an article in *Overland Monthly* (Vol. LII, No. 1), July 1908, author Kensett Rossiter waxed poetic about the legal requirement for trains to stop and provide water in the desert: "An iron road has come to cut the desert in two, and the prospector, if he is hard driven, knows that he can but reach that road and hail a passing train, it will stop and give him water. The railroad has to obey, for it is a law that man has made. The passengers, watching from their windows, see him start off again across the burning sands, and verily they do know that ten feet from the iron rails the country is as new and as strange as it was when the world began."

639. The "California Limited" ran from Chicago to Los Angeles. The "Overland Limited" service connected Chicago to San Francisco. It does not appear there was any dedicated "Limited" train service from New York to San Francisco at the time.

640. The San Gabriel Mountains are a mountain range located in northern Los Angeles County and western San Bernardino County, California. The mountain range is part of the Transverse Ranges and lies between the Los Angeles Basin and the Mojave Desert. This range lies in—and is surrounded by—the Angeles National Forest, with the San Andreas Fault as the northern border of the range. The highest peak in the range is Mount San Antonio—commonly referred to as Mt. Baldy (10,064 feet)—and rises towards the eastern extremity of the range which extends westward from the Cajon Pass (currently, the I-15 Freeway).

641. In *History of San Bernardino and Riverside Counties* (1922), Victorville was described as, "a town of about 750 people, and is not incorporated. It lies about in the center of Victor Valley, on the Mojave River, 44 miles north of San Bernardino. The main lines of the Santa Fe and Salt Lake railroads pass through it. The town has good schools, with eleven teachers; an M. E. church; a weekly newspaper, the Victor-Valley-News-Herald; one drug store, ice manufacturing plant, three hotels, and one bank... There is in Victorville a plant which manufactures fibre from a desert plant commonly called Spanish dagger. This fibre is used for binding twine and rope." Figure 218 is from a 1920s postcard of Victorville depicting the road out of Hesperia towards Cajon Pass heading into the mountains.

Figure 218: Postcard—Bird's Eye View—Victorville, Calif., *ca.* 1920.

642. Describing the condition of the road from Victorville through Cajon Pass, the *Blue Book* avoided describing the bad road up, instead describing it as consisting "mostly sand and gravel... to summit... balance concrete and macadam" and adding that there was a "fine view from top of [Cajon] Pass." It was not until 1922 when California paved the road from the summit down to Victorville (bypassing Hesperia). Figure 219, is an excerpt from *Auto Club Map 3*; although the elevation is not annotated on this map, the summit was twenty-seven miles from San Bernardino.

Figure 219: Map of Cajon Pass Summit, *ca.* 1915.
Source: *Auto Club Map 3.*

Figure 220: Composite Panoramic Photo of Summit at Cajon Pass, *ca.* 1919.
Source: USGS.

643. Figure 220 is a USGS image they made by "stitching together" a series of photographs to create a panoramic view from the summit of Cajon Pass looking back toward Victorville and down toward San Bernardino.

644. Given the sand and gravel condition of the road on the northern section of the road up to Cajon Pass, it is not surprising that C.K. felt as if had he climbed a mile in elevation from Victorville until reaching the summit. In reality, it was less than 3,000 feet to the summit from Victorville.

645. He had reached the section of twenty-six miles of paved highway from the city of San Bernardino at the top of Cajon Pass, built by San Bernardino County. This section of road was officially completed and opened to the public in around August 1916. It took seven years, until 1922, for the road to be paved from the summit to Victorville.

646. C.K. says he had seventy miles remaining to Los Angeles after passing through Cajon Pass. This is reasonable, depending on where he made this assessment. The *Blue Book* Route 612 states it is 62.8 miles from San Bernardino to Los Angeles. Route 608 in the same volume reflects 26.3 miles from the summit of Cajon Pass to San Bernardino, totaling 89.1 miles. Thus, C.K.'s estimate was highly accurate if he was twenty miles down the road from the summit of Cajon Pass—still six miles north of the city of San Bernardino—when he estimated seventy miles remaining to Los Angeles.

647. This area had recently emerged as an orange-growing center, known as the "Orange Empire." In 1911, the town of San Bernardino inaugurated its annual National Orange Show. By 1919, the Pacific Electric Railway was marketing a special "Trolley Trip" transporting tourists from Los Angeles to San Bernardino to see the orange groves.

648. The "sump," as used here, is a reference to the bottom half of the aluminum engine case.

649. In Figure 221, Ontario is reflected as being thirty-nine miles from Los Angeles.

650. In this context, "free engine" means taking the transmission out of gear—placing it in "neutral"—so that the clutch may be released and the engine can still idle while the motorcycle coasts along.

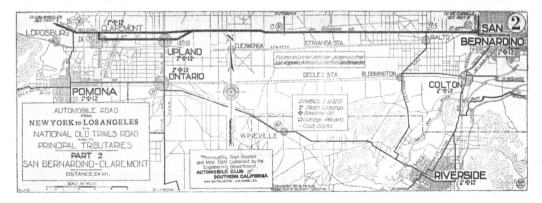

Figure 221: Map of San Bernardino to Claremont, 1915.
Source: *Auto Club Map 2.*

Figure 222: Map of Claremont to Los Angeles, 1915.
Source: *Auto Club Map 1.*

651. If C.K. hung onto the car for exactly ten miles, Figure 222 shows that he would have been past Pomona; this is just west of Spadra, which is shown as 29.3 miles from Los Angeles.

652. In 1919, the Henderson agent in Los Angeles was the Henderson Motorcycle Sales Co., located at 907 S. Main Street, Los Angeles. The officers were: Charles A. Hubbard, president; Tennant Lee, vice president; and Allen B. Monks, treasurer. Among these individuals, Tennant Lee was the representative of Henderson in California most visible to the public.

653. Hotel Clark, located at 426 S. Hill Street, was a fancy hotel in 1919 that was just a few blocks north of Henderson Motorcycle Sales Co. The Hotel Clark still stands, but has not operated as a hotel in many decades. Including the current owners, at least three entities have acquired and attempted to restore and restart the hotel—but none has been successful. The hotel is located in an area that is now less desirable than it was in 1919. Figure 223 is a 1917 display advertisement for the Hotel Clark.

654. "grip": A leather handbag that opens from the top.

655. Although C.K. wrote earlier in this chapter (see Note 630) that he had shipped a suitcase from Santa Fe, he apparently shipped *two* bags. Ordinarily, this would suggest that he travelled "light" from Santa Fe through the rest of New Mexico, Arizona, and southern California, but he also strapped on a couple of two-gallon water bags to cross the desert which, when full, would have added thirty-three pounds to the total weight of the bike.

Figure 223: Hotel Clark Advertisement, *ca.* 1917.
Source: *The Official Hotel Red Book and Directory,* 1917. Page 33.

CHAPTER XXI

LOS ANGELES TO SAN FRANCISCO

In full, the real name of Los Angeles is "La Puebla de Nuestra Señora la Reina de los Angeles"[656]—"The City of our Lady the Queen of the Angels." Founded by Spanish settlers about 1780, it is built upon the plains that roll from the foothills of the Sierra Madre down to the sea. It represents the very last word in the civilization of the Far West.

Los Angeles is a city of which to be proud. It is a hustling metropolis, but not too hustling. Its streets are wide and well-laid, its buildings clean, and its residences are just too wonderful for any words of mine. It is moreover the "movie centre" *par excellence*[657] of the world. "Duggie" and "Mary" and "Charlie"[658] are not merely familiar characters on the screen. They are your neighbours. You see them pass in the streets and go shopping with them in the stores, like ordinary human beings. Undoubtedly the development of Los Angeles in recent years is due largely to this industry. So also is the amazing beauty of its feminine population. Going deeper still, we find that the secret of its success lies in the wonderful climate. There is but one rainy season in Los Angeles during the year, and that is the month of December.

Strange to say, Los Angeles is not on the sea-coast. It is twelve miles to the nearest part of the beach.[659] This seemed rather extraordinary to me, particularly as San Francisco, with whom they are so eagerly competing, stands on one of the finest and largest harbours in the world. I remarked so to the *Times* reporter one day.[660] "But why," I asked," did they build Los Angeles so far from the sea?" "Oh well, you see," he replied in all seriousness, "they had a mighty good idea about things. They reckoned that by the time Los Angeles had really started growing she'd be right on top of the Pacific, so they gave her a chance and laid the place out twelve miles away." "Oh, was that it? I see," was my innocent retort.

Be that as it may, there is a network of beautiful, straight, concrete roads leading from the city down to the coast in all directions. Dozens of small residential towns are springing up amid this network of roads—towns that some day will be suburbs of

Los Angeles. At least that is the way to think of them. And the roads themselves? On Saturday afternoons and Sundays they are like great living arteries along which flows an endless stream of motor-cars. The Californians know how to enjoy themselves. There is not one fragment of the art of exterminating boredom that they have not studied. They frivol *en masse*,[661] and to do it they naturally choose the sea-beach as a habitat. Consequently the coast is strung with dozens of seaside resorts of every type and shade of description, and with only a mile or two between them.

A trip to one of these "Los Angeles Beaches"[662] is essential to the education of the true student of Southern Californian civilization. Never at any time have I seen public highways so completely covered with motorcars. The number seen approaches the incredible, in the eyes of the astonished European. Frequently there were two almost endless rows of cars with but a few feet between them, moving slowly along like a gigantic procession several miles in length. Occasionally there would be a hold-up, and the whole string of cars, one after the other, would pull up, each car close upon its forerunner. Without exception, all American cars are provided with buffers at front and rear so that the car does not suffer any damage when one touches another even with quite a severe impact. The obstruction is removed, and on the procession goes again. Perhaps some unfortunate is changing a wheel at the roadside. Then there is a big curve in the long, straight line where the more fortunate Fords and Maxwells and Buicks and Overlands, etc., etc., swerve round him. And thus we carry on until the coast is reached.

Naturally the first glimpse I had of the Pacific Ocean gave me feelings of unbounded joy. I even confess to having obeyed the childish instinct to pick up shells and seaweed on the beach. It was a sight to look upon until the majesty of the breakers and the infinite expanse of the deep blue ocean eclipsed one's sense of magnitude altogether and one became lost in a world of vision and fantasy.

I spent over a week in Los Angeles.[663] During that time I was almost overwhelmed with hospitality. The Californians I found easily the most hospitable people in America. At every hand I found people, whom I had neither seen nor heard of before, inviting me to dinner, and taking me rides in their cars. Further, I found I was friends with the police, and that without any difficulty either! In fact, the very air of California is charged with friendliness. Consequently, I was sorry when the day came when I should leave it behind.

Lizzie was finished. She had had a complete overhaul and several parts of the engine replaced. Numerous telegrams and letters had been flashed across the States to the works at Chicago. They were in vain. Although still under the makers' guarantee, they would accept no responsibility.[664] I paid the last bill that made Lizzie's repair account just exceed the amount I originally paid for her three months before and started out to complete the journey to San Francisco.[665] I cannot, however, omit to mention the extreme courtesy and hospitality with which I was met at the Henderson Agency itself. I could never at any time wish for better attention or hope to make better friends in foreign countries than I was fortunate enough to do in the "City of Angels." I left it with a pang of regret.

It was late in the evening when I started. I found to my annoyance that the lights were defective. The headlight was *hors de combat.* Only the "dimmer" remained to light me on my way. I had about sixty dollars in my pocket, though, so I was the perfection of happiness withal.

I am afraid those sixty dollars need some explanation. I arrived in Los Angeles a week before with about twenty. The Post Office, as ever, maintained an inexplicable silence. Having now quite reconciled myself to being mailless wherever I went, save for a letter or two forwarded through my friends in Cincinnati,[666] I decided to direct my energies to a profitable purpose while waiting for Lizzie's return from hospital.

I scanned the newspapers night and day.[667] Had I been a tram-driver or a page-boy I could have made a hit at once without any difficulty. There was also a big demand for boot-blacks,[668] but for anything that suited my tastes and inclinations there was nothing. My small stock of "greenbacks" (paper dollars) was slowly diminishing the while. Something had to be done.

So I started in on journalism. Strange to say, I made money at it. With the one exception of Kansas City, it is the only time I ever have. Americans seemed interested in the impressions of stray Englishmen through "God's own country." Better still, Californians seemed interested to learn what one stray Englishman in particular had to say about California on the one hand, and all the other States on the other![669]

I have the best of reasons for believing that they were perfectly satisfied with my report. So that is how, after paying for Lizzie's operation, I still had sixty odd dollars left to my credit.[670]

The broad, well-lighted city streets with their trolley-cars[671] soon were left behind, and we rode for miles along boulevards of wondrous surface through the residential quarters of Los Angeles. There were magnificent bungalows of countless variety, the homes of both poor and rich. Further on, we passed through Hollywood, the home of the homes of the "movie" people.[672] Occasionally would be seen a great block of buildings, unpretentious in architecture but palatial in extent. These were the "studios" where the films are made that instruct, amuse, and annoy the world's population.[673]

Finally, the last bungalow receded into the background and ahead was inky blackness,[674] a beautiful concrete highway, and the faint forms of mountain ranges. In the darkness, dispelled only within a radius of a few feet by the small pea-lamp that remained in service, everything looked mystic, shadowy, and strange. It seemed just the night, just the surroundings for adventure, the kind of environment that makes the vagrant life so much worth living.

The road ran parallel with the coastline, some ten or more miles away, but in between lay the Santa Monica Mountains, whose feet the highway skirted.[675] Sometimes the hill-sides were barren and rocky; other times they were clothed in gloomy cedar forests. I wondered what strange animals lurked in them and whether I should make the acquaintance of any mountain lions, bears, wolves, wild cats and other animals that still are plentiful in the mountain regions of California. Occasionally a car passed, the glare of its headlights transforming the sombre surroundings into a still stranger world of silver and gold. The road for a few moments changed to a path of glistening white leading to the unknown. And then, when the car dashed by, everything plunged instantaneously into a sea of blackness so intense that it could almost be felt.

I had intended to polish off a couple of hundred miles before morning. I love nothing better than a long night ride on a good road. But lack of illumination defied my intentions. After thirty miles I pulled in to the side of the road where a great beech tree overhung its branches, and laid down my ground-sheet upon the soft bed of dead leaves and nuts that lay beneath.

It was the softest mattress that I have ever lain upon in the open. In a few minutes I was fast asleep.

In the early hours of the morning I began to dream, I dreamt that some great animal was walking slowly around me as I lay. It snuffled about, grunting at intervals in a most dissatisfied manner. It is not a habit of mine to dream about anything. I remember reflecting subconsciously that I had ceased to dream of bears and such like when I reached the age of four. Why then should I dream about them now? Oh, hang the fellow! What is he making that confounded noise for?

A few minutes later I discovered that I was not dreaming at all. I was wide awake. Without moving anything but my eyes I peered into the darkness that still enshrouded everything. Sure enough I could make out a huge black mass somewhere near my feet, but could not discern its actual form. . . . Slowly, gently, I slipped my hand underneath my pillow. At last, I thought, I shall have a chance of shooting at something bigger than prairie-dogs! And then the thought struck me, how strange it was that in all these thousands of miles of travelling through plains and deserts and forests, my slumbers had never been interrupted by any nocturnal visitor—I had not even SEEN anything that could possibly annoy the most domesticated young person who loves his feather-bed.

The big black thing became more distinct as I looked. His head was down and he was engaged in wondering just exactly what my feet were and who put them there; whether they'd be nice to eat if vegetable, and if not, whether they were animal or mineral, and if so, why? I waited my time. He put his head closer to smell the offending object. With a sudden kick I landed out straight for his nose with my right foot. A yell rent the air and the big black thing leapt away squealing into the darkness. A 33 bullet followed him there just for luck.[676]

His squeaks gradually died down as he scampered helter-skelter down the road. It was only a poor harmless pig[677] looking for nuts—but he had no right to disturb my slumbers!

In the morning we continued towards the west. The end of the Santa Monica Range came in sight and soon the road descended in long winding "grades" towards the sea-coast. For the first time by daylight I saw California in its true colours. Here I should mention that the height of summer is not the best time to explore California. It is in the winter and the spring that the country is arrayed in its greatest glory. The lack of rain, even near the sea-coast, is so marked that by the time summer is reaching its zenith, there is not a green blade of grass to be seen. The face of the country, where it remains uncultivated and unirrigated, is an eternal brown. At first this brings a sense of disappointment to the traveller who has heard so much of California's meadows of wonderful green mingled with the hues of countless kinds of wild flowers. In summer-time there are none. But in spring-time, when the sun has not started to blaze and the rain has worked its miracles, the charm of the country must be beyond description.

At Ventura, a pretty town on the sea-coast,[678] Lizzie's speedometer ticked off the 4,500th mile.[679] There remained another 450 to be done,[680] and the journey would be at an end. I had little doubt now of getting there. The roads were so good that motor-cycling was child's play. Indeed it often became monotonous. At most times one could travel at almost any speed of which one's machine was capable, and still the straight, flat roads would be tiring to the point of boredom.

The towns and villages one passed, however, were full of charm. The most famous road through California, El Camino Real—which means "The Highway of the King"[681]—was one which I was following and had its origin in the old trail which the historic padres followed in the romantic days of the Spanish occupation two and three hundred years ago. This trail, blazed by the padres "by God's will for the reigning monarch of Spain," stretches for 900 miles from Mexico to Oregon,[682] and along it there still stand the old Mission Houses that are so prominent a feature of Californian history. There are nineteen of them, each "a day's journey apart," and each of an entirely distinct and characteristic type of architecture.

These Missions stand to-day, having with few exceptions been maintained intact in their original form, and they serve as beautiful testimonies to the genius of their builders. So admired is their style of architecture that they are religiously copied, more so now than ever before, in public buildings and sometimes private dwellings in all parts of the West. One even sees railway stations and tramway termini[683] modelled in the form of one of these ancient Franciscan Missions!

If I was charmed with Ventura, I was thrice charmed with Santa Barbara, another wonderful coast town of modern style built on an ancient site. The old Santa Barbara Mission[684] stands away up on the hill-sides of the Santa Ynez Range above the town and looks over the blue waters of the Pacific towards the craggy islands of Santa Cruz that lie beyond.[685] For sheer delight of climate, scenery, and surroundings I would forsake any home in any town in any country that I have yet seen to live in Santa Barbara, had I the wherewithal to do so.

Following the coast-line, and in many places separated from it only by a ridge of stones or a strip of vegetation, the road continues on its happy way for many miles.[686] On the left splash the deep blue waters of the Pacific. On the right rise steeply the Santa Ynez Mountains,[687] which like a link in a great chain form, with many others, more or less disjointed, the "coast range" that fringes the sea from Mexico to Oregon. Sometimes the road is bordered with Yucca palms, sometimes with pepper trees, and sometimes with eucalyptus.[688] One even sees, almost simultaneously, cactus plants and prickly pears growing amid the parched-up grass on the sun-swept side of some unfriendly hill!

At Caviota,[689] a few miles south of the famous "Point Conception,"[690] the road leaves the coast and swerves inland. Across the tip of the Santa Ynez Range it goes, swerving now to the left, then to the right, climbing, dipping, and swerving again for sixty or seventy miles until once more it catches a glimpse of the Pacific at El Pismo beach.[691]

Near here I left the beaten track and followed a narrow pathway that led around a hill-side to the cliffs.[692] Here I made my bed down once again in the long, dry grass that clothed the top. I could say with tolerable certainty that never before had a motor-cycle followed that path. It was soon no more than a little rut scarcely visible in the grassy slope. But I achieved my objective. With the murmur of the sea, as it dashed against the rocks a few hundred feet below, singing always in my ears, I passed one more night of exquisite repose and magic charm.

I awoke in the morning and sniffed the sea air. It was very attractive certainly, but was there not something the matter with it somehow? Or was it my imagination? I wriggled half out of bed and peered over the edge of the cliff. I stopped; I looked; I listened. Down there, on a little bed of white sand, lay a dead seal stretched out flat, as one would lay a tablecloth. He looked a dismal sight, poor fellow.

Ten miles more, inland again, and it was breakfast-time. We were at San Luis Obispo,[693] a fine little town at the foot of the Santa Margarita—one more link in the coast range.[694] San Luis Obispo took its name from an old Mission founded in 1772,[695] and once was the centre of wealth among the Spaniards of the country.[696]

Afterwards we cross the hills and continue northward. Always the Southern Pacific Railroad is on our right, sometimes just a few feet from the highway.[697] The concrete has stopped and at intervals we have our old friend, the natural gravel. The laying of concrete is being proceeded with at many places, a hundred yards or so at a time, and detours running parallel at the side connect us up with the road ahead. Many little seedling towns are passed—all of them well planned and well advertised—and at last we come to Paso Robles (Pass of the Oaks), a larger town which derives its name from a great natural oak park. I should mention that oak trees are abundant in California and they grow often to a very great size.

We are now in the Salinas Valley, in proportion like a long, narrow groove 100 miles long cut in the face of the country. Through it runs the Salinas River, winding and bending with great sweeps through its sandy bed. At midsummer it is dried up completely,[698] and, from the long wooden bridges that cross and re-cross it, looks like a sandy sea-beach, with fences across from one bank to the other to stop the cattle straying!

Along this valley blows a constant cool wind from the sea in the north.[699] All day long it blows, week in, week out. The further north one proceeds the stronger it becomes, until it approaches almost a gale that whistles down the narrow channel like a cold blast, even in the broiling heat of the cloudless sun. Where, here and there, were to be seen bunches of poplar trees and eucalyptus, they were invariably leaning distinctly to the south, their gaunt trunks permanently moulded by the inexorable wind.[700] On the smaller trees, the sycamores and the cedars, there was often not a branch nor a leaf to be seen on the northern side of the trunk, the foliage almost touching the ground on the southern side. Those hundred miles were the coldest I had known in the whole journey, and always I found the head wind so strong that the power of the machine seemed half absorbed in merely combating it.

San Miguel, San Ardo, King City, Soledad, Gonzales, and finally, at five in the afternoon, Salinas was reached at the end of the valley. San Francisco was now but little more than 100 miles beyond. To-morrow would be the last day. The end was in sight.

But what of Lizzie? Alas, she was in a sorry condition. Gradually since we left Los Angeles two days before she had fallen off in power. The old rattles and noises had recurred with astonishing alacrity. I had had many stops for minor adjustments and examinations, and even feared another breakdown before the skyscrapers of Frisco loomed in sight. The reader may be in as good a position as I to judge of the merits of American compared with English motor-cycles, but he will admit that seldom could occur a worse combination of bad luck and pig-headed pertinacity than is witnessed in the wanderings of Lizzie and me through the United States of America.

At Salinas I ate and drank right heartily, and drowned my sorrows in wistful contemplation of the blue eyes of the gentle damsel who served apple pie across the counter of the "quick-meal" luncheon bar.[701]

"Lizzie, would you like to sleep by the sea to-night for the last time? Think we can get there, old girl? It's twenty miles there and twenty back, y'know![702]—Righto, c'mon!" and she burst once again into an animated confusion of noise and life.

Monterey is on the coast. It stands surrounded by hills on a magnificent bay which, with its yachts, motor-launches, and fishing-boats, is one of the most famous beauty-spots of the Californian coast. Monterey was once an important centre of history in the early days of Spanish and Mexican sovereignty. Later, it enjoyed the distinction of being the first spot in California where the American flag was hoisted.[703] Now it is little more than a seaside resort, but as famous in California as is Naples in Italy.

A splendid highway leads from Salinas and cuts through beautiful hills clothed in cedar and oak. The journey was worth doing, if only to breathe the sea air again and sleep to its murmur.

It was rather a pathetic affair—that last night out. I hated to leave Lizzie propped up on her stand on the low cliffs while I made a comfortable bed in the sand on the beach. The tide was out, but I was determined to get as near to the sea as possible. I chose a spot where, nestled in a sandy cove in the rocks, I could see the breakers just a score of yards from my feet.

I awoke in the early morning to find the sea barely a foot from my feet. The tide rose higher than I had expected, but I had time to enjoy a few delightful minutes of lying half awake in bed before I finally proved discretion to be better than damp bedclothes and dragged my belongings to a less obtrusive spot.

Thus dawned another day, the day that was to see the end. I had ample time and lingered on the way, now administering friendly attention to Lizzie, now stopping for a light refreshment or to take a leisurely photograph. It was all too glorious—that last day.

But poor old Lizzie again showed signs of exhaustion. I nursed her tenderly and rode as slowly as I felt inclined throughout the day.

Monterey was left behind after breakfast. Then Salinas was reached once more, and now we were again on the road to Frisco.

Over the mountains to the east once again, down the San Juan Grade,[704] that wound and screwed itself round the rocky slopes, and we got to San Juan, where the tall eucalyptus and waving pepper trees gave an air of majesty to the fine old Mexican town it proved to be.

Then we turn to the north once more and enter another valley, the valley of Santa Clara. The towns become larger and more frequent, the country more developed. Orchards and fruit-groves are frequently seen. At the road-sides, built up on trestles, are great water-tanks that are used for irrigation. I notice that here and there, where the pipes that lead to them have leaked a little, the dark brown soil below has burst into great masses of fresh green grass, while all around is parched and lifeless.

At San José we find a great fruit-growing centre, and at the same time a beautiful city of many thousand inhabitants. Its streets are lined with palms and its suburbs extend into the orange groves that abound on every hand.

Simultaneously one cylinder starts to misfire, and then another. Soon they are all missing. At intervals they would all chip in for a second or two, and as suddenly chip out again. I smelt magneto trouble.

I also smelt prunes, millions of them. O Californian Prune, how often have I eaten of thy tasty endocarp in far-off England! And here thou art in myriads about me![705]

I stopped a dozen times, changed plugs, examined leads, and tinkered with the magneto. Evidently there was something the matter inside the magneto. I would trust to luck to get to 'Frisco—only forty miles more.

And thus we continued, sometimes dawdling along at fifteen and then suddenly bursting into full power and shooting along at forty for a minute or two, as Lizzie's peculiar whim would have it. It was annoying, tiring, disheartening, but I felt I should get there. I had long since planned a trip to the Yosemite National Park, returning thence to the north across the border and eastward through Canada back to New York. That little project would certainly never come off. I had had enough already. I made one great big oath to sell Lizzie's carcase[706] for what it would bring in San Francisco. Poor old Lizzie! I pitied her in a way. She must have been born with a curse on her head. But she would have to go, if only for 100 dollars. Already I began wondering who would get her after we had parted.

After ten miles appeared the southern tip of the great harbour that stretches inland to north and south from San Francisco. This bay is fifty miles long and ten miles wide[707] and forms one of the grandest harbours in the world. All the navies of all the nations of the earth could be comfortably tucked away in a corner of it. The road follows within a few miles of the western shore of this inland sea, and at every few miles are small, fast-growing cities comparable with nothing but their prototypes that cluster around

Los Angeles. For here we are absolutely in the centre of the wine-making district.[708] Sixty years ago cuttings and rooted vines of every variety found in Europe were brought to California and planted,[709] mostly around this great bay of San Francisco, where the frequent sea-fogs contribute so much to the maintenance of perfect conditions for the growing of vines. They flourished, and now we have Médocs and Sauternes and Moselles and countless others from California, as well as from France.

For miles and miles we see nothing but vineyards and fruit-groves. There is no fence, no ditch, no railing. The orange trees and plum trees fringe the very road. It is not possible to say where one estate ends and another begins. The owners probably know.

The towns are now so thick that with them also it is difficult to say where one ends and another begins. Only another fifteen miles! Poor old Lizzie, she may peg out altogether.

But no. She keeps at it. Sometimes she ceases firing altogether, but only for a moment. On she goes again, now on one, now on four cylinders. Hey ho! We shall get there all right.

'Buses and cars in hundreds pass in both directions. We shall soon be in 'Frisco now.

Tram-lines appear and then trams. Trolley-cars, they call them in America. 'Frisco at last!

I dodge in and out of the traffic as best I may. It is very thick indeed, and in very much of a hurry. I sail down Market Street, the "Strand"[710] of San Francisco. What matter if Lizzie clatters and rattles and stops and shoots on again? She has brought me here. And as I say so, the little indicator on the speedometer moves to 4,950.[711] Just 50 miles short of 5,000 from New York! Gee! it seems like an extract from another life, that departure from far-off New York. And how long? Three months? It feels like twelve at the least!

I found the post office and sang out for mail.[712] Sure enough there was some— forwarded from Cincinnati. I learnt for the first time that the detailed "Schedules" that I had dispatched three months ago at New York had not yet reached England.[713] Hence the reason for the seeming unkindliness of the Post Office en route. But where were they? I was not to know until a week after my return to England, when they arrived suddenly, without any warning, and simultaneously, to all my friends and relatives there.[714] They had been all round British East Africa; Heaven and the New York postal authorities alone know why! I had not counted on such waywardness on their part when in my innocence of American ways I had dropped them in the post-box at New York.

Thus ends my tale of woe. It is a strange thing, but nevertheless true, that now I have done with it and written about it and done with writing about it, I still think what a glorious trip it was and what a perfect ass I was to do it, and what a still greater ass I was to say anything about it!

CHAPTER 21 NOTES

656. El Pueblo de Nuestra Señora la Reina de los Ángeles (The Town of Our Lady the Queen of the Angels) was the Spanish civilian pueblo founded in 1781. By the 20th century, it became the American metropolis of Los Angeles.

657. "*par excellence*": A French term with the literal meaning "by excellence," but used to describe something that was better or more than all others.

658. C.K. is referring to the United Artists: Mary Pickford (film actress known in the early days of her career as "America's Sweetheart"), Charlie Chaplin (renowned comedian and film director who portrayed the character "the Tramp" in numerous films), and Douglas Fairbanks (swashbuckling film actor) who, on February 5, 1919, formed United Artists along with D.W. Griffiths. The intent of the enterprise was to protect independence for the film artists, create their own distributorships, and give them complete artistic control over their films and the profits they generated.

659. Although C.K. said it was twelve miles from Los Angeles to the nearest beach, it was actually a bit more than that. Figure 224 (next page) is an excerpt from a 1915 map produced by the Automobile Club of Southern California. Venice Beach, then known as "Playland of the Pacific," was reported as being fourteen miles from downtown, while Santa Monica and Playa Del Ray were sixteen miles, and Long Beach was twenty-one miles away.

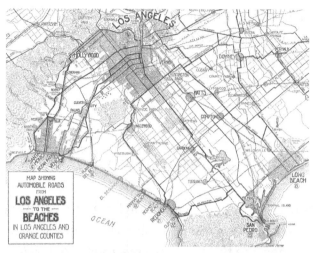

Figure 224: Map Showing Automobile Roads from Los Angeles to the Beaches, 1915.
Source: Automobile Club of Southern California.

660. Figure 225 is an article that appeared in the *Los Angeles Sunday Times* on August 10, 1919, the third day of C.K.'s presence in Los Angeles. The article makes it clear that he had already abandoned the idea of riding his motorcycle back East. It also describes patent-related business he planned to conduct on the east coast before heading back to England.

CROSS COUNTRY ON MOTORBIKE.

Royal Air Force Captain is Here for Stay.

———◆———

Will Proceed Up Coast, then Back to East.

———◆———

Thinks California Roads are Magnificent.

After serving for four years in the Royal Air Force, Capt. C.K. Shepherd of Birmingham, Eng., is in Los Angeles on a motorcycle tour through America. Capt. Shepherd, who is a member of the firm X-L-All, Ltd., motor manufacturers, is devoting his energy to the discussion of eastern roads. He says that east of the California State line good roads are of such rarity that they have special paths built for the use of cows. These, he said, refused to travel on the regular highways.

"After leaving Barstow," he said last night, "it was just like getting into paradise. When I came down the long pass and saw stretched before me the miles and miles of good roads, I felt that my journey had not been in vain."

Capt. Shepherd says he is "somewhat of a pen-pusher" himself, and intends to write a book upon his return about his trip. He has written "Through England by Motorbike" and will supplement it with his experiences in America.

He was loud in his condemnation of the eastern roads and equally loud in his praise of those of California. He says that in England everyone has a motorcycle. All the men of means, he says, have at least three—light, medium and heavy. He says that the good roads of that country are responsible for their popularity.

He expects to stay at the Clark for a few days, when he will leave for the north. Then he will return to the East by rail to conclude negotiations for several patents to be manufactured by his company.

Figure 225: "Cross Country on Motorbike" Article.
Source: *Los Angeles Sunday Times*, Part VI, Page 4, August 10, 1919.

661. *"en masse"*: French term for "all together."

662. In 1919, both Venice Beach and Long Beach had popular amusement parks built on piers into the Pacific Ocean. Venice Beach amusement park billed itself as the "Coney Island of the West." Figures 226 and 227 show the throngs of beach-goers and amusement-seekers at Long Beach and Venice Beach in 1920. By coincidence, C.K. arrived in Los Angeles the same week as the US Navy: It was Fleet Week! A large naval contingent was moored off Long Beach, adding even more traffic to the roads to Long Beach. Since C.K. does not mention seeing the US Navy at the beach, he probably took in the beach scene at the closer Venice Beach.

Figure 226: Long Beach and "The Pike" Amusement Park, *ca.* 1920.
Source: Los Angeles Public Library.

Figure 227: Venice Beach with Abbot Kinney's Amusement Park in the Distance, *ca.* 1920.
Source: Los Angeles Public Library.

663. The length of C.K.'s stay was likely driven by the time it took to repair his motorcycle.

664. As illustrated in Chapter 7, Note 196, Figure 59, the 1919 Henderson came with a 90-day guarantee.

665. C.K. spent about $480 on the motorcycle in New York, so his characterization of his final expense meant that he could have expended $900 in total on the motorcycle and its maintenance during the trip—an inflation-adjusted amount of almost $13,000 today.

666. It seems clear here that, before leaving England, C.K. had given his family and friends Steve's mailing address in Cincinnati. Steve would then forward any mail received to addresses or post offices that C.K. gave him for such purposes.

667. The 166 "Men Wanted" classified advertisements in the *Los Angeles Times*, August 7, 1919 seemed mostly to be for positions that were permanent and therefore longer term than C.K. was seeking. For example, it seems like C.K. was imminently qualified to fill this advertised post: "WANTED–TOOL ROOM MAN WHO HAS HAD actual experience on knowledge in selecting tools for workmen in machine shop, and also capable of acting as time-keeper. Do not apply unless fully qualified to fill position. AMERICAN ENGINE & AIRPLANE CO., 2869 W. Pico."

668. "boot-black": A British term for someone who shines shoes for money. Although C.K. stated there was a big demand for such work, the "Men Wanted" classifieds in the *Los Angeles Times*, August 7, 1919 contained only one advertisement for a "shoe shine," a job in Long Beach to work on commission. It seems possible that C.K. used "boot-black" only as an example of a low-paying job, of which there were countless such positions advertised.

669. Although C.K. says he wrote several popular articles—providing his views as an Englishman on the roads in California and elsewhere—and published them while he was in Los Angeles, no such articles have been located.

670. If C.K. arrived at Los Angeles with twenty dollars and left Los Angeles with sixty dollars after paying for his motorcycle to be overhauled yet again in addition to hotel, dining, and other expenses over a week, it seems like he would

have needed to be paid up to one hundred dollars for his articles. However, this amount would call for a great deal of writing, or an extraordinarily higher rate of pay than the "dime a line" he had received for the same work in Kansas City. If C.K. was also paid a "dime a line" in Los Angeles and he netted one hundred dollars for his work, it suggests that there are as many as a thousand lines of his thoughts published in Los Angeles in the first two weeks of August 1919.

671. Although the photograph in Figure 228 was not taken at night, it illustrates the traffic conditions of 7th Street and Broadway in Los Angeles. C.K. was likely pleased to no longer need to negotiate these kinds of circumstances.

Figure 228: View of the Intersection of 7th Street and Broadway in Downtown Los Angeles. **Source:** Los Angeles Public Library.

672. The *Blue Book* Route 391 from Los Angeles toward San Francisco tracked along Sunset Blvd., west on Hollywood Blvd. and then north on Cahuenga Blvd.— directly through Hollywood. Although the residences of major motion picture actors changed over time, many did reside in the area. In a long multi-page article by an unnamed author in *The Literary Digest* (Vol. LV, No. 19, November 10, 1917), the lives and times of the film stars were commented upon including noting— on Page 86—that "Mary Pickford occupies the beautiful Bogardus home at the corner of Sunset and Western, which she has leased during her stay in California. The house is surrounded by fine gardens and the driveway is lined with palms

and orange-trees." Figure 229 is an excerpt from a special tour map from the Automobile Club of Southern California titled "Automobile Road Map from Los Angeles to Topanga Cañon & Return." The depicted routing north and west of downtown Los Angeles is consistent with the *Blue Book* route. Mary Pickford's "Bogardus home" in 1917 would have been a couple blocks south of Hollywood Blvd., due south of the road coming out of Griffith Park between Vermont Ave. and Cahuenga Blvd.

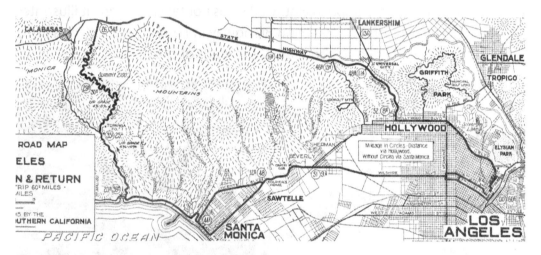

Figure 229: Automobile Road Map from Los Angeles to Topanga Cañon & Return, *ca.* 1915. **Source:** Automobile Club of Southern California.

673. Many of the motion picture studios were on or near Sunset Blvd., a main thoroughfare parallel to Hollywood Blvd. that was one quarter of a mile south. But Universal Film Manufacturing Company (now Universal Studios) created Universal City, which is located about four miles north on Cahuenga Blvd., as shown in Figure 229 cited in Note 672.

674. C.K. had probably reached Calabasas, shown at left in the upper left corner of Figure 229 cited in Note 672. A small community noted on in the *Blue Book* Route 391, Calabasas was located 27.8 miles from Los Angeles and yet was still twenty-six miles before reaching Camarillo.

675. C.K.'s estimate that the road paralleled the coastline about ten miles away was accurate. The Santa Monica Mountains extend about forty miles to the west from the Hollywood Hills in Los Angeles to Point Mugu in Ventura County.

676. C.K. reports that he fired his gun using a .33 caliber bullet at the wild pig. Because this is an odd size, however, it is more likely he fired a .38 caliber bullet from his Smith & Wesson revolver. The book's typesetter probably did not notice that the second "3" in the manuscript was an "8."

677. In 1919, wild pigs in California were descendant from domestic swine first troduced by European settlers in the 1700s. Large colonies of such animals lived on Santa Cruz—the largest of what are now called the Channel Islands, about thirty-five miles offshore of Ventura—and were often hunted in organized outings. Around 1920, some European wild boars (*Sus scrofa*) were released in the Monterey area. Most of the wild boar in California today are descendants of the interbreeding of these populations. They are considered an invasive species and continue to be hunted year round.

678. Ventura was first named San Buenaventura and also became known as the Poinsettia City by the Sea due to its preeminence in this sector of the flower industry. Figure 230 is a photo of Main Street approaching Chestnut Street in Ventura, facing west as C.K. would have been riding—paralleling the Pacific Ocean about 2,000 feet to the left—with Mercer's Garage on the left and, diagonally across the intersection on the right, the Hotel De Leon.

Figure 230: Main and Chestnut Streets, Ventura, California, *ca.* 1919.
Source: Courtesy of the Museum of Ventura County.

679. C.K.'s reported odometer reading of 4,500 miles at Ventura is reasonable. The *Blue Book* Route 391 reflects that it was 68.7 miles from Los Angeles to Ventura. He earlier wrote that he arrived in Los Angeles with 4,422 on the odometer, so it is credible that 4,500 could have been on the odometer in Ventura being that it reflects only 9.3 more miles than the published distance over the road from Los Angeles to Ventura.

680. C.K.'s estimate that it was 450 miles from Ventura to San Francisco is generally accurate, since the routes in the *Blue Book* total 487 miles. However, that number does not include the side trip to Monterey C.K. references. As discussed later, there is evidence that C.K. did not actually make the side trip to Monterey.

681. "El Camino Real" translates to "The Royal Road," but it was also known as The King's Highway. It is the 600-mile trail connecting the twenty-one Spanish missions in California: from the Mission San Diego de Alcalá (San Diego) to the Mission San Francisco Solano (in Sonoma).

682. Although San Diego is perhaps close enough to Mexico to be say that El Camino Real starts in Mexico, Sonoma is 300 miles of road south of Oregon, making the total length of El Camino Real about 600 miles, not 900. C.K.'s source that it was 900 miles long and ran all the way to Oregon it not known, but author David Andrew Hufford confirms the essence of C.K.'s characterization of in his 1901 book, *El Camino Real: The Original Highway Connecting the Twenty-One Missions from South to North*, including:

> "I was described as a road connecting five presidios, three pueblos, and twenty-one missions "extending in an irregular line from San Diego county on the south to Sonoma county on the north, at intervals of a day's ride on horseback was located their beautiful missions, each in the midst of a small community of peaceful, indolent, happy people, affords a marked contrast to anything familiar to average American eyes."

683. C.K. was describing what is known as the Mission Revival style of architecture, born in the 1890s in California and adopted by the Santa Fe and Southern Pacific Railways as the style for many of their buildings.

684. Figure 231 is a photo of the Mission Santa Barbara, which was dedicated December 4, 1786.

Figure 231: Mission Santa Barbara, *ca.* 1901.
Source: *El Camino Real,* 1901.

685. The ocean is about 2.5 miles southeast of Mission Santa Barbara at its closest point. The island of Santa Cruz is about thirty miles south of Mission Santa Barbara.

686. Figure 232 (next page) is a photo of Lizzie (also displayed on the cover of this book) taken by C.K. by the side of the road along the California coast, probably just north of Ventura on what is now Emma Wood State Beach, Faria Beach, or Mussel Shoals. In addition to the road behind the motorcycle at right, there is also a fence separating the road from at least one set of railroad tracks.

Figure 232: Lizzie at the Beach in California, *ca.* 1919.
Source: C.K.'s personal slide collection.

687. The Santa Ynez Mountains are principally in Santa Barbara County, with an eastward extension into Ventura County.

688. "Yucca Palm" is usually another name for the Joshua Tree (*Yucca brevifolia*), the same type of plant included in the book in Chapter 19 with the sign for the Hotel Georgia affixed to it. The California pepper tree (*Schinus molle*) is a shade tree that grows bright pink berries. Eucalyptus trees were introduced to California by Australians in the 1850s in the hope they could quickly produce wood for railroad ties, but it was not found suitable. One of the tallest species (*Eucalyptus globulus*), also known as Tasmanian blue gum, has proven valuable in California for use as windbreaks near highways and farms, as well as a shade tree in cities and gardens.

689. The actual name is Gaviota (beginning with a "G"). It is the Spanish word for "seagull" and is the name given to a nearby mountain peak. Figure 233 is a postcard of a general store and gas station at Gaviota in about 1915. C.K. almost certainly stopped here for fuel because he was soon to be heading into the hills for the night. This store and gas station remained in operation until 1970 when it was demolished to make way for a development that was never completed.

Figure 233: Postcard of Newland's General Merchandise, Gaviota, *ca.* 1915.

690. It is unclear what C.K. meant by referring to Point Conception as "famous," but it is a landmark about thirteen miles further up the coast from where he went inland up Gaviota Pass. Point Conception is the point where the Santa Barbara Channel meets the Pacific Ocean, making a natural division between Southern and Central California. The landmark was first named Cabo de Galera in 1542 by the Spanish explorer Juan Rodriguez Cabrillo. However, in 1602, Sebastian Vizcaíno sailed past and named it Punta de la Limpia Concepción ("Point of the Immaculate Conception") and that became the name that stuck.

691. C.K.'s estimate that he saw El Pismo Beach sixty or seventy miles past Gaviota is very close. The *Blue Book* Route 392 reflects that it was 74.8 miles from Gaviota Station to Pismo Beach. C.K. would have driven through Santa Maria, Nipomo, and Arroyo Grande, and probably would have seen Pismo Beach on the left in the vicinity of Arroyo Grande. Also, the town of Pismo was originally named *El* Pismo. It was based upon the name the native Chumash people had long called the area by their word for tar, *pismu*. It is identified as El Pismo Beach the 1915 map from the Automobile Club of Southern California (see Figure 234, next page).

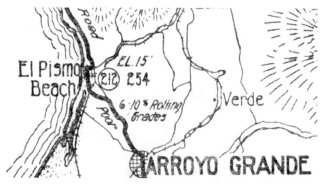

Figure 234: Excerpt from "Los Angeles to San Francisco via Coast Route, Part 3," 1915. **Source:** Automobile Club of Southern California.

692. It is not easy to determine where C.K. slept that night, other than to observe that he said it was ten miles further to San Louis Obispo. Based upon his description of how he got there, it is possible that he camped in the hills above what is now Sunset Palisades.

693. It seems most likely that C.K. had breakfast at the Liberty Cafe in San Luis Obispo. This was the sole dining establishment that advertised in the only newspaper in San Luis Obispo at the time. The Liberty Cafe was located in the middle of town, at 897 Monterey Street—a main street that C.K. would have used on his way through San Luis Obispo. Figure 235 is the advertisement for the Liberty Cafe that was in the newspaper the day after C.K. came through town.

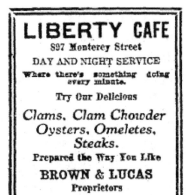

Figure 235: Liberty Cafe Advertisement.
Source: *San Luis Obispo Daily Telegram*, August 14, 1919. Page 7.

694. C.K. may have misread his map or his map had a printing error. The Santa Margarita mountains are much further south, in San Diego County. However, C.K. would pass through the town of Santa Margarita after leaving San Luis Obispo and getting through the Santa Lucia Mountain Range.

695. Figure 236 is a photo of the Mission San Luis Obispo de Tolosa as it appeared in 1901. It was dedicated on September 1, 1772. The mission fell into ruins in the mid-1800s, but began decades of improvement and restoration efforts with the Mission's centennial in 1872.

Figure 236: San Luis Obispo de Tolosa, *ca.* 1901.
Source: *El Camino Real,* 1901.

696. It is not known where C.K. received the information that the San Luis Obispo de Tolosa Mission (or San Luis Obispo itself) was the center of wealth for local Spaniards.

697. C.K. was correct in saying this was the Southern Pacific railroad. But he would have been experienced enough by then to know it was common practice for wagon trails and auto roads to be established next to railroad tracks throughout the west. Thus, in order for him to remark about this, these tracks must have seemed more present, closer, and/or for longer stretches than he had previously seen. The road from San Luis Obispo closely followed the tracks northeast through the canyon in the Santa Lucia Mountain Range, but the proximity continued after

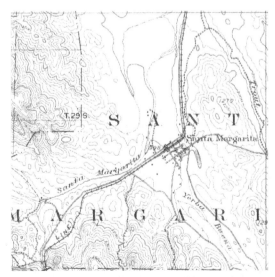

Figure 237: Topographical Map of Santa Margarita, California.
Source: *USGS: California San Louis Obispo Quadrangle,* 15 Minute Series, 1916.

clearing the mountains and coming into Santa Margarita and beyond. Figure 237 is an excerpt from a 1916 edition of the USGS topographical map, including the area of Santa Margarita that shows the road and tracks running parallel coming all the way through town.

698. Figure 238 is a photograph taken by C.K. of the dried riverbed of the Salinas River.

Figure 238: Dried Salinas River, *ca*. August 1919.
Source: C.K.'s personal slide collection.

699. The "sea in the north" refers to the San Francisco Bay.

700. Figure 239 is a photograph taken by C.K. of a wind-bent tree in California.

701. A directory for Salinas in 1919 has not been located. The *Salinas, Monterey and Pacific Grove Directory* (1926) includes listings for nineteen restaurants in Salinas—some as part of a hotel—others on their own. Thus, it is virtually impossible to determine where C.K. ate breakfast that morning.

Figure 239: Wind-Bent Tree in California, *ca.* August 1919.
Source: C.K.'s personal slide collection.

702. Although the weight of evidence indicates that C.K. did not take a side trip to Monterey, his characterization that it was twenty miles from Salinas to Monterey is accurate. The *Blue Book* Route 48 reflects that it was 19.2 miles from Salinas to Monterey, and 2.5 miles further to Pacific Grove. Figure 240 (next page) is a 1915 tour map of the area. Figure 241 (next page) is a map of the Pacific southwest that C.K. drew several years after his journey for apparent use in public presentations. The map depicts a bold dashed line showing "route taken"; it is conspicuous that it does not reflect the excursion to Monterey, although it does show the excursions to the Royal Gorge and Grand Canyon. Between this map and mileage discrepancies that cannot be reconciled, the weight of evidence is that C.K. did not spend his last night in the hills above Monterey. It seems more likely he spent the last night in one of the numerous hotels in Salinas.

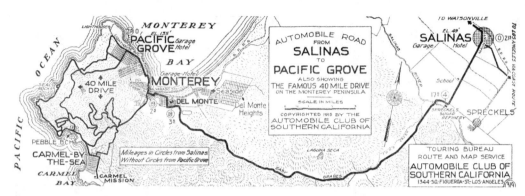

Figure 240: "Automobile Road from Salinas to Pacific Grove," *ca.* 1915.
Source: Automobile Club of Southern California.

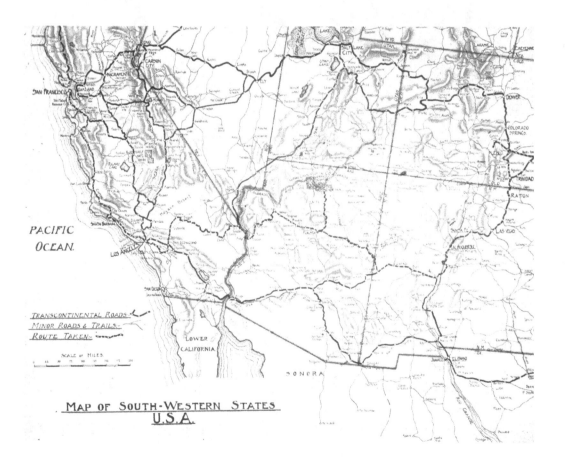

Figure 241: C.K. Drawing of Map of South-Western States with Route Taken, *ca.* 1930.
Source: C.K.'s personal slide collection.

703. The American flag was first raised in California on July 7, 1846 in Monterey. Commodore John D. Sloat, commanding the U.S. Navy's Pacific Squadron, landed 225 sailors and marines on the beach and, within minutes, the American flag was hoisted. Commodore Sloat then read his proclamation of the annexation of "Alta California" to the US.

704. The San Juan Grade Road remains a popular road for motorcycle riders.

705. Besides being the first capitol of California, San Jose was a major agricultural community, producing a significant amount of fruits and vegetables, such as prunes, grapes, and apricots. The orchards in the Santa Clara Valley reportedly were so fragrant with the smell of ripening fruit that it was sometimes called the Valley of Heart's Delight.

706. "carcase": the British spelling for carcass.

707. C.K.'s dimensions for San Francisco Bay (fifty by ten miles) are pretty close. The maximum dimensions currently used are sixty by twelve miles.

708. Grapes were one of the major crops in the area, but the advent of Prohibition changed the economy such that more fruits and vegetables were soon being grown. The first broccoli grown in the US was planted in the area in 1922.

709. Although wine was made in the US for hundreds of years using the native muscadine grape, it is almost correct to say that it was not until the middle of the 19th century when *Vitis vinifera* grapes from Europe finally found a good living space in northern California. Earlier attempts to grow them failed due to black rot and phylloxera. Besides muscadine, most wine in the United States was made with Concord or Niagara or hybrids such as Catawba and Marechal Foch. In 1629, Spanish missionaries discovered that *Vitis vinifera* would grow in New Mexico. But these grapes did not make it to California until 1769, when they were planted at the vineyards at the new Mission San Diego. In 1823, Father José Altimira established the northern-most mission, Mission San Francisco Solano, in Sonoma and planted the grapes there. That was the beginning of the wine industry in northern California, slightly less than one hundred years before C.K. rolled through town.

710. C.K. is referring to "The Strand," a major thoroughfare in Westminster, Central London. It spans just over ¾ mile from Trafalgar Square eastwards to Temple Bar, where the road becomes Fleet Street.

711. The inference is that the odometer read 4,950 when C.K. reached San Francisco and stopped riding. This is consistent with his statement that the odometer read 4,500 in Ventura and that he had another 450 miles to go. However, the *Blue Book* reflects it is 487 miles from Ventura to San Francisco, even without including the reported trip to Monterey. If C.K. was at 4,500 in Ventura and did not go to Monterey, he still would have arrived in San Francisco with 4,988 miles on the odometer. In an attempt to resolve this, we could consider that the 4,500 reading "in Ventura" was actually nearly forty miles past Ventura. Thus, if he started with a reading of 4,422 miles in Los Angeles, it was 555.6 miles of road from Los Angeles to San Francisco (without Monterey), meaning that his odometer would read 4,977.6 in San Francisco. Unless there was some way for C.K. to reduce the distance from Los Angeles to San Francisco by 5%, the only practical explanation seems to be that the 4,422 reading in Los Angeles is *also* unreliable. The previous reported odometer was back in Kansas City (1,919). After Kansas City, there were 2,945 miles of published road distance to San Francisco (without Monterey), which would have him arriving in San Francisco with 4,864 on the odometer. It is reasonable to believe C.K. drove eighty-four additional miles between Kansas City and San Francisco than were on the published routes. Alternatively, if the odometer actually read over 5,000 miles in San Francisco, it seems certain C.K. would have proudly reported that fact.

712. The U.S. Post Office and Court Building, 7th and Mission Street, San Francisco, was completed in 1901. Figure 242 shows the route C.K. would have used, driving up Market Street to the post office (larger dark rectangle). The location of the Clift Hotel has been added to this image (small dark rectangle at upper center) and is about six blocks north of the post office, two blocks west of Union Square.

713. This again implies that C.K. received mail from England that had been sent to Cincinnati and then forwarded to San Francisco. The context of the word "schedules" as C.K. used it is not clear, but he seems to be saying that he had been periodically mailing his itinerary and updates back to family and friends in England; however, they apparently had not received any of his communications.

714. This makes clear that he had sent these "schedules" to numerous people—namely, family and friends. None of these correspondences survive in C.K.'s archives kept by his son, but he would almost certainly have sent them to his brother George and sister Maud, whose records have been lost to time.

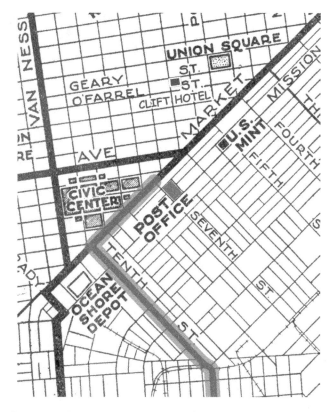

Figure 242: Principle Automobile Routes in and out of San Francisco, 1915 (annotated 2019). **Source:** Automobile Club of Southern California.

EPILOGUE

SCENE I

SCENE.—*Outside the Post Office,*[715] *San Francisco, Cal.*
TIME.—*August, 1919.*[716]

CHARACTERS

LIZZIE.

MYSELF.

AN ARMENIAN.

CROWD OF LOUNGERS, SMALL BOYS, AND WOMEN OF VARIOUS NATIONALITIES.

(SELF *emerges from portals of Post Office. Chorus of voices from crowd.*)

"'Ere 'e is; look at his face; look at his chest. You're one globe-trotter, I'll reckon. How long did it take? How much has it cost? What did you do it for? How'd you like San Francisco?" etc., etc., etc.

MYSELF (*dangerously ruffled at not having received a cheque*). "Well, and what are you all gaping at, like a lot of half-witted school-kids? Never seen a motor-cycle before? Here, you (*to* ARMENIAN), where's the Clift Hotel?"[717]

ARMENIAN. "Do you vont to zell zis machine?"

MYSELF (*successfully concealing rapture at the suggestion*). "Sell her, after she's brought me all the way from New York? SELL HER? Why, I'd sooner sell my mother-in-law."[718]

ARMENIAN. "I vill gif you 'undred dollar right 'ere."

MYSELF. "Hundred dollars be damned, and you with 'em! Where's the Clift?"

CHORUS OF VOICES. "Up the hill here and second on the right. Von 'undred dollar. Follow the trams. Give us yer waterbag, boss. Look at his boots. There's a cop on the corner. Von 'undred ten dollar, right now. Look at 'is 'air," etc., etc.

(*Exit slowly in procession,* SELF *leading; Alarums and Excursions.*[719])

393

SCENE II

SCENE.—*My room at the Clift Hotel.*
Half an hour has elapsed.

(SELF *discovered, washing, face. There is a knock at the door.*)

SELF. "Come in."

(*Enter* ARMENIAN.)

ARMENIAN. "Ah, 'ere you vos. Ze manager tolt me your room. I come right up."

SELF. "Apparently."

ARMENIAN. "I vont to buy your motorsickle; vot you vont for 'im?"

SELF. "Speak respectfully, please. I want 500 dollars for HER."

ARMENIAN (*throwing up his hands in horror*). "Ah, zat vos too much, my frent! Dot vos more zan you give for 'im—for 'ER."

SELF. "And how the devil do you know what I gave for her?"

ARMENIAN. "I haf made enquiries, jhust. I af bin to ze aghency 'ere. Zey say it vos 480 dollars."[720]

SELF. "Well, any fool knows a machine improves with running (*the blush is unnoticed beneath my Indian complexion*); and what's more, if a machine can stick it all the way across THE UNITED STATES OF AMERICA it must be a dem good one. I should have asked 600, but I like your face (*cold shivers down spine*), so I only want 500."

ARMENIAN. "Ah, zat vos far too much. I vill gif you von 'undred fifteen—no more."

SELF. "Nothin' doin', bo. Five hundred. Here's my card; you can call round any time between now and to-morrow midday with the money. If you can't do it by then, you can drop in and see me at Salt Lake City after next Wednesday, or Chicago after next Saturday.[721] Cheerio; close the door as you go out."

ARMENIAN (*reading card and much awed by same*). "Ah, you vos Mistaire Sh—Captin Sheffer, R.A.F.? I tink you vos vaire rich man. You could afford to GIF me ze machine! Not so? Me vaire poor man, Captain Sheffer, R.A.F."

SELF. "If you knew as much about the Air Force as I do, you'd know better, my friend. Now, for Heaven's sake, BUZZ OFF,[722] and don't worry me."

(*Exit* ARMENIAN *with bows, shuffles of the feet, and salaams.*[723])

SCENE III

SCENE.—*The same. Half an hour later. A knock.*
SELF. "Come right in."
(*Enter* ARMENIAN.)

SELF. "What, again? Got the 500?"

ARMENIAN. "Grieved to trouble you vonce more, Captin Sheffer, R.A.F., but all ze money I 'af in ze world vos von 'undred twenty-five dollar. Me vaire poor man, Capt—"

SELF. "Yes, I've heard you say so. I believe you. Now we're both liars."

ARMENIAN. "Ah no, you insult me, Captin Sheffer, R.A.F. I am poor, but I am 'onorable man. I tell always ze truth. Zat vos all I 'af in all ze vorld."

SELF. "Look here, Mister—I don't know what your name is, but I guess you're a Hebrew of some kind—"

ARMENIAN. "My name is Mistaire Karachan, and I come from Armenia."[724]

SELF (*aside*—"I might have guessed it."). "Well, Mr. Karachan, I'll take your word for it. Give me 125 right now and you can take the machine away with you. She's outside on the pavement. But mind, I shall never want to see your face again."

ARMENIAN (*moved almost to tears*). "Ah, you vos a torough zhentleman, Mistaire Sheffer; all ze Englishmen are zhentlemen. Zer is only von contry in all ze vorld vaire zer are such zhentlemen."

SELF. "Well, you can hand over the wealth right now, here."

ARMENIAN. "Ah, but I 'af not got it wiz me, Mistaire Sheffer. It is too much to carry about in my pocket. But I can gif you fifty dollar and bring ze rest zis afternoon. Zat vos alright? I can take ze machine now, yes no?"

SELF. "You can take the machine when you've paid me 125 dollars IN CASH, and not till then. Get me? I shall be in again at two this afternoon. You can meet me in the hall with the money. Good-bye till then."

ARMENIAN. "Vell, you vill gif me written undertaking not to sell it to anyvon till then, Captin Sheffer, R.A.F.?"

SCENE IV

SCENE.—*The same.*

TIME.—*3 p.m.*

(*A knock on the door, followed by* ARMENIAN.)

ARMENIAN. "Mistaire Sheffer, I 'af come to make you a good bargain. You see zis gold votch? It vos giffen me by my fazer and it is solid gold wiz twenty-von jewels. You could sell it anywhere for fifty dollar. Now you 'af bin zhentleman to me, I vill be zhentleman to you. I vill give you ze votch and von 'undred dollar for your motorsickle! Is it not a bargain, Mistaire Sheffer?"

SELF. "Get out!"

SCENE V

SCENE.—*The same.*

TIME.—*An hour later. A knock on the door.*

(*Enter* ARMENIAN.)

ARMENIAN. "Oh, Mistaire Sheffer, I 'af jhust von more offer to—"

SELF. "Look here, Mr. Karachan, I'm getting fed up with you. Better quit before I bang this water-jug on your head. You've wasted all my day as it is."

ARMENIAN. "Ah, you vill not do zat. I know you vill not do zat. You are too much zhentleman. But wait, Mistaire Sheffer. Hear me vot I say. I 'af von great big suggestion to make for you. I make my living viz growing fruit. I 'af small plantation only five mile from 'ere.[725] I vill pay you for your motorsickle viz grapes. I vill gif you five ton of beautiful grapes and send them wherever you like in United States. Or if you not like zat, I vill gif you 'undred dollar and von ton of grapes. Is zat not good offer, yes no?"

SELF (*recovering from momentary speechlessness at the thought of swapping Lizzie for five tons of grapes*). "Look here, Mr. Karachan, I've had enough of this fooling. I've undertaken to sell you the machine for 125 dollars, and if you don't bring me the money, and all of it, right now, I'll report you to the police. Now there's an end of it. Get out."

(*Exit* ARMENIAN *amid more alarums and excursions.*)

SCENE VI
SCENE.—*The same.*
TIME.—7 *p.m. A knock.* (*Enter* ARMENIAN.)

ARMENIAN. "Oh, Captin Sheffer, R.A.F., I 'af got your money 'ere, but I 'af bin to ze police to register ze machine and zey say I 'af stolen it and vould not let me come away. After much trouble we telephone a big frend of mine who know police and zey let me come away. But zey vont your address and ze registration certificate you 'af in New York."

SELF. "But, Good Lord, man, who the devil said you could register it? It isn't yours yet! Give me the money."

ARMENIAN (*handing me fifty dollars and a cheque for seventy-five*). "'Ere it vos, but you vos not angry, Captin Sheffer, R.A.F? I vonted only to save time, because I vont to use ze machine to-morrow."

SELF. "Yes, but this is no good (*showing the cheque*). This isn't CASH. How do I know this'll be honoured? Besides, the banks are closed now and won't be open till Monday,[726] and I'm leaving to-morrow."

ARMENIAN. "Ah, but no, zey vill 'onour ze cheque. Mistaire—[727] is vaire well known in San Francisco. You can speak to 'im on ze telephone if you like and 'e vill tell you ze cheque is all right."

SELF. "No doubt, but all the same I'll see if the hotel manager here will cash it. If he won't, that's good enough for me. Come along, and we'll see him together."

ARMENIAN. "But you vill gif me receipt now, yes no? Ah, but vot is zis? (*picking up a small adjustable spanner[728] that lay on the dressing-table*). It is part of ze machine! You vould not surely make me pay for a motor-sickle vizout no tools? Ah, Captin Sheffer, R.A.F., it is not jhust; I must 'ave everyzing. Are zer any more—" (*At this juncture* ARMENIAN *is successfully extruded through the doorway, still protesting volubly.*)

SCENE VII

SCENE.—*In the hall of the Hotel. Manager behind desk.*

SELF. "Excuse me, but I have a favour to ask. I have just done a deal with this gentleman, but as all the banks are closed till Monday, I am wondering if you would be good enough to cash this cheque for me as I am leaving for the East to-morrow."

(MANAGER *looks closely at me and proceeds to open till; then, looking at* ARMENIAN, *pauses for a moment. Ultimately the money is paid over.*)

(ARMENIAN *and* SELF *walk toward door opening on to street.*)

SELF. "What the blazes! Where's Lizzie? I left her up against the pavement. She's gone!"

ARMENIAN. "Oh, zat vos alright. I move 'er zis afternoon to a garage round ze corner. Jhust zink how terrible it would be if some one stole 'im!"

SELF. "Well, I'll be goldarned!"

SCENE VIII

SCENE.—*Garage "round the corner." Lizzie stands surrounded by darkness,* ARMENIAN, *and* SELF. SELF *discovered explaining to* ARMENIAN *how the wheels go round and why.*

SELF. "Well, good-bye, Lizzie, old girl. I grieve to let you go into the hands of this being, but it is all for the best. We've had some jolly times together, but the time is come to part. Good-bye, once and for all; good-bye, GOOD-BYE—"

ARMENIAN. "Ah, Mistaire Sheffer, you 'av forgot ze adjustable spanner!"

EPILOGUE NOTES

715. The US Post Office and Court Building, 7th and Mission Street, San Francisco, was completed in 1901 (see Chapter 21, Note 712, Figure 242).

716. Analysis of activities preceding this event indicates these events occurred in the afternoon and on the evening of Friday, August 15, 1919. Later in the conversation, he states that the banks were no longer open and he would be leaving on Monday so, again, this implies these events occurred on Friday, August 15, 1919.

717. The Clift Hotel is at 495 Geary St. at the corner of Taylor (see Figure 243). It was opened in 1915 to serve visitors to the 1915 World's Fair. In 1919, it was about a twelve-minute walk, about a half a mile from the main post office (see Chapter 21, Note 712, Figure 242).

718. C.K. was not married in 1919, so he had no mother in law to sell.

719. "alarums and excursions": A phrase used to describe martial sounds and the movement of soldiers across the stage and as a stage direction in Elizabethan drama. Also used to characterize "clamor, excitement, and feverish or disordered activity."

Figure 243: Postcard of the Clift Hotel, Geary & Taylor Streets, *ca.* 1915.

720. The Henderson agent in San Francisco in 1919 was "Motorcycle Sales Company," which was located at 1446 Market Street, one mile away from the Clift Hotel (see Figure 244, next page). The price of $480 is consistent with period advertisements for the Henderson Z-2 Electric with all the options.

Figure 244: Excelsior Henderson Agent, San Francisco, *ca.* 1918.
Source: *Motorcycle and Bicycle Illustrated*, July 18, 1918, Page 29.

721. This may simply be a generalization, since it is subsequently implied that this conversation occurred on Friday, August 15, 1919. C.K. previously stated he would be leaving "tomorrow" (on Saturday) and then arriving "next Wednesday" in Salt Lake City, which would be on August 20, 1919. This suggests that he had already arranged his trip homeward (or backfilled the days in his book to conform to what he ended up doing) and that the train from San Francisco to Salt Lake City took three days, and then he would arrive in Chicago three days later. This itinerary allows for stops to engage in whatever patent-related business he intended and is consistent with his eventual departure from New York on the SS *Celtic* on September 10, 1919.

722. "buzz off": This means "go away" and may seem like a more modern term, but it was published almost one hundred years earlier. It can be found in a Samuel Griswold Goodrich poem entitled "To a Fly in Midwinter" published in *Parley's Magazine for Children and Youth*, Vol. I, No. 2, March 30, 1833. In the poem, the author—publishing under the nom de plume Peter Parley—addresses a fly and tells him to "buzz off."

723. *"salaam"*: An Arabic word referring to a gesture of greeting or respect—with or without a spoken salutation—typically consisting of a low bow of the head and body with the hand or fingers touching the forehead.

724. The problem is that there is no evidence of anyone named Karachan ever living in California during that period. (Additionally, there is no census data for anyone named Karachan, or similar, in California from 1910 to 1930.) It seems C.K. used the name to create a literary "caricature" of the person to whom he sold the bike as a means of illustrating a man of questionable integrity. L.M. Karachan was—at the time—a senior advisor within the Bolshevik government in Russia and was well-known as such by Europeans and even in America including articles in *The Times of London* on April 7, 1919 and, later, in the *Los Angeles Times* on July 24, 1921 and again on December 25, 1922—the first of which referred to Karachan as a "shifty Armenian." Thus, it seems likely that the name Karachan was simply employed by C.K. as a quickly recognizable caricature of the man's behavior.

725. An exhaustive search of the data from the 1920 census for any adult males in California who were born in Armenia yielded no owners of vineyards or plantations (or even laborers on farms) within ten miles of San Francisco (even as far away as Napa Valley). Thus, it is completely unclear who this person may have been, what his name actually was, or what he did with Lizzie after he bought her.

726. The indication that the banks are closed "now" implies they were open earlier in the day but later closed. Again, combined with the statement that the banks would not open until Monday indicates this conversation and sale took place late in the day on Friday, August 15, 1919. See previous Note 721.

727. This 2-em dash (——) represents a missing word or part of a missing word. In this context, it means that the Armenian did not write the check himself, but spoke the name of the person who did write the check and, for whatever reason, C.K. did not include the name of the third party.

728. "adjustable spanner": A British term for what is called an adjustable wrench in the US.

ACKNOWLEDGEMENTS

I would like to acknowledge the following people whose contributions helped make this book what it is:

My wonderful wife, Laura Sue, without whose patience, encouragement, tolerance, and love I never would have been able to have the dream, much less live it.

My father, Ken Hunnibell—who passed on without knowing of this dream—but nonetheless contributed greatly to its inception and outcome.

C.K.'s son, Dr. Charles Drury Shaw, who literally opened the doors of his home office to me, granting me access to the vast depth and breadth of material from his father's archives.

Steve's grandsons, Tom and Andy Stevenson, who welcomed me into their home and provided documents and information that offer important context to C.K.'s life and times.

Lloyd Hill, who supported, encouraged, and guided my research and writing on this subject over many years.

Brian Blue and Tom Martin of the Grand Canyon Historical Society for their early assistance with all things Flagstaff and the Grand Canyon.

Kevin Schindler at the Lowell Observatory in Flagstaff for opening the Observatory's logs and finding records of C.K.'s visit.

Chris Baker for his research and report helping me understand and decode the meanings and relevance of key details in C.K.'s RFC/RAF records.

Bruce Linsday, whose antique motorcycle literature collection proved to be the only source for copies of a series of articles C.K. wrote about his ride and published in 1919.

Countless librarians, research assistants, records clerks, government officials who each provided their unique insights and relevance to many of the details included in this book.

Gary Krebs for his patience with this first-time author with an unconventional book and his cheerful enthusiasm for the subject matter itself, and Larry Baker for his professional and thoughtful work on the index.

The team at Union Square Publishing—including Rick and Scott Frishman, Karen Strauss, and Claudia Volkman—for helping this new author get his first book into print.

ABOUT THE AUTHOR

CAPTAIN CHARLES KENILWORTH ("C.K.") SHEPHERD

Born on May 31, 1895 at home at 108 Oakfield Road, Balsall Heath, Edgbaston, Birmingham, England, Charles Kenilworth Shepherd was the last of seven children of Timothy Stephen Shepherd and Elizabeth Alice Dale. The Shepherds had only recently relocated to the Birmingham area from Richmond, Surrey, England when C.K. entered this world. The home at 108 Oakfield Road, still standing today, is a "terraced house"—homes built next to each other as part of a residential development in the early 1890s on the estate around Oakfield Villa. When the Shepherds moved into the home, the name "Kenilworth" was already affixed to the iron gate at the street, apparently put there by the first owner. Although it was uncommon to give formal names to such small homes, Timothy Shepherd often used the name "Kenilworth" to identify his home at 108 Oakfield.

C.K. grew up in a family of entrepreneurs and inventors. By the time Timothy Shepherd died in 1937, he had been granted over four-dozen patents in England and other countries. Timothy Shepherd's company, XL-ALL, Ltd., manufactured bicycle and motorcycle accessories, including leather saddles. For a short time in the early 1900s, XL-ALL manufactured two-cylinder motorcycles under the model name "Eclipse."

C.K. idolized his brother, George Frederick Shepherd, who was ten years his elder. At age fourteen, inspired by the new field of aviation, C.K. helped George build an "aeroplane" in hopes of collecting a prize of £1,000 offered by the *Daily Mail* for the first Englishman to operate an entirely British aircraft over a one mile circular course. Unfortunately, their plans were dashed following a catastrophic engine failure in the XL-ALL yard during testing.

Undaunted, George went on to be granted some nineteen patents worldwide and, from 1948-1971, received patents in eight countries around the world related to his invention of "the Shepherd Caster"—a commercially successful piece of office hardware in use even today. C.K. himself accumulated over a dozen patents during his life. He applied for four of those patents immediately prior to his 1919 trip across America, all related to improvements to internal combustion engines.

In 1910, when C.K. was fifteen years old, he passed a competitive examination at Birmingham's Tindal Street Council School to earn a scholarship at Suffolk Street's Council Central Secondary School. On January 11, 1915, when C.K. was nineteen, he volunteered for enlistment in the Royal Flying Corps. This was just six months after the beginning of what was subsequently dubbed World War I. Apparently seeking a better assignment, he touted his technical knowledge and qualifications. Also, as was common practice at the time, C.K. claimed to be five years older than his actual age. It worked. C.K. was sent to South Farnborough in Hampshire, where he was quickly confirmed as an Air Mechanic 2nd Class. By the end of January 1915, he was in the theater of war in France.

While in France, C.K. worked at the British Expeditionary Force's "Engine Repair Shops" (ERS) at Pont de l'Arche, near Rouen, under the auspices of the No. 1 Air Depot at the Air Park near Saint Omer. He rapidly rose through the enlisted ranks: from private, to corporal, to sergeant. On July 2, 1916, less than a year and a half after enlisting, he received a field commission to 2nd Lieutenant and was assigned a position as equipment officer, 3rd class. Over the next two years, as the Royal Flying Corps became the Royal Air Force, C.K. was promoted to captain and was responsible for about 300 men at ERS. His time there ended after he violated a direct order to stop his work on inventing a new method to test machine gun gearing. He was subsequently shipped off to the new No. 3 Air Depot at Chaumont in southern France. The circumstances of his departure from France are unknown but records reflect that, on July 8, 1918, he was transferred back to the "home establishment" to work at XL-ALL for the remainder of the war. By 1918, XL-ALL had converted at least some of its production line to leather and brass to make belts, fittings, and even ammunition for use by British soldiers in the war.

As he wrote about in *Across America by Motor-Cycle*, a few months after the war ended, C.K. met in London with a fellow officer from his Engine Repair Shop days: Captain Thomas Stevenson, Jr. (known to him as "Steve"). They pondered their future. Steve, who had been born in Scotland, was heading to Cincinnati to reconnect with his family who had emigrated to the United States in 1913. C.K. decided he would "cross yon herring pond to take a trot 'round America." And so the trip described in *Across America by Motor-Cycle* was born.

The planning for his trip could not have lasted more than five months. C.K. departed Liverpool on May 23, 1919 bound for Montreal, Canada. Before leaving, he applied for the first four of his patents that were granted later that year. Although

C.K. didn't mention it in *Across America by Motor-Cycle*, he had a business purpose for his trip. When he entered the United States from Canada, C.K. stated that his destination was Persons Manufacturing Company in Worcester, Massachusetts. Persons made motorcycle saddles, Timothy Shepherd owned some patents for motorcycle saddles, and XL-ALL made saddles—so it seems likely that part of the trip was directly related to pursuit of the family interest in motorcycle saddles. Also not mentioned is the fact that, when he made his way through Washington, D.C., C.K. met with a patent attorney and intended to meet with manufacturers after finishing his ride in San Francisco before heading back to England in September.

After completing his fascinating cross-country journey on August 16, 1919, C.K. spontaneously sold his motorcycle to a man he met by happenstance outside the San Francisco Post Office. The next day, C.K. boarded a train to arrive in New York in time to board the SS *Celtic* to England, departing New York on September 10, 1919 and arriving in Liverpool nine days later.

Three years later, *Across America by Motor-Cycle* was published. Almost simultaneously, on November 21, 1922, C.K. married Ursula Mary Edwards, the granddaughter of Samuel Edwards, who had been Lord Mayor of Birmingham in 1900. C.K. and Ursula had two daughters, Verity Jean Shepherd and Helen Shepherd.

It became apparent that C.K. was not a traditional "family man" who adhered to a regular lifestyle or occupation. Late in his life, he described his lifestyle as that of a "vagabond." He traveled extensively—often by himself and on a shoestring—but made at least one expedition with Ursula on a Harley-Davidson motorcycle with a sidecar in Tunisia. He set up offices and businesses in England and France as an engineer, architect, surveyor, author, bookseller, artist, and art supply dealer.

C.K.'s' innovative spirit was evident in his architectural vision as he sought to build what we would call "affordable housing" today, including speedy construction methods utilizing pre-fabricated concrete components. But he felt ostracized and even persecuted by the establishment architects who had no appreciation for new ideas or his lack of formal schooling and social connections. Still, he designed and oversaw construction of a number of homes in the Birmingham area, many of which stand today. Unfortunately, his businesses did not always thrive and he found himself bankrupt more than once.

Although C.K. never divorced Ursula, they seem to have lived separately beginning around 1930. C.K. suffered from what today is called fibromyalgia, was in frequent pain, and often sought relief in other locales either due to climate or availability of medical practitioners to help him. His physical condition, as well as adverse business outcomes in England, appear to have motivated him to move to France and began similar businesses there.

Ursula died at the age of 42 from cancer on December 23, 1938. Five months later, C.K. legally changed his name to Charles Kay Shaw. He claimed that people in France had a difficult time pronouncing his last name and that he had written under the pen name of Charles Shaw. However, it seems more likely the name change was to seek a fresh start in life because his given name had become tarnished through years of unsuccessful business outcomes. Less than five months after he changed his name—and just three days after England declared war on Germany beginning what would become World War II— C.K. married Honorah ("Nora") Tarpey, a woman fifteen years his junior he had hired into his architectural practice fresh out of secretarial school around 1925. The family took up residence in London, at #12 Drury Lane.

One year later, while London was enduring frequent aerial bombardment by Germany, C.K. wrote to his old friend Steve in Cincinnati that he had married Nora then because he did not want her to be without means if something happened to him. C.K. and Nora ran an artist's supply and bookstore on the ground floor and lived two floors up. At the same time, he served as a civil servant with the British Ministry of Aircraft Production. His primary work there was in "industrial publicity," an internal corporate communications program that sought to inspire workers to increase productivity. In 1944, after WWII, C.K. published a book, *Industrial Publicity*, in which he documented the efficacy of his work and advanced the value of its application in a post-war commercial economy.

During World War I, within six months of enlisting, C.K. had submitted an invention to the Royal Flying Corps for a "Land Speed Indicator for Aeroplanes." During World War II, he had advanced a number of additional inventions to the British government, including: a "phonoscope" (a device for detection of enemy night bombers); a sub-surface transportation scheme to move supplies on ships (barges that floated just below the surface of the water); and even a helicopter design.

In 1941, C.K. and Nora had a daughter, Claire Michelle Shaw. Three years later, they welcomed a son, Charles Drury Shaw, into the family. By the 1950s, they had moved out of London to a large house C.K. dubbed "Drury Lodge," located in East Grinstead, Sussex. At Drury Lodge, C.K. set up a photographic darkroom, a machine shop, and a laboratory, all supporting his various curiosities and scientific investigations and increasing research into what had apparently interested him for of his for most of his life: "spirituality" and survival of life after death, more currently characterized as "the occult."

Near the end of his life, C.K. penned several accounts (some published, some not) in which he recounted his own near-death experience as a four-year-old boy, running home after his first day of Sunday School and being run over by a horse-drawn carriage. He recalled what we would characterize today as an "out of body experience" while he was physically unconscious. A few years later, while still a student and member of a nature club at the school, he caused quite a stir when he invited noted naturalist Sir Oliver Lodge—then the Principal of Birmingham University—to speak at his school. Sir Oliver was perhaps then—and certainly since—a well-known proponent of "survival."

It seems C.K. became acquainted with author Francis Rolt-Wheeler prior to 1922, since several photographs in *Across America by Motor-Cycle* are credited to him. Although Rolt-Wheeler was a prolific author of boys' educational adventure books such as *The Boy with the United States Survey* and *The Boy with the American Red Cross*, Rolt-Wheeler had also ventured into science, with a ten-volume series *Science-History of the Universe*. Rolt-Wheeler was living in New York in 1919 when C.K. passed through twice that year but, by 1930, was publishing a French-language occult periodical in Tunisia, *L'Astrosophie*, in addition to *The Seer*—a comparable English-language journal in Nice, France. C.K. wrote articles for Rolt-Wheeler's publications and they remained lifelong acquaintances.

C.K.'s creative energies never ceased. Based in Drury Lodge,[729] he continued to travel and conduct complex experiments on light refraction and, among other things, continue his adventures in inventions and patents; he was granted British patents for luminescent paints and artist paintbrushes. He was granted patents in six countries for inventing the idea of publishing phonographic recordings on film mounted on cardboard substrate. He also produced a series of paper model books, providing pre-cut cardboard templates for children and adults to fold and assemble to create 3D model collections of airplanes, cars, and even more elaborate models like *Thomas the Tank Engine* and the coronation of Queen Elizabeth II in 1953.

C.K. had a number of unpublished written works and even came back to the United States in 1956 to meet with publishers, but was unsuccessful in selling anything. During the 1950s and 1960s, C.K. regularly traveled and was a frequent participant at the Spiritualist Association of Great Britain (SAGB) in London. Although he did not profess to be a medium himself, he advanced the subject matter from a lay perspective in two of his books: *Yes, We Do Survive* (published in Bombay, India in 1965) and *Introduction to Spiritualism* (published in January 1968 by SAGB). In the works, he describes specific personal experiences and how they influenced his life.

On January 16, 1971, three years after *Introduction to Spiritualism*, C.K. passed on at the age of seventy-five following complications from stomach cancer. His wife, Nora, survived him but passed away in 1998. All four of his children also survived him and two remain alive as of this date (Helen Shepherd and Charles Drury Shaw).

ABOUT THE AUTHOR NOTES

729. Drury Lodge was the name C.K. gave his home. Figure 245 is a pen-and-ink illustration by C.K. that he drew of his home in 1966.

Figure 245: Drury Lodge, September 1, 1966.
Source: Ilustration by C.K. Shaw.

ABOUT THE AUTHOR

CAPTAIN MARK LESLIE HUNNIBELL

Born on August 22, 1957 in Providence, Rhode Island, Mark Leslie Hunnibell is the second of four children of Kenneth Lee Hunnibell and Carol Linda Dutra. Both Kenneth and Carol had been students at the Rhode Island School of Design (RISD), as had many in Mark's extended family. Shortly after Mark was born, his father bought and then moved the family to an old farm homestead (originally built in 1786) in Rehoboth, Massachusetts. When Mark was about six years old, his parents divorced and he moved with his mother and three sisters to a home in a subdivision about forty-five miles north of the old farm homestead. Six years later, they moved to Kensington, California—a small community just north of Berkeley. Mark attended junior and senior high schools in Richmond, California, where he graduated in June 1975. Two months later, he flew back to live with his father in Rehoboth while continuing the family legacy at RISD in Providence, Rhode Island.

Although Mark frequently demonstrated his creative abilities in studies at RISD, he spent more time with extra-curricular activities and, when it came time for him to graduate in June 1979, he was nine credits short to receive his Bachelor of Fine Arts in Industrial Design. Intent on moving back to California, Mark drove across the country in the summer of 1979. He remedied his credit shortfall by taking a full semester of journalism and psychology classes at the University of California, Berkeley, and had the credits transferred back to RISD. After completing his coursework at Cal Berkeley, he took a job as an automotive machinist in Albany, California. While there, he began work on the 1919 Henderson motorcycle "basket case" that his father had given to him a couple years earlier, disassembling it and beginning to repair the engine.

In September 1980, finally motivated to put his RISD degree to use, Mark and Geoff, his friend from RISD, drove across the country from California to the east coast. Geoff was taking a new position in Washington, DC. Mark was going to live with his father in Rehoboth while he assembled his design portfolio to begin his career as a designer in New York. Mark and Geoff were on an extremely tight budget for the trip (they each started with $100), so they camped and stayed with friends along the way on their ten-day trip.

One overnight stop was in Lubbock, Texas, visiting with Rich—a high school friend of Geoff's who was going through pilot training in the US Air Force (USAF). Although Mark recalled being told that his father had served as a mechanic in the Rhode Island National Guard before he was born, Mark had never been around anyone "in the service" and was surprised at how "normal" Rich and his peers were. Rich informed Mark that anyone with a college degree could become an Air Force pilot if he or she completed the training. The next morning, before leaving, Rich brought Mark out to the base and arranged to have Mark take a seat in one of the T-38 supersonic jets sitting on the ramp. The experience left an indelible impression on him.

Soon thereafter, now living with his father back in Rehoboth and after a long night working on his design portfolio, Mark announced one morning that, rather than pursue a design career, he planned to join the Air Force to be a pilot. He knew he would be forever restless if he did not explore this opportunity. The announcement was so unexpected and the concept so preposterous that his father—always the practical man—insisted he immediately go into Providence to meet with the USAF recruiter to find out if anything Mark was talking about was true. At dinner that evening, Mark reported that it was a real program and that he qualified for it with his RISD degree. His father asked what he was going to do. Mark replied, "Oh, it's done," explaining that he had already signed up and the first exams had already been scheduled.

Less than a year later, Mark made his solo flight in an Air Force T-41—a Cessna 172 airplane the Air Force used to determine if a flight candidate had the skills to complete jet training. Mark passed this screening program and in December 1981 received his commission as a 2nd lieutenant. In May 1983, after more than a year of intensive military pilot training, Mark arrived at his first assignment as a C-130 pilot at Clark Air Base in the Republic of the Philippines. In October 1985, he transferred to a WC-130 unit at Keesler Air Force Base in Mississippi, "the Hurricane Hunters." Mark completed his military service at the rank of captain and was honorably discharged from the Air Force effective January 5, 1989. Two months later he began what would become his twenty-nine-year career as a pilot for American Airlines.

Beginning during his time in the Philippines, Mark acquired substantial knowledge and expertise in computer programming and was a pioneer in using desktop computers to write and run custom applications to support operational

Air Force missions. He received an account on the Defense Data Network—one of the first applications of the of TCP/IP communications protocol originally called ARPANET—and later forming the basis of "the Internet."

While at American Airlines, Mark became active in the Allied Pilots Association, the labor union exclusively representing the pilots at American Airlines. He personally developed the union's first "members only" web site and suite of services. Beginning in 1998, he was elected and served as a representative union officer for two years. From 1998-2009, he oversaw the professional Information Technology department within the union that administered the second and third generations of the Internet services he had brought forth.

In 2000, Mark decided it was time to dust off the baskets of the old 1919 Henderson project if he was ever going to complete the restoration. He began researching the history of the make and model, while also searching for competent experts to help him with what he knew would be substantial machine work to get the bike running. Early on, he discovered C.K. Shepherd's book, *Across America by Motor-Cycle*, igniting the first spark of what has become a wildfire: the dream of recreating Shepherd's ride one hundred years later.

By 2002, Mark had joined the Antique Motorcycle Club of America (AMCA) and had begun building a network of people to assist him with his own restoration and the growing plans for the cross-country trip. He volunteered to help at a northeast regional "meet" of AMCA and within a couple years was the chairman of a key committee for that meet. Later, he helped AMCA to stabilize and re-catalogue its "Virtual Library" collection of digital copies of hundreds of books, catalogues, photos, and documents relating to antique motorcycles.

Without a machine shop of his own, Mark was reliant on others to complete the "heavy lifting" of the restoration. After one disappointing engagement with a supposed expert for engine restoration, Mark was forced to start over. Knowing that he planned to ride this motorcycle cross-country, he engaged Mark Hill: a highly sought after machinist and veteran of Henderson motorcycle preparation for such endeavors. Thus began what became nearly a decade-long process during which experts went to extraordinary lengths to bring both the engine and frame back from what would normally be considered their graves.

In June 2018, Mark retired from American Airlines as a Boeing 737 captain, having previously been a captain on the McDonnell-Douglas MD-80, Airbus A300, and Boeing 767/757, as well as a first officer on the Boeing 727 and Airbus A300, and a flight engineer on the McDonnell Douglas DC-10.

Shortly after Mark's retirement, his 1919 Henderson was—at long last—running and drivable, and he was able to devote his full energies to attending to final restoration, "driver training," and installation of safety equipment on top of the endless chores associated with researching and planning his cross-country trip in 2019.

Across America by Motor-Cycle: Fully Annotated Centennial Edition is the product of Mark's dogged determination to discover and tell the rest of the story of Charles Kenilworth Shepherd's amazing journey. He also plans to document his own journey in a subsequent book with the working title *Chasing Charles: Across America by Motor-Cycle II.*

BIBLIOGRAPHY

Authored Books and Manuscripts

Albuquerque Auto Trades Association. *National Old Trails Highway*. Albuquerque: Albuquerque Auto Trades Association, 1920.

Alford, Steven E. and Ferriss, Suzanne. *An Alternative History of Bicycles and Motorcycles*. Lanham, Maryland: Roman & Littlefield, 2016.

Arizona Automobile Association & Rocky Mountain Motorists, Inc. *Travel Directory of Arizona*. Phoenix: Arizona Automobile Association & Rocky Mountain Motorists, Inc., 1931.

Bacon, Roy and Hallworth, Ken. *The British Motorcycle Directory—Over 1,100 Marques from 1888*. Ramsbury, Marlborough, England: The Crowood Press, 2004.

Bagby, George P., ed. *The Annotated Code of the Public Civil Laws of Maryland, Vol 1 of 2*. Baltimore: King Brothers, State Printers, 1911.

Bagby, George P., ed. *The Annotated Code of the Public General Laws of Maryland, Vol 4*. Baltimore: King Brothers, State Printers, 1918.

Baggs, Mae Lacy. *Colorado—The Queen Jewel of Rockies*. Boston: The Page Company, 1918.

Baker, T. Lindsay. *Portrait of Route 66: Images from the Curt Teich Postcard Archives*. Norman, Oklahoma: University of Oklahoma Press, 2016.

Baring, Maurice. *Flying Corps Headquarters, 1914-18*. London: William Blackwood & Sons, Ltd., 1968.

Bisbee, Frederick A. *A California Pilgrimage*. Boston: The Murray Press, 1915.

Blackmar, Frank W., ed. *Kansas: A Cyclopedia of State History, Embracing Events, Institutions, Industries, Counties, Cities, Towns, Prominent Persons, Etc., Volumes I and II.* Chicago: Standard Publishing Co., 1912.

Blanchard, Arthur H., ed. *American Highway Engineers' Handbook, First Edition.* New York: John Wiley & Sons, 1919. Page 535.

Boyd, Varna G. and Furgerson, Kathleen A. *The Mystery of the Monongahela Indians.* Laurel, MD: Greenhorne & O'Mara, Inc., 1999.

Britton, N.L. and Rose, J.N.. *The Cactaceae—Descriptions and Illustrations of Plants of the Cactus Family, Volume I.* Washington, DC: The Carnegie Institution of Washington, 1919. Page 180, Plate XXXIV.

Brown, John, Jr. and Boyd, James. *History of San Bernardino and Riverside Counties—Volume I.* Chicago: Lewis Publishing Company, 1922.

Bunyan, John. *The Pilgrim's Progress from This World, to That Which Is to Come.* London: Nath. Ponder at the Peacock in the Poultrey near Cornhil, 1678.

Campbell, Marius R. *Bulletin 707: Guidebook of the Western United States - Part E. The Denver & Rio Grande Western Route.* Washington, DC: US Geological Survey, 1922.

Carlson, W.G. *Directory of Flagstaff.* Flagstaff: The Coconino Sun, 1929.

Chamier, John Adrian. *The Birth of the Royal Air Force: The Early History And Experiences Of The Flying Services.* London: I. Pitman & Sons, 1943.

Charles Mason Dow, LLC. *Anthology and Bibliography of Niagara Falls, Volume II.* Albany, New York: State of New York, 1921.

Cormack, Andrew and Cormack, Peter. *British Air Forces 1914-1918(2).* Wellingborough, England: Osprey Publishing Ltd., 2001.

Craig, Charles F. *Bulletin No. 6: The Prophylaxis of Malaria with Special Reference to the Military Service.* Washington, DC: Office of the Surgeon General, US War Department, August 1919. Page 77.

Darton, N.H. and Others. *Bulletin 613: Guidebook of the Western United States—Part C. The Santa Fe Route with a Side Trip to the Grand Canyon of the Colorado.* Washington, DC: US Geological Survey, 1915.

Dye, Peter John. *Air Power's Midwife—Logistics Support For Royal Flying Corps Operations On The Western Front 1914-1918.* Birmingham, England: University of Birmingham, October 2013.

Dyke, A.L. *Dyke's Automobile and Gasoline Engine Encyclopedia, Eighth Edition.* St. Louis: A.L. Dyke, 1918.

Dzierzak, Lou. *Schwinn.* St. Paul, MN: MBI Publishing, 2002.

Ebel, Charles O. ed. *Ebel's Decatur City Directory.* Decatur: Review Printing & Stationary Company, 1911. Pages 902-903.

Environmental & Enhancement Group. *Historic Route 66 Corridor Management Plan.* Phoenix: Arizona Department of Transportation, March 2005.

Farmer, John S. and Henley, W.E. *A Dictionary of Slang and Colloquial English.* London: George Routledge & Sons, Ltd., 1905.

Fransen, Tim, ed. *An Anthology Of Early British Motorcycle Travel Literature.* London: Essex-Dakar Books, 2009.

Frazier, Dr. Gregory W. *Motorcycle Adventurer: Carl Stearns Clancy: First Motorcyclist To Ride Around The World 1912-1913.* iUniverse, 2010.

Guilford, W.S. *California Hog Book.* San Francisco: Pacific Rural Press, September 1915.

Hall, Alice Eby. *The Cajon Pass.* Charleston, SC: Arcadia Publishing, 2009.

Hammett, Kingsley. *Santa Fe: A Walk Through Time.* Layton, UT: Gibbs Smith, 2004.

Harper, Jared V. *Santa Fe's Raton Pass.* Dallas, TX: Kachina Press, 1983.

Henshaw, Peter. *The Encyclopedia of the Motorcycle: An Illustrated Guide to the Classic Marques with 600 Photographs*. Leicester, England: Lorenz Books, 2007.

Hewston, Norman. *A History of Moseley Village: Volume One*. Gloucestershire, England: Amberley Publishing, 2009.

Higgins, C.A. *Titan of Chasms—The Grand Canyon of Arizona*. Chicago: Passenger Department of the Santa Fe Railroad. 1905. Page 24.

Hubbard, Elbert. *Power or the Story of Niagara Falls*. East Aurora, New York: Roycrofters, 1914.

Hufford, David Andrew. *El Camino Real: The Original Highway Connecting the Twenty-One Missions from South to North*. Los Angeles: D.A. Hufford & Co., 1901.

James, George Wharton. *The Grand Canyon of Arizona: How to See It*. Boston: Little, Brown, and Company, 1918.

James, George Wharton. *The Wonders of the Colorado Desert, Volume I*. Boston: Little, Brown, and Company, 1906.

Jones, Richard Cumpston. *Saint-Omer and the British Connection*. CreateSpace Independent Publishing Platform, 2013.

Kaszynski, William. *The American Highway: The History and Culture of Roads in the United States*. Jefferson, NC: McFarland Publishing, 2000.

Keble, John. *The Christian Year*. Oxford, England: W. Baxter, 1827. Vol. I, Pages 1-3.

Lacy, Lester D. *A History of the Social Phases of the Temperance Movement in Kansas*. Lawrence, Kansas: University of Kansas, 1916.

League for Industrial Rights. *Law and Labor, Volume I*. New York: League for Industrial Rights, 1919.

Mangum, Richard K. and Mangum, Sherry G. *Grand Canyon-Flagstaff Stage Coach Line : A History & Exploration Guide*. Flagstaff, Arizona: Hexagon Press, 1999.

Marquis, Albert Nelson, ed. *Who's Who in America, Volume VI*. Chicago: A.N. Marquis & Company, 1910. Page 1638.

Maule, Mary K. *A Prairie-Schooner Princess*. Boston: Lothrop, Lee & Shepard Co., 1920.

McGregor, Ewan and Boorman, Charley. *Long Way Round: Chasing Shadows Across the World*. New York: Atria Books, 2004.

McInnes, I. and Webb, J.V. *A Contemptible Little Flying Corps*. London: The London Stamp Exchange, 1991.

Mencken, H.L. *The American Language: An Inquiry into the Development of English in the United States, 2nd ed.* New York: Alfred A. Knopf, 1921.

Morrison, Annie L. and Haydon, John H. *History of San Luis Obispo County and Environs*. Los Angeles: Historic Record Company, 1917.

Parrish, Randall. *The Great Plains: The Romance of Western American Exploration, Warfare, and Settlement, 1527-1870*. Chicago: A.C. McClurg & Co., 1907.

Philpott, Ian. *The Birth of the Royal Air Force*. Barnsley, England: Pen and Sword Books, Ltd., 2013.

Pinkerton, Allan. *The Expressman and the Detective*. Chicago: W.B. Keen, Cooke & Co. 1874.

Ramer, John E. *Biennial Report of the Bureau of Labor Statistics of the State of Colorado—1915-1916*. Denver Colorado: State of Colorado, 1916.

Rider, Gary L. *Marshall County*. Charleston, SC: Arcadia Publishing, 2018.

Rolt-Wheeler, Francis. *The Boy With the U.S. Inventors*. Boston: Lothrop, Lee & Shepard Co., 1921.

Schindler, Kevin. *Lowell Observatory*. Charleston, SC: Arcadia Publishing, 2016.

Schramm, Robert W. *Moundsville WV*. Charleston, SC: Arcadia Publishing, 2004.

Scott, Sir Walter. *Kenilworth*. Paris: Julius Didot, Senior, January 8, 1821.

Searight, Thomas B. *The Old Pike—A History of the National Road*. Uniontown, PA: Thomas B. Searight, 1894.

Shaw, C.K. *Angry Old Man*. Unpublished, *ca.* 1960.

Shaw, C.K. *C.K. Shaw—30-Year Brief History*. Unpublished, September 12, 1958.

Shaw, C.K. *God Speaking*. Unpublished, *ca.* 1950.

Shaw, C.K. *Industrial Publicity*. London: C.&J. Temple Limited, 1944.

Shaw, C.K. *Introduction to Spiritualism*. London: Spiritualist Association of Great Britain, 1968.

Shaw, C.K. *A Lesson in Practical Psychology*. Unpublished, *ca.* 1939.

Shaw, C.K. *Life of a Vagabond*. Unpublished, *ca.* 1958.

Shaw, C.K. *Manuscripts Available for Publication*. Unpublished, *ca.* 1967.

Shaw, C.K. *My Philosophy*. Unpublished, January 1, 1943.

Shaw, C.K. *Painting in Oils*. London: Shaw Correspondence of Art, *ca.* 1946.

Shaw, C.K. *Return to Sanity*. Unpublished, *ca.* 1947.

Shaw, C.K. *Tunisian Landscape*. Unpublished, *ca.* 1943.

Shaw, C.K. *Yes, We Do Survive*. Bombay, India: D.B. Taraporevala Sons, 1965.

Shepherd, C.K. *Death in the Desert*. Unpublished, *ca.* 1933.

Shepherd, C.K. *Devis Descriptifs et Plans*. Nice, France: Building Society of Nice, *ca.* 1930.

Shepherd, C.K. *Diary*. Unpublished. September 26, 1935-May 12, 1936.

Shepherd, C.K. *Music in the Desert*. Unpublished, ca. 1933.

Shepherd, C.K. *Particulars of the £350 Type House*. Birmingham, England: The Alpha Building Corporation, *ca*. 1928.

Shepherd, C.K. *Vagabond in Morocco*. Unpublished, *ca*. 1935.

Simpson, J.A. and Weiner, E.S.C., eds. *The Oxford English Dictionary, Second Edition*. Oxford, England: Clarendon Press, 1989.

Smith, Joseph D. *The Propeller, 840th Aero Squadron*. Harrisburg, Pennsylvania: The Courier Press, 1919.

Thomas and Gordon, eds. *Florence City Directory 1905-1906*. Florence, CO: The Tribune Printing & Publishing Co., 1905.

Thompson, J Lee. *Politicians, the Press, and Propaganda: Lord Northcliffe and the Great War, 1914-1919*. Kent, OH: The Kent State University Press, 2000. Page 166.

US Department of Commerce. *Abstract of the Fourteenth Census of the United States*. Washington, DC: Government Printing Office, 1910.

US Department of Commerce. *Abstract of the Thirteenth Census of the United States*. Washington, DC: Government Printing Office, 1910.

US Department of the Interior Washington. *Rules And Regulations: Grand Canyon National Park*. Washington, DC: US Department of the Interior, 1920.

US Forest Service. *The San Gabriel, San Bernardino, and San Jacinto Forest Reserves*. Washington, DC: US Forest Service, 1900.

US National Park Service. *Day Hike—Bright Angel Trail*. Grand Canyon, Arizona: US National Park Service, 2015.

US National Park Service. *Special Resource Study: Route 66*. Denver: US National Park Service, July 1995.

Villiers, George. *The Rehearsal*, 1671.

Wallace, Laurel T. *Historic Highways in the NMDot System*. Santa Fe, New Mexico: New Mexico Department of Transportation, October 2004.

Waugh, Frank A. *A Plan for the Development of the Village of Grand Canyon, Ariz.* Washington, DC: Government Printing Office, 1918.

Weingroff, Richard F. *The National Old Trails Road—Part 1: The Quest for a National Road*. Washington, DC: US Federal Highway Administration, 2003.

Weingroff, Richard F. *The National Old Trails Road—Part 2: See America First in 1915*. Washington, DC: US Federal Highway Administration, 2004.

Westgard, A.L. *Tales of a Pathfinder*. New York: A.L. Westgard, 1920.

Wheeler, H.A. *Vitrified Paving Brick: A Review of Present Practice in the Manufacture, Testing and Uses of Vitrified Paving Brick, 2nd Ed.* Indianapolis: T.A. Randall & Co., 1910.

Wood, Ruth Kedzie. *The Tourist's California*. New York: Dodd, Mead and Company, 1914.

Wood, Ruth Kedzie. *The Tourist's California*. New York: Dodd, Mead and Company, 1915.

Wood, Stanley and Hooper, C.E. *Over the Range to the Golden Gate*. Chicago: R.R. Donnelley & Sons Co., 1904.

Wright, Joseph, Ed. *The English Dialect Dictionary, Being the Complete Vocabulary of All Dialect Words Still in Use, or Known to Have Been in Use During the Last Two Hundred Years*:

- *Vol. I (A-C)*. London: Henry Frowde, Amen Corner, E.C., 1898.
- *Vol. II (D-G)*. London: Henry Frowde, Amen Corner, E.C., 1900.
- *Vol. II (D-G)*. London: Oxford University Press, 1923.
- *Vol. II (F-M)*. London: Henry Frowde, Amen Corner, E.C., 1900.
- *Vol. III (H-L)*. London: Henry Frowde, 1905.
- *Vol. IV (M-Q)*. London: Henry Frowde, 1905.
- *Vol. V (R-S)*. London: Henry Frowde, 1905.
- *Vol. VI (T-Z)*. London: Henry Frowde, 1905.

Wrobel, David M. *Global West, American Frontier*. Albuquerque: University of New Mexico Press, 2013.

Unattributed Books and Manuscripts

The American Florist Company's Directory. Chicago: American Florist Co., 1914.

Arizona State Business Directory. Denver: The Gazetteer Publishing and Printing Co., 1920.

Bennett's Business Directory—Warwickshire. Shropshire, England: T.F. Wycherly, 1914.

Boyd's Directory of the District of Columbia. Washington, DC: R.L. Polk & Co., 1919.

Boyd's Philadelphia Combined City and Business Directory. Philadelphia: C.E. Howe Co., October 1916.

Bradstreet's Book of Commercial Ratings of Banker's, Merchants, Manufacturers, etc., in a Portion of the United States, Volume 214. New York: The Bradstreet Company, July, 1921.

Britain At War. Stamford, England: Key Publishing, July 2015.

The Burlington's Number One. Chicago: Chicago, Burlington & Quincy Railroad Company, 1904. Chapter 1—Colorado, Page 18.

Cracking the GED® Test with 2 Practice Tests—2017 Edition. Framingham, MA: Princeton Review, 2016. Pages 580-582.

Decatur City Directory. Peoria: Leshnick Directory Co., 1921. Pages 586-587.

Directory of Syracuse Telephone Exchange—Issue Number Two. Syracuse, Kansas: Republican News Press, September 1915.

The Existing Law of Boroughs in Pennsylvania. Philadelphia: George T. Bisel Co., 1917.

Hagerstown, Maryland Directory. Hagerstown, MD: Franklin Directory Company, 1922.

Hagerstown, Maryland Directory. Richmond, VA and Hagerstown, MD: Hill Directory Company, 1910-1911.

The Hotel World. Chicago: Hotel World Interests, Inc., January 4, 1919.

Interstate Automobile Register and Tourists' Guide, Number One, New England. Worcester, Massachusetts: F. S. Blanchard & Company, 1905.

Kansas City Directory. Kansas City, MO: Standard Press, 1919. Page 126.

Kelly's Directory. London: Kelly's Directories Ltd., 1903-1934.

Laws of New York, Volume I. Albany: J.B. Lyon Company, 1916.

Laws of New York, Volume I. Albany: J.B. Lyon Company, 1918.

Laws of New York, Volume III. Albany: J.B. Lyon Company, 1917.

Laws of the State of Indiana. Indianapolis: W.M. Burford, 1913.

Laws of the State of Maryland. Baltimore: King Brothers, State Printers, 1916.

Motion Picture Studio Directory. New York: Motion Picture News, 1918.

Motion Picture Studio Directory. New York: Motion Picture News, 1920.

Moundsville City Directory. Pittsburgh: R.L. Polk & Co., 1924.

New Mexico State Business Directory. Denver: The Gazetteer Publishing and Printing Co., 1913.

New Mexico State Business Directory. Denver: The Gazetteer Publishing and Printing Co., 1920.

New York—The Metropolis of the Western World. New York: The Foster & Reynolds Co., 1917.

The New York Central Railroad Company Timetable. New York: New York Central Lines, June 30, 1918.

Official Guide of the Railways and Steam Navigation Lines of the United States. New York: The National Railway Publication Company, June 1907.

Official Guide of the Railways and Steam Navigation Lines of the United States. New York: The National Railway Publication Company, June 1921.

The Official Hotel Red Book and Directory. New York: Official Hotel Red Book and Directory Co., 1917.

The Official Hotel Red Book and Directory. New York: Official Hotel Red Book and Directory Co., 1920.

Poor's Manual of Railroads. New York: Poor's Publishing Company, 1919. Page 1592.

The Revised Statutes of the State of Missouri. Jefferson City, Missouri: The Hugh Stephens Co., 1919.

Salinas, Monterey and Pacific Grove Directory. San Francisco: R.L. Polk & Co., 1926.

Williams' Cincinnati Directory, 72nd Edition. Cincinnati: The William Directory Company, 1922.

Periodicals

Advertising & Selling. "How Much is Two and a Half Million?" Vol. 29, No. 38, Page 18. New York: Advertising & Selling Co., Inc., March 13, 1920.

The American Florist. Chicago: American Florist Co.:
  • Vol. LI, Nos. 1572-1597, July 20, 1918-January 11, 1919.
  • Vol. LII, Nos. 1598-1621, January 18-June 28, 1919.
  • Vol. LIII, Nos. 1624-1649, July 24, 1919-January 10, 1920.

The Appian Way. Vols. I-II. St. Joseph, MO: Pikes Peak Highway Association, January 1923-December 1924.

Arizona—The State Magazine. Vol. X, Nos. 1-2. Phoenix, Arizona: State Publishing Co., February 1919.

Arizona Republican. "Weather Report." Phoenix, Arizona: Arizona Republican:
  • July 30, 1919.
  • July 31, 1919.
  • August 1, 1919.
  • August 2, 1919.

Automobile Journal. "Pikes Peak Highway." Vol. LVXI, No. 12, Insert Page 16. Pawtucket, RI: Automobile Journal Publishing Co., July 1919.

Automobile Journal. Vol. XLI. Pawtucket, RI: Automobile Journal Publishing Co., 1916.

The Automobile Trade Directory. Vol. X, No. 1, Pages 74 and 378. New York: The Automobile Trade Directory, January 1912.

Automobile Trade Journal. "Passenger Car Review." Vol. XXIII, No. 7. Pages 179-208. Philadelphia: Chilton Company, January 1, 1919.

Automobile Trade Journal. Vol. XXI, Nos. 3-6. Philadelphia: Chilton Company, September-December 1916.

Automotive Industries. Vol. XXXIX, Nos. 1-26. New York: The Class Journal Company, July 4 December 26, 1918.

Bellevue College Bulletin. Vol. 12, No 3. Bellevue, Nebraska: Bellevue College, March 1913.

Better Roads and Streets. "Modern Highway Construction, Maintenance and Equipment" Steele, George D. Vol. IV, No. 3. Pages 15-22, 54. Dayton, Ohio: The Otterbein Press, March 1914.

Birmingham Daily Gazette. Birmingham, England:
- "£75 Conversion Charge." Page 12. January 25, 1933.
- "Birmingham Wedding." Page 6. July 7, 1922.
- "Colmore-Row Theft." Page 10. March 1, 1927.
- "Custom of a Bank." Page 6. July 31, 1906.
- "Registrar's Protest." Page 11. June 23, 1932.
- "Woman Builder's Debts." Page 9. March 10, 1932.

Birmingham Daily Post. "Nisi Prius Court – Before Mr. Justice Bucknill." Page 8. Birmingham, England: Birmingham Daily Post, August 24, 1900.

Birmingham Natural History Society Newsletter. "A strange request re C.K. Shepherd—Hon Sec BNHS 1921." Jarvis, Peter. No. 107. Page 3. Birmingham, England: Birmingham Natural History Society, December 2015.

Cartographic Perspectives. "The Official Automobile Blue Book, 1901–1929: Precursor to the American Road Map." Bauer, John T. No. 62, Pages 4-27. Milwaukee: North American Cartographic Information Society, Winter 2009.

Cassier's Magazine—Engineering Illustrated. "Mechanical Energy and Industrial Progress" Unwin, W. Cawthorne. Vol. VIII. New York: The Cassier Magazine Company, July 1895.

The Cement Era. "Arizona Bridges and Culverts." Vol. XV, No. 8, Page 40. Chicago: The Cement Era Publishing Company, August 1917.

The Coconino Sun. "Local Brevities." Vol. XXXVI, No. 44, Page 16. Flagstaff, Arizona: The Coconino Sun, August 29, 1919.

Colorado Highways Bulletin. Vol II, No. 9, Page 7. Denver, Colorado: State of Colorado, September 1919.

Daily News. "Springs and Tyres—Final Gleanings at the Stanley Cycle Show." "Kuklos." Page 12. London: Daily News, November 29, 1907.

The Desert. Vol. 13, No. 11. Palm Desert, California: Desert Press, September 1950.

The Echo. "The Speed Mania: More Heavy Fines." Page 6. Gloucestershire, England: The Echo, September 26, 1924.

The Edinburgh Gazette. "The Bankruptcy Act, 1914." From The London Gazette—Receiving Orders. Issue 14130, Page 587. Edinburgh, Scotland: *Edinburgh Gazette,* May 26, 1925.

The Edinburgh Gazette. "The Bankruptcy Acts, 1914 and 1926." From The London Gazette—Receiving Orders. Issue 14838, Page 178. Edinburgh, Scotland: *Edinburgh Gazette,* February 26, 1932.

Eighteenth-Century Studies. "Rewriting the Savage: The Extraordinary Fictions of the 'Wild Girl of Champagne.'" Douthwaite, Julia. Vol. 28, No. 2, Pages 163-192. Baltimore: Johns Hopkins University Press, 1994.

Electric Railway Journal. "The Ohio Electric Railway." Vol. 34, No. 15, Pages 873-875. New York: McGraw Publishing Company, October 16, 1909.

Engineering and Contracting. "An Englishman's Views of American Roads." From Municipal Engineering and Sanitary Record, London. Vol. LVIII, No. 1, Page 13. Chicago: Engineering and Contracting Publishing Co., November 29, 1922.

Engineering and Mining Journal. Vol. CVI. New York: McGraw-Hill Co. July-December 1918.

Flight. "£1,000 'All British' Prize Won." Aero Club of the United Kingdom. Vol. I, No. 45, Page 703. London: F. King & Co., November 6, 1909.

Flight. "On the Offering of Prizes." Aero Club of the United Kingdom. Vol. I, No. 16, Pages 215, 217, 226. London: F. King & Co., April 17, 1909.

Gazetteer of Modern Houses in the United Kingdom and the Republic of Ireland. "The Modern House Revisited." Gould, Jeremy. No. 2, Pages 112-128. London: The Twentieth Century Society, 1996.

Gloucester Citizen. "Debtors Accusation 'Blackmail and Slander' Allegation." Page 6. Gloucestershire, England: Gloucester Citizen, October 20, 1932.

Good Roads: Devoted to the Construction and Maintenance of Roads and Streets. Volume XII. New York: The E. L. Powers Co., July-December 1916.

The Graphic. "Two Motor Wanderers." Vol. CVI, No. 2762, Page 678. London: The Graphic, November 4, 1922.

The Holbrook News. Vol. 11, No. 13, Pages 5-6. Holbrook, Arizona: The Holbrook News, July 18, 1919.

The Idler. "A Variation from the Programme" Thomas, Leslie. Vol 28. London: Chatto and Windus, October 1905.

Illinois Archaeology. "Lamanitish Arrows and Eagles with Lead Eyes: Tales of the First Recorded Explorations in an Illinois Valley Hopewell Mound." Farnsworth, Ken. Vol. 22, No. 1, Pages 25-48. Champaign, IL: Illinois Archaeological Survey, Inc., 2010.

Indiana Magazine of History. "Names of the Ohio River." Dunn, J.P. Vol. 8, No. 4. Bloomington, IN: Indiana University Department of History, December 1912.

The International Studio. "Recent Designs in Domestic Architecture." Vol. 43, No. 171, Pages 212-216. New York: New York Offices of the International Studio, May 1911.

Iowa Service Bulletin. "Iowa's Natural Roads Shame Illinois Highways" Burton, J.C. Vol. IV, No. 11, Page 9. Ames, IA: Iowa State Highway Commission, November 1916.

Iowa Service Bulletin. "The Trail of the Painted Posts—A tale of the organized Middle West Tourist Routes" Spears, Raymond S. Vol. IV, Nos. 1-2, Pages 7-8. Ames, IA: Iowa State Highway Commission, November 1916.

Journal of the Royal Aeronautical Society. "The Engine Repair Shops Pont de L'Arche." Fell, L.F.R. Vol 70, Pages 167-168. London: Royal Aeronautical Society, January 1966.

Journal of the Royal Astronomical Society of Canada. "Percival Lowell's Last Year." Sheehan, William. Vol. 110, No. 6, Page 224. Toronto: Royal Astronomical Society of Canada, December 2016.

L'Astrosophie. Rolt-Wheeler, Francis. Vols. I-XVI. Carthage, Tunisia: Institut Astrologique de Carthage, 1919-1937.

Language in India. "Mother Tongues of India According to the 1961 Census." Mallikarjun, B. Vol. 2, August 5, 2002.

The Leeds and Yorkshire Mercury. Page 2. Yorkshire, England: The Leeds and Yorkshire Mercury, June 17, 1907.

The Literary Digest. Vol. LV, No. 19. Page 86. New York: Funk & Wagnalls, November 10, 1917.

The London Gazette. London: London Gazette:
- "Adjudications." Issue 41534, Page 6616. October 28, 1958.
- "Appointments of Trustees." Issue 41542, Page 6835. November 7, 1958.
- "Asst. Equipment Officers." Issue 29779, Page 9816. October 11, 1916.
- "The Bankruptcy Acts 1914 and 1926 - Receiving Orders." Issue 41495, Page 5634. September 12, 1958.
- "Equipment Officers, 1st Cl." Issue 30385, Page 11903. November 16, 1917.
- "Equipment Officers, 2nd Cl." Issue 29910, Page 808. January 19, 1917.
- "Memoranda." Issue 29687, Page 7482. July 28, 1916.
- "Notice." Issue 34621, Page 2967. May 2, 1939.
- "Notice." Issue 39067, Page 5705. November 14, 1950.
- "Release of Trustees." Issue 44064, Pages 8429-8430. July 26, 1966.
- "Transfers." Issue 31336, Page 5923. May 13, 1919.

Los Angeles Times. Los Angeles: Los Angeles Times, August 7, 1919.

Magazine of Western History Illustrated. "Trinidad Upon the Las Animas" Teetor, Henry Dudley. Vol. XIV, No. 1, Pages 85-90. New York: Magazine of Western History Publishing Co., May 1891.

The Mercury. "Case Against Lichfield Girl Fails." Page 5. Lichfield, England: The Mercury, July 26, 1935.

Mohave County Miner and Our Mineral Wealth. Vol. XXXVII, No. 40, Page 2. Kingman, Arizona: Mohave Printing and Publishing Company, August 2, 1919.

Mohave County Miner. Page 2. Kingman, Arizona: Mohave Printing and Publishing Company, August 3, 1918.

Motor Age. Chicago: Class Journal Company:
- "Convicts a Big Asset in Road Building." Hatch, Darwin S. Vol. XXI, No. 17, Pages 5-12. April 25, 1912.
- "Motor Roads of the U.S." Vol. XXXI, No. 14, Pages 32-50. April 5, 1917.
- "The 1917 Automobile Blue Books and What Each Volume Covers." Vol. XXXI, No. 14, Pages 88-89. April 5, 1917.

The Motor Cycle. London: The Motor Cycle:
- "The Evolution of the Motor Cycle." B.H.D. Vol. 20, Pages 700-706. June 1, 1922.
- Vol. 9, Nos. 432-457. July 6-December 28, 1911.
- Vol. 11, Nos. 536-561. July 3-December 25, 1913.
- Vol. 16, Nos. 667-692. January 6-June 29, 1916.
- Vol. 17, Nos. 693-717. July 6-December 21, 1916.

Motorcycle and Bicycle Illustrated. New York: Trade Journal Corporation:
- "'Cannonball' Baker Stopped by Mud" Vol. 15, No. 6. Page 19. June 26, 1919.
- "Capt. C.K. Shepherd Arrives on Coast." Vol. 15, No. 36, Page 48. September 4, 1919.
- "Hap Scherer Back East." Vol. 15, No. 29, Page 31. July 17, 1919.
- "Sherer Finishes Transcontinental Trip." Vol. 15, No. 33, Page 17. August 14, 1919.
- "Stephens Reports Gain" Vol. 15, No. 20, Page 31. May 15, 1919.
- "Touring Country on a Motorcycle." Vol. 15, No. 31, Page 31. July 31, 1919.
Vol. 18, Nos. 40-52. October-December 1922.

MotorCycling and Bicycling. Chicago: Tradepress Publishing Corporation:
- "Across the Continent by Motorcycle - Part I" Scherer, "Hap." Vol. XVIII, No. 9. Pages 20-21. August 27, 1919.
- "Across the Continent by Motorcycle - Part II" Scherer, "Hap." Vol. XVIII, No. 11. Pages 13-14. September 10, 1919.
- "Across the Continent by Motorcycle - Part III" Scherer, "Hap." Vol. XVIII, No. 12. Pages 23-24. September 17, 1919.
- "British Henderson Tourist Reaches the Pacific Coast" Vol. XVIII, No. 11. Page 22. September 10, 1919.
- "Britisher Praises American Scenery" Vol. XVIII, No. 4. Page 22. July 23, 1919.

Motor Travel. New York: Automobile Club of America:
- Vol. X, Nos. 1-10. June 1918-March 1919.
- Vol. XI, Nos. 1-12. April 1919-March 1920.
- Vol. XIII, Nos. 1-12. April 1921-March 1922.

Moving Picture World. New York: Chalmer's Publishing Co.:
- Vol. 29, Nos. 1-14. July-September 1916.
- Vol. 41, Nos. 1-4. July 1919.

Municipal Engineering and the Sanitary Record. "Are the Americans Successful Road Builders?." Vol. LXX, No. 1701, Page 502. London: Municipal Engineering Publications, July 6, 1922.

New Mexico Historical Review. "Beyond Pie Town: Mapping West Central New Mexico." Jensen, Joan M. Vol. 90, No. 1. Albuquerque: Department of History, University of New Mexico, 2015.

Our Journal. Metal Polishers International Union. Vol XXVIII. Cincinnati: Metal Polishers International Union, 1919.

The Overland Monthly. Vol. LII. San Francisco: The Overland Monthly Co., July-December 1908.

Pacific Motorcyclist and Western Wheelman. "A Britisher's Impressions of Transcontinental Motoring in America." Shepherd, C.K. Los Angeles: Pacific Motorcyclist and Western Wheelman:
- "Part 1." Pages 14-15, 18. August 21, 1919.
- "Part 2." Pages 28-29, 39. September 4, 1919.
- "Part 3." Pages 13, 27. September 18, 1919.
- "Part 4." Pages 26-27, 46. October 2, 1919.
- "Part 5." Page 26-27. October 16, 1919.

El Palacio. "Address of Hon. Frank Springer at the Dedication of the New Museum, Santa Fe, N.M. November 26th, 1917." Walter, Paul A.F., ed. Vol. IV, No. 4. Pages 1-18. Santa Fe: Journal of the Museum of New Mexico, Archaeological Society of New Mexico, and Santa Fe Society of the Archaeological Institute of America, November 1917.

The Pan American Geologist. Charles Keyes, ed. "Earth's Future Mirrored on Face of Mars." Hamilton, George H. Vol. XXXVII, No. 4, Pages 267-271. Des Moines: Geological Publishing Company, May 1922.

Parley's Magazine for Children and Youth. "To a Fly in Midwinter." Goodrich, Samuel Griswold. Vol. I, No. 2, Page 25. Boston: Lilly, Wait, and Company, March 30, 1833.

Popular Science Monthly. Vol. 93, No. 96, Page 103. New York: Popular Science Publishing Co., December 1918.

Proceedings of the Academy of Natural Sciences. "Further Notes on Meteor Crater, Arizona." Barringer, Daniel Moreau. Philadelphia: Academy of Natural Sciences, September 1914.

Punch, or the London Charivari. Vol. 26, No. 660, Page 82. London: Punch, March 4, 1854.

The San Bernardino County Sun. "Pioneer Motor Travelers Faced Trying Ordeals." Belden, L. Burr. Page 40. San Bernardino, California: The San Bernardino County Sun, October 10, 1954.

The Santa Fe Magazine. Chicago: Santa Fe Railway:
- Vol. X, Nos. 1-12. December 1915-November 1916.
- Vol. XIII, Nos. 1-12. December 1918-November 1919.
- Vol. XIV, Nos. 1-12. December 1919-November 1920.

Santa Fe New Mexican. Santa Fe, New Mexico:
- January 3, 1919.
- July 14, 1919.
- July 21, 1919.
- July 21, 1919.
- July 22, 1919.
- July 23 1919.

Scientific American. "A Mine in a Meteor-Made Crater." Chapman, Arthur. Vol. CXII, No. 3, Page 70. New York: Munn & Co., January 16, 1915.

The Scotsman. "Motor Show in Edinburgh – Some of the Specialties." Page 12. Edinburgh: The Scotsman, March 20, 1907.

See America First. Sheboygan, Wisconsin: The Bureau of American Travel, Inc.:
- "By Auto from Chicago to Los Angeles." McGaffey, Ernest. Vol. 7, No. 2. January 1921.
- "Canon City, Colorado." Bradbury, E.A. Vol. 7, No. 1, Page 9. November 1920.

The Seer (Cover Pages Only). Nice, France: The Seer Publishing Co., September 1933-February 1934.

The Seer. "How Bert Hinkler Crashed." Shepherd, C.K. Pages 47-50. Nice, France: The Seer Publishing Co., September 1933.

The Spanish-American (Roy, New Mexico). "Wagon Mound" Vol. III, No. 43. Page 5, November 16, 1907.

Superscience Quarterly. Vol. 1, No. 1, Cover. Cannes, France: C.K. Shepherd, July 1934.

Technical World Magazine. "Motorcycle as Powerplant." Vol XX, No. 5, Page 748. Chicago: R.T. Miller, January 1914.

Temple Bar. "The Fowl in the Pot." Weyman, Stanley J. Vol. LXXXV, Pages 203-220. London: Richard Bentley & Son, 1889.

Transactions. "Head-Lamp Glare-What Is It?" Replogle, J.B. Part I, Vol. XII, Pages 297-311. New York: Society of Automotive Engineers, 1917.

Twentieth Century Magazine. "Women Road Builders." Gentry, Elizabeth. Vol. V, No. 5, Page 88. Boston: The Twentieth Century Company, March 1912.

The Two Worlds. "Full Story of Capt. Hinkler's Death and Return." Shepherd, C.K. Vol. XLVI, No. 2398, Pages 863-864. Manchester, England: Two Worlds Publishing Company, November 10, 1933.

Western Highways Builder. Vol. 1, Nos. 1-22. Los Angeles: Western Journal Company, February 1-December 20, 1919.

Western Liberal. "New Mexico is Hard Hit by Drouth." Page 8. Lordsburg, New Mexico: Western Liberal, January 4, 1918.

Maps and Navigation

Arizona Good Roads Association Illustrated Road Maps and Tour Book. Page 122. Prescott, AZ: Arizona Good Roads Association, 1913.

Highways Green Book, Second Annual Edition. American Automobile Association. Washington, DC: Andrew B. Graham Co., 1921.

Map of the Dixie Highway. National Highways Association, Washington, DC. Baltimore: A. Hoen & Co., 1915.

The National Old Trails Road to California, Part 1. Los Angeles: Automobile Club of Southern California, 1916.

Official Auto Trails Map of the United States. Chicago: Rand McNally & Co., 1915.

Road Map of the State of Arizona. Automobile Club of Arizona. Phoenix: Automobile Club of Arizona, 1922.

Sanborn Fire Insurance Maps for Santa Fe, New Mexico. New York: Sanborn Map Company, 1913 and 1921.

Sanborn Fire Insurance Map from Cincinnati, Hamilton County, Ohio. Vol. 8. New York: Sanborn Map Company, 1917.

Pikes Peak Ocean to Ocean Highway Strip Map. Touring Information Bureau of America. Waterloo, Iowa: Touring Information Bureau of America, 1915.

Official Automobile Blue Book. New York: The Automobile Blue Book Publishing Company:

- Volume 1. *New York State and Canada*. 1919.
- Volume 2. *New England States & Maritime Provinces*. 1919.
- Volume 3. *N.J., Pa., Md., Del., Va., W.Va., D.C.* 1919:
    - Route 116—Atlantic City, N. J., to Philadelphia, Pa.—64.2 m. Pages 188-190.
    - Route 119—Atlantic City, N. J., to Philadelphia, Pa.—66.2 m. Pages 191-192.
    - Route 710—Uniontown, Pa., to Wheeling, W. Va.—68.2 m. Pages 645-647.
    - Route 814—Washington, D. C., to Hagerstown, Md.—76.7 m. Pages 740-741.
- Volume 4. *Ohio, Indiana, Michigan, Kentucky*. 1919:
    - Route 615—Columbus to Zanesville, Ohio—54.3 m. Page 639.
- Volume 5. *Ill., Wis., Minn., Ia., Mo., & Upper Mich*. 1919:
    - Route 229—Decatur to Springfield, Ill.—43.0 m. Pages 271-272.
    - Route 250—Springfield, Ill., to Hannibal, Mo.—105.3 m. Pages 295-297.
    - Route 406—Hannibal to Chillicothe, Mo.—138.8 m. Pages 445-447.
- Volume 6. *Southeastern States*. 1919.
- Volume 7. *Mont., Wyo., N. Dak., S. Dak., Neb., Colo., Kan., Ark., Tex., N.M., Okla., & La*. 1918:
    - Route 177—La Junta to Pueblo, Colo.—66.0 m. Pages 221-222.
    - Route 178—La Junta to Trinidad, Colo.—85.2 m. Pages 222-223.
    - Route 729—Las Vegas to Santa Fe, N. M.—73.0 m. Pages 754-755.
    - Route 835—Magdalena, N. M., to Springerville, Ariz.—135.7 m. Pages 845-846.
    - Route 836—Springerville to Winslow, Ariz.—137.6 m. Pages 846-848.
    - Route 837—Winslow to Flagstaff, Ariz.—64.7 m. Page 848.

Volume 8. *California, Nev., Utah & Ariz*. 1919:
    - Route 48—Salinas to Pacific Grove, Cal.—21.7 m. Page 118.
    - Route 391—Los Angeles to Santa Barbara, Cal.—98.5 m. Pages 454-458.
    - Route 392—Santa Barbara to Paso Robles, Cal.—148.9 m. Pages 458-461.
    - Route 441—Flagstaff to Grand Canyon, Ariz.—84.9 m. Page 507.

- Route 602—Flagstaff to Kingman, Ariz.—175.6 m. Pages 612-613.
- Route 603—Kingman, Ariz. to Needles, Cal.—71.5 m. Pages 613-614.
- Route 607—Needles to Barstow, Cal.—164.6 m. Pages 616-617.
- Route 608—Barstow to San Bernardino, Cal.—82.6 m. Pages 617-618.
- Route 612—San Bernardino to Los Angeles, Cal.—62.8 m. Pages 618-620.
- Volume 9. *Washington, Oregon, Idaho, & B.C.* 1919.
- Volume 10. *Mont., Wyo., N. Dak., So. Dak., Neb., Col., No. Kan., E. Ida., Alta., Sask., & Manit.* 1920:
  - Route 249—Pueblo to Canon City, Colo.—44.1 m. Page 267.
  - Route 269—Canon City to Royal Gorge, Colo.—10.2 m. Page 275.
- Volume T. *Main Trunkline Highways of the United States.* 1920:
  Route 616—Springerville to Winslow, Ariz.—135.8 m. Pages 773-774.

US Geological Survey. Washington, DC: US Geological Survey:
- *Arlington Quadrangle, Indiana.* 1:24,000. 7.5 Minute Series. 1960.
- *Ash Fork Quadrangle, Arizona.* 1:63,360. 15 Minute Series. 1948.
- *Brilliant Quadrangle, New Mexico-Colorado.* 1:62,500. 15 Minute Series. 1915.
- *Brookfield Quadrangle, Missouri.* 1:62,500. 15 Minute Series. 1948.
- Cajon Quadrangle, California. 1:24,000. 7.5 Minute Series. 1956.
- *Cameron Quadrangle, West Virginia-Pennsylvania-Ohio.* 1:62,500. 15 Minute Series. 1904.
- *Camp Mohave Quadrangle, Arizona.* 1:250,000. 1x1 Degree Series. 1892.
- *Canon City Quadrangle, Colorado.* 1:125,000. 30 Minute Series. 1892.
- *Carthage Quadrangle, Indiana.* 1:24,000. 7.5 Minute Series. 1960.
- *Cathedral Caves Quadrangle, Arizona.* 1:24,000. 7.5 Minute Series. 2018.
- *Chino Quadrangle, Arizona.* 1:250,000. 1x1 Degree Series. 1891.
- *East Cincinnati Quadrangle, Ohio.* 1:62,500. 15 Minute Series. 1914.
- *Elmoro Quadrangle, Colorado.* 1:125,000. 30 Minute Series. 1897.
- *Flagstaff Quadrangle, Arizona.* 1:125,000. 30 Minute Series. 1912.
- *Florence Quadrangle, Colorado.* 1:24,000. 7.5 Minute Series. 1959.
- *Hannibal Quadrangle, Illinois-Missouri.* 1:62,500. 15 Minute Series. 1932.
- *Lyman Lake SW Quadrangle, Arizona.* 1:24,000. 7.5 Minute Series. 1971.
- *Mechanicsburg Quadrangle, Illinois.* 1:62,500. 15 Minute Series. 1954.
- *Morristown Quadrangle, Indiana.* 1:24,000. 7.5 Minute Series. 1956.

- *Niantic Quadrangle, Illinois.* 1:62,500. 15 Minute Series. 1954.
- *Picacho Butte Quadrangle, Arizona.* 1:62,500. 15 Minute Series. 1947.
- *Pitas Point Quadrangle, California.* 1:24,000. 7.5 Minute Series. 1951.
- *Raton Quadrangle, New Mexico.* 1:62,500. 15 Minute Series. 1914.
- *San Louis Obispo Quadrangle, California.* 1:62,500. 15 Minute Series. 1916.
- *Socorro Quadrangle, New Mexico.* 1:250,000. 1x1 Degree Series. 1958.
- *Spanish Peaks Quadrangle, Colorado.* 1:125,000. 30 Minute Series. 1900.
- *Springfield Quadrangle, Illinois.* 1:62,500. 15 Minute Series. 1922.
- *St. Johns Quadrangle, Arizona.* 1:250,000. 1x1 Degree Series. 1892.
- *Starkville Quadrangle, Colorado.* 1:24,000. 7.5 Minute Series. 2013.
- *Tetilla Peak Quadrangle, New Mexico.* 1:24,000. 7.5 Minute Series. 1945.
- Thurston Quadrangle, Ohio. 1:62,500. 15 Minute Series. 1909.
- *Tin Pan Canyon Quadrangle, New Mexico.* 1:24,000. 7.5 Minute Series. 1971.
- *Trinidad East Quadrangle, Colorado.* 1:24,000. 7.5 Minute Series. 2013 and 1951.
- *Trinidad West Quadrangle, Colorado.* 1:24,000. 7.5 Minute Series. 2013.
- *Tuscola Quadrangle, Illinois.* 1:62,500. 15 Minute Series. 1952.
- *Ventura Quadrangle, California.* 1:24,000. 7.5 Minute Series. 1951.
- West Cincinnati Quadrangle, Ohio. 1:62,500. 15 Minute Series. 1914.
- *White Ledge Peak Quadrangle, California.* 1:24,000. 7.5 Minute Series. 1952.
- *Yucca Quadrangle, Arizona.* 1:62,500. 15 Minute Series. 1929.

Other Documents and Resources

Across America By Motorcycle. Landers, Chris B. 2010.
http://acrossamericabymotorcycle.blogspot.com.

"C.K. Shepherd Departure from Liverpool." Liverpool, England. May 22, 1919.
http://search.findmypast.com/record?id=tna%2fbt27%2f0894000033%2f00065.

"Cincinnati Speedway." Niemeyer, Kurt. *Cincy Magazine Online.* December 2011.
http://cincymagazine.com/Main/Articles/Cincinnati_Speedway_3464.aspx

"Commencement Certificate." Tindal Street Council School. July 14, 1910. Birmingham, England: Tindal Street Council School.

Confidential Files Re-Officers. London: Royal Flying Corps., January 1918-January 1919.

Consumer Price Index, 1913-. Minneapolis: Federal Reserve Bank of Minneapolis. https://www.minneapolisfed.org.

"Death Certificate—Charles K. Shaw." Herefordshire, England: Herefordshire Council Offices, January 16, 1971.

Electoral Registers. Council Office: Warwickshire, England. 1918-1936.

"Evolution of the New York Driver's License." NYTimes.com, March 16, 2013. https://archive.nytimes.com/www.nytimes.com/interactive/2013/03/17/nyregion/17licenses-evolution.html.

"Feature Class Definitions" *Geographic Names Information System (GNIS)* Washington, DC: US Geological Survey. https://geonames.usgs.gov/.

"Feature Films Released between 1919-01-01 and 1919-12-31" IMDb. https://www.imdb.com/search/title?year=1919&title_type=feature

Fossil Trees or Petrified Wood. Baisan, Christopher H. Tucson, Arizona: University of Arizona, February 2013. http://www.ltrr.arizona.edu/~cbaisan/BBTRB/Petrified1.pdf

"Francis Rolt Wheeler: The Productive Years." ethelroltwheeler.wordpress.com. March 1, 2013. https://ethelroltwheeler.wordpress.com/2013/03/01/francis-rolt-wheeler-the-productive-years/

"Francis Rolt-Wheeler: 1876-1960." Demarest, Marc. ehbritten.blogspot.com. February 23, 2013. http://ehbritten.blogspot.com/2013/02/francis-rolt-wheeler-1876-1960.html

"The General" IMDb. https://www.imdb.com/title/tt0017925/

Google Earth. https://www.google.com/earth/.

"Immigration and Naturalization Service Form 548." *Vermont, St. Albans Canadian Border Crossings, 1895-1954*. US Department of Labor, June 3, 1919.

"Last Will and Testament." Shaw, Honorah Margaret (Tarpey). May 31, 1989.

Letter to Thomas Stevenson, Jr. C.K. Shepherd. Unpublished, March 28, 1928.

Letter Draft to C.K. Shepherd. Thomas Stevenson, Jr. Unpublished, February 3, 1940.

Letter to Thomas Stevenson, Jr. C.K. Shaw. Unpublished, September 19, 1940.

Letter to Thomas Stevenson, Jr. C.K. Shaw. Unpublished, March 19, 1958.

The Military Service History of Charles Kenilworth Shepherd (Report). Baker, Chris. Warwickshire, England: fourteeneighteen|research, July 4, 2017.

"The Ministry of Aircraft Production." *Battle of Britain Day by Day*. battleofbritain. wordpress.com. https://battleofbritain.wordpress.com/unsung-heroes/the-ministry-of-aircraft-production/

"Peach Springs Trading Post—Route 66: A Discover Our Shared Heritage Travel Itinerary." US National Park Service. http://www.nps.gov/nr/travel/route66/peach_springs_trading_post.html

"Pueblo Languages" Redish, Laura and Orrin Lewis. *Native Languages of the Americas*. http://native-languages.org/pueblo.htm. © 1998-2015.

"Raton Pass 2011." sangres.com. 2011. http://sangres.com/photos/ratonpass.htm

"results view." *Espacenet Patent Search*. https://worldwide.espacenet.com/

"Riverside Drive." Catasus, Edgar. *I love the Upper West Side.com*. March 20, 2017. https://ilovetheupperwestside.com/riverside-drive/.

"Stories of the Battle of Britain 1940—Lord Beaverbrook, a Week at the Office." spitfiresite.com. May 27, 2010. http://spitfiresite.com/2010/05/battle-of-britain-1940-lord-beaverbrook-a-week-at-the-office.html

USDA-NRCS Plants Database. Greensboro, NC: USDA, NRCS - National Plant Data Team, January 2019. http://plants.usda.gov.

"Where Is the Oldest City in the United States?"Wonderopolis®. Louisville: National Center for Families Learning. https://wonderopolis.org/wonder/where-is-the-oldest-city-in-the-united-states.

Z. Wiggs' Railway Cattle Guard. Washington, DC: US Patent and Trademark Office, November 23, 1897.

INDEX

CPSIA information can be obtained
at www.ICGtesting.com
Printed in the USA
FFHW010932180619
52996284-58621FF